Islam and Muslim History in South Asia

This collection of essays by Francis Robinson, a leading scholar on Islam in South Asia, brings together the author's best-known writings, many of which have been central to academic debates in the field. The essays address key themes in the history of the Muslims of South Asia, among them, conversion to Islam, the impact of print, the emergence of this-worldly religion, the process of 'secularization', and the relationship between religion and politics. The collection also includes reviews of some of the most important scholarly contributions to the field of South Asian Islamic history over the last two decades. Essential reading for scholars and students, this volume will also attract informed general readers interested in South Asia's Islamic heritage.

Francis Robinson is Professor of the History of South Asia, Royal Holloway, University of London.

Islam and Muslim History in South Asia

Francis Robinson

YMCA Library Building, Jai Singh Road, New Delhi 110 001

Oxford University Press is a department of the University of Oxford. It furthers the University's objective of excellence in research, scholarship, and education by publishing worldwide in

Oxford New York

Auckland Bangkok Buenos Aires Cape Town Chennai
Dar es Salaam Delhi Hong Kong Istanbul Karachi Kolkata
Kuala Lumpur Madrid Melbourne Mexico City Mumbai Nairobi
São Paulo Shanghai Taipei Tokyo Toronto

Oxford is a registered trade mark of Oxford University Press in the UK and in certain other countries

Published in India
By Oxford University Press, New Delhi

First published 2000
Second impression 2001
Oxford India Paperbacks 2003

ISBN 0 19 566359 4

Printed at Saurabh Printers Pvt. Ltd., Noida
Published by Manzar Khan, Oxford University Press
YMCA Library Building, Jai Singh Road, New Delhi 110 001

Dedicated

to

the memory of

Professor Mohibbul Hasan

scholar and gentleman,

who guided me in my early days in India

and

to my pupils

IAT, KHA, SFDA, DHE, MS, ARK,

CL, YS, AAA, AD, RH MD, PD, EH

Acknowledgements

'Islam and Muslim Society in South Asia' was originally published in *Contributions to Indian Sociology*, vol. XVII, no. 2 (1983). Copyright © Institute of Economic Growth, Delhi, 1983. All rights reserved. Reproduced with the permission of the copyright holders and the publishers, Sage Publications India Pvt Ltd, New Delhi.

'Islam and the Impact of Print in South Asia' was originally published in N. Crook (ed.), *Transmission of Knowledge in South Asia* (New Delhi, 1997).

'Religious Change and the Self in Muslim South Asia since 1800' was originally published in *South Asia*, vol. XX, no. 1 (1997).

'Secularization, Weber and Islam' was originally published in Toby Huff (ed.), *Weber, Secularization and Islam*. I thank Toby Huff and Transaction Books for permission to publish.

'The Muslims of Upper India and the Shock of the Mutiny' was originally published in M. Hasan and N. Gupta (eds), *India's Colonial Encounter: Essays in Memory of Eric Stokes* (New Delhi, 1993). I thank the editors for permission to publish.

'Nation-formation: The Brass Thesis and Muslim Separatism' was originally published in *Journal of Commonwealth and Comparative Politics*, XV, 1997. I thank the editor of the journal and Frank Cass for permission to publish.

'Islam and Muslim Separatism' was originally published in D. Taylor and M. Yapp (eds), *Political Identity in South Asia* (London, 1979). I thank the South Asia Centre of The School of Oriental and African Studies and the Curzon Press for permission to publish.

'The Congress and the Muslims' was originally published in F. Robinson and P. Brass (eds), *The Indian National Congress and the Indian Society* (New Delhi, 1987); I thank co-editor, Paul Brass for permission to publish.

All the reviews were published in *Modern Asian Studies*.

'Sufis and Islamization', XIV, 4 October 1980.

'Nineteenth-Century Indian Islam' XIV, 4 Oct. 1980.

'Islam in Malabar', XVIII, 1 February 1984.

'Islamic Revival', XVIII, 2 April 1984.

'The Jinnah Story', XX, 3 July 1986.

'The Congress Muslims and Indian Nationalism', XXIII, 3 July 1989.

I thank the Syndics of Cambridge University Press for permission to publish.

Contents

Introduction

Islam and Muslim History in South Asia

One of the features of modern academic life is that much is published in collected volumes with short print runs, misleading titles and high prices. Other works are published in journals that are not always easy to locate. In consequence, the cumulative impact of individual contributions to a subject can be lost. Indeed, it might barely be sensed at all. This last point was brought home to me in India in 1997 when I learned that scholars with substantial interest in my field had little knowledge, for instance, of most of the essays I had written relating to Firangi Mahal. To remedy this situation I have made two selections of essays and long reviews. This volume of work devoted to aspects of Islam and Muslim history is the first. It is to be followed by a volume devoted to the *ulama* of Firangi Mahal and Islamic culture.

Every piece of work has a context both personal and intellectual. Some even develop a history as they are noted and responded to. I shall, where appropriate, sketch that context and history. Before doing so, it is worth reflecting for a moment on the extraordinary changes that have taken place in the world and in our intellectual climate over the past twenty-five years. In the 1970s socialist understandings of life, of varying depth, were dominant; the study of the material world and material forces was all. The study of religious ideas, religious change, or the transmitters of religious ideas, was not an attractive or, for some, even an appropriate thing to do. I have vivid memories of being lambasted by my good friend, the late Anwar Jamal Qidwai, who at the time was Vice-Chancellor of the Jamia Millia Islamia, for doing research on the *ulama* of Firangi Mahal. 'Why', he asked, 'do you pay attention to these retrogressive forces? There was a time when Western academics used to work hand in hand with the "progressive" forces in our society.' I had no answer except to say that I thought the subject interesting, that it was one of the privileges of the scholar to study what he thought was important rather than to follow a particular political agenda. Now, after the Iranian Revolution, the failure of so many socialist regimes, and the emergence of religious revivalism as a fact of major significance in world affairs, few would question the value of studying religious ideas, their interpretations and transmission. Indeed, they are a prime concern, for better or worse, of governments and intelligence services throughout the world. This said, in all fairness to Anwar Jamal, I should point out that he spoke with the angst of a secular intellectual painfully aware of the tribulations which the politics of religion had brought and could bring to his society.

The past is always another country, another culture. One of the greatest quests for the historian, and also the greatest pleasure, is to reach out to and to try to bring to life what it was to be alive in that other country and at another time. I seek to explore and to savour the lives of those who have lived in that past, and to give it value. The aim is to get well behind, indeed to strip, the veils set up by language, history, discourses of power or mere forgetfulness. Two historians have affirmed this direction most powerfully. Peter Brown is the first, a colleague for some years, and a friend in every sense. His *Augustine of Hippo* remains the most extraordinary evocation of what it was to be human in another era.[1] Richard Cobb is the second, whose valuing of the individual and the particular in the past, whose unrivalled capacity to set before us French lives with lavish quantities of what Geertz would term 'thick description' revealed, for my generation, a different and enthralling way of being a historian.[2]

My concern to understand and value the humanity of those who had lived in 'another country' meant that in the mid-1990s, along with many other scholars especially of Asia, I was disturbed by a new thesis promulgated by the American political scientist, Samuel P. Huntington, which was much discussed among international relations and foreign policy experts. Huntington argued that in the post-Cold-War era the prime distinctions between people were less ideological and economic than cultural. World politics was being reconfigured along civilizational lines. As that process took place, deep fault lines were emerging between the Muslim world and the West. Indeed, it had 'bloody borders' and represented the greatest danger to world peace.[3] Huntington's civilizational paradigm for the study of global politics threatened to establish a new orientalism. Different civilizations were being endowed with different 'essences' and, of these, Muslim civilization was given the role with which it had been endowed for too much of Western history—of being the hostile 'other', and the mirror in which the West perceived its unique world destiny.

The invitation to give a plenary lecture at the annual Anglo-American Conference at London's Institute of Historical Research in July 1997 provided an opportunity to offer a historian's corrective to the Huntington paradigm. The conference was devoted to global history. The corrective, which forms the first essay in this volume 'The Muslim and the Christian Worlds: Shapers of Each Other', demonstrates the long history of influence and interdependence between the Muslim and the Christian worlds, a long history which too many on both sides have found it in their interests either to overlook or even actively conceal. Ironically, this corrective was very much in harmony with Huntington's vision for the way forward: 'the futures of both peace and Civilization depend on understanding and cooperation among the political, spiritual and intellectual leaders of the world's major civilizations.'[4] What better way to enhance understanding between the Western and the Muslim civilizations than to demonstrate how much they have shared and continue to share! The lecture is published for the first time.

'Islam and Muslim Society in South Asia', the second essay, started as a public lecture given in the University of Cambridge in February 1983. One context in which it was written was in the aftermath of my *Atlas of the Islamic World since 1500*.[5] The two powerful influences over this work were first my own research on the *ulama* and sufis of the Firangi Mahal family of Lucknow, which had led to an understanding of the key role of *ulama* and sufis in Muslim history as guardians and transmitters of the central messages of their civilization and as interpreters of the messages to the society in their time.[6] This understanding together with the growing research on *ulama* and sufis in the 1960s and 1970s created the central strand of argument in the one hundred-thousand-word *Atlas'* text, and a good number of its dynamic maps.[7] The second influence was a masterwork of Islamic history, Marshall Hodgson's

Venture of Islam: Conscience and History in a World Civilization.[8] The subtitle indicates what was so influential in the work; the illustration of the interaction of ideas and piety on the one hand and power and material life on the other in fashioning a world civilization. It was, moreover, a treatment which from its very first page was imbued with a powerful desire to show the utmost respect for the people and values it explored.

The second context was the important intellectual leadership offered by Imtiaz Ahmad of Jawaharlal Nehru University in editing a four-volume study of Islam in South Asia. At the time the lecture was given, three volumes had been published: the fourth was about to be.[9] In the introduction to volume three Ahmad set out his credo. He asserted the superiority of the sociological vision over that of the Islamicist. 'The sociological and the social anthropological understandings of religion,' we were told, 'is at once more comprehensive and more concrete.' He noted that scholars of Indian Islam, indeed of Islamic societies in general, had explained the differences between law and practice in historical development—in terms of long processes of Islamization—from heterodox and heteroprax forms of Islam towards more orthodox and orthoprax forms. Ahmad rejected this understanding of a dynamic relationship between ideas and society through time in favour of a concept of coexistence. For him the high Islamic and custom-centred traditions peacefully 'coexist as complementary and integral parts of a common religious system'. They do so, moreover, and have done so, because of 'the constraints of Islam's own struggle for survival in an alien environment'.[10]

The aim of the lecture was to assert the understanding, given to me by my research on the Firangi Mahal family and by work for the *Atlas*, that there was a dynamic relationship between Islamic knowledge and society through history. This was evident, surely, in the fact that in 610 AD there was not a single Muslim and now the world has more than a billion. It was no less evident in the fact that the first Muslims appeared in the Indian subcontinent in the seventh century and now the region contains c̄ 350 million. Arguably it was evident, too, in the great movement of revival and reform which had swept through the Islamic world since the eighteenth century. This revival had mingled with great processes of economic, social, technological and political change to produce substantial shifts in belief and behaviour from those profoundly influenced by magic and superstition to those in which the formal requirements and understandings of Islam were more fully realized. South Asia, itself, has been one of the most fertile and powerful sites of this Islam-wide movement, generating ideas and organizations of great influence elsewhere. Indeed, the past two hundred years have seen South Asia's leadership at a peak in the Muslim world.[11] In this context mass reform movements have emerged which shattered any sense that there might be equilibrium maintained between the high Isla- mic and the custom-centred traditions. There is the *Tablighi-Jama'at* or Preaching society, which has grown from a movement to purify the Meos of Mewat in the era of communal competition of the 1920s and 1930s to become the most widely followed movement in the Muslim world. Its annual conferences at Raiwind in Pakistan and Tongi in Bangladesh are, after the Haj, the largest annual gatherings of Muslims in the world.[12] There is the extraordinary growth of *madrasas* in Pakistan, in which the reformist Deobandis have played the leading role. Amongst the elements which help this movement forward are processes of urbanization, the failures of the state, the competition of religious world views, the struggle for power between organizations, as well as funding from outside sources. The *madrasa* movements seek their particular routes to the further Islamization of Pakistani society and are often prepared to use force to realize their ends.[13]

The published lecture elicited strong responses from Gail Minault and Veena Das. For Minault my criticism of Ahmad was unfair because we were operating form different perspectives—his anthropological, mine historical. My assault on the concept of the uniqueness of Indian Islam was wrong because there were some unique Indian resolutions to Islamic problems. Moreover, my understanding was clearly flawed because I seemed to think that God or history was on the side of Islamic reassertion.[14] For Das I was wrong-headed to talk of a 'pattern of perfection' in Islam to which Muslims aspired; I ignored the interpretative role of learned and holy men; and I was mistaken in privileging the practices of the religious elite as normative over those of 'folk theologies'.[15]

These and other criticisms were answered.[16] There was, however, an issue I raised which clearly struck a raw nerve. It was my suggestion that Ahmad came from a world-view, shared by other Indian Muslim scholars, which was concerned to emphasize the essential Indianness of Indian Muslims. This was not to suggest that there was any manipulation of results, only to note, as Ahmad himself had stated, that Islam in India was constrained by the wider Indian world in which it existed, and to register that certain assumptions, for instance Nehruvian ones about the 'essential unity of India' were in the very air that people breathed. It was such an atmosphere, I would hazard, which prompted Anwar Jamal Qidwai to bemoan the preference of some Western scholars for 'retrogressive' rather than 'progressive' subjects of study. It is such an atmosphere, too, perhaps, which has meant that over the past fifty years there has been no major study by an Indian Muslim of Syed Ahmad Khan, arguably the greatest Indian Muslim of the nineteenth century, and no major study of the rise of the All-India Muslim League, arguably one of the most important movements of the twentieth century. There has, however, been much work, for instance the output of Mushirul Hasan, on the contributions of Indian Muslims to Indian nationalism.[17] Subconsciously, perhaps consciously, there have been forms of self-censorship. The past fifteen years of severe contestation of Indian national identity have only underscored the need for intellectuals, in particular from the minority communities, to raise their voices with care.

'Islam and the Impact of Print in South Asia' began life in 1992 as an inaugural lecture. It was entitled 'Technology and Religious Change: Islam and the Impact of Print' and was substantially shorter.[18] The fifty-five minute time-span of the lecture had prevented me from exploring the theme in full; the longer version enabled me to pay attention to the all-important psychological changes flowing from the introduction of print. My starting point was that the introduction of print, and the revolution in the transmission of knowledge that it helped to bring about, had transformed the religious life of Western Christendom. It had enabled a massive attack on religious authority, shaped new weapons of religious proselytization, and helped to fashion new religious understandings. If this was the case for the Christian world, why should it not also be the case for the Muslim world? The impact of print, moreover, was a process which we were privileged to be able to observe much more closely in the Muslim than in the Christian case, in part because it had only begun to be felt in the nineteenth century and in part because, in much of the Muslim world, mass literacy was still making headway. Major differences between Muslim and Christian civilizations were, of course, not be ignored, nor were the different circumstances in which the change was experienced—in Europe, one of dominance and expansion, in the Islamic world, one of declining power and colonial rule.

One of the great advantages of working in a large university history department is the range of one's colleagues' interests and the pleasures and profit to be had from sharing ideas with them. In this case I had the good fortune to sit at the feet of Rosalind Thomas who had for some years been exploring the growth of literacy in the oral world of classical Greece, the relationship which existed between these two forms of transmitting knowledge, and their meaning for society and human understanding.[19] Her work led me to a host of scholars in the field, but most particularly to Marshall McLuhan, the first great proponent of the social and psychological implication of change in the media of communication, Walter Ong, McLuhan's early pupil and leading intellectual disciple, and Bill Graham of Harvard, who has thought long and deeply about the impact of the spoken holy word as compared with the silently read page in major religious traditions. A whole new world was opened up with many tempting vistas to explore.

Pondering upon these prospects in the context of South Asia, it seemed not unreasonable to suggest that the introduction of print, working alongside the great complex of changes introduced by colonial rule, had been little short of revolutionary. There was, as I wrote:

> the emergence of a Protestant or scriptural Islam; the strengthening of the Pan-Islamic layer in the Muslim sense of identity; the levelling of an assault on the *ulama* as the sole interpreters of Islam; the outflanking of oral, person to person, systems for the transmission of knowledge; and colonising of Muslim minds with Western knowledge; the opening of the way towards new understandings of Islam such as those of the modernists and the 'fundamentalists'.[20]

Most of these processes have been the subject of research. On the other hand, the psychological effects of print—the process of 'distancing', which helped to bring about a new historical consciousness; the reification of religion, and an emphasis in piety on this-worldly action; 'the process of interiorization' which was manifest in an increasingly personal and private encounter with the Quran; and a new and more powerful focus on the person of the Prophet Muhammad in Muslim faith—was worthy of much further investigation.

One topic of particular interest which emerged from the consideration of the impact of print was the potential relationship between forms of religious change and understanding, on the one hand, and the religious underpinning of forms of individualism, on the other. This was the subject of 'Religious change and the Self in Muslim South Asia since 1800', which was a keynote lecture at the conference of the Asian Studies Association of Australia in July 1996. I began with that process of great importance—the shift in Muslim piety in the nineteenth and twentieth centuries from otherworldly to this-worldly religion. Islam, of course, had always had its profoundly this-worldly aspects but these had been balanced by powerful traditions of mystical thought and belief in God's capacity to intercede for men on earth. Now, as a consequence of the great movement of revival and reform, there was a widespread assault on all ideas of intercession and increasing awareness on the part of many Indian Muslims that they, and they alone, were responsible for creating Islamic society on earth. Again, as in the case of the impact of print, it seemed worth considering what a similar shift had meant in the history of the Christian West. Again, of course, the distinctively different historical contexts in which the process took place was kept firmly in view. So, too, was the particular quality of an Islamic environment, in which revelation created the community, in which the law and the values it generated all supported the community, and in which the individual only acquired rights by entering the community and subordinating his will to the common will.

Taking the lead from recent scholarship on the Christian Reformation and its long-term ramifications, in particular noting the insights of Charles Taylor's fine work, *Sources of the Self: The Making of Modern Identity*,[21] it was possible to discern in the lives and culture of nineteenth- and twentieth-century Indian Muslims, developments that were not dissimilar from those experienced by post-Reformation Western Europeans. From the new sense of personal responsibility for the achievement of salvation which came with this-worldly religion, there emerged the idea of individual instrumentality in this world. Man was the prime mover in God's creation and it was his duty to act to fulfil His guidance. From the knowledge that it was individual Muslims who willed the existence of their Muslim society, it became possible for individuals to become increasingly autonomous and self-affirmative. They could choose whether to build a Muslim society on earth or not. They could choose, indeed, whether to be Muslims or not. From affirmation of the self followed affirmation of the ordinary things of the self—the ordinary things of life. Such affirmation is a powerful theme of both secular and religious writing of the period. Then, that sense of personal responsibility which lies at the heart of this-worldly Islam was a feeble driving force without the complementary process of self-examination. This-worldly Islam helped to develop the more reflective believer, thus staking out an interior territory for the Muslim in which the struggle for Islam took place. It stimulated a new self-consciousness, an inward turn. All of these processes were clearly present among South Asian Muslims. Certainly, they were supported by the influence of the West, by economic forces and by aspects of the growth of the state. But, what is important from our point of view is that they were also underpinned and validated, and quite unwittingly so, by the central thrust of the Muslim movement of revival and reform. This has set up a central tension between the aspects of individualism enhanced by the nature and forms of this-worldly religion and the central fact of community obligation in Islam. It is a tension, I suggest, which has been felt most acutely by Muslim women, who have had to bear so much of the burden of upholding community values and identity through this period of extraordinary changes of all kinds.

Many avenues for further research present themselves. The themes of self-instrumentality, self-affirmation, the affirmation of the ordinary things of life and the inward turn, all offer fascinating prospects for further literary and anthropological study.[22] The tensions in this-worldly Islam set up by its underpinning of aspects of individualism in order to generate the mass force to sustain the community on the one hand and community obligation on the other would appear to have considerable potential for generating new religious understandings, indeed, for finding new positionings for the faith in social and political life. Exploring these tensions in the life of Muslim societies, discovering the different forms of resolution of them achieved by individuals and religious thinkers, and assessing the capacity of these resolutions to satisfy those involved is one of the most important and exciting research frontiers. Here is the living, and always shifting, interface between a great religious tradition and social reality.[23] Finally, the whole phenomenon of the shift from other-worldly to this-worldly religion in

Islamic piety requires major study. So far, research has been restricted, and probably properly so, to discreet study of revivalist, reformist and Islamist movements. This shift, however, is the most important development in the orientation of religious thought since the thirteenth century when the ideas of Ibn 'Arabi spread through the Muslim world. It intersects, in ways full of possibilities, with dominant ideas of the twentieth-century world whether they be human rights, individual empowerment, personal fulfilment or free-market capitalism. It is a major source of the energy, which has flowed through the Muslim world over the past two centuries, and which will continue to flow shaping Muslim lives for the future.

'Secularization, Weber and Islam' owes its beginning to the first complete English edition of *Economy and Society*,[24] Weber's masterpiece of sociological thought, which stimulated a series of workshops on Weber and the great religious traditions led by Guenther Roth of the University of Washington, Seattle, one of its editors, and Wolfgang Schluchter of the University of Heidelberg. One was devoted to Weber and Islam, the results of which were published in German in *Max Weber's Sicht des Islams*.[25] This piece, first published under the title 'Saekulisierung im Islam' is published in English for the first time in 1999; a small amount of material has been added to bring it up-to-date.

My concern was to see what Weber's theories might tell us about secularization in the Indo-Muslim context. In the mid-1980s the outcome seemed to be conflicting signals. Taking his theory of secularization, it certainly seemed that Indo-Muslim society had travelled down the path of disenchantment and fragmentation, his secularizing path.[26] On the other hand, if we took his approach of considering secularization within the unique 'developmental history' of Islam, the process looked rather more complex; elements of both secularization and Islamization were clearly visible. Looking back on this essay from the vantage point of subsequent research and thought, there is the realization that some of the underpinnings of individualism and their manifestations, are emerging from the 'developmental history' of Islam itself. Growing individualism has challenged and will challenge the obligations of community, and may form the leading edge of an Islamic process of secularization.

In 1981, Eric Stokes, Smuts Professor of Commonwealth History in the University of Cambridge, died. Few British scholars of India have been more loved and respected. He offered leadership in the arts of writing history, wide-ranging intellectual companionship, and much personal kindness to all. It was a wholly appropriate tribute that his *festschrift*, *India's Colonial Encounter*, should have been organized and edited by two scholars from Delhi, Narayani Gupta and Mushirul Hasan. Gupta's appreciation of Stokes, which prefaces the volume, celebrates qualities which will not be forgotten by those who knew him.[27]

The Mutiny Revolt of 1857 and the world of the Indian Landlord and peasant lay at the heart of Stokes' teaching for many years. 'The Muslims of Upper India and the Shock of the Mutiny' which was my contribution to the *festschrift*, was the natural bridge between the prime focus of his scholarly engagement and mine. The object of the piece was simple: to demonstrate the extent to which Muslim leaders of the second half of the nineteenth century—leaders of the modernist movement of Aligarh, leaders of the *ulama* of Deoband, and leaders of the *ulama* of Firangi Mahal—had been caught up in the events of 1857; to show how far their worlds—political, cultural, physical—had been shattered by them; and to illustrate their impact on their subsequent actions. Apart from the neatness of the connection between Stokes and myself, I chose the subject because the impact of the Mutiny experience and the brutal British retribution which followed it on the minds of the north Indian Muslim elite always seemed to have been underestimated. Yet, it was central to the urgency, the drive and the radical approach, which led to Aligarh modernism and the ideological thrusts and institutional development that formed the background to Muslim separatism and the eventual demand for Pakistan, and which also led to the institutionalization of Islamic protestantism in the Deoband movement whose various developments and offshoots have not just subcontinental but global importance.[28]

The central concern of this article with the impact of the Mutiny and its aftermath have been fleshed out in two important recent books. There is Christopher Shackle and Javed Majeed's translation of Hali's *Musaddas*, which is the first readily accessible version of the poem in English, and boasts a full and excellent introduction. The opening *rubai* sets the tone of elegiac lament over the sorry state into which the Muslims have fallen:

> If anyone sees the way our downfall passes all bounds
> the way that Islam, once fallen, does not rise again,

He will never believe that the tide flows after every ebb,
once he sees the way our sea has gone out.[29]

Half the poem is then devoted to attacking the failure of Muslim contemporaries—the rich, aristocrats, mystics, scholars, doctors, poets, fanatics, and bigots. European and British achievements are lauded explicitly and implicitly as the Prophet is made the preacher of Victorian values, stressing the virtues of frugality, cleanliness, sobriety, self-discipline, self-improvement, punctuality and philanthropy. Little more than two decades after the Mutiny, the new directions for Muslim society are being made very clear.[30]

A similar picture, in this case of the massive impact of the destruction of the old literary and aristocratic culture of Delhi and Lucknow in the Mutiny, is most sensitively drawn in Frances Pritchett's excellent *Nets of Awareness*. Muhammad Husain Azad and Altaf Husain Hali are the focal points of her study. In her preface she quotes Azad on the completeness of the transformation brought about by the Mutiny experience:

The important thing is that the glory of the winner's ascendant fortune gives everything of theirs—even their dress, their gait, their conversation—a radiance that makes them desirable. And people do not merely adopt them, but are proud to adopt them.[31]

The bulk of this work demonstrates how these great poets 'survivors of the great historical collision', as she characterizes them, set out to ensure, by incorporating English poetics, that Urdu literature survived.

Three essays on Muslim separatism follow logically from the 'shock of the Mutiny'. They embrace my developing thoughts on the subject. This had been the topic of my first book published in 1974.[32] In the same year the distinguished political scientist, Paul Brass, published his *Language, Religion and Politics in North India.*[33] Brass was exploring the political dimensions of nationalism and ethnicity; he was particularly concerned to explain why some nationalist movements succeeded while others did not. As far as Muslim separatism was concerned, he argued that there had been few objective differences between Hindus and Muslims in northern India and little in Hindu or Muslim revivalism to make Muslim separatism inevitable. What had been crucial was that Muslim elites had been themselves in danger of losing power in northern India and, as modern politics developed under the colonial state, chose divisive rather than composite symbols as the focus of political action. In selecting these divisive symbols rather than composite ones these elites acted rationally, standing apart from their culture and traditions.[34] 'Nation-formation: The Brass Thesis and Muslim Separatism' was my first response to Brass' argument. I proposed that he underestimated the influence of Hindu and Muslim revivalism, and greatly underestimated that of the colonial state. Moreover, he also overestimated the freedom of Muslim elites to choose one set of political symbols over another. They were constrained by their relationships with other groups and by the framework for political development created by the state. They were, furthermore, particularly constrained by the society that shaped them and by that society's fears and aspirations. Brass, in his response, was prepared to concede that elites might be constrained by the cultures of the groups they wished to represent. But he continued to argue that, if Muslims chose Islamic symbols for political action, it was not because those might be the symbols they instinctively preferred, or because they were the most desirable of the limited range available, but because they happened to be the best designed to protect and promote their interests.[35] 'Islam and Muslim Separatism' was the next stage in my response. My concern was to question yet further the possibility of 'rational choice', of best self-interest choice, by proposing that in the development of Muslim separatism many Muslim leaders had been constrained by political ideas derived from the Islamic culture, indeed, on occasion they had been constrained by religious belief itself.

In terms of the debate on nation-formation there were two poles, that of the instrumentalists and that of the primordialists. Brass ended up inclining towards the instrumentalist pole and I towards primordialist. That said, in describing my position, on reflection I would rather the term primordialist had not been used at all, however qualified. Scholars in referring to the Brass–Robinson debate found it too easy to ignore the attempted subtleties of my position and push me into some unreflecting camp of primordialist determinism. My position was not to deny politicians degrees of political choice, but only to indicate that they were more constrained by personal histories and cultural forces than Brass would have one believe.

The debate with Paul Brass, a chivalrous academic opponent if ever there was one, helped to form a friendship which I greatly value. One outcome of that friendship was a colloquium held at the University of Washington under the auspices of the South Asian Studies Programme in which we set out to celebrate the centenary of the Indian National Congress, which for all its vicissitudes of recent decades, remains one of the world's great political parties. The colloquium led to a volume of essays; my contribution to the volume was 'The Congress and the Muslims'. A decade after the commencement of the Brass–Robinson debate, I used it as an opportunity to review how the arguments over Muslim separatism had been advanced by recent scholarship. It refers to the work of Chris Bayly who demonstrated how the commercialization of royal power in the seventeenth and eighteenth centuries helped to bring about the development of a rooted Islamic service gentry and a largely Hindu merchant class which were to be the socio-economic formations that sustained Muslim and Hindu high culture and also Muslim and Hindu politics in the nineteenth and twentieth centuries. It refers to the work of Barbara Metcalf and others who had expanded our understanding of the drives and development of the various forms of Muslim revival and reform. It deals in particular with Farzana Shaikh's exploration in depth of the argument in 'Islam and Muslim Separatism' that in making political choices Indian Muslims were constrained by values derived from their Islamic background.[36] Recent work on Hindu revivalism is surveyed which reveals growing awareness of the obstacles it presented to Muslims being part of Congress, an awareness which has of course only grown over the past fifteen years. Also surveyed is the work of David Page and Ayesha Jalal on the frameworks for politics fashioned by the British in the 1919 and 1935 Government of India Acts and the ways in which the federal aspects of the framework increasingly brought conflict between Hindu and Muslim to mingle with conflict between centre and province. The basis for a much richer and more complex understanding of Muslim separatism was revealed.

Since then major contributions have focused either on the role of colonialism in constructing a communal discourse or on the origins, development and impact of Hindu nationalist consciousness. Gyanendra Pandey has been the standard bearer of the former understanding. He argues that the British constructed India for themselves primarily in terms of religious communities—Hindu, Muslim, Sikh and so on. Indian elites in their interactions with the colonial state, as well as with each other, aided and abetted this construction; they made for themselves communal histories with their roots deep in the past. At the same time, in opposition both to the communal vision and to the colonial state, they fashioned a national history built around the 'fundamental unity of India'.[37] This understanding has had wide support.[38] Since the Babri Masjid affair, the rise of Hindu nationalist parties to power in Indian politics, and the clear importance of religious community in political life elsewhere in the world of the 1990s, the answers have not seemed quite so simple. For Peter van der Veer, India's religious nationalisms (a term he prefers to the pejorative communalisms) are not just a product of India's colonial past. Nor are they primordial attachments inculcated by tradition. They are about changing identities spread by institutionalized devotionalism and shaped by pilgrimage, migration, print and the visual media. They are the framework within which the discourses of religious and national community come together. They have their own history and are much more than some 'master narrative of European modernity'.[39]

As the emergence of Hindu nationalism in all its glory has placed the Nehruvian vision of the 'essential unity of India' in a new perspective, we have become increasingly aware of the power of Hindu revivalism and Hindu imagery in the politics of the last thirty years of British rule. Joya Chatterji has revealed the importance of the religious nationalism of the Bengali Bhadralok in the 1930s and 1940s and how they welcomed partition with open arms.[40] Christophe Jaffrelot has offered a powerful analysis of the rise of Hindu nationalism from the 1920s.[41] Recent research has shown how aspects of this phenomenon drove Muslims into countervailing action. Hindu attempts at the mass conversion of Muslims in Mewat in the 1920s led to the foundation of the Tablighi Jama'at, an organization which has had a major role from the bottom up in sustaining and enhancing a Muslim identity.[42] Saiyid Abu'l Ala Maududi, who was to found the Jama'ati Islami in 1940 travelled from Hyderabad to Delhi in the late 1930s for the first time in seven years. He found the atmosphere so changed, and the attitude towards Muslims of at least one leading Congress politician so high-handed, that from that moment he identified Congress nationalism with a drive for Hindu supremacy.[43] In 1992, in writing the introduction to the Oxford edition of *Separatism among Indian Muslims* I declared that 'we now have the materials for a much richer understanding of the complex processes at work in the making of Muslim separatism'.[44] Now, seven years later, with yet more perspectives offered by fresh research and the passage of time, the possibilities for richer understanding only increase.

Over the past twenty years scholarship devoted to the world of Islam and that of Muslims in South Asia has expanded substantially. In addition to the South Asian and British interest long present, there has been growing attention in Europe, Australia and especially in the USA. Indeed, arguably the last three decades of the twentieth century saw a rich harvest from the investment made from the 1950s by the US in area studies.

It has been my custom to review at length major new contributions to the field. The aim has always been in part to pay tribute to major scholarly achievement and also to share with fellow scholars my pleasure and excitement in the new understandings made available and the new vistas opened up.

Dick Eaton has devoted much of his scholarly life to investigating and explaining the processes of Islamization in the subcontinent, to developing major insights into the processes by which South Asia was transformed from a society with few Muslims under the Delhi sultanate to one with c. 350 millions today—at least one-third of the Muslims of the planet. The *Sufis of Bijapur* was Eaton's first great contribution to the subject. He demonstrates how by understanding the social roles which sufis have performed it is possible to understand their Islamizing effect. Mirroring scholarly approaches which were being adopted elsewhere in the study of the Muslim world, it represented a major step forward in the study both of sufism and of Islamization in South Asia. This fine book was followed fifteen years later by *The Rise of Islam and the Bengal Frontier 1204–1760*. In this remarkable study based on sources in Persian, Arabic, Bengali, Sanskrit and European languages, as well as notably fruitful research in the Persian records of the Sylhet and Chittagong collectorates, Eaton shows how Mughal attempts to exploit the resources of Bengal, as well as to entrench their rule, created the drives behind Islamization. Islam, in fact, was 'a civilization-building ideology associated both with settling and populating the land and with constructing a transcendent reality associated with that process'.[45] With these two outstanding pieces of research Eaton blew away old arguments of Islamization being achieved by the sword or being a popular revolt against a

Brahminically dominated society and set a new level of understanding of the mechanics of religio-cultural change against which all who enter the field will have to measure their work.

The year 1978 was a vintage one for the history of South Asian Muslims. In addition to Eaton's first book, it also saw the publication of David Lelyveld's *Aligarh's First Generation: Muslim Solidarity in British India* and Christian Troll's *Sayyid Ahmad Khan: A Reinterpretation of Muslim Theology*, which jointly represented a great step forward in our understanding of the ideas and achievement of Syed Ahmed Khan, indeed, as the review suggests, the greatest step forward since Hali wrote *Hayat-i Javed*. Traces of my concerns at the time about the role of ideas in social action are clearly evident in the review; the debate with Paul Brass had only just concluded. Hence I was unhappy with the way Lelyveld seemed to make ideas of what it was to be a Muslim a function of the changing social and political context and happy with Troll's view that Syed Ahmed's life 'exemplifies that change of ideas, rather than being a mere epiphenomenon or ideological superstructure of changes in the economic, social and political field, is in fact related to all of them by way of mutual interaction'.[46]

This said, *Aligarh's First Generation* was unrivalled as an analysis and evocation of the world from which the creators of the MAO College came and of the society and values that were fostered there. Recently we have been fortunate enough to be presented with Gail Minault's *Secluded Scholars* which could be regarded as the companion volume to Lelyveld's work. The emergence of 'modern' education for Muslim girls was in large part, though certainly not entirely, the work of the Aligarh movement. The products of this initiative were to play leading roles in literary and public life not dissimilar from those of the Aligarh brothers. Like Lelyveld, Minault explores the 'sharif' or respectable world from which the first generations of 'modern' educated Muslim women came. Like Lelyveld she is also dealing with the social, cultural and institutional dimensions of Muslim modernism. But arguably in her case the themes are much larger, more revolutionary. Lelyveld was dealing with yet another stage in Muslim history in which the male Muslim world negotiated new technologies, new institutions and new ideas. Minault, on the other hand, addresses the early stages of one of the great themes of change in contemporary Muslim societies—the ways in which Muslim women and men negotiate the passage of

Muslim women from a world of concealment to become major, even equal, players in all aspects of Muslim public life.[47]

Christian Troll's study of Syed Ahmed Khan as a theologian was a source of delight. As a work revealing the quality of an individual Muslim, as well as the huge challenges Muslims confronted in nineteenth-century India, it belongs with Ralph Russell's portrait of Ghalib,[48] Frances Pritchett's portraits of Muhammad Husain Azad and Altaf Husain Hali,[49] and to a lesser extent with Barbara Metcalf's treatment of Rashid Ahmad Gangohi and Muhammad Qasim Nanautvi.[50] It is hard not to imagine that he brought especial understanding to his interpretation from his own religious commitment and training. Believers, whatever their particular form of belief, have advantage in studying other believers. Equally, I have no doubt that time spent labouring with Christian theology is no disadvantage when studying a Muslim striving his utmost to meet the theological challenges of his time. No less important than the particular sensitivities and skills which Troll brought to his work on Syed Ahmed was the way in which he shows just how much Syed owed to, and was shaped by, the reforming impulse of the late-eighteenth and early-nineteenth century Delhi. It is our good fortune that Troll did not end his interest in major Indo–Muslim theologians with Syed Ahmed. Together with Gail Minault he was responsible for recovering from obscurity and making available the first major study in English of Abul Kalam Azad, another great religious and intellectual pilgrim.[51] Azad owed much in his early life to Syed Ahmed Khan, and was amongst his true heirs in Syed's great struggle to be a true Muslim in the modern Indian world.

In commencing my review of these two good books, I asserted that it was about time that someone took on the task of writing the life of Syed Ahmed Khan. Twenty years have passed and still nobody has yet risen to the task of interpreting the achievement of this extraordinary man. For a biographer of mature historical and literary talents there is a marvellous opportunity.

The study of the Muslim world of India, as we might expect, has tended to be dominated by the study of the Muslims of the north. For this reason major monographs devoted to the Muslims of other regions are particularly welcome. We think, of course, of the work of Eaton on Golkonda and Bengal,[52] of that of Asim Roy and Rafiuddin Ahmed on Bengal,[53] of Susan Bayly and J.B.P. More on the Muslims of Tamilnadu,[54] and of the potential revealed in the essays collected in Dallapiccola and Lallemant's *Islam and the Indian Regions*.[55] The publication of Miller's *Mappila Muslims of Kerala* in 1976[56] and Stephen Dale's *Islamic Society on the South Asian Frontier* in 1980 brought our understanding of the distinctive Muslim world of south-west India, so very different from that of the north, into a new era. It was now possible for scholars to have a detailed understanding of the Muslim topography of Malabar, and significant learned and holy families, like the Ponnani Makhdums and the Mambram Tannals, were brought into view to be placed beside the Waliullahis and Firangi Mahalis of the north. In reviewing Dale's book, one response was how clearly the picture which he drew of assertive Islamization in Malabar, in particular over the past two hundred years, was clearly at odds with Imtiaz Ahmad's view that in India the high Islamic and custom-centred traditions peacefully 'co-exist as complementary and integral parts of a common religious system'.[57] The second was that Dale gave too much weight to 'a long tradition of religiously expressed violence' interacting with economic and social conditions in explaining the nineteenth-century *jihads* in the region and not enough to influences from the worldwide movement of revival and reform. Tantalizing connections were set out for us between the Mambram Tannals and the scholarly world of the Yemen. As time goes on, research in family and other libraries in Kerala, the Yemen, the Hijaz and Egypt should reveal more of the connections that existed and the value which should be put upon them. There is benefit to be gained not just from understanding the broader 'Islamic world' context of the Muslims of Malabar but also that of the Muslims of much of India.

Barbara Metcalf's *Islamic Revival in British India* is one of the most important books published during the past thirty years not just on Islam in India but on the Islamic world in general. My review sets out some of the book's notable achievements: the analysis of the rich range of the reactions of the north Indian *ulama* to Muslim decline and British dominance; the demonstration of the extraordinary vitality and creativity of Indian Islam in the eighteenth and nineteenth centuries; the exploration of how the Deoband movement was such a successful response to the challenges of colonial rule; and the illustration of the remarkable way in which the reforming *ulama* embraced a communications revolution in order to build a constituency for themselves in Muslim society. With the benefit of hindsight one would wish to emphasize further achievements. *Islamic Revival* is the first study, of which I am aware, of an example of the great reorientation of Muslim piety over the past two centuries from other-worldly to this-worldly religion. It is also the book to which one must turn to discover the roots of major movements in the Muslim world today. The South Asian diaspora, and the growing significance of religious organization in the politics of many areas, mean that there is growing need to understand the ideas and purposes of groups such as the Deobandis, the Tablighi Jama'atis, the Ahl-i Hadiths[58]and the Barelvis, and Metcalf's book is where all should begin. Since the publication of *Islamic Revival* Metcalf herself has carried forward the study of Islamic reform with work on the Tablighi Jama'at and her edition of Thanvi's *Behishti Zewar*.[59] Other aspects of this field which she has done so much to open up have been pursued by Friedmann, Sanyal, Malik, Sikand and myself.[60]

Muhammad Ali Jinnah is the dominating figure of the Muslim politics of twentieth-century South Asia—a key shaper of those politics in the first half of the century and a towering legacy, an endlessly manipulated icon, for the second half. For a quarter of a century after Jinnah's death there was little reassessment of his aims and achievements. However, the publication between 1970 and 1982 of the twelve volumes of British documents relating to the transfer of power, the deposit of the 80,000 pages of the *Quaid-i-Azam* papers in the National Archives of Pakistan, and the availability of growing quantities of the archives of the All-India Muslim League began to make such reassessment possible. In 1984 and 1985 two such reassessments appeared; Stanley Wolpert's *Jinnah of Pakistan* and Ayesha Jalal's *The Sole Spokesman: Jinnah, the Muslim League and the Demand for Pakistan*. The achievements of Wolpert was to make Jinnah accessible to a new generation, and to reveal the human side of a man so often portrayed as cold and distant by his political colleagues. Wolpert's weakness was that he had not had the advantage of reading Jalal and still followed the orthodox Pakistani view of Jinnah as a man who from the late 1930s had perceived Muslims to be a separate nation on the Indian subcontinent and from 1940 fought for the creation of a separate, sovereign state of Pakistan. This mixture of the human Jinnah and the heroic fighter for the sovereign state of Pakistan was also the line adopted by Akbar Ahmed's recent book and feature film on the subject.[61] Interestingly, however, a documentary on Jinnah, produced by Café Productions, and with which Ahmed was also substantially involved, made clear Jinnah's much more complex approach to the issue of Pakistan, and contains a striking interview with Jinnah's daughter, Dina Wadia, in which she asserts that her father never intended to divide British India into separate sovereign states at Independence.[62]

Jalal's achievement was to demonstrate convincingly that Jinnah's aims were quite the reverse of the orthodox Pakistani version, that right up to June 1946 he pursued a Muslim future within India and then spent the last thirteen months of British rule desperately trying to manage the failure of his strategy. It is an argument supported by the publication of the unexpurgated version of Abul Kalam Azad's *India Wins Freedom* in 1988 which asserted Azad's view that Pakistan was for Jinnah a bargaining counter 'perhaps to the very end' and that it was Patel who was responsible for the division of India.[63] This position, as we have seen, is also supported by Jinnah's daughter. In the review I described Jalal's thesis as 'novel', a point on which I was quite properly corrected by Asim Roy.[64] It was not novel to me as I had heard it from Jalal's thesis supervisor, Anil Seal, in the 1960s, and had the impression that it had been a view in Delhi in the 1940s. What was truly novel was the detailed working out of the argument in terms of the play of power at the time and the large quantity of records now available. This said, we should note the view of the editor of the Jinnah papers that all current assessments of Jinnah must be incomplete. Because no one yet has been able to work through the entire body of Jinnah's papers, declares Z.H. Zaidi, 'no complete analytical and objective study of Jinnah and his time has been possible.'[65]

If the 1980s saw major steps forward in our understanding of Jinnah, they saw similar steps forward in our understanding of the nationalist Muslims. The latter came with Mushirul Hasan's biography of Dr M.A. Ansari and Ian Henderson Douglas' biography of Abul Kalam Azad. I chose to review the books together because they offered an opportunity to consider some of the concerns and drives behind the Muslim nationalists. Hasan's biography of Ansari forms part of his major effort to ensure that the great Muslim figures in the nationalist movement, Muhammad and Shaukat Ali, Ansari and Azad, should not be forgotten. It is interesting to speculate on the extent to which Hasan's driving concern was due in part to piety towards the three of the four who had been involved in founding the Jamia Millia Islamia where he worked, in part to concern that historical justice should be done, and in part, and perhaps subconsciously, to a concern to engage, as historians must often do, in a discourse of national identity.

Douglas' biography of Azad, which was completed as long ago as 1969, and which was only published as a result of the entrepreneurial persistence of Gail Minault, is a most important book. It brings our understanding of this most gifted and complex of national leaders to a new level. By revealing the humanity of the man it gives us a better sense of his greatness. By showing the interaction between his personal life and his religious ideas, it gives a real sense of Azad's spiritual struggle and growth. By setting before us Azad's belief in the essential oneness of all religions, which the combination of Douglas' research and editor Troll's detective work was able to demonstrate had been achieved by 1910, the work revealed the profound religious underpinning of Azad's nationalist vision. This was a fine achievement and perhaps one that benefited from the fact that the author was a Christian missionary, a man who approached Azad first of all as a fellow struggler in the way of faith. It is unfortunate that the book, which tells us so much about how a great man strove to live a Muslim life, and which compares strikingly with Seyyed Vali Reza Nasr's recent biography of Maulana Azad's opposite number in Indo–Muslim thought, Maulana Maududi, would seem to have received relatively little notice, certainly not enough to merit a paperback edition.[66]

These reviews, which cover but a tithe of the books produced in the field, reveal the vigour with which the study of Islam and Muslim history in South Asia has been undertaken over the last quarter of a century. Old shibboleths have been overturned. Some, indeed, with a significance that reaches into the Muslim world at large. And this is as it should be. The study of Islam and Muslim history in South Asia should be no small or meagre branch of study for it involves the history of one-third of the Muslim peoples of the world and one-third of the people of South Asia. As a subject it is only in its infancy. Huge quantities of archives and materials in Persian remain to be broached. Large quantities of papers in various South Asian languages lie with families and private institutions. The field is a sumptuous theatre in which some of the great themes of historiography can be explored, an arena where it is always a privilege to strive to discover what it was to be human in that place at another time.

NOTES

1. Peter Brown, *Augustine of Hippo: A Biography* (London, 1967).
2. Representative of Cobb's style at its most influential is his collection of essays *A Second Identity; Essays on France and French History* (London, 1969). This style, however, was not acceptable to all. The response of the historian of the crusades, Jonathan Riley–Smith, to a brilliantly atmospheric lecture given by Cobb at Royal Holloway on Thermidor was that such an approach would be totally unacceptable in Cambridge. Riley–Smith now holds the Chair of Medieval History in Cambridge.
3. Samuel P. Huntington, *The Clash of Civilizations and the Remaking of World Order* (New York, 1996).
4. Ibid., p. 321.
5. Francis Robinson, *Atlas of the Islamic World since 1500* (Oxford, 1982).
6. See the second volume of essays, *The Ulama of Firangi Mahal and Islamic Culture* (New Delhi, forthcoming).
7. For a summary of this argument see Francis Robinson, 'Islamic History as the History of Learned and Holy Men' in *La Transmission du Savoir dans le Monde Musulman Peripherique: Lettre d'information*, no. 5, Avril 1986, pp. 1–10.
8. Marshall G.S. Hodgson, *Venture of Islam: Conscience and History in a World Civilization*, 3 vols (Chicago, 1974).
9. The three volumes already published were: *Caste and Social Stratification among the Muslims* (New Delhi, 1973); *Family, Kinship and Marriage among Muslims in India* (New Delhi, 1976); and *Ritual and Religion among Muslims in India* (New Delhi, 1981). The fourth volume was: *Modernisation and Social Change among Muslims in India* (New Delhi, 1983).
10. Ahmad (ed.), *Ritual and Religion*, Introduction.
11. This theme was developed in 'South Asia as Part of an Islamic World System', a lecture given in Oxford as part of a series on Wallerstein, world-system theory and the Islamic world, November 1998.
12. For a substantial analysis of the Tabligh see Yoginder Singh Sikand 'The Origins and Development of the Tablighi Jama'at (1920s–1990s): A Cross-Country Comparative Study', University of London, PhD, 1998.
13. For the growth of madrasas in Pakistan see Muhammad Qasim Zaman, 'Sectarianism in Pakistan: The Radicalization of Shi'i and Sunni Identities', *Modern Asian Studies*, 32, 3, July 1998, pp. 689–716, and for the growth of madrasas and their relationship to a new Sunni militancy see S.V.R. Nasr, 'The Rise of Sunni Militancy in Pakistan: The Changing Role of Islamism and the ulama in Society and Politics', *Modern Asian Studies*, forthcoming.
14. Gail Minault, 'Some Reflections on Islamic Revivalism vs. Assimilation among Muslims in India', *Contributions to Indian Sociology*, n.s., 18, 2, 1984, pp. 301–5.

15. Veena Das, 'For a Folk-theology and Theological Anthropology of Islam', *Contibutions to Indian Sociology*, n.s. 18, 2, 1984, pp. 293–300.
16. Francis Robinson, 'Islam and Muslim Society in South Asia; A Reply to Das and Minault', *Contributions to Indian Sociology*, n.s. 20, 1, 1986, pp. 97–104.
17. See, in particular: Mushirul Hasan, *Nationalism and Communal Politics in India, 1885–1930* (Delhi, 1991); *A Nationalist Conscience; M.A. Ansari, the Congress and the Raj* (Delhi, 1987); *Legacy of a Divided Nation: India's Muslims since Independence* (Delhi, 1997).
18. Francis Robinson, 'Islam and the Impact of Print' *Modern Asian Studies*, 27, 1, February 1993, pp. 229–51.
19. See Rosalind Thomas, *Oral Tradition and Written Record in Classical Athens* (Cambridge, 1989), and *Literacy and Orality in Ancient Greece* (Cambridge, 1992).
20. Francis Robinson, 'Islam and the Impact of Print in South Asia', Nigel Crook (ed.), *The Transmission of Knowledge in South Asia: Essays on Education, History, and Politics* (Delhi, 1996), p. 90.
21. Charles Taylor, *Sources of the Self: The Making of Modern Identity* (Cambridge, 1989).
22. Major work has been done on the theme of the self and the fashioning of identity in the colonial and post-colonial years by Katherine Pratt Ewing. Through a reading of al-Ghazzali's understanding of desire as central to human action and through an analysis of long-standing sufi practice she argues that the reflexive critical consciousness normally associated with the 'modern' self can be found in the sufi tradition. Iqbal, she argues, drew on this tradition in reconstituting the Muslim self as a powerful active force in the face of European domination. Katherine Pratt Ewing, *Arguing Sainthood: Modernity, Psychoanalaysis and Islam* (Durham NC, 1997).
23. A. fascinating example of such a resolution between religious tradition and social reality is former President Rafsanjani's advocacy in 1990 of temporary or *muta* marriage to enable Iranian youth, now often unable to marry until 25 or 30, to satisfy their sexual needs within the framework of the law. Shahla Haeri 'Temporary Marriage: An Islamic Discourse on Female Sexuality in Iran', in Mahnaz Afkhami and Erika Friedl (eds), *In the Eye of the Storm; Women in Post-revolutionary Iran* (London, 1994), pp. 98–114. The tension between individual and community is not, of course, just a feature of Muslim societies but a common feature of non-Western societies. See, for instance, Nancy R. Rosenberger (ed.), *Japanese Sense of Self* (Cambridge, 1992) and Mattison Mines, *Public Faces, Private Voices: Community and Individuality in South India* (Berkeley and Los Angeles, 1994).
24. Guenther Roth and Claus Wittich (eds), Max Weber, *Economy and Society: An Outline of Interpretive Sociology*, 2 vols (Berkeley and Los Angeles, 1978).

25. Wolfgang Schluchter (ed.), *Max Weber's Sicht des Islams* (Frankfurt am Main, 1987).
26. For an exploration of Weberian themes in a sufi context see Claudia Liebeskind, *Piety on its Knees: Three Sufi Traditions in South Asia in Modern Times* (Delhi, 1998).
27. Narayani Gupta, 'Eric Stokes (10 July 1924 – 5 February 1981)', Mushirul Hasan and Narayani Gupta (eds), *India's Colonial Encounter: Essays in Memory of Eric Stokes* (Delhi, 1993), pp. vii–ix.
28. 'South Asia as part of an Islamic World System', *supra*.
29. Christopher Shackle and Javed Majeed, *Hali's Musaddas: The Flow and Ebb of Islam* (Delhi, 1997), p. 103; for my review of Shackle and Majeed see, Francis Robinson, 'House of Mirrors', *Times Literary Supplement*, 23 April 1999, pp. 4–5.
30. Ibid., 'Introduction', pp. 76–8. This point also comes through clearly in an analysis made by my PhD student, Amit Dey, of a substantial number of nineteenth- and twentieth-century biographies of the Prophet in Bengali.
31. Muhammad Husain Azad, *Ab-e Hayat* (Water of Life), cited in Frances W. Pritchett, *Nets of Awareness: Urdu Poetry and Its Critics* (Berkeley and Los Angeles, 1994), p. xvi.
32. Francis Robinson, *Separatism Among Indian Muslims: The Politics of the United Provinces' Muslims, 1860–1923* (Cambridge, 1974).
33. P.R. Brass, *Language, Religion and Politics in North India* (Cambridge, 1974).
34. Ibid. pp. 119–81.
35. P.R. Brass, 'Elite Groups, Symbol Manipulation and Ethnic Identity among the Muslims of South Asia', in D. Taylor and M. Yapp (eds), *Political Identity in South Asia* (London, 1979), pp. 35–77.
36. Gyanendra Pandey, *The Construction of Communalism in Colonial North India* (Delhi, 1990).
37. Carol A. Breckenridge and Peter Van der Veer (eds), *Orientalism and the Postcolonial Predicament* (Delhi, 1994).
38. Peter Van der Veer, *Religious Nationalism: Hindus and Muslims in India* (Berkeley and Los Angeles, 1994).
39. Joya Chatterji, *Bengal Divided: Hindu Communalism and Partition, 1932–1947* (Delhi, 1995).
40. Christophe Jaffrelot, *The Hindu Nationalist Movement and Indian Politics 1925 to the 1990s* (London, 1996).
41. Sikand, 'Tablighi Jama'at', pp. 139–216.
42. Sayyed Vali Reza Nasr, *Mawdudi and the Makings of Islamic Revivalism* (New York, 1996), pp. 31–2.
43. Francis Robinson, *Separatism Among Indian Muslims: The Politics of the United Provinces' Muslim 1860–1923* (Delhi, 1992), p. xxiv.
44. Richard M. Eaton, *The Rise of Islam and the Bengal Frontier, 1204–1760*

(Berkeley and Los Angeles, 1993); see also my review of this book in *Journal of Islamic Studies*, 7, 1, January 1996, pp. 113–15.

45. Christian W. Troll, *Sayyid Ahmad Khan: A Reinterpretation of Muslim Theology* (Delhi, 1978), p. xx.
46. Farzana Shaikh, *Community and Consensus in Islam: Muslim Representation in Colonial India, 1860–1947* (Cambridge, 1989).
47. Gail Minault, *Secluded Scholars: Women's Education and Muslim Social Reform in Colonial India* (Delhi, 1998); see also Azra Asghar Ali, 'The Emergence of Feminism Among Indian Muslim Women, 1920–47', University of London, PhD, 1996.
48. Ralph Russell and Khurshidul Islam, *Ghalib 1797–1869: Volume I: Life and Letters* (London, 1969).
49. Pritchett, *Nets*, op. cit.
50. Barbara Daly Metcalf, *Islamic Revival in British India: Deoband, 1860–1900* (Princeton NJ, 1982).
51. Ian Henderson Douglas, *Abul Kalam Azad: An Intellectual and Religious Biography*, Gail Minault and Christian W. Troll (eds) (Delhi, 1988).
52. Eaton, *Islam on the Bengal Frontier*, op. cit. and *Sufis of Bijapur 1300– 1700: Social Roles of Sufis in Medieval India* (Princeton NJ, 1978).
53. Rafiuddin Ahmad, *The Bengal Muslims 1871–1906: A Quest for Modernity* (Delhi, 1981), and Asim Roy, *The Islamic Syncretistic Tradition in Bengal* (Princeton NJ, 1983).
54. Susan Bayly, *Saints, Goddesses and Kings: Muslims and Christians in South Indian Society, 1700–1900* (Cambridge, 1989); J.B.P. More, *The Political Evolution of Muslims in Tamilnadu and Madras 1930–1947* (Hyderabad, 1997).
55. Anna Libera Dallapiccola and Stephanie Zingel-Ave Lallemant, *Islam and Indian Regions*, 2 vols (Stuttgart, 1993).
56. Roland E. Miller, *Mappila Muslims of Kerala: A Study in Islamic Trends* (Delhi, 1976).
57. Ahmad, *Ritual and Religion*, Introduction.
58. The need to broadcast the understandings offered by Metcalf's book was recently underlined when the leading Anglo-Pakistani journalist, Tariq Ali, described the Ahl-i Hadiths as 'a creation of the ISI'. Tariq Ali, 'Try and disarm us, if you can', *London Review of Books*, 15 April 1999, pp. 19–22.
59. Barbara D. Metcalf, *Perfecting Women: Maulana Ashraf 'Ali Thanawi's Bihishti Zewar: A Partial Translation with Commentary* (Berkeley and Los Angeles, 1990).
60. Sikand, 'Tablighi Jama'at'; Robinson, 'Ulama of Firangi Mahal'; Yohanan Friedman, *Prophecy Continuous: Aspects of Ahmadi Religious Thought and its Medieval Background* (Berkeley and Los Angeles, 1989; Usha Sanyal, *Devotional Islam and Politics in British India: Ahmad Riza Khan Barelwi and his Movement, 1870–1920* (Delhi, 1996); Jamal S. Malik,

Islamische Gelehrtenkultur in Nordindien: Entwicklungsgeschichte und Tendenzen am Beispiel von Lucknow (Leiden, 1997).

61. Akbar Ahmad, *Jinnah, Pakistan and Islam Identity: The Search for Saladin* (London, 1997). The feature film was entitled 'Jinnah'.
62. 'Mr Jinnah—The Making of Pakistan' (Café Productions, 1997).
63. Maulana Abul Kalam Azad, *India Wins Freedom; the Complete Version* (Delhi, 1988), p. 197.
64. Asim Roy, 'The High Politics of Partition: The Revisionist Perspective', *Modern Asian Studies*, 24, 2, May 1990, pp. 385–408.
65. Z.H. Zaidi, *Jinnah Papers: Prelude to Pakistan 20 February–2 June 1947*, First Series, vol. I, part 1, Islamabad, 1993, p. xxii.
66. Douglas, *Azad* and Nasr, *Mawdudi*.

Chapter One

The Muslim and the Christian Worlds: Shapers of Each Other[1]

This essay is framed in the spirit of global historical enquiry. The brush strokes are broad and likely to sweep over sensibilities. Some strokes may well be made in the wrong place or the wrong direction. Nevertheless, I hope you feel the price is worth paying for the big story I propose to address.

Let us be clear about our Muslim and Christian worlds. We are dealing with a Muslim world which, from the eighth to the eighteenth century was a leading player in global affairs, indeed, which some have called an Islamic world system. We are dealing with a Western Christian world which from the eighteenth century became in its turn the leading player in global affairs and formed, of course, the archetypal world system. Through fourteen centuries of world history these two civilizations have lived cheek by jowl, from time to time, rubbing up against each other, penetrating each other, borrowing from each other, learning from each other, despising each other, fighting each other and fantasizing about each other. Arguably, Muslim and Christian civilizations have influenced each other, and continue to do so, as no two other civilizaions have done before.

Given this long and not always harmonious relationship we need to remind ourselves that it carries with it much baggage. On the Western–Christian side, there is the polemic against Islam dating back to the Middle Ages; there is the Enlightenment use of the Muslim world as a free-range area for the imagination; there is the orientalist legacy which rendered this Muslim world into some undifferentiated and unchanging essence; and there still remains a legacy of fear from the old days of Muslim power that combines with an arrogant superiority towards an inferior civilization which Europeans once ruled. On the Muslim side the legacies go back no more than two hundred years; it is only over this period that Muslims have taken the West seriously. These legacies are a mixture of admiration for the Western achievement, fear of the Western power, resentment at Muslim subordination to Western power, and a serious questioning of whether the Western model of progress is the right one for them. This last issue lies right at the heart of Muslim discourses about their present and future.

The last fact—the Muslim questioning of the Western model of progress—has led the distinguished US political scientist, Samuel P. Huntington, to propose his thesis of the *Clash of Civilizations*.[2] In the post-Cold-War era, he argues, the crucial distinctions between people are not primarily ideological or economic, but cultural. World politics is now being reconfigured along cultural lines. As that process takes place, the Muslim world is emerging with deep faultlines between it and the West. It has 'bloody borders' and represents the greatest danger to world peace. I do not wish to engage in a critique of Huntington's argument; it is enough for the moment to suggest that it seems powerfully informed by orientalist assumptions and is supported by a selective use of evidence. But, Huntington's intervention has attracted enormous attention. This makes it of value to review the long history of influence and interdependence between the Christian and the Muslim worlds. It is worthwhile, when some are focusing on what may divide us to remind ourselves of the many bridges which have lain between us in the past, and which may still have their uses in the present and future. So, first, I propose to examine the impact of the classical and late antique worlds on the development of Islamic civilization; second, I propose to examine the impact of the Islamic world on the development of Europe from the Middle Ages onwards; third, I want to look at the role of the West in shaping the modern Muslim world; and fourth, the continuing role of the Muslim world in helping to shape the West.

THE IMPACT OF THE CLASSICAL AND LATE ANTIQUE WORLDS ON THE DEVELOPMENT OF ISLAMIC CIVILIZATION

It is well known, but I often think not well-known enough, that the learning of the classical and late antique worlds made an immense contribution to the development of Muslim civilization. The creation of an Arab–Muslim empire in the seventh and eighth centuries, stretching from the Atlantic in the West to Central Asia and the Indus Valley in the East, created a huge new nexus for the exchange of goods, the movement of peoples and the mingling of cultures and ideas. In the new high civilization which developed from the eighth century onwards, Islam drew on Indian and Iranian strands as well as Jewish and Hellenistic ones.

Let us consider the contributions of Greek learning to the development of Muslim civilization. We should say first of all that it came to the Islamic world not in its classical form but as it had come to be elaborated in the late antique world. The Hellenistic traditions of Athens were sustained by Nestorian Christians working under Sasanian patronage at the educational centre at Jundishapur in southern Iran. The Hellenistic traditions of Alexandria were sustained successively at Antioch in Syria, at Marw in Khorasan, and at Harran in Mesopotamia. Theological debate in the eighth and ninth centuries led to curiosity about Greek thought and both traditions were transferred to Abbasid Baghdad. A great programme of translation of works from Greek, and also from Syriac, was set in place. By the eleventh century at least eighty Greek authors had been translated, major figures such as Aristotle, Plato, Galen and Euclid being represented by several works. Amongst the subjects covered were: philosophy, medicine, mathematics, physics, optics, astronomy, geography, and the occult sciences of astrology, alchemy and magic.

This heritage from the ancient world was not allowed to lie fallow. Amongst the more important areas of further cultivation was mathematics, from the development of Arabic numerals, through the invention of Algebra and Trigonometry, to the discovery of decimal fractions and al-Hazen's problem. In astronomy, Muslims moved from accepting Ptolemy's geocentric view of interplanetary motion to becoming increasingly critical of it. By the thirteenth and fourteenth centuries Nasiruddin Tusi at Maragha and Ibn al-Shatir in Damascus were on the verge of making the breakthrough to the heliocentric theory of Copernicus. In medicine, there was the work of Ibn Zuhr on diet, of al-Nafisi on the circulation of blood, and of Abul Qasim al Zahrawi on surgery. But most important, there were the great encyclopaedists of medicine, al-Razi (Rhazes) and Ibn Sina (Avicenna) whose *Qanun*, which had great influence in Europe, is arguably the most important book in the history of medicine. Finally, there is that majestic series of philosophers inspired by the challenge of Greek thought: Ibn Sina, who helped develop the powerful strand of neo-platonic thought in Islam; the great commentators on Aristotle and Plato—al-Farabi, Ibn Rushd (Averroes) and, once again, the remarkable, Ibn Sina.[3]

This Hellenistic inheritance had a great and enduring impact on the development of Islamic civilization. Without the inheritance in the mathematical sciences, and their further development, the marvellous Muslim achievements in architecture would not have been possible. Without the inheritance in medicine, and its further development, Muslim achievements in healthcare, the development of hospitals, and most notably the great teaching hospitals of the central Islamic lands, would have been unlikely. Without the Muslim advances in astronomy and geography, the Islamic world would have been much less effectively knitted together as a 'world system' across which trader, scholars and mystics moved with ease. Without the legacies of philosophy this world would surely have been a different place: skills in logic have assisted Muslim jurists in the daily necessity down the ages of building bridges between revelation and changing human circumstance; the background of neo-platonic thought in sufism, the Islamic mystical tradition, enabled innumerable bridges to be built between the monotheistic heart of the faith and thousands of local pietistic traditions. This said, we should note that philosophy, as classically understood, was, by the eleventh century, found to be too great a threat to revelation. Its claims were refuted and banished to the margins of Muslim civilization by 'Abd al-Hamid al-Ghazzali—for some Muslims the greatest Muslim since Muhammad, for others the greatest disaster to strike the Muslim world.

In our world of scholarship, once Islam had transmitted its classical inheritance to Europe, interest quickly flagged. Nevertheless, this inheritance continues to have influence and inspire ideas right down to the present. Greek medicine is still practised in India and Iran. Greek learning in the rational sciences still figure in some traditional Islamic educational curriculums—in the *madrasas* of India they still refer to Aristotle as the 'first teacher'. Moreover, without the bridge-building role of neo-platonic ideas working through the thought of Ibn 'Arabi of Murcia in Spain, the greatest of the sufi thinkers, the remarkable spread of Islam from the thirteenth century onwards, in which sufis had a leading part to play, would have been much less effective. As it happens, the greatest enemy of the classical inheritance in Islam has been modern Western knowledge; so Greek medicine in the twentieth century has given way before Western biomedicine, and the classical inheritance of the *madrasa* curriculum before Western mathematical and natural sciences. Nevertheless, even now the legacy of Greece can be most powerfully felt; there is a remarkably close resemblance, as my colleague Vanessa Martin has demonstrated, between Ayatollah Khomeini's theory of Islamic government, expounded in his lectures at Qum in 1971, and Ibn Rushd's commentary on Plato's Republic.[4] Khomeini's theory lies behind the current constitution of the Islamic Republic of Iran.

We could leave the impact of the classical and late antique worlds there, but there is a further element which commands attention. This derives from the recent work of Garth Fowden presented in his recently published *From Empire to Commonwealth: the Consequences of Monotheism in Late Antiquity*. On the one hand he emphasizes the power of the vision of universal empire in late antiquity—the potent shadows of Cyrus and Alexander. On the other, he emphasizes the great importance, as a step in the direction of universal empire, of the Emperor Constantine's marriage of Christian monotheism with the Roman imperial structure. The early Islamic empire, he argues, realized to the full the ambitions in late antiquity to create a politico-cultural world empire.[5] This is symbolized in the triumphal proclamations on the Dome of the Rock in Jerusalem:

O ye People of the Book, overstep not bounds in your religion; and of God speak only truth. The Messiah, Jesus, son of Mary, is only an apostle of God, and His Word which he conveyed into Mary, and a Spirit proceeding from Him. Believe therefore in God and His apostles, and say not 'Three'. ... God witnesses that there is no God but He; and the angels, and men endowed with knowledge, established in righteousness, proclaim there is no God but He, the Mighty, the Wise. The true religion with God is Islam.

He it is who has sent His messenger with the guidance and the religion of truth, so that he may cause it to prevail over all religion, however much the idolators may hate it.[6]

It is there in the six kings of the world depicted in the throne room of the Ummayyad palace at Qusayr Amra: the defeated emperors of Byzantium and Iran, the defeated Roderick the Visigoth of Spain, the Negus of Ethiopia, and perhaps the rulers of China and Central Asia. The early Caliphs too, like the Emperor Constantine, drew their authority directly from God. Whereas the traditional view has been to regard the Islamic conquests as meaning the end of the late antique world, Fowden argues that the Muslim victory means the fulfilment, the culmination of the late antique world.[7] Such a re-reading of the founding legend of Muslim history, not to mention the death rattle of Classical civilization, is likely to be unpopular with Muslims, and probably with Byzantine and late antique specialists too. It is, however, worthy of serious consideration. And, if this is the case, we must see the Emperor Constantine's marriage of political and religious universalism as one of the greatest legacies of the late antique world to Islam. It lived in the extraordinarily powerful idea of the universal caliphate. It lives in the pan-Islamic ideal down to the present, and the Islamic mission to all of humankind.

THE IMPACT OF THE ISLAMIC WORLD ON THE DEVELOPMENT OF EUROPE

If rewriting the founding legends of Islam is likely to be unpopular, with Muslims at least, chipping away at the founding legends of European civilization may be no less unpopular with Westerners. Consideration of Arab–Muslim contributions to the making of medieval Europe has long been problematic. Too great an emphasis on the Arab–Muslim role has tended to threaten long-cherished ideas of Europeanness, or Westernness, buried fundamentally in a pre-conceived Latin, Christian past. These ideas, moreover, mingle with, and are confused by, that powerful tendency in European civilization since the Crusades for Europeans to define themselves, and they do so in different ways at different times, against the Muslim 'other'.

This said, traditionally there have been few problems in acknowledging Muslim contributions to European material culture. We accept the impact of Muslim achievements in textiles, carpets, metal- and leather-working, glass-making and bookbinding, which can be found across medieval and early modern Europe. We have little trouble with the fact that silk and paper came to the West by Muslim hands, as did the cultivation of sugar, cotton and citrus fruits. We acknowledge a host of Muslim contributions in shipbuilding, navigation, agriculture and the arts of fine living. We cannot ignore a substantial Arabic input into European languages across a broad range of activities, not least among them being commerce with words such as 'magazine' from the Arabic *makhazin* meaning storehouse, 'traffic' from the Arabic *tafriq* meaning distribution, 'tariff' from the Arabic *Ta'rifah* and 'check' from the Arabic *sakk*.[8]

Since the work of the great American scholar Charles Haskins, there has been a powerful argument for accepting that Arab–Muslim scholarship played a significant role, alongside the revival of classical Latin prose, poetry and law, in stimulating what he called the Twelfth-Century Renaissance. 'It befits us to imitate the Arabs especially,' declared Hugo of Santalla, the twelfth-century Aragonese scholar of astrology, 'for they are as it were our teachers and precursors in this art.'[9]

And this was surely the spirit that motivated the host of venturesome twelfth- and thirteenth-century scholars who made their way to Toledo, Seville, Barcelona and Sicily to translate into Latin, Arab–Muslim works on science and philosophy, Arab–Muslim versions of Greek texts, and Arab–Muslim commentaries on these texts. The excitement of the great translators—Gerard of Cremona, Adelard of Bath, Robert of Ketton, Micheal Scott, and many others—must have matched that of our experimental scientists today as they uncover seam after seam of new knowledge about the natural world. Through Arabic came advanced knowledge in mathematics, astronomy, optics, astrology, alchemy, geography and of course medicine which, as Haskins declared, 'profoundly coloured European thought'.[10] Through Arabic came the neo-platonism of Avicenna and the Aristotelianism of Averroes. Indeed, through Arabic came a whole new world of logic and metaphysics to which European thinkers of all kinds had to respond, and which many used as intellectual tools. Haskins talks of the 'spirit of devotion to science', the 'rationalistic habit of mind', and the 'experimental temper' found amongst the ancient Greeks but 'fostered and kept alive in the Mohammedan countries, and it was chiefly from these that they passed to Western Christendom'.[11]

One senses, however, that not all have been comfortable with work which gives the Arab–Muslim contribution a seminal role in fashioning the new European spirit—which brings the Arab–Muslim contribution from the margins towards the centre of the making of Europe. In considering Muslim influence over the emergence of European colleges and universities, historians from Rashdall to Powicke have only been willing somewhat grudgingly to give that influence a little room. In considering the origins of European humanism, scholars from B.L. Ullmann to Paul Kristeller have pointed to a series of key unresolved problems and issues but have been unwilling, as far as one can see, to explore how these problems and issues might have been resolved by calling into play earlier and cognate developments in the Islamic world.[12] In considering the origins of the troubador and the lyric of courtly love, one surveys a battlefield littered with the carcasses of academic reputations. Nor is the unease all on the side of the historians of Europe. A leading historian of the Islamic world, Gustave von Grunebaum, was prepared to admit that Islam contributed a good bit in detail to the development of European civilization 'but', he said, 'it would be preposterous so much as to ask whether any of its essentials are of Muslim inspiration ... except for Averroism.'[13]

In spite of this scepticism and unease the work of bringing Arab–Muslim influence more towards the heart of European development has gone on apace in recent years. The process has benefited from scholars steeped both in Arabic and European sources. Foremost amongst these has been George Makdisi. With regard to the origins of colleges, for instance, he has demonstrated the extraordinary number of parallels between their development in the European world and that of *madrasas* in the Muslim world a century before, from the close resemblance of the legal framework used to the subordination of the literary arts to law, theology and medicine. He has also shown the many points of correspondence between the two systems, whether in academic posts and subjects studied or in the technical Latin terms peculiar to scholasticism and their precise Arabic equivalents. It would all appear to point to a Muslim origin for the scholastic method, whose late echo now dies in Western universities under pressures of funding and which many might regard as the foundation of the scientific achievements of the modern world. Using very much the same techniques, Makdisi has also discerned the origins of Renaissance humanism in that of classical Islam, focusing in particular on the study of grammar, rhetoric and poetry, and in general, on all the striking parallel aspects in the Arab–Muslim and European systems of learning, from the organization of knowledge through to the cult of fame and glory, the practice of ridicule and wit, and the celebration of indi- vidualism.[14]

This process of assessing more favourably the Arab–Muslim contribution has benefited, too, from a touch of Spanish pride. I think here of the work of Maria Menocal, who not only values greatly the Arab–Muslim influence on Spanish culture but, by the same coin, wishes that the influence of the high culture of al-Andalus on the development of Europe should be more widely understood and accepted. She makes a powerful case for a reconsideration of the extent of Arab influence on medieval literature from the lyrics of courtly love through to Dante's *Divina Commedia*.[15] The particular concerns of Maria Menocal are part of a more general move in Spanish historiography, as I understand it, to reassess Arab–Muslim influence on Spanish culture in everything from Catholic mysticism and the wealth of Spanish literature through to music and dance. All such efforts, of course, carry with them the risk of overcompensation for the denials that have gone before. They also invite support from politically motivated sources eager to see a historical record more favourable to Muslims appear. Nevertheless, the signs are that Arab–Muslim influence on the de- velopment of European civilization is coming to be seen as less and less marginal.[16]

We have not, however, finished with Arab–Muslim influence yet. So far we have been concerned with cultural elements which, once absorbed, worked their influence from within. But no less important was the mighty presence of the Islamic world in moulding European civilization from without. It is useful, I would suggest, to conceive of medieval Europe as a third-world civilization lying cheek by jowl with the first-world civilization of Islam. This was a first-world civilization which was seen to embrace much of the known world, which was rich, advanced, and disturbing in its arrogant presumption of superiority.

Europeans defined themselves against this world. They did so in the great crusading movement whose first objective was to capture the holy city of Jerusalem. Arguably the crusades were great founding events of Christian Europe, in which, as one historian has put it, 'Europe found its soul'.[17] They were, moreover, through centuries of warlike Christian–Muslim interaction, to be a great force in European history. During the crusades Europeans also came to define themselves in their polemic against Islam, a polemic as unjust in its content as anything that Islamic groups might hurl against the

West today. The religion of the Europeans was the true way, while Muhammad was in impostor and his revelation a distortion of the truth. Their religion was one of peace, spread by persuasion, while Islam was one of violence, spread by the sword. Their religion was one of sexual restraint and lifelong monogamous marriage, while Islam endorsed sexual indulgence in this life and an endless diet of sexual ecstasy in the life to come. Their religion was that of Christ, whereas Muhammad was the anti-Christ, the agent of the devil, whom Dante placed in the ninth of the ten ditches around Satan's stronghold and condemned to being split continually from his chin to his anus.

Once established as the significant other of European civilization, the Islamic world never lost the role, except for the brief interlude of the Cold War. For Enlightenment scholars eager to undermine Christianity, it was helpful to reinterpret Islam as a civilizing force which had transmitted ancient learning to the West, and whose Prophet was a profound thinker and the founder of rational religion. For creative minds from the eighteenth to the twentieth centuries, it was an exotic playground full of possibilities. Some of these were supplied by Galland's translation of the Arabian Nights in 1704 with its rich store of caliphs, genies and fabulous happenings. More were supplied by the lush and romantic images conjured up by the great nineteenth-century school of orientalist painters. For the venturesome from Hester Stanhope to T.E. Lawrence the Islamic world was a destination of allure and new human possibilities which could be exploited to expand the potential of their lives. But, by the time the Europeans were the rulers of this world, they were also using it as the measure of their enlightenment, their progress, and the superiority of their civilization. Manifold have been the European uses of the Islamic world from the twelfth to the twentieth centuries. We cannot fully understand European history without taking into account what Europe has taken from its Muslim neighbour and the uses to which that Muslim neighbour has been put.[18]

THE IMPACT OF THE WEST IN SHAPING THE MODERN MUSLIM WORLD

If we now turn to the modern period, there is no doubting the Western role in helping to shape the modern Muslim world. Politically it is, of course, in large part the outcome of the European imperial era. By 1920 the whole of the Muslim world except Iran, Central Anatolia, Arabia and Afghanistan was under European rule. European power played a large part in deciding what states there would be in the Muslim world and where. It often helped build the frameworks of the modern state within the boundaries of these new states. European interests strove to shape their political regimes.

Economically, Muslim societies were bent to the purposes of European capital whether it was the plantation economies of the Malay States and the Dutch East Indies, the cotton monoculture of Egypt, or the concessions hunted by so many in Iran. Dual economies became the order of the day and the shapers of much political action.

The physical environment of Muslim societies was, of course, moulded by European economic and political power. Nowhere is the process more dramatically seen than in the great cities. Here a new European city built on a grid pattern might be set beside the old Muslim city with its arabesques of closed quarters, blind alleys and infinite numbers of seemingly unattainable private spaces, as in Fez or Tunis. Or, alternatively, grand Haussmanlike boulevards and wide open spaces were bulldozed throu. the old jungle of alleyways, as in Cairo, Delhi or Lucknow. This, moreover, was just part of a broader process of imposing Western forms of order, as is well set out in Timothy Mitchell's *Colonizing Egypt*.[19]

Socially, at least two major developments are worthy of note. The first is the division which opened up between those who have been absorbed into the modern economy and the modern state, and those who have not. A good number of the former acquired Western languages, Western education, Western habits; they came to eat, dress, and often organize their domestic space, Western style. They became the first rulers of Muslim peoples when independence was achieved. The second development cuts across the first. The Western example presented new possibilities for Muslim women. They sought to move in public spaces as never before. They sought education at all levels. They sought jobs. They demanded the vote and a role in public life. This is the most disturbing change for Muslim societies which the West has helped to set loose. It is one, too, in which women are clearly in the forefront of the battle for the Muslim future, and have been, and are, made to bear the wounds and scars of bruising change. Much of the discourse on modernity has taken place over how women should clothe themselves and move in public.[20]

In terms of knowledge, the learning which had shaped and informed Muslim societies over one thousand years was, during the nineteenth century, in large part discarded and replaced by that which came from the West. Avicenna was replaced by Western medical texts, Nasiruddin Tusi by Western mathematical texts, and so on. In general, the old learning persisted only in the economically more backward areas of society and in one or two great traditional universities such as Egypt's al-Azhar and India's Deoband. As time went on, there was the fearful development of deracinated Muslims learning about their faith and its past not from their own learned men but from the books of Western scholars.

As they have experienced this revolutionary change, Muslims have gone through a gamut of feelings. They have admired the military strength and achievements of the West. 'So it went on until all had passed', declared a Moroccan visitor to Paris in 1846 after watching a review of French troops:

> leaving our hearts consumed with fire for what we had seen of their overwhelming power and mastery ... In comparison with the weakness of Islam ... how confident they are, how impressive their state of readiness, how firm their laws, how capable in war.[21]

Muslims have been obsessed by a sense of lost glory, what Akbar Ahmad calls the al-Andalus syndrome. 'When autumn has set in over the garden,' sighed the late-nineteenth century Indian poet Hali in his classic elegy on the rise and fall of Islam:

> Why speak of the spring time of flowers?
> When shadows of adversity hang over the present,
> Why harp on the pomp and glory of the past?
> Yes, these are things to forget;
> But how can you with the dawn
> Forget the scene of the night before?
> The assembly has just dispersed;
> The smoke is still rising from the burnt candle;
> The footprints on the sands of India still say,
> A graceful caravan has passed this way.[22]

Muslims have shown increasing resentment of the West and its power over them. 'Against Europe I protest,' proclaimed Iqbal, the poet-philosopher of Pakistan who died in 1938:

And the attraction of the West.
Woe for Europe and her charm,
Swift to capture and disarm!
Europe's hordes with flame and fire,
Desolate the world entire.
Architect of Sanctuaries,
Earth awaits rebuilding; rise![23]

Ultimately, large numbers of Muslims have rejected the Western way forward for humankind. 'Come friends,' exhorted 'Ali Shariati, ideologue of the Iranian revolution, who died in 1977:

let us abandon Europe; let us cease this nauseating apish imitation of Europe. Let us leave behind this Europe that always speaks of humanity, but destroys human beings wherever it finds them.[24]

So overwhelming was the Western embrace of the Islamic world, as the twentieth century went on, that for some Muslims, known as fundamentalists, but much better known as Islamists, the only answer seemed to be to strive to seal off the Muslim world hermetically from the West. For them revelation was to be the only arbiter of human affairs, state power must be used to put this into effect. So all behaviour must be held within an Islamic frame, all culture, and all knowledge—hence Islamic economics, Islamic sociology, and Islamized natural sciences. If you think about it, the Islamists follow the pattern of the medieval Christian polemic against Islam; the Islamic way is the only true way; the West is demonized as the 'Great Satan'; the West is attacked as a sink of unspeakable sexual indulgence. Thus, the weak seek to gather strength, to preserve their identity, in the face of the strong.

But even this most fundamental of rejections has not been achieved without interaction with the West and Western knowledge. Maulana Maududi, the great South Asian progenitor of Islamist thought began to develop his ideas after a period of serious study of Western social and political thought.[25] Saiyid Qutb, the leading Egyptian Islamist thinker, was much influenced by the French Fascist thinker Alexis Carrel and a trip as a visiting professor to the USA.[26] Ali Shariati was no less influenced by Sartre, Fanon and Louis Massignon, and period as a student in France.[27] Moreover, this influence can also be discovered amongst more traditionally educated Muslim scholars. At a recent meeting between Christian and Shia theologians from Iran, the Christians were amazed to discover that not only did the Iranians know of the classical Hellenic philosophers, but also the work of Descartes, Kant, Hegel and Heidegger, as well as that of the Christian thinkers, Barth, Tillich and Bultmann.[28]

Even the great plans to seal off Muslim societies have been shown to have their limits. Revelation may control public space, but Islamic law, derived from revelation, has always made private space sacrosanct. There is now the irony in the age of global communication that it is possible in the home to enjoy much of the Western culture and knowledge that is forbidden in the public arena ... . And that is what numbers of Muslims do.[29]

CONTINUING MUSLIM SHAPING OF THE WEST

The fact that the West has had such power in relation to the Muslim world over the past century has not brought Muslim influence in the West to an end. The attraction of economic opportunity as well as freedom from persecution has led to the development of substantial Muslim communities in the West—some 20 million in Europe not counting the Muslim population of the Balkans so recently discovered by many Europeans and a further 8 million in North America. In Europe, these Muslims are slowly redefining Europeanness by giving it a Muslim strand; by challenging the essentialism of much European understanding about the Muslim world, often by revealing their own myriad differences; and by working for a fuller understanding of the Muslim past, and not least, the Muslim past of Europe.

Then, Christian believers in an increasingly non-believing European world are beginning to find common cause with their Muslim cousins, with whom they share so much of the same semitic prophetic tradition. It is a process signalled in the words of the second Vatican Council which, as long as ago as the early 1960s, emphasized how much Christians and Muslims share; it continues today in growing amounts of interfaith discussion and celebration.

And then, at the end of the twentieth century, the Muslim world still has its enduring role in confirming aspects of Western identity by offering reverse images of the West. The old strands of the medieval Christian polemic are still there but in new form. The old objection to Islam, which focused on sex and sexuality, has become a new objection to the position of Muslim women; the old worry about violence has become disapproval of Muslim approaches to human rights; and the old accusation of heresy now takes new shape for the denizens of a post-Enlightenment and post-Christian world, who see the Islamist aim to subordinate all of human life to revelation in the modern era as the worst of heresies.

What light does all of this shed on Huntington and his 'battle of civilizations'? I do not deny his most serious purpose, but it is difficult not to see it, at least in part, drawing on the old Western polemic against Islam, Western fears of Islam, and a strong dose of orientalism. On the other hand, and this is what I wish to emphasize today, there is a long history of the Muslim and the Christian civilizations drawing on each other, and being enriched by each other, and this is a process which, whatever the rhetoric, still continues. There have been, and still are, many bridges across the so-called fault lines between the two civilizations. Historians can help to make them better signposted and better used.

NOTES

1. Plenary lecture given at the Anglo-American Conference of historians at the Institute of Historical Research, University of London, July 1977.
2. S.P. Huntington, *The Clash of Civilizations and the Remaking of World Order* (New York, 1996)
3. Islam's heritage from the ancient world and the further developments achieved by Muslim efforts are well surveyed in two publications associated with the World of Islam Festival of the mid-1970s. S.H. Nasr, *Islamic Science: An Illustrated Survey* (Westerham, 1976) and J.R. Hayes (ed.), *The Genius of Arab Civilization: Source of Renaissance* (Westerham, 1975)
4. V. Martin, 'A comparison between Khumaini's *Government of the Jurist* and *The Commentary on Plato's Republic* of Ibn Rushd', *Journal of Islamic Studies*, VII, 1, January 1996, pp. 16–31.
5. G. Fowden, *From Empire to Commonwealth: Consequences of Monotheism in Late Antiquity* (Princeton, NJ, 1993), in particular pp. 138–68.
6. Ibid., p. 142.
7. Ibid., pp. 143–9.
8. Raggaei El Mallakh, 'Trade and Commerce', Hayes (ed.), *Genius of Arab Civilization*, pp. 221–33; S.K. Jayyusi (ed.), *The Legacy of Muslim Spain*, 2 vols (Leiden, 1994); J. Schacht and C.E. Bosworth (eds), *The Legacy of Islam* 2nd edn (Oxford, 1979).
9. C. Burnett, 'The Translating Activity in Medieval Spain', Jayyusi, *Legacy*, vol. 2, p. 1051.

10. C.H. Haskins, *The Renaissance of the 12th Century* (Cleveland, 1957), p. 301.
11. Ibid., p. 302.
12. See the chapter entitled 'Studies on the origins and antecedents of humanism' in G. Makdisi, *The Rise of Humanism in Classical Islam and the Christian West* (Edinburgh, 1990), pp. 294–302.
13. Gustave E. Von Grunebaum, *Medieval Islam: A Study in Cultural Orientation*, 2nd edn (Chicago, 1953), p. 342.
14. G. Makdisi, *The Rise of Colleges: Institutes of Learning in Islam and the West* (Edinburgh, 1981) and *The Rise of Humanism*.
15. M. Menocal, *The Arabic Role in Medieval Literary History: A Forgotten Heritage* (Philadelphia, 1987).
16. See the magisterial survey of the current state of scholarship in Jayyusi, *Legacy*.
17. Watt, *Influence of Islam*, p. 56.
18. N. Daniel, *Islam and the West: The Making of an Image* (Edinburgh, 1960); *Islam, Europe and Empire* (Edinburgh, 1966); R.W. Southern, *Western Views of Islam in the Middle Ages* (Cambridge, Mass., 1962); M. Rodinson, *Europe and the Mystique of Islam* (Seattle, 1987); A. Hourani, *Islam in European Thought* (Chicago, 1991).
19. T. Mitchell, *Colonising Egypt* (Cambridge, 1988).
20. See, for instance, L. Ahmed, *Women and Gender in Islam* (New Haven, 1992); D. Kandiyoti (ed.), *Women, Islam and the State* (Basingstoke, 1991); Z. Hasan, *Forging Identities: Gender, Communities and the State* (New Delhi, 1994).
21. S.C. Miller (trans and ed.), *Disconcerting Encounters: Travels of a Moroccan Scholar in France in 1845–46* (Berkeley, 1992), pp. 193–94.
22. Excerpt from the *Musaddas o Jazr-e-Islam* by Altaf Husain Hali in Syed Abdul Latif, *The Influence of English Literature on Urdu Literature* (London, 1924), p. 130.
23. A.J. Arberrry (trans), *Persian Psalms (Zabur-i 'Ajam) parts I and II translated into English verse from the Persian of the late Sir Muhammad Iqbal* (Lahore, 1948), p. 76.
24. Quoted in the translator's Introduction, H. Algar, trans, *On the Sociology of Islam: Lectures by Ali Shari'ati* (Berkeley, 1979), p. 23.
25. S.V.R. Nasr, *Mawdudi and the Making of Islamic Revivalism* (New York, 1996), p. 15.
26. A. Al-Azmeh, *Islams and Modernities* (London, 1993), p. 30.
27. Algar, *On the Sociology*, pp. 21–5.
28. C. Hewer, 'Iranian Islam in Dialogue with European Christianity', *Islam and Christian Muslim Relations*, III, 2, December 1992, pp. 304–11.
29. For a discussion of the relationship of public and private worlds in Muslim societies see B. Musallam, 'The Ordering of Muslim Societies' in F. Robinson (ed.), *The Cambridge Illustrated History of the Muslim World* (Cambridge, 1996), pp. 164–207.

Chapter Two

*Islam and Muslim Society in South Asia**

There has been a tendency, in recent years, for some anthropologists, and those who feel they have anthropological insights, to emphasize that Muslim society in South Asia, particularly in India, is much more Indian in its beliefs and practice than has been thought in the past. This tendency has its greatest protagonist in Imtiaz Ahmad, a professor of sociology at the Centre for Political Studies in New Delhi's Jawaharlal Nehru University. Since 1975, Ahmad (assisted by both Indian and non-Indian scholars) has been steadily revealing his vision of Indian Islam in what is to be a four volume series of essays. Three volumes have been published—*Caste and Social Stratification among Muslims in India* (1973), *Family, Kinship and Marriage among Muslims in India* (1976), and *Ritual and Religion among Muslims in India* (1981). In the introduction to the third volume, a part of which has been published in *Islam and the Modern Age* (Ahmad 1981a), Ahmad sets out the main lines of his argument.

He begins with what, for many Islamic sociologists, has come to be an almost obligatory attack on Islamicists. They know languages and texts, but they do not know how Muslims actually behave. They have, in consequence, projected a normative idea of Islam and have deceived us to the great variety of Muslim practices throughout the world. 'The sociological or social anthropological understanding of religion,' we are told, 'is at once more comprehensive and more concrete' (Ahmad 1981b: 2). There is some truth in this. But we also sense a dismissiveness towards the achievements of

* This article is an amended version of a public lecture given at the University of Cambridge on 14 February 1983.

other disciplines, as well as a jarring confidence in the superiority of the sociological vision.

Ahmad pursues his point by emphasizing the gulf which exists between Islamic law and Muslim practice in India. He observes that all the Muslims he has dealt with acknowledge the five pillars of Islam—creed, prayer, fasting, alms and pilgrimage—and in doing so, acknowledge their duty to follow the pattern for a perfect Muslim existence laid down in the Quran, the example of the Prophet, and the holy law. But, the Islam they practise 'is heavily underlined by elements which are accretions from the local environment and contradict the fundamentalist view of the beliefs and practices to which Muslims must adhere' (Ahmad 1981b: 7).

Ahmad notes that, in the past, Islamicists and anthropologists have explained the contradictions between law and local practice by pointing to the historical development of Islamic society. According to them, such contradictions were inevitable for a faith which, by and large, had only slowly intruded into other societies, come to exist side by side with other systems of belief and practice, and often had to accommodate itself to them in order to survive. In such a situation, there were bound to be some who lived lives closer to the Islamic ideal than others, whose religious behaviour was profoundly influenced by local custom. Nevertheless, the tendency would be for local custom to give way before the slow but sure progress of the Islamic ideal in Muslim hearts and lives. So Aziz Ahmad, doyen of Muslim scholars of South Asia, considered the folk and syncretic elements in Indian Islam, the worshipping of saints, the barely disguised presence of Hindu godlings, the hint of pollution and the traces of caste, as mere temporary anomalies which would eventually be eliminated by the actions of Muslim reformers. So also the influential anthropologist Clifford Geertz assumed that the process of Islamization meant a similar victory of an orthodox, orthoprax great tradition over a heterodox, heteroprax little tradition. 'The typical mode of Islamization,' he declares, is:

> painfully gradual. First comes the Confession of faith, then the other pillars, then a certain degree of observance of the law, and finally, perhaps, especially as a scholarly tradition develops and takes hold, a certain amount of learning in the law and the Quran and Hadith upon which it rests. The intricate norms, doctrines, explications, and annotations that make up Islam, or at least Sunni Islam, can be apprehended only step by step, as one comes to control, to a greater or lesser degree, the scriptural sources upon

which it rests. ... Islamic conversion is not, as a rule, a sudden, total, overwhelming illumination but a slow turning toward a new light (Ahmad 1981b: 8–11).[1]

Ahmad does not accept that the insights of either Aziz Ahmad or Clifford Greetz apply to India. He notes the revivalist and reformist movements of nineteenth- and twentieth-century Islam in India (movements of a kind which Aziz Ahmad saw bringing eventual victory to the high Islamic tradition), but discounts their importance because syncretic and folk beliefs are still widely found in Indian Islamic practice. He cannot find Clifford Geertz's pattern in Islamization in India because he finds the orthodox and orthoprax living harmoniously side by side with the heterodox and heteroprax. Ahmad can discover no dynamic situation in which a high Islamic tradition is steadily eating into local custom-centred traditions. Nor, for that matter, does he discover one in which custom-centred traditions are edging into the territory of a high Islamic tradition. He would rather talk of co-existence. High Islamic and custom-centred traditions peacefully 'co-exist as complementary and integral parts of single common religious system'. They do so, and have done so, because of 'the constraints of Islam's own struggle for survival in an alien environment'. Muslims came to India bearing a distinct religious tradition characterized by a vigorous iconoclastic zeal; 'they would probably liked to have conquered the indigenous religious traditions wholesale.' But, he declares, 'this could not be possible to achieve because the indigenous mores and traditions were already an integral part of the life of the people and their total displacement could be achieved only at the cost of Islam's own rejection' (Ahmad 1981b: 15). The suggestion seems to be that the co-existence of high Islamic and custom-centred religious traditions developed in the past, is established in the present, and is the distinctive, unique, pattern of Indian Islam which will probably persist into the future.

Those who know their map of intellectual India will probably have a shrewd idea of where Ahmad might be located. His anthropology of Muslim India seems to have much in common with scholarship long associated with the Jamia Millia Islamia. He offers a picture of Indo–Muslim society which seems similar to that of Indo–Muslim history painted by Muhammad Mujeeb, Ziya-ul-Hassan Faruqi, and now by Mushirul Hasan.[2] It emphasizes that Indian Muslims have their roots deep in Indian society, that they are natural inhabitants of an Indian world. It implies that there is no reason why they should not be good and loyal citizens of the Republic of India. Just as there is a sense in which all history is contemporary history, so there is also one in which all sociology is contemporary sociology.

This is not to suggest that Ahmad, or any of these scholars, have a political purpose but merely that they have a distinctive angle of vision. Ahmad's perspective, moreover, is important, because it is crucial that Islam should be understood in its Indian, indeed, in its Hindu context. It is a context too long neglected. Further, he has powerfully stated his perspective by drawing together the work of many who share in it. Nevertheless, the investigations conducted so far do not seem to have explored the subject to the full. They appear limited in understanding, place and time; these limitations raise doubts about Ahmad's conclusions regarding the nature of Indian Islam. I shall examine the nature of these limitations, and put forward alternative conclusions which emerge from investigations conducted along a broader front.

One limitation concerns the style of investigation that Ahmad and his followers have adopted. Much of their purpose is devoted to showing how Muslims actually behave, and how this behaviour is at variance with preferred Islamic practice, indeed is similar to much Hindu practice. In one sense, this emphasis on behaviour is correct because none of the revealed religions place as much emphasis on right conduct (as opposed to right thinking) as Islam. But, if the investigator goes no further than behaviour, understanding of the extent to which genuine shifts in religious orientation may have taken place must be limited. Men often maintain old customs but, as time passes, attach different meanings to them. Some of the problems of perception of the mere observer of religious practice are illuminated by a passage adapted from one of Basil Davidson's many books on Africa. He makes an African describe what he heard and saw on a visit to Coventry cathedral. The African reports that:

> The English claim to have some notion of a high God, but in fact this God is thought of as a man. They claim not to worship images but with my own eyes I saw many kneel before a huge image which filled the east end of the cathedral. They claim only to worship one God, but I counted at least three not to mention many lesser Gods whom they call saints. They claim not to be cannibals, and that their communion rite, in which we have long

suspected cannibalism, is and always was symbolic, and that what they eat is only bread and wine. I observed the rite myself and at least on this occasion they were telling the truth (Davidson 1969: 168–69).

Anthropologists who give little weight to the written word, one senses, are likely to suffer some of the same problems as Davidson's apocryphal African. Ahmad and some of his fellow scholars make much of Muslim attendance at saint's shrines. Although the possibility of injecting old forms with new content is acknowledged (Ahmad 1981b: 16; Fruzzetti 1981), it is always referred to as 'saint worship' and regarded, despite attendance at shrines in every other Muslim society, as an *essentially* Hindu institution absorbed within Indian Islam. Not once do they refer to the important distinction between the worship of a saint and the worship of God in a saint's presence which is to be found in the writings of the Indian *ulama* and sufis. Many who attend saints' shrines are, of course, either worshipping the saint or begging him to intercede for them with God. But there are others who do none of these: they are praying to God in the presence of the saint. The late eighteenth-century holy man of Firangi Mahal, Anwar al-Haq, always emphasized the importance of prayer in the family graveyard; prayer in the company of those who were already close to God was much more likely to be efficacious (Wali Allah n.d.: 43–4). There is, moreover, considerable literature devoted to conduct at saints' tombs, particular forms of behaviour indicating the proper difference in attitude towards the saints and towards God. It is not good enough to bundle all attendance at saints' tombs into the category of 'saint worship'. Even a cursory acquaintance with the *fatawa* and *malfuzat* literature indicates that very few Muslims see anything wrong in such activity. What is crucial is the intention with which it is pursued and the manner in which it is done.[3] Study with the help of interviews would help reveal the intentions of those attending shrines; study with the help of texts would illuminate the significance of different forms of behaviour at shrines. What often might seem to be saint worship would reveal a range of Islamic understandings, a range of positions on the gradient of Islamization. While the thoughts of some still sought the benefit of old superstitions, those of others were coming to be riveted on God.

A second limitation flows from Ahmad's concentration on Indian Muslims alone, which I suspect may have eased his progress towards hinting that Indian Islam has something of a unique quality, in which orthodox, orthoprax Islam co-exists with heterodox, heteroprax Islam as complementary and integral parts of a single common religious system. Of course, Islam in India is unique in one sense; it is only here that we might find a sufi shrine ordering its festivals according to the Hindu calendar, as at the shrine of Hajji Waris Ali Shah of Deva; it is only here that a Hindu festival might be included with Islamic festivals in the celebrations of the year, as at Nizam al-Din Awliya of Delhi; or, again, that we might find many features common to Hindu and Christian festivals, as Susan Bayly has found in the celebrations of the Urs of Shah Hamid of Nagore (Bayly, 1986). But all Islamic societies contain a mixture of local pre-Islamic practice and high Islamic culture. In Java, Muslims are known to pray to the Goddess of the Southern Ocean as well as to Muslim saints and to God himself (Ricklefs 1979). In Ottoman Turkey the Bektashi sufi order, which was powerful in the Balkans and Anatolia and closely associated with the famed Janissary corps of once Christian slave soldiers, recognized an Islamic Trinity of Allah, Muhammad and Ali, and included a version of the Christian communion service in their rites (Birge 1937: 210–18). Further, in nineteenth-century southern Arabia the Swiss Arabist and traveller, Johann Burckhardt, noted that the Bedouin still observed the pre-Islamic practice of sexual hospitality (Burckhardt 1829: 453).

Even in long great Islamic centres many dubious customs and beliefs could be found flourishing within earshot and eyeshot of paragons of Islamic right conduct. Consider the picture Snouck Hurgronje paints of late nineteenth century Mecca, the recorded behaviour of its women, the many visits to saints' tombs; the inhabitants of that holy city had every right to fear Wahhabi rule (Hurgronje 1931: 39–93). Consider, too, the picture painted by Edward Lane of mid-nineteenth century Cairo; here within a muezzin's cry of al-Azhar he finds every kind of superstition and belief in magic flourishing with vigour (Lane 1871: 281–347). Snapshots of these Muslim worlds taken by investigators at various times in the past two centuries reveal pictures not dissimilar in form from those recently taken by Ahmad and his associates of Muslim communities in India. Far from being unique, the shape of Indian Islam, the relationship between law and actual practice, seems to have much in common with Islamic societies elsewhere.

Mention of the snapshot technique, or what is sometimes

called the synchronic view, introduces a crucial third limitation to Ahmad's work which is the little weight he gives to moving film—the historical dimension—a dimension to which scholars as varied as Aziz Ahmad and Clifford Geertz attribute great importance. In the long run we can only understand the relationship between Islam and a particular society by investigating what is happening to that relationship through time. To do this, it is worth digressing to understand how Islamic history moves.

Islam offers a pattern of perfection for man to follow. It is contained in the Quran, the word of God spoken to man through the Prophet Muhammad. It is also contained in the traditions which relate what the Prophet, who is believed to have been divinely inspired, said and did. It is summed up in the law, in which the divine guidance for man is gathered together in a comprehensive system of rules designed to direct all human activity. Although the law came to be formed in the two hundred years following the Prophet's death, and drew on the customary practice of the time, most Muslims have believed that it was fashioned quite independently of historical or social influences. It is known as the *Sharia*, a word derived from Arabic meaning 'the straight way leading to the water'. We should not be deceived into thinking that there are strongly conflicting patterns of perfection by the fact the there are four *mazhab* or ways of Sunni law. There are only minor differences between them and, from the eighteenth century at least, many Muslim scholars, Hanbalis apart, have had little problem drawing from all four. Moreover, we should not be deceived by the fact that in many societies non-Islamic practices had acquired the force of law in Muslim minds. This is often a matter of imperfect knowledge or temporary expedient, although temporary in this sense may well be several hundred years. Nevertheless, such is the desire to follow the true path, a desire noted by many anthropologists, that, as knowledge of the law has grown more widespread, its provisions have tended to oust false practice. Ideally, then, the law stands above society as a pattern of perfection, a standard which all should strive to reach. The more completely a man follows the law in his life, the greater his chance of salvation at the Day of Judgement. The more completely the law is realized in society, the greater the chance that society will be healthy, powerful and just. There is continual tension in Islamic history between the need to strive to realize the pattern of perfection and the necessities of ordinary human life.

The pattern of perfection has been preserved down the ages, and exemplified and administered to Muslim peoples by learned and holy men. The learned men are, of course, the *ulama*, those with *ilm* (knowledge), men learned in the Quran, the traditions and the law, and skilled in ways to make these precious gifts to man socially useful. The holy men are the sufis, or Muslim mystics, men expert in techniques of spiritual development, who teach Muslims how to make God's revelation live in their hearts. I will treat ulama and sufis as different human beings, although often the two functions they perform are united in one man, being no more than the two sides of a fully rounded Islamic personality. But, whether one or two, both are concerned to guard and to broadcast Islamic knowledge in their time, and to raise fresh guardians and transmitters of the central messages of Islamic culture. When a teacher finished teaching a particular book, and was satisfied with his pupil's progress, he gave him an *ejaza* or licence to teach, and on that licence were recorded all the previous teachers of the book back to its author many hundreds of years before. The pupil could see how he had become the most recent bearer of Islamic knowledge transmitted down the ages. Similarly, when a sufi master, or shaikh, decided that a follower was suited to be a disciple, he gave him a *shijra* or mystical genealogy which stated the stages by which mystic knowledge had passed down from the Prophet to the founding saint of the order, and from the founding saint to his shaikh, and thence to him. The gratitude, love, respect, veneration of pupil for teacher, and disciple for master was boundless; they knew the central importance in Islamic life of the responsibilities which had been bestowed upon them. Their connections, criss-crossing regions and continents,form throughout most of Islamic history the essential moulding framework of the Islamic community. We might regard them as the scaffolding of the Islamic community; this is, for instance, how Peter Holt has described them in the Sudan (Holt 1967: 5). However, I prefer to think of them as the network of arteries and veins along which the life-giving blood of knowledge has flowed through time, and along which it is pumped to the corners of the Islamic world. The central themes of Islamic history focus on the activities of learned and holy men, or their interactions with each other and with the world in which they move. These themes are—their attempts to bring Islamic knowledge to pagan and Islamizing societies; their relationships with the state, which are often difficult because ideally the state exists only to put the law as they interpret it into practice; and their connections with each other, in particular the flow of ideas and of knowledge along the connections of pupils and teachers, and of disciples and masters, through time and throughout the Islamic world. The more widely Islamic knowledge was known and acted upon, the more widely Islamic society would be realized on earth.

The extent to which the pattern of perfection is realized in Muslim societies is always changing. There will be learned and holy men eager to raise Muslims to a higher Islamic standard; there will be Muslims who will know that, whether they like it or not, this is what they ought to be striving to achieve. But the fate of such a process does not, of course, depend merely on the leadership of learned and holy men or the deepening religious vision of those claiming to be Muslim. It interacts with the wider context—social, economic and political—and it is factors such as these which need to be considered to understand how Islamic knowledge might come to be spread more widely and applied more vigorously. They also suggest how its forward progress might on occasion be checked, and put into reverse.

Consider, for instance, the impact of the social roles which holy men often used to play. They were the pioneers and frontiersmen of the Islamic world, men who from the thirteenth century played the crucial role in drawing new peoples, pagans, Hindus, Buddhists, Shamanists, into an Islamic cultural milieu. According to tradition, nine saints introduced Islam to Java; wandering holy men, we are told, first brought Islam to West Africa. What the holy men did, it appears, was to find points of contact and social roles within the host community. They shared their knowledge of religious experience with men of other spiritual traditions. They helped propitiate the supernatural forces which hemmed in and always seemed to threaten the lives of common folk. They interpreted dreams, brought rain, healed the sick and made the barren fertile. They mediated between rulers and ruled, natives and newcomers, weak and strong. In fact, by accommodating themselves to local needs and customs, they gradually built a position from which they might draw people into an Islamic milieu, and gradually educate them in

Islamic behaviour. It is a process which Richard Eaton has demonstrated in one of the most original recent books on South Asia, in which we see sufis at this very task around the shrines of Bijapur from the fourteenth to the eighteenth centuries (Eaton 1978).

Consider, too, the significance of increasing contact with cultures which are thought to represent more fully the pattern of perfection, cultures in which Islamic knowledge is more widely spread and manifest. Such contact often seems to draw men towards higher Islamic standards, and often, though not always, the stronger and more frequent the contact, the greater the impact on local Islamic practice. One crucial source of contact between the central and the further Islamic lands has been trade. From its inception in Arabia to the growth of European seaborne commerce, it was Islam's great good fortune that its main cultural centres lay on the trade routes of the world. Indian and Arab Muslim traders first brought Islam to the port cities of island Indonesia; it was their continuing activity which sustained its development. So northern Sumatran Atjeh, where Arab Hadramauti traders have settled and where associations with the Gulf, Arabia and Egypt have been most close, has always been the most Islamized of Indonesian lands. We can see a similar process in sixteenth-century West Africa where great entrepots at the end of trade routes, East-West across the savannah and North-South across the desert (Ngazargamu, Kano, Jenne, Walata and Timbuctoo), were also leading centres of Islamic learning. To this day, the gaunt, sticklebacked mosques of Timbuctoo remain eloquent reminders of a time, four hundred years ago, when it was re- nowned for its libraries and *madrasas*, and its scholarship was known and respected from Egypt to the Maghrib.

A second source of contact can be found in the pilgrimage to Mecca, a subject which has only just begun to be studied seriously. Nevertheless, we know enough already to have some idea of its Islamizing effect. For instance, in the case of nineteenth- and twentieth-century Indonesia, the tremendous increase in the performance of the Meccan pilgrimage had a great impact on spreading Islamic knowledge in the area and on establishing new standards of Islamic practice (Roff 1970: 172–73; Benda 1970: 182–83). Then, the idea should be taken further to consider the new forms of contact and communication which have become available through technological advance and the spread of education. There is the great, but as yet unmeasured, influence of the printing press in the Islamic world, introduced during the nineteenth century, which, combined with the vigorous publishing activity of the ulama and the spread of popular literacy, has meant that for the first time millions of Muslims have been able to discover for themselves what the pattern of perfect Muslim life should be.

The power of the state has had its part to play, even though Muslim rulers have often found *raison d'etat* running counter to the demands of revelation. If learned and holy men have been supported in their work, Islamic knowledge has had a chance to spread more widely in society. If the state has patronized scholarship and teaching, Islamic knowledge may have grown, the number of people transmitting it, perhaps, increased. If the state has enforced the holy law, there have been inducements to proper Islamic behaviour, in public acts at least. From the late sixteenth century, Bornu came to be the most Islamized society south of the Sahara, because its rulers gave the holy law uncompromising support: 'evil went and hid herself,' declared a local chronicler, 'and the path of righteousness was plainly established without let or hindrance' (Adeleye 1971: 500). Where some form of the holy law has come to be applied by the modern state, with all its great coercive force and power of social penetration, we may be sure that large groups of Muslims have probably come closer to the pattern of perfection than ever before. In Indonesia, in spite of the determination of the national leadership to stand against an Islamization of the state, the institution of a Ministry of Religion in the 1940s has led to the Islamic pro- visions concerning marriage, divorce and inheritance being more widely enforced than ever before (Lev 1972). In Iran and Pakistan, despite the distaste which some Iranians and Pakistanis may have for their government's recent and powerful support for forms of the holy law, the result has already been a shift towards Islamic as opposed to Western or other forms of behaviour.

Yet, if the power of the state has played its part in spreading Islamic knowledge, so paradoxically has its decline; indeed, the Islamic response which it evoked has provided one of the strongest boosts to the process of Islamization in the past two centuries. In the eighteenth century, Muslim power was waning: the Safavid empire was in shreds, the Mughal empire restricted to Delhi, the Ottoman empire in sickly decline, the sultanates of Java and Sumatra were pale shadows of their former selves, the great Islamic cities of West Africa's upper Niger were under heathen rule. Learned and holy men in their different societies, but also increasingly in contact with and influencing each other, responded by striving as never before to promote a purer vision of Islamic life and society. If Muslim power was weakening, if the fabric of Islamic society was breaking down, the feeling seemed to go it was because Muslims had deserted the straight path towards perfection. By and large, they went back to the first principle, the Quran and the traditions, and rejected much of the scholastic superstructure built up as Islam had encountered other cultures through the centuries. Whether it was the movement of Muhammad Abd al-Wahhab in Arabia or that of Imam Shamil in the Caucasus, that of Usuman dan Fodio in North Nigeria or Dipanegoro in Central Java, men with economic, social and political grievances were swept into campaigns to create a new Islamic order in which they hoped, often after a millenarian fashion, that a just order would rule the land in which they lived. Many such movements were violent *jihads* (holy wars): some were peaceful. They all had the effect of spreading Islamic knowledge and bringing about a wider observance of Islamic law. The results of many have been felt right down to the present (Robinson 1982: 110–29).

However, great historical processes should not lead us to ignore the special chemistry of personal contact, or the influence of learned and holy men whose lives where thought to demonstrate command or outward and inner Islamic knowledge, whose community thought them to be models of true Islamic life. Thus one mid-nineteenth century biography of an Indian learned man declares that:

> Muhammad Yaqub was not only learned in the revealed and rational sciences, but he was a sojourner on the mystic path. ... He was not only a doctor for spiritual ills, but for bodily ills as well. All in his family, young and old, considered him their elder. Indeed, not only his family, but the entire city accepted the influence of his dignity and majesty. ... He was a man of great perfections and a recipient of revelations. He had hundreds of disciples and pupils (Metcalf 1982: 138).

Indeed, the instant in which a man might suddenly acquire from another a fuller understanding of what an Islamic life might be is often recorded in the *malfuzat* literature. So Abd al-Razzaq of Firangi Mahal was afraid to pray behind his uncle Abd al-Wali, fearing his mystical tendencies. However, one day he was late for prayers and found that he had to pray behind his uncle if he was not to miss prayers altogether. He did so and 'enjoyed these prayers more than ever before'; he now began to add spiritual understanding to his command of formal religious knowledge (Qidwai n.d.: 8). We should never forget the power of personal example and personal contact in the many small communities in which most Muslims lived.

All these processes, and more, have helped in the diffusion and application of Islamic knowledge. It is, as Geertz reminded us in the passage quoted earlier, a painfully slow process. Small changes in the culture of island Java between 1500 and 1800, for instance, mark its slow shift in orientation from a Hindu–Buddhist towards a Muslim world. Men stopped cremating their dead, women danced with more modesty, batik patterns became more formal, the devil-shaped kris handle became stylized, and an Islamic story was included amongst the cycles of the Wayang theatre (Robinson 1982: 92–3). Important new work by Richard Eaton, using the genealogies of the Sail tribe (which has been associated with the great Punjab shrine of Baba Farid and Pak Pattan over six centuries), suggests a similarly slow rate of change. He follows the technique pioneered by Richard Bulliet in Iran of noting the shift towards the use of Muslim names as an indicator of Islamization (Bulliet 1979). Between 1200 and 1400 he found no Muslim names; they were all Punjabi secular names. From 1415 to 1580 the proportion of Muslim names mover from 10 per cent to 30 per cent, from 1580 to 1782 from 30 per cent to 60 per cent, and from 1782 to 1862 it moved from 60 per cent to 100 per cent. At least six centuries of Islamic contact was required for all to give Muslim names to their children (Eaton 1984). But if this process is slow, we should also recognize that the combination of many such processes, wherever Islam has gained a footing, from the seventh century to the present, has brought, as Marshal Hodgson declares, perceptible movement towards similar beliefs, similar forms of behaviour and similar religious practice (Hodgson 1974, 2: 329–68).

This said, we should note that the progress of Islam has never been triumphant: the drives behind Islamization have faltered and been thrust back. Take, as a simple example, the impact of that remarkable medieval traveller, Ibn Battuta, on the Maldives. The arrival of this paragon of high Islamic culture had an immediate Islamizing effect. He was made a judge and began to impose the holy law, forcing women to cover their breasts and beating men who were late for prayers. Soon the people grew restless and the Wazir asked him to leave (Ibn Battuta 1859). Following this, we can be sure the islanders quickly fell back into their old ways. Consider southern Java in the eighteenth century, after Mataram was cut off from the more highly Islamized northern coast, as Merle Ricklefs observes, Muslims began to slip back into their old Hindu–Buddhist ways (Ricklefs 1974). Consider, too, the impact of modernization after a Western fashion in the nineteenth and twentieth centuries. Although, on the one hand, few processes can have done more to spread Islamic knowledge widely in Islamic societies, on the other hand, it has also nourished powerful rival cultures and raised rival systems of knowledge. Men have gained power in Muslim societies who are Muslim only by culture and who have striven to impart the knowledge and the outlook of the West wholesale: the number of learned and holy men has declined, their authority has waned.

Islamic history, therefore, offers abundant evidence that there is a dynamic relationship between Muslim societies and the pattern of perfection transmitted and exemplified by learned and holy men. More often than not, over the past fourteen centuries, Muslim societies have moved towards a greater realization of that pattern of perfection; on occasion, when they have been cut off from sources of cultural leadership, or when faced with powerful rival cultures, they have slipped away from it. The crucial point is that some form of traffic is always taking place between visions of the ideal Muslim life and the lives which Muslims lead.

Indian Islam is no exception to this rule. Consider what has taken place in the past two hundred and fifty years. This may not appear to be a period of great vigour in Islamic life. There is the decline of Mughal power, the rise of the Marattas, the British and the Indian nationalist—a world where Muslim culture and power went hand in hand, comes to be dominated by a culture in part Western, in part secular, and in part Hindu. But, in fact, this has been a period of extraordinary, probably unprecedented, vitality in Indian Islam. Albert Hourani, whose perspective is from the central Islamic lands and whose concern is with ideas rather than with power, has no doubt about this vitality. He is said to rate India as the leading force in the Islamic world at the time (Metcalf 1982: 9). He has good reason to do so—it was from India that in the seventeenth and eighteenth centuries new drive had been put into the Naqshbandiyya, the sufi order most prominently involved in Muslim revivalism throughout Asia; India supplied leading teachers to the great cosmopolitan centres of eighteenth-century Islamic scholarship at Mecca and Medina; India's contributions to Islamic scholarship were causing comment in Cairo's al-Azhar; and in the nineteenth century, Indian textbooks were coming to be used in many parts of the Islamic world.[4]

This period of extraordinary vitality coincides with the time when learned and holy men were stronger and more prominent than ever before in Indian history. Cantwell Smith has reminded us that generally, in Islamic history, the ulama do not emerge until much later than is usually supposed, and that in India they were not consolidated as a group until almost the modern period (Smith 1963: 42). It was at this time, when Islam had lost its hold on power in India, that paradoxically the ulama were best placed to lead their fellow Muslims and to spread knowledge of the faith. Their efforts to respond to Muslim political weakness, and the dangers which it threatened, are the prime source of the vitality of Indian Islam. They explain, for instance, both the new vigour in branches of the Naqshbandi and Chishti orders, and the great attempts of Shah Wali Allah to create the intellectual and doctrinal bases of unity for Indian Muslims. But, most important from our point of view, they explain how learned and holy men strove as never before to bring the pattern of a perfect Muslim life to each individual Muslim, how in fact there came to be a revolution in the availability of Islamic knowledge.

One way in which learned and holy men sought to spread Islamic knowledge more widely was through aggressive movements of revival and reform. These were similar to the movements taking place throughout the Islamic world in the nineteenth century; indeed, they had some connections with them. There was the Mujahidin movement of Saiyid Ahmad of Rae Bareli. Saiyid Ahmad aimed to rid Islam of Hindu practices, to end belief in the intercessionary power of saints and to establish an ideal Muslim community where Muslims could live according to the holy law. The movement became a *jihad* and Ahmad himself was killed in 1831, although his followers continued to create a stir in many parts of India till the end of the nineteenth century. There was also the Faraizi movement of Hajji Shariat Allah in Bengal; its aims were similar to those of the Mujahidin; it also became a violent movement whose organization existed at least until the end of the nineteenth century. But these Indian militant movements had little success as compared with those of Usuman dan Fodio in West

Africa, Muhammad Ahmad al-Mahdi in the Sudan, or even Sultan Sulaiman in south-western China.

The main way in which learned and holy men spread Islamic knowledge more widely was by developing a whole new range of new methods of transmission and broadcasting; in doing so, they were quick to exploit new forms of organization and new technological developments. Up to this time, most had taught informally in their homes. Now schools, maktabs and *madrasas* began to be established, institutions which were greater than individuals. Most nineteenth-century movements had their schools, but by far the most important were those of Deoband. The first school was founded in 1867; by the 1880s there were twelve schools, by 1900 forty odd, and by the centenary in 1967, there were apparently 8,934 (Metcalf 1982: 136). All taught a reformed Islam. All, as far as we know, were supported by public subscription, and owed nothing to the state. The Deobandi ulama, moreover, also established an office for issuing *fatawa*, or decisions on debatable points of Islamic law. Over the years it has published its decisions. Indeed, the custom of publishing their collected *fatawa* has grown up amongst the most leading ulama, offering guidance as never before to their less expert colleagues and to the community at large.[5]

Another new method of communication stemmed primarily from sufi practice. In India, as in many parts of the Islamic world in the eighteenth and nineteenth centuries, there was growing emphasis on the person of the Prophet as the exemplar of perfect human life, and the presentation of the sufi shaikh or pir as the model of the Prophet in the current generation. So one leading pir of the early twentieth century declared:

> The pir is the gateway to absorption in the Holy Prophet. Through him we reach the congregation of the Prophet, and to reach this congregation is to become close to God. ... Before the arrival of the Prophet, these spiritual physicians were Prophets themselves, and since the arrival of the Prophet they succeeded him, wearing his cloak (Abd al-Bari 1926: 15; Schimmel 1975: 98–116, 236–39).

Side by side with this new emphasis there developed a great new interest in *mawlid* ceremonies, that is ceremonies on each of the first twelve days of Rabi al-Awwal, and culminating with the Prophet's birthday, in which the lives of the Prophets would be told. Firangi Mahalis introduced this practice in Lucknow, Allahabad and Madras: it was a new way of communicating Islamic knowledge to the masses. The process of guidance, moreover, was supplemented by the publication of lives of the Prophet, biographies of learned and holy men, and *tazkiras*, collections of such biographies.[6]

Yet another new method was to make Islamic knowledge immediately comprehensible and readily available. As was happening elsewhere in the Islamic world at the time, learned and holy men were translating Islamic knowledge into languages everyone could understand. In India, the Quran was translated into Persian in the early eighteenth century, into Urdu in the early nineteenth century, and into Bengali in the late nineteenth century. By the 1870s several competing Urdu translations of the Quran were circulating. The major works of the reformist Mujahidin were written in Urdu, so were major guides to Islamic behaviour. Then, this new readily comprehensible presentation of Islamic knowledge was harnessed to the lithographic printing press, which at last made it possible to mass-produce works in Islamic scripts in the way that it had been possible to reproduce European Christian works since the fifteenth century. Imagine the limitations on communication when restricted to word of mouth, copying by hand, and the labour of an expert few. The ulama leapt at the opportunities provided by the lithographic press; some made it the basis of big business. Everything was published large-scale, from Islamic classics to the simplest textbooks, from significant achievements of seventeenth- and eighteenth-century Indian scholarship to the biographies and collections of *fatawa* through which the ulama hoped to provide new guidance for the community. In 1871, the government of the North-Western Provinces and Oudh noted that 23,000 Qurans had been published in the previous year; in 1877 that 70 per cent of all religious titles were Muslim, although Muslims were only 13 per cent of the population (Metcalf 1982: 202–3). 'Now God has been gracious in providing books', rejoiced Mawlana Nazir Husain in 1895. 'Books which one could not see in dreams or conceive of in imagination are now available for cowries' (Metcalf 1982: 205). No development made a greater contribution to the availability of Islamic knowledge.

Evidently, something remarkable was taking place in nineteenth-century Muslim India. Learned and holy men were developing many new ways of making contact with the Muslim masses; Indian Muslims were able, as never before, to know the pattern of perfect Muslim life. Historical scholarship has only just begun to probe be- neath the surface of political events to recognize this phenomenon: its overall significance has yet to be assessed. There is, however, enough evidence to suggest that it was accompanied by a continuing process of Islamization.

There are examples of the process of Islamization actually taking place. There is the impact of the 'Faith Movement' of Muhammad Ilyas, which drew its inspiration from the major streams of nineteenth-century revival and reform on the Mewatis, and others, over the past fifty years. The Mewatis are described as building mosques, opening Arabic school, growing beards, adopting Muslim clothes, and slowly abandoning unlawful customs (Anwarul Haq 1972). There is the detailed work in which Rafiuddin Ahmed describes the Islamizing of a Bengali world in the late nineteenth century, a process which built on the earlier activities of the Faraizis and the Mujahidin. He notes how Bengali Muslims no longer invoked God as 'Sri Sri Iswar' or as 'Sri Sri Karim' but as 'Allaho Akbar'; how they dropped Hindu surnames (Chand, Pal, Dutt) and adopted Muslim ones (Siddiqui, Yusufzai, Qureshi); how they stopped giving their newspapers Bengali names and began to give them all Arabic or Persian ones; how their desire to be identified as Bengalis lessened. 'Sir,' he quotes a Bengali villager addressing a government official some seventy years ago, 'only Muslims live in this village. There are no Bengalis here' (Ahmad 1981: 72–132). Other indicators ought to be taken into account. There is the fact that in the late nineteenth century, India, from time to time, supplied the largest number of pilgrims to Mecca (Metcalf 1982: 359). There is the enormous interest in pan-Islamic affairs, which led to an extraordinary increase in the circulation of Muslim newspapers whenever the wider Islamic world suffered crises, like the Russo–Turkish war of 1877–78, the Graeco–Turkish war of 1897, the Balkan wars of 1911–13, or the last throes of the Ottoman empire and caliphate from 1918 to 1924. There are the hundreds of thousands, perhaps millions, of Muslims who have supported from their own pockets the growth of the Deoband movement from one to over 8,000 schools, and who, by their help towards diffusing Islamic knowledge, have made a most positive statement in favour of Islamization. Then, finally, there are the connections which have been made between movements of revival and reform and support for what in many ways must be the crowning achievement of Islamization, the creation of an Islamic polity. Stephen Dale (1980) has demonstrated how a nineteenth-century movement for Islamic reform in Malabar grew into a warlike attempt to establish an Islamic state in the 1920s, and into a political demand for the foundation of a Mappilastan from the 1930s. Likewise, David Gilmartin (1979) has shown how the eighteenth-century Chishti revival in the Punjab bred a tradition of sufi leadership which was to be in the forefront in fighting for an Islamic state of Pakistan in the 1940s. All this raises the general problem of the relationship between Islamization and Muslim separatist politics. Here, it is enough to state that, although research has yet to indicate what weight it should be given, a connection undoubtedly exists.

The evidence set out here raises doubts about Imtiaz Ahmad's conclusion that the high Islamic and the custom-centred traditions have come to be integrated 'to a point that they should come to co-exist as complementary and integral parts of a common religious system'. Rather, it would appear to support the positions of Aziz Ahmad or more especially of Clifford Geertz. In Islamic history, in general, there has been a movement towards, or occasionally away from, the pattern of perfection. In South Asia, in particular, over the past two hundred years, learned and holy men have shown unusual activity and imagination in spreading knowledge of that pattern more widely. The evidence suggests, moreover, that many Muslims have made steps towards realizing that pattern more fully. It may be that over that past thirty-six years the process has continued more obviously in Pakistan and Bangladesh. It may be that in India the process has slackened, even gone into reverse. What there cannot be, as Ahmad asserts, is a state of equilibrium. He is able to make his assertion, one senses, because the case studies he has brought together embrace too short a period of time, because, perhaps, the sociological understanding of religion, and religious change, is not as 'comprehensive' as he would like to think. The historian's extended view suggests that there is continual, if sometimes slow and barely perceptible, movement between visions of perfect Muslim life and those which ordinary Muslims lead.

NOTES

1. Here Ahmad quotes (Geertz 1965: 96–7). Earlier he refers to Aziz Ahmad (1969: 51); he also places Faruqi (1978/1979) in the same category of thinking.

2. This position is reflected particularly in some of the specific statements and the underlying concerns of Mujeeb (1967), Faruqi (1963) and Hasan (1979a, 1979b).
3. For a *fatawa* on this subject delivered by a mufti of a reformist school of thought, see Lajpuri (n.d.: 258–60). On the attitude of the ulama of Firangi Mahal towards behaviour at saints' shrines see Robinson (1984: 333–56).
4. It is interesting to note how at the same time the Indian branch of another community spread throughout the world; the Armenians had also asserted a temporary intellectual leadership (Walker 1980: 50–1).
5. Amongst the more influential collections were the *Fatawa-i Azizi* of Shah Abd al-Aziz of Delhi, the *Fatawa-i Rashidiyya* of Mawlana Rashid Ahmad Gangohi of Deoband, and the *Majmua-i Fatawa* of Mawlana Abd al-Hayy of Firangi Mahal.
6. For instance, much of the *malfuzat* literature generated by the saints of Firangi Mahal and of Bansa was published for the first time in the early twentieth century. In Sumatra, moreover, Siegel notes how the Atjehnese journal *Penjoeloeh* began to feature biogrphies of the ulama in the 1940s at a time when they were particulary concerned to give their community Islamic leadership (Siegel 1969: 128–99).

REFERENCES

Abd al-Bari, M.Q., *Malfuz-i Razzaqi*, Kanpur, 1926.

Adeleye, R.A., 'Hausaland and Bornu 1600–1800', in J.F.A. Ajayi and M. Crowder (eds), *History of West Africa*, vol. 1 (London: Longman, 1971), pp. 485–530.

Ahmad, Aziz, *An Intellectual History of Islam in India* (Edinburgh: University of Edinburgh Press, 1969).

Ahmad, Imtiaz (ed.), *Caste and Social Stratification among the Muslims* (New Delhi: Manohar, 1973).

—— (ed.), *Family, Kinship and Marriage among Muslims in India* (New Delhi: Manohar, 1976).

—— 'The Islamic Tradition in India', in *Islam and the Modern Age* 12, 1981a., 1: 44–62.

—— (ed.), *Ritual and Religion among Muslims in India* (New Delhi: Manohar, 1981b).

Ahmad, Rafiuddin, *The Bengal Muslims 1871–1906: A Quest for Identity* (Delhi: Oxford University Press, 1981).

Bayly, S., 'Islam in Southern India', in D.H.A. Kolff and C.A. Bayly (eds), *Comparative Studies in Colonial History: India and Indonesia* (Dordrecht: Martinus Nijhoff, 1986), pp. 35–73.

Benda, Harry J., 'South-east Asian Islam in the Twentieth Century', in

P.M. Holt, A.K.S. Lambton and B. Lewis (eds), *The Cambridge History of Islam*, vol. 2. (Cambridge: University Press, 1970), pp. 182–207.

Birge, J.K., *The Bektashi Order of Dervishes* (London: Luzac and Co., 1937).

Bulliet, Richard W., *Conversion to Islam in the Medieval Period: An Essay in Quantitative History* (Cambridge Mass.: Harvard University Press, 1979).

Burckhardt, J.L., *Travels in Arabia* (London: Henry Colburn, 1829).

Dale, Stephen Frederic, *Islamic Society on the South Asian Frontier: The Mappilas of Malabar 1498–1922* (Oxford: Clarendon Press, 1980).

Davidson, Basil, *The Africans: An Entry to Cultural History* (London: Longmans, 1969).

Eaton, Richard M., *Sufis of Bijapur 1300–1700: Social Roles of Sufis in Medieval India* (Princeton: Princeton University Press, 1978).

—— 'The Political and Religious Authority of the Shrine of Baba Farid in Pakpattan, Punjab', in B. Metcalf (ed.), *Moral Conduct and Authority: The Place of Adab in South Asian Islam* (Berkeley and Los Angeles: University California Press, 1984).

Faruqi, Ziya-ul-Hasan, *The Deoband School and the Demand for Pakistan* (Bombay: Asia Publishing House, 1963).

—— 'Orthodoxy and Heterodoxy in Indian Islam', *Islam and the Modern Age* 9, 4/10, 1, 1978/1979.

Fruzzetti, Lina M., 'Muslim Rituals: The Household Rites vs. the Public Festivals in Rural India', in Imtiaz Ahmad (ed.), *Ritual and Religion among Muslims in India* (New Delhi: Manohar, 1981).

Geertz, Clifford, 'Modernization in a Muslim Society: The Indonesian Case', in R.N. Bellah (ed.), *Religion and Progress in Modern Asia* (New York: The Free Press, 1965).

Gilmartin, David, 'Religious Leadership and the Pakistan Movement in the Punjab', *Modern Asian Studies*, 13, 1979, 3: 485–517.

Haq, Anwarul M., *The Faith Movement of Mawlana Muhammad Ilyas* (London: George Allen and Unwin, 1972).

Hasan, Mushirul, *Nationalism and Communal Politics in India, 1916–1928* (New Delhi: Manohar, 1979a).

—— (ed.), *Muslims and the Congress: Select Correspondence of Dr M.A. Ansari 1912–1935* (New Delhi: Manohar, 1979b).

Hodgson, Marshal G.S., *The Venture of Islam: Conscience and History in a World Civilization*, vol. 2 (Chicago: University of Chicago Press, 1974).

Holt, P.M., *Holy Families and Islam in the Sudan*, Princeton Near East Papers No. 4. Princeton: Program in Near Eastern Studies, 1967.

Hurgronje, C. Snouck, *Mekka in the Latter Part of the Nineteenth Century*, J.H. Monahan (trans), (Leiden: E.J. Brill, 1931).

Ibn Battuta, *Rihla*, C. Defrémery and B.R. Sanguinetti (eds), vol. 4 (Paris: Imprimerie Imperiale, 1859).

Lajpuri, Mufti Sayyid Abdurrahim, *Fatawa Rahimiyyah*, vol. 2. M.F. Qurshishi (trans), (Surat: 'Attarsthan', n.d.).

Lane, Edward William, *An Account of the Manners and Customs of Egyptians*, 5th ed., 2 vols. (London: John Murray, 1871).

Lev, Daniel S., *Islamic Courts in Indonesia: A Study in the Political Bases of Legal Institutions* (Berkeley and Los Angeles: University of California Press, 1972).

Metcalf, Barbara Daly, *Islamic Revival in British India: Deoband, 1860–1900* (Princeton: Princeton University Press, 1982).

Mujeeb, Muhammad, *The Indian Muslims* (London: George Allen and Unwin, 1967).

Qidwai, Altaf al-Rahman, *Anwar-i Razzaqiya*, Lucknow, n.d.

Ricklefs, M.C., *Jogjakarta under Sultan Mangkubumi, 1749–1792: A History of the Division of Java* (London: Oxford University Press, 1974).

—— 'Six Centuries of Islamization in Java', in Nehemia Levtzion (ed.), *Conversion to Islam* (New York: Holmes and Meier, 1979).

Robinson, Francis, *Atlas of the Islamic World since 1500* (Oxford: Phaidon, 1982).

—— 'The Ulama of Firangi Mahal and their Adab', in B. Metcalf (ed.), *Moral Conduct and Authority: The Place of Adab in South Asian Islam* (Berkeley and Los Angeles: University of California Press, 1984), pp. 152–83.

Roff, William R., 'South-east Asian Islam in the Nineteenth Century', in P.M. Holt, A.K.S. Lambton and B. Lewis (eds), *The Cambridge History of Islam*, vol. 2 (Cambridge: Cambridge University Press, 1970). pp. 155–81.

Schimmel, A., *Mystical Dimensions of Islam* (Chapel Hill: University of North Carolina Press, 1975).

Siegel, James T., *The Rope of God* (Berkeley and Los Angeles: University of California Press, 1969).

Smith, William Cantwell, 'The Ulama in Indian Politics', in C.H. Philips (ed.), *Politics and Society in India* (London: George Allen and Unwin, 1963).

Wali Allah, Firangi Mahali, *Al-Aghsan al-arbaa* (Lucknow: Nadwa Ms., n.d.).

Walker, Christopher J., *Armenia: The Survival of a Nation* (London: Croom Helm, 1980).

Chapter Three

Islam and the Impact of Print in South Asia

Print brought about a revolution in the transmission of knowledge.[1] Down to the Middle Ages, oral transmission was the normal way in which knowledge was passed on. Knowledge was stored up in men; memorizing was amongst the most highly prized of arts; scholars were masters of mnemonic tricks. This system was steadily transformed by Gutenberg's introduction of the moveable type printing press for the Roman alphabet.[2] The advent of mass-produced printed books reduced dependence on oral systems of transmission, until they became no more than trace elements in language and values. The British, for instance, still talk of auditing accounts; they still worry about the loss of the art of memory in educating their young. Gutenburg's press also accelerated a revolution in human consciousness. This is, of course, the particular insight in which Marshall McLuhan led a host of academics who perceived a transformation of human consciousness as it moved from the oral to the written word, as it moved from a consciousness dominated by sound to one dominated by visual space. Knowledge became less warm, less personal, less immediate and more cold, abstract, and intellectual.[3]

This revolution in the transmission of knowledge helped to bring about a transformation of the religious life of Western Christendom. Print lay at the heart of that great challenge to religious authority, the Protestant Reformation; Lutheranism was the child of the printed book.[4] Print also lay at the heart of the Catholic counter-offensive, whether it meant harnessing the press for the work of the Jesuits and the office of Propaganda, or controlling the press through the machinery of the Papal Index and the Papal

Imprimatur. Print, and the enormous stimulus to literacy which the desire to read the Bible gave, was at the heart of that slow change in northern European Christianity from a time when a Church building and its decoration might be read as one great iconic book to one which was increasingly focused on the Bible, the Word, which many could read and all might understand, because at last it was in their language.[5] In the end, as Elizabeth Eisenstein, the historian of the influence of print tells us, the impact of printing on Western scriptural faith points in two quite opposite directions: towards '"Erasmian" trends and ultimately higher criticism and modernism, and towards more rigid orthodoxy culminating in literal fundamentalism and Bible Belts'.[6]

Print, and the revolution in the transmission of knowledge which it brought about, was not established in the Islamic world until the nineteenth century, four hundred years after it started getting established in Christendom. Where Muslim regimes still wielded power, but were threatened by the expansion of the West, such as Egypt, Iran and the Ottoman Empire, presses were started in the early nineteenth century but were not widely used until the second half of the century. According to Mehmet Kaplan, it is not until the years 1870–90, that it is possible to see the Ottoman elite beginning to be transformed by book knowledge.[7] Where Muslims were under some form of colonial rule, and the threat of the West was more evident, the response was much more rapid and much more urgent. Within two decades of the beginning of the century, the Muslims of Tsarist Russia had seventeen presses in operation. By the 1820s, Muslim reformist leaders in the Indian subcontinent were busily printing tracts. By the 1830s the first Muslim newspapers were being printed. By the 1870s, editions of the Quran, and other religious books, were selling in tens of thousands. In the last thirty years of the century, over seven hundred newspapers and magazines in Urdu were started. All who observed the world of printing noted how Muslims understood the power of the press. In Upper India (mainly North-West Provinces and Punjab), at the beginning of the twentieth century, four to five thousand books were being published in Urdu every decade and there was a newspaper circulation of tens of thousands.[8]

Print, therefore, has had an influence on Muslims for a century and a half. Given the power of industrial technology and the power of the modern state, print has been understood to have had a significantly greater impact than in its first one and a half centuries of influence in the West. It is now worth assessing its impact on religious change. We propose to do so in the context of South Asia, the region of the Islamic world in which the influence of print has been, arguably, longest and most deeply felt. It is also the region which over the past century has been as fertile in producing new Islamic understandings and influential over religious thinking elsewhere as any other.

To comprehend the impact of print on Islamic understandings, we need to have some insight into why print technology was not adopted by Muslims when it was first available. We also need to know why during the nineteenth century, South Asian Muslims felt able to change their approach. Such investigations will help to lay the foundations for an exploration of the impact on religious change of the two main innovations wrought by print in the transmission of knowledge: the mass production of sources of knowledge and the moving of the main vehicle of its transmission from sound to sight. After religious changes have been identified, their significance will be weighed in the context of Muslim society in South Asia as a whole.

WHY DID MUSLIMS FAIL TO ADOPT PRINT UNTIL THE NINETEENTH CENTURY

It was not because Muslims did not know about printing presses that they failed to adopt print until the nineteenth century. As early as 1493 Jewish refugees from Spain set up printing presses in Istanbul, printing Bibles and secular books. Jewish and Christian communities, moreover, continued to use printing presses in various parts of the Muslim world. Nor was it that the rather more difficult problems of printing in Islamic cursive scripts (in which letters have four different forms depending on their position in the word, and vowels and inflections are signalled by a complex system of pointing) had not been overcome. As early as the fifteenth century the Quran was printed in Arabic in Italy; in the sixteenth-century Christians were using the press of Arabic printing in Syria.[9]

In fact, current scholarship is unsure about why Muslims rejected printing for so long—indeed it is a problem that does not seem to have been seriously studied. Doubtless, the great guilds of *khatibs* or scribes would have been opposed to printing. But, if this was the case, why should they have carried greater weight than the occupants of the Christian *scriptoria*? Certainly, orthodox *ulema*, ever wary of the possibility of religious innovation (i.e. *bida*, the nearest that Islam gets to the Christian concept of heresy) would have been deeply concerned about the introduction of printing; the one printing press operated by Muslims in Istanbul in the 1730s and 1740s aroused so much opposition that it had to be closed down. More generally, there would have been the doubt which many pious Muslims would have felt about associating with *kufr*—the products of non-Islamic civilization. Such doubts never lasted for long in the case of seriously useful items like military technology, or significant sources of pleasure like tobacco, but they have dogged all initial Muslim responses to new things from the West—from clocks to electric light. Such consideration apart, however, there is good reason for arguing that the source of the negative Muslim response to printing lay much more deeply than this. The problem was that printing attacked the very heart of Islamic systems for the transmission of knowledge; it attacked what was understood to make knowledge trustworthy, what gave it value and authority.

To understand why this might be so, we need to examine the system for transmitting knowledge as it flourished over 1200 years from the beginning of Islam. At the heart of this system of transmission is the very essence of knowledge for the Muslim, the Quran. For Muslims the Quran is the word of God—His very word. It is more central to Islamic theology than the Bible is for Christians or the Torah is for Jews. It is the divine presence. It is the mediator of divine will and grace. For instance, as Christian theological discussion might focus on the virgin birth of Christ as the proof of his divine nature, so Islamic theological discussion might focus on the Quran, on its matchlessness, as the guarantee of its divine character. 'Quran' itself means 'recitation', *al-Quran*, the recitation or the reading out aloud. It is through being read out aloud that the Quran is realized and received as divine.[10] Pious Muslims strive to learn as much of it as possible by heart. They recite it constantly through the daily round, at prayer times, through the passage of the year, most notably in the month of Ramadan, and through all the stages of life. It is like a sacrament, ever on their lips. For its words are not mere words. 'They are', in Constance Padwick's magical phrase, 'the twigs of the burning bush aflame with God.'[11]

The Quran was always transmitted orally. This was how the

Prophet transmitted the messages he had received from God to his followers. When, a few years after the Prophet's death, these messages came to be written down, it was only as an aid to memory and oral transmission. This has been the function of the written Quran ever since. Telling evidence for the essential orality of the Quran and its transmission is that in the 1920s the Egyptian standard edi- tion was produced not from a study of variant manuscript versions but from a study of the fourteen different traditions of recitation.[12]

The oral transmission of the Quran has been the backbone of Muslim education. Learning the Quran by heart and then reciting it aloud has been traditionally the first task of young Muslim boys and girls. It is a process begun with celebration, a *Bismillah* ceremony, celebrating the first words the child will learn. It is a process which, if completed successfully, i.e. the whole Quran being committed to memory, will be celebrated with great joy. It is not given to many to learn to recite the whole Quran, and the title thus won of *Hafiz* or *Hafizah al-Quran* is greatly respected. The usual method of learning was that each day the teacher would write some verses on the pupil's slate, and the pupil would spend the rest of day learning them. Those who were able to recite them successfully the next day, in addition to what they already knew, would be entitled to wash their slates and have more verses written on them. This is still the method of transmission in much of the Islamic world, and it is why, as you wander through the neighbourhoods of a Muslim town, you are likely to hear a polyphonic hum—it will be the chanting of young children as they learn the word of God.

The methods of learning and of transmitting the Quran laid their impresses on the transmission of all other knowledge. 'The Quran,' declared that great fourteenth-century Muslim historian, Ibn Khaldun, in a disquisition on the art of teaching, 'has become the basis of instruction, the foundation of all habits that may be acquired later on.'[13] Take, for instance, the publication of a book in the early Islamic centuries. Its writing down like that of the Quran was merely an aid to oral publication. The author would dictate his first draft, either from memory or from his own writing; the copyist would then read it back to him. Publication would take place through the copyist reading the text to the author in public, usually in a mosque. During this process the author might make additions and emendations and several readings might be required before it was given his authorization. This was known as his *ijaza*, which means 'to make lawful'. Thus the author gave permission for the work 'to be transmitted from him'. Further copies had real authority only when they had been read back to the author and approved.[14]

Now let us assume that this book enters the *madrasa* curriculum, indeed becomes one of the great texts of the school curriculum. It would be transmitted in a very similar way. The teacher would dictate the text to his pupils, who might write it down, or frequently would commit it to memory—many Islamic pedagogical texts were written in rhyme to help the memory. Subsequently, there might be an explanation of the text, depending on its nature. The completion of the study of the book would involve a reading back of the text with an explanation. If this was done to the teacher's satisfaction, the pupil would then be given an *ijaza*, a licence to teach that text. On that *ijaza*—and such *ijazas* are still given today—would be the names of all those who had transmitted the text going back to the original author. The pupil was left in no doubt that he was the trustee in his generation of part of the great tradition of Islamic learning handed down from the past.

The question arises, why should the style of Quranic transmission have had such an impact on the transmission of Islamic knowledge in general? Why should Muslims memorize and recite out loud when writing was in wide use throughout urban society? It was not as if Islam had anything against writing. 'Good writing,' declares a tradition of the Prophet, 'makes the truth stand out.' Calligraphy is the highest of the Islamic arts. The beautiful writing of the words of God is the typical adornment of Islamic space. Yet, writing and literacy have always remained subservient to superior oral tradition in the transmission of knowledge. For us, who are so deeply im- bued with the culture of print, this is hard to understand. For us writing is a vehicle which can carry words and ideas across time and space. It is a fairly mechanical process which can make an absent author present. Of course, there can be ambiguities and misunderstandings, and the further away we get from an author in time or in culture the greater the chance of there being those ambiguities and misunderstandings. But they are not a central problem of writing. Writing is for us reliable communication; speech is unreliable communication. If in doubt, we get it in writing.[15]

Muslims, on the other hand, were always fundamentally sceptical of the written word. 'Language,' declares Ibn Khaldun, 'is merely the interpretation of ideas that are in the mind. ... Words and expressions are media and veils between the ideas. ... The student of ideas must extract them from the words that express them.' Oral expression was crucial to success. 'But,' Ibn Khaldun goes on, 'when a student has to rely on the study of books and written material and must understand scientific problems from the forms of written letters in books, he is confronted with another veil ... that separates handwriting and the form of letters found in writing from the spoken words found in the imagination.'[16] To understand the words properly and to approach their meaning, the student must read them aloud. So, as the Quran gained full realization only by being recited aloud, so too did the academic book give of its full meaning by being read aloud. Muslims were always in doubt about writing. They got at the truth in speech.[17]

Thus, person to person transmission was at the heart of the transmission of Islamic knowledge. The best way of getting at the truth was to listen to the author himself. Muslim scholars constantly travelled across the Islamic world so that they could receive in person the reliable transmission of knowledge. The custom grew with the early collectors of the traditions relating to the Prophet. It was steadfastly maintained by later scholars. So the great Spanish mystic, Ibn Arabi (b. 1165) travelled from Murcia to Seville, Tunis, Fez, Cordoba, Almeria, to Tunis again, twice each to Cairo, Jerusalem, Mecca and Baghdad, and to Mosul, Malatya, Sivas, Aksaray, Konya and Damascus where he died in 1240. So, too, the remarkable writer of pedagogical texts, Saiyid Sharif al-Jurjani (b. 1339) travelled from Taju (by the Caspian) to Herat, Karaman (Anatolia), Alexandria, Constantinople, Shiraz, and to Samarqand, where he became a great figure at the court of Timur, dying in 1413. When a scholar could not get knowledge from an author in person, he strove to get it from a scholar whose *isnad*, or chain of transmission from the original author, was thought to be the most reliable. The personal nature of the transmission is captured by the words of this tenth-century *ijaza*:

> I entrust my book to you with my writing from my hand to yours. I give you authorization for the poem and you may transmit it from me. It has been produced after having been heard and read.[18]

Knowledge was being transmitted from man to man. Moreover, this practice cannot be explained away merely by asserting the preference for the oral over the written text. It is to be explained by a central concern for the transmission of the author's meaning, the true meaning of the text. Person to person transmission through time was the most reliable way of making up for the absence of the original author in the text. It enabled the student to read the white lines on the page, as the Muslim teachers used to say, as well as the black lines.[19]

Much Islamic scholarship, its form and its method, was designed to compensate for the absence of the author in the text. So, the history of this scholarship, indeed for many, Islamic history itself, was the history of its transmission from person to person. This was exemplified in that classic literary form, the *tazkirah* or collective biography. The *tazkirah* might deal with the scholars of a particular time, place or a family. It recorded, after family details, who a man's teachers were, what he learned and who his pupils were. His own contributions to knowledge would be listed along with anecdotal evidence bearing on the scholar's reliability as a transmitter of knowledge. Related to the same concern to compensate for the absence of the author in the text, we have the enormous respect given to the teacher in the Islamic tradition. The teacher was after all the living embodiment of knowledge; he cherished truth in his heart. 'Know that ... one does not acquire learning nor profit from it,' declared a thirteenth-century educational manual, 'unless one holds in esteem knowledge those who possess it. One [must also] glorify and venerate the teacher.'[20] The situation was little different at the beginning of the twentieth century. The pupil 'should walk several paces behind his teacher', declared a leading north Indian scholar, 'he should strive to be the first to do his teacher's bidding ... and should they differ his teacher's word is final.'[21] Such was the impact of person to person transmission on respect for the teacher. Moreover, it was such an influential model that it was the method of transmission not just of formal religious knowledge, but of all knowledge. It did not matter whether it was music, or calligraphy, or the spiritual dimension of Islam, i.e. sufism—authoritative knowledge was transmitted from person to person.

With this understanding, the objections which Muslims might have had to printing become a lot more clear. Printing, by multiplying texts willy nilly, struck right at the heart of person to person transmission of knowledge; it struck right at the heart of Islamic authority. No Muslim was likely to adopt it until he saw the good in printing greater than the evil it might cause. In fact, Muslims only came to adopt printing when they felt Islam itself was at stake and print was a necessary weapon in the defence of the faith.

Lest it be felt that Muslims were unique in the cultural barriers that they threw up against the adoption of printing it should be noted that Hindus, who knew about the printing press at least from the time that Jesuits began printing in Indian languages in the sixteenth century, were no more willing to adopt the technology. Their reasons, moreover, seem not dissimilar from those of the Muslims. Although they had commanded the art of writing for more than two millennia, and used it for commercial or bureaucratic purposes, oral transmission was regarded as the only appropriate way of communicating holy words. Graham tells us:

> The ancient Vedic tradition represents the paradigmatic instance of scripture as spoken, recited word ... Written texts have been used, certainly, but a text without a teacher to teach it directly and orally to a pupil is only so many useless leaves or pages ... Knowledge or truth, especially salvific knowledge or truth, is tied to the living words of authentic persons, not authentic documents ... these living words can only be valid on the lips of one who has been given the authority from a valid teacher to use them.[22]

The oral transmission of Vedic texts, moreover, has provided the model for the transmission of popular scriptural texts whether they be the Puranas and the Tantras or the *Ramayana* and the *Gitagovinda*. This is the case with the relatively recent retelling of the *Ramayana*, the *Ramacaritamanasa* of Tulsi Das (d. 1623), which has acquired enormous popularity.[23]

On the other hand, it might also be noted that, where no strong tradition of orally transmitted salvific literature existed, and perhaps where the state anticipated benefit rather than threat from the adoption of the technology, as in Confucian China, there seem to have been few barriers to the development of printing. Woodblock printing was already well-developed under the Tang dynasty (618–907) and was greatly expanded under the Sung dynasty (960–1279). The state controlled the printing of the Confucian canonical scriptures. The entire Buddhist canon (involving the cutting of 130,000 blocks) and the entire Taoist canon were also printed as were an enormous number of literary works, medical guides, practical handbooks and so on. At the same time commercial printing for the mass public developed. By the seventeenth century there was vast China-wide industry which produced everything from fine editions of literary works to crudely-printed ephemera for popular reading.[24]

WHY DID SOUTH ASIAN MUSLIMS COME TO ADOPT PRINT IN THE NINETEENTH CENTURY?

The overcoming of the obstacles to print in Muslim South Asia,[25] as in other parts of the Islamic world, interacted with a wide range of factors. Muslims were coming to realize the extent to which, after six hundred years of domination on the subcontinent, they had lost power: they were coming to understand the severity of their competition with the European civilization which ruled them, and the Hindu world which rivalled them. They were undergoing an intense period of religious revival in which there was strong pressure to renew Islam both inside and outside South Asia. They were faced with rapid economic and social changes as their colonial rulers sought to harmonize their productive and consumptive activities more closely with the international economy. They were faced, too, with mrginalization of much that made sense of their world and gave meaning to their deepest beings, as European science, literature and Enlightenment thought filled the public spaces of their lives, becoming the meat of the educational system, offering the route to success in life and informing the substance of the dominant political discourse. Indeed, they were faced with the problem of how they could still be good Muslims and at the same time enable their community to survive under foreign Christian power.

We have already noticed the alacrity and vigour with which print was adopted by Urdu-speaking Muslims, from the tracts and newspapers that were published in the 1820s and 1830s to the thousands of books published at the beginning of the twentieth century. This vigorous exploitation of print was led by the *ulema*, that is by the scholars and teachers who were the custodians of 1200 years of oral transmission of Islamic knowledge. Two of the earliest Muslim books to be printed were Saiyid Ahmad Barelvi's *Taqwiyat al-Iman* and his *Sirat al-Mustaqim*, both key works in the Muslim revival of the early nineteenth century. A great family of *ulema*, that of Shah Abdul Aziz of Delhi, played a major role in bringing both these works to a wider public. In the latter part of the nineteenth century, the equally distinguished Firangi Mahal family of *ulema* from Lucknow were big publishers of Islamic texts which were sold throughout upper India and through Afghanistan in Central Asia. They also published some of the earliest Urdu newspapers, among them *Tilism-i Lakhnaw* which was published for two years before the Mutiny and *Karnamah*, which came out for three decades afterwards.[26] Then, Deoband, the most important centre of Islamic scholarship in late nineteenth-century India, was already by this time, as it is today, a town of printed books and bookshops.[27] It now houses what many regard as the most important traditional university in the Islamic world after Cairo's al-Azhar.

The question remains why did *ulema* in north India embrace printing with such vigour? Simply, without power they were fearful for Islam. They were apprehensive that the community, the vast majority of whom were converts from Hinduism, might slip back into the maw of Hindu India. They were frightened by the activities of Christian missionaries who attacked Islam on the streets and in the press—although when missionaries ventured on set-piece debates with the *ulema* they were often worsted. They were frightened because there was no legitimate power to put the holy law of Islam, the *sharia*, into operation. Their answer to this challenge was better religious knowledge. Muslims should know, much more clearly and much more certainly than before, how to behave as Muslims. The printing press was a crucial means to this end. It worked side by side, moreover, with a great programme of translation of the Islamic classics from Arabic and Persian into the vernacular. Many of the more important works of the Islamic educational curriculum were translated into Urdu in the nineteenth century. There were at least twelve attempts to translate the Quran into Urdu during the century. Moreover, the process of translation not just into Urdu but into other vernaculars of South Asia continues to the present day.[28] Knowledge was no longer to be the special possession of an élite but open to all those who could read, memorize and listen with understanding.

The *ulema* were delighted by the huge increase in the number of books and the great improvements it brought to education. Declared one scholar in 1895:

> Now God has been gracious by providing books. Books which one could not see in dreams or conceive of in imagination are now sold for cowries.

And going on to talk of his schooldays in Delhi in the first half of the century:

There were only eighteen copies of Bukhari, and of these, generous people had divided copies into parts and distributed them amongst students so that they could study them. When I studied Tirmizi from Miyan Sahib three of us shared one copy; and we three lived in different sections of the city ... One of us would study it for a few hours, then another would carry it off ... No one had a chance to study a whole book ... Because of reading incompletely and out of order [the study of] every book was deficient.[29]

Thus, the *ulema* used the new technology of the printing press to compensate for the loss of political power. If Islam could no longer be supported by the swords of Muslim princes, it could now be supported by the enhanced religious understanding of Muslims themselves.

But the most powerful reason why the *ulema* felt able to adopt printing with such vigour was that it was not seen, at least initially, as involving any abandonment of the oral tradition of person to person transmission. The printed book was designed to reinforce learning systems that already existed, to improve them, not to transform them. No one was to read a book without the help of a scholar. This was made very clear in one of the most influential works of popularization written over the past two centuries, Ashraf Ali Thanawi's *Bihishti Zewar* (Jewels of Paradise), a companion for Muslim women, a book designed to take the cause of Islamic reform into the harem. Rounding off the *Jewels of Paradise* Thanawi warns his readers against the dangers of the unsupervised reading of books:

To avoid all this first show to a scholar any book being bought or read. If he says it is useful, then read it. If he says it is harmful, do not look at it or even keep it in the house ... In short do not read any book without consulting a scholar. In fact, without a scholar do nothing at all.[30]

THE MASS PRODUCTION EFFECTS OF PRINT AND RELIGIOUS CHANGE

Throughout the nineteenth and twentieth centuries the popularization of formal religious knowledge through print in South Asia has been closely intertwined with Muslim religious revival. This revival has been accompanied by a whole series of religious changes associated, to a greater or lesser degree, with the use of print. The first set of changes is primarily a result of the mass-production effects of print.

A new way of being Muslim developed alongside those that

already existed. It has come to be called Islamic protestantism and bears comparison with Christian protestantism. It was a significant answer to the problem of how to be Muslim under British rule. For Muslim protestants the route to survival was scriptural knowledge, knowledge of the Quran, and the traditions, and how to be a Muslim. Print was central to broadcasting this knowledge and making it available. Print was essential, too, to the successful working of their school system, independent of the colonial state and based on Deoband, which was to transmit and spread this knowledge. The idea was that, with better Islamic knowledge, Muslims would be able to live a proper Muslim life for themselves. It would not matter if a Christian colonial state occupied the public arena. Their knowledge would tell them what God's will was; their conscience would make them obey it. This Islamic way, moreover, was reinforced by an approach to Islamic mysticism which forbade any thought of intercession at saints' tombs. Nothing was to dilute the powerful mixture of God's word and human conscience.[31] Supporters of this way of being Muslim, by and large, had little interest in state power; they opposed the Muslim demand for Pakistan in the 1940s. Similar responses to colonial rule emerged both in Indonesia and in North Africa.

Islamic vision broadened to embrace much of the Muslim community in the world at large. Traditionally, of course, the idea of the *Ummah*—the community of the Muslims in the world at large —had a sense of magic for Muslims; it was after all a community created through the grace of God's revelation through Muhammad. But the writings of Indian Muslims in the eighteenth and early nineteenth centuries give little sense of much involvement with the world outside South Asia, except with the Hijaz, Iran and perhaps Central Asia. However, during the second half of the nineteenth century, it is evident that South Asian Muslims were coming to experience an increasingly intense imaginative and emotional relationship with the wider Islamic world. The reasons for this expanding vision were many: the impact of colonial rule; the realization that the encroachment of the West was an experience being shared by almost all Muslims; the increasing ease with which Muslims were able to travel to be with Muslims in other lands; the need to find a sense of identity as they grappled with the meaning of the modern state in colonial form. This expansion of vision could not have taken place without the development of a large and vigorous

Muslim press. Indeed, there was a symbiotic relationship between the growth of pan-Islamic consciousness and of the press; it bears comparison with the relationship which Benedict Anderson has noted between the rapid march of print capitalism and the emergence of national consciousness in early modern Europe.[32] The more Indian Muslims discovered about the fate of their brethren elsewhere in the Islamic world, the more they wished to know. When Russia and the Ottoman Empire went to war in the late 1870s, the press boomed. When the British invaded Egypt in 1882, it boomed again. When the Ottoman Empire entered its terminal stages from 1911 onwards, the press boomed as never before. Great newspapers flourished—Abul Kalam Azad's *al-Hilal*, Muhammad Ali's *Comrade* Zafar Ali Khan's *Zamindar*.[33] Such was the fervour and the excitement that many Muslims came to live a significant part of their imaginative lives in thoughts about the wider Islamic world. Muslims adopted headwear and other forms of dress to indicate their identification with the Middle East.[34] Their writings betrayed an absorption with the Muslims of other counties. At the leading edge of this pan-Islamic vision of the Muslim community, and of course exploring its religious meaning, was the poet Muhammad Iqbal. When he wanted to emphasize the decline of Islam, he wrote a tearful poem about the end of Arab rule in Sicily; when he wanted to reflect upon human creativity, he wrote his finest Urdu poem on the mosque at Cordoba; when he wanted to emphasize that the Muslim community was not confined by any space, he wrote:

> Our essence is not bound to any place;
> The vigour of our wine is not contained
> In any bowl; Chinese and Indian
> Alike the shard that constitutes our jar,
> Turkish and Syrian alike the clay
> Forming our body; neither is our heart
> Of India, or Syria, or Rum,
> Nor any fatherland do we profess
> Except Islam.[35]

Iqbal's sweeping vision magnifies a broadening horizon that many Muslims were coming to sense, to some extent at least. They were discovering that there was a part of themselves which was mentally and emotionally integrated with the wider Islamic world. They had a pan-Islamic layer in their identity. Without the press this pan-Islamic horizon could never have been seriously explored.

A third religious change, and one in which print played a large and arguably, the most important part, was the erosion of the authority of the *ulema* as interpreters of Islam. However, a glance at public affairs in the nineteenth- and early twentieth-century India would not necessarily suggest that this was the case. At no stage in the history of Islam on the Indian subcontinent were the *ulema* so influential. In a situation in which Muslim power was destroyed, and in which the Muslim landed and government service classes were compromised by their association with the colonial power, the *ulema* were able to push themselves forward as the defenders of Muslim culture and Muslim values in a modernizing and Westernizing world. As we have seen, they used print and the press as a major weapon in their struggle. They achieved considerable success in building a constituency in Muslim society at large to compensate for the loss of the support of Muslim state power. By the end of the nineteenth century, Shibli Nomani was urging the first conference of *ulema* to take control of the Muslim community.[36] In 1917, when the British were considering a major devolution of power to Indians, the *ulema* sent in addresses to the Viceroy and the Secretary of State for India claiming that power should be devolved on them.[37] Such was their influence, moreover, that when they protested against British rule—the biggest since the Mutiny of 1857—to try to save the Turkish Caliphate and to protect the holy places of Islam, they were able to blow constitutional politics off course for a good four years.[38]

But, ironically, while print enabled the *ulema* to extend their influence greatly in public affairs, it also seriously damaged the roots of their authority. By printing the Islamic classics—and the print run for a major text could be as many as ten thousand copies —and by translating them into the vernaculars they undermined their authority; they were no longer necessarily around when the book was read to make up for the absence of the author in the text; their precious *ijazas*, which brought the authority of the past of their learning in the present, were made less significant; their monopoly over the transmission of knowledge was broken. Books, which they literally possessed and carried in their hearts, and which they transmitted with a whole series of mnemonic aids to memory, could now be consulted by any Ahmad, Mahmud or Muhammad, who could make what they willed of them. Increasingly from now on any Ahmad, Mahmud or Muhammad could claim to speak for Islam. No longer was a sheaf of impeccable *ijazas* the buttress of authority; strong Islamic commitment was enough. The force of 1200 years of oral transmission, of person to person transmission, came increasingly to be ignored. As a consequence, as Akbar Ahmad so often says, no one knows nowadays who speaks for Islam.[39]

In fact, the twentieth century has witnessed a steady decline in the authority of the *ulema*. Of course, they still command respect. Of course, many still comport themselves as men who cherish the knowledge of God's word in their hearts should, their dignity and manners reflecting their sense of their awesome responsibilities. Nevertheless, their authority has been draining away and they do not walk so tall; their gowns and turbans do not signify as much. Doubtless they will end up like teachers in the universities of the West; like scholars, who wear their finery on special occasions, but with little sense of its meaning—a mere sartorial echo of the time when they had real authority.

By breaking the stranglehold of 1200 years of oral transmission and of the madrasa-trained *ulema* on the interpretation of Islamic knowledge, print helped to make possible an era of vigorous religious experiment. Print came to be the main forum in which religious debate was conducted; it was an era of pamphlet wars and of religiously partisan newspapers and magazines. Scholars—some madrasa-trained and some not—delved with increasing vigour into the resources of both the Islamic tradition and Western civilization, now made freely available by print, to find answers to contemporary challenges. The result was a rapid florescence of sectarianism. Group after group sprang up: Deobandis, Barelvis, Ahmadis, Necharis, Ahl-i Hadiths, Ahl-i Quran, Jamaatis and so on.

Some of the more extreme responses to contemporary challenges, some of the more radical leaps forward in religious thinking, came from men who were not formally trained *ulema* but were from outside the oral system of transmission. One of these was Mirza Ghulam Ahmad of Qadian, the founder of the Ahmadiyya sect, who died in 1908. Drawing on strands in medieval Islamic thought as well as the spurious claims of a European explorer in the Himalayas and the Gospel of Barnabas, a medieval forgery, he made a series of assertions. Among them were the following: that Christ did not die on the cross but survived to preach to a lost tribe of

Israel in the Punjab and is buried in Kashmir; that Ghulam Ahmad himself was the Promised Messiah of the Christian and Muslim traditions; and that he, Ghulam Ahmad, was a prophet—suggesting that prophecy had not come to an end with the Prophet Muhammad. Ghulam Ahmad was not popular with his fellow Muslims; his ten million or so followers are persecuted throughout much of the Islamic world. However, it is unlikely that Ghulam Ahmad would have been able to develop his views outside the much freer access to knowledge offered by print. Certainly his followers in Britain know the value of print; at the heart of the complex they have recently built at Tilford, near Guildford, is a printing press with facilities for computer typesetting in thirty different languages.[40]

Ghulam Ahmad is something of a curiosity, albeit an interesting one. Much more important in developing new trajectories of religious thought were Saiyid Ahmad Khan, who died in 1898, and Saiyid Abul Ala Maududi, who died in 1979. Saiyid Ahmad Khan was the founder of Islamic modernism, that is, the development in Islamic thought which bears comparison with the development of higher criticism and modernism in Christian thought. He was deeply concerned that Islam should make sense in the light of Western science; he was no less concerned that Muslims should be reconciled to Western civilization and British rule. A largely self-taught scholar, Saiyid Ahmad explored the Islamic tradition for himself. He also explored contemporary Western science and biblical criticism. He knew William Paley's *Natural Theology* and John Herschel's *Outlines of Astronomy*. He approved of Unitarians such as Spinoza and Toland, but disapproved of radical German theologians of the Tubingen school such as David Strauss and Ferdinand Baur. He was certainly aware of the great achievements in natural history of Charles Lyell and Charles Darwin, if not directly, at least through their impact on Bishop Colenso's questioning of the historical nature of the Pentateuch.[41] Saiyid Ahmad remains the only Muslim, to my knowledge, to have produced a commentary on the Bible. He also produced his own vast commentary on the Quran. In developing a new Islamic theology, he echoed the natural theologians amongst the Christians of his time: the word of God and the work of God cannot be in conflict.[42] If they seemed to be in conflict, it was the fault of Muslim understanding. With a new sense of history, he drew a distinction between the essence of the Quran and what belonged to the time when it was revealed. At the heart of his modernist approach was his concern to draw this essence, the intention of revelation, into the modern world and to cut away the shackles of the past. Now Islam could fearlessly keep in step with the advance of modern science and of social change. It was an Islamic understanding which could never have been generated in the madrasas with their oral systems for transmitting knowledge. It was entirely a product of the world of print. To this day it flourishes only amongst those subject to Western-style systems of education.

Saiyid Abul Ala Maududi was the founder of Islamic 'fundamentalism'—or, better put, the Islamist movement—in South Asia, and the most powerful influence on its development worldwide. Like Saiyid Ahmad Khan he was not madrasa-educated and stood outside the traditional oral systems of transmission; he was also self-educated in European social and political thought. His prime concern was that Islam and Islamic society should be able to withstand its increasingly corrosive encounter with the West. To do this, rightly-guided Muslims had to take control of the modern state; he had no time at all for the Muslims protestants who avoided the realities of modern politics and relied on individual human wills to make Islamic society. Political power was to be used to put revelation into operation on earth. All the guidance that was needed already existed in the holy law, the *sharia*, which embraced all human activity. God was sovereign on earth, not man; the state, manned by the rightly-guided, was His agent. This is the basic blueprint of Islamic fundamentalism. It has been carried forward by the organization of the rightly-guided, the Jamaat-i Islami, whose influence in Pakistan and elsewhere is out of all proportion to its numbers.

Maududi's Islamic understanding, which appeals to many educated Muslims throughout the world, particularly those educated in the modern sciences, is entirely a product of print culture. Moreover, the Jamaat-i Islami is in significant measure sustained by print, a large part of its income coming from the sale of Maududi's works. Furthermore, its message is spread by print. The young Muslim 'fundamentalist' gets much of his Islamic knowledge from books which will often be read without a teacher. The printed book is the chief vehicle of Maudud's ideas, as it is for other Islamizing forces, whether they be the offshoots of the Muslim Brotherhood in the Arab world or the Nurcular in Turkey.[43] Indeed, the founder of the Nurcular actually insisted that books should replace people as guides in faith. 'They are *gazis*,' he said pointing to a pile of the writings of his followers, 'they have waged a battle against unbelief.'[44]

THE PSYCHOLOGICAL EFFECTS OF PRINT AND RELIGIOUS CHANGE

Here we are concerned with the changes in consciousness which take place as the mind comes to be less informed by sound and more by sight. This is one of the great revolutions in human history involving a basic shift in what McLuhan terms the 'ratio of the senses'. There followed 'a new posture of mind charged with new preferences and desires, as well as with [sic] new patterns of perception'.[45] Such new postures and new patterns were also to have their effect on religious expression and understanding.

Some guidance as to the nature and the meaning of the change can be gathered from the experience of the West. One issue that most scholarship has made clear is that, in the shift from sound to sight, writing was relatively unimportant. There was remarkable continuity, as we have seen in the Islamic world, between oral and manuscript culture. Books in scribal hands certainly did begin the work of restructuring consciousness, but more often than not they were aids to the oral reproduction of knowledge and not replacements for it; most people still read out loud and university teachers tested their students not in written examination but by oral dispute.[46] Even the arrival of print, although decisive in the long run, did not mean the immediate overwhelming of oral communication. The 'human voice' was not at once 'closed down', in McLuhan's words, 'as Gutenberg typography filled the world'.[47] For centuries afterwards the learned in even the most advanced countries of Europe regarded books, as they had done in classical times, as something to be read out loud. Printed texts carried forward the Reformation not by destroying oral communication but by augmenting its possibilities. Punctuation systems remained for the ear and not the eye. Until the end of the seventeenth century oral communication was common for public and private purposes in the family, village and town. Indeed, it was not until the eighteenth and nineteenth centuries that the transforming impact of print was widely felt on the mind. As Graham declared:

> In terms of change in modes of consciousness as well as sheer material change the great chasm in forms of communication turns out to be not that

between literate societies and non-literate societies, but that to which McLuhan's eccentric, often infuriating, but also prescient *Gutenberg Galaxy* pointed—the gulf between our own modern Western post-Enlightenment world of the printed page and all past cultures ... as well as most contemporary ones.[48]

So profoundly has the printed page come to form the mind of the literate today that we have to struggle to recapture a sense of what the word means to people of purely oral culture and how it might fashion the workings of their minds. Imagine a world in which words have no visual form, in which they are always dynamic and evanescent. In this world all words involve human interaction, their impact fills the present, indeed floods the consciousness, leaving little room for anything else. Consider the techniques of producing words in this environment: man can only speak what he can recall, so his speech is dependent on formulas, patterns, rhythms—it is full of mnemonics; he piles idea upon idea rather than systematically organizing his speech into subordinate clauses; he heaps epithet upon epithet, cliché upon cliché rather than presenting his thinking in analytical form; his language is fluent, fulsome, voluble—replete with what the rhetoricians term *copia*; he tends to be conservative in thought because precious knowledge which is not repeated soon vanishes; he expounds his ideas in terms of the world about him because abstractions would be of little value; he is involved with his story rather than objectively distanced; he subordinates the past to the present within which his whole being takes place. The experience for the speaker and for the audience is intensely participatory; it strikes at the very heart of consciousness. As Walter Ong declares:

> In a primary oral culture, where the word has its existence only in sound, with no reference whatsoever to any visually perceptible text, and no awareness of even the possibility of such a text, the phenomenology of sound enters deeply into the human being's feel for existence, as processed by the spoken word. For the way in which the word is experienced is always momentous in psychic life.[49]

In such a world there is little distancing from experience; there is little room for introspection, for objectivity or for analysis.[50]

Such aspects of orality and of oral experience help us to understand better the great transformation of human consciousness which began with the adoption of writing in the ancient world and reached its fullness in the West in the eighteenth century. One crucial outcome of the migration of the world from oral/aural into visual space was the distancing or the separation of the knower from the known. A text comes to lie between them as a tangible object, the existence of which enables knowledge to be distinguished from the knower. In the same way it becomes possible to draw a distinction between data, the text, and interpretation. Then, the existence of the text separates it from the living context of spoken words and the many non-verbal communications which may accompany them; it is placed instead simply in the context of other texts. The existence of the text, furthermore, both enforces verbal precision and makes possible the separation of past from present. The mind thus rises out of its immersion in the present to embrace the possibilities of abstract thought.[51]

Connected with this, there is a second outcome of the migration of the word into visual space; man's opening up of his interior world. One way of charting this process, alongside developing technologies of the word, is to trace the growing complexity and roundedness of human characters as depicted in the plays of the ancient Greeks, through those of Shakespeare down to the novel, which achieves its full flowering in the nineteenth and twentieth centuries along with those widespread monuments to the insatiable contemporary fascination with the individual and the self, the biography and autobiography. These developments have, of course, been paralleled by the growth of modern psychology. That this transformation of consciousness crosses a watershed in the eighteenth and nineteenth centuries is demonstrated by the 'silencing' of the human voice: dialectics gave way to silent cerebration, rhetoric to the art of literary composition; logic was no longer the art of discourse but that of thinking, and silent reading spread across the face of Europe. Western Europeans now developed a growing inward orientation as they faced the struggles of life; they were more aware of themselves, were developing inner resources and fostering their consciences; Protestants privately interpreted the Bible, Catholics privately confessed their sins. Such men were less likely to be moved by shame, the institutionalized pressure for conformity of a largely oral community, and rather more likely to be guided by the personal resources they had developed in cultivating themselves. As new technologies of the word were helping to give man untold power over the physical world, they also threw open windows over the broad vistas of his interior landscape.

This transformation of human consciousness, which made slow and uneven progress in the time of manuscript culture, but moved more rapidly towards a peak in that of print, led to new forms of mental behaviour and new qualities of the mind. The process of interiorization brought an increasing introspectiveness; that of distancing led to a growing capacity for objectivity and analytical thought. The disciplines of history and philosophy, the analytical and conceptual understandings of literature, art and human affairs were all the natural offspring of this change. So, too, alongside the new levels of precision made possible by print—the locking of words into well-defined spaces, the capacity for accurate and endless repetition, the ability to reproduce exactly-worded descriptions of carefully-observed objects and processes, and in the form of pictures, graphs, tables, maps and diagrams—was the rise of modern science.[52]

Such developments, of course, had implications for religious understanding. As a direct result of the growing power of the visual media, Christianity became increasingly cut off from the oral/aural roots of its revelation. For those able to ponder over revelation on the printed page, the Word could never be so dynamically and so sensually present as it had been when communicated by the voice of man alone. For those who no longer needed to commit scripture to memory, the Word was never likely to suffuse the workings of their minds and to inform their daily speech and action as it was for those who have the word of God with them. The modern West, as Graham tells us, 'appears to be historically anomalous in its understanding of scripture largely because of its general loss of a significant oral/aural relationship to the scriptural word and, indeed, to the written word altogether'.[53] Yet more important, for those for whom religious knowledge had become just one of several ways of understanding man's relationship to this life and the hereafter, religion may no longer be central to this process but marginal, perhaps irrelevant. Moreover, it has become an object amongst other objects, a system of explanation amongst other systems, an ideology amongst other ideologies. The migration of the word from sound to sight seems to have gone hand in hand with the marginalization of the Word in Western life.

There are dangers in trying to apply ideas derived from one set of historical circumstances to another. Nineteenth- and twentieth-century South Asia is not fifteenth- or sixteenth-century Europe.

The Islamic context in general, moreover, as well as that in South Asia in particular, is one in which a higher cultural value has been placed on the oral transmission of scripture than in Christianity. Nevertheless, South Asia in the nineteenth and twentieth centuries has experienced the onset of print after a substantial fashion, a development which must be placed in the context of a process of modernization which is much more rapid and much more compressed than that experienced by the West. South Asian Muslims have moved some way down the path travelled by European Christians in the transfer of the word from sound to sight. It is, therefore, not unreasonable to suggest that religious understandings have come to be influenced by the processes of distancing and interiorization similar to those experienced in Christian Europe.

DISTANCING AND RELIGIOUS CHANGE

The emergence of new strands of historical understanding had vast significance for religious understanding. Oral tradition and madrasa methods of teaching had bred distinctive attitudes to the past. For one thing it was an undifferentiated country. Certainly, it was the home of the Quran, the Hadiths, the *sharia* and the commentaries of the learned; certainly, too, it was the realm in which the wisdom of hundreds of saints had been elaborated. This country was there to be plundered without care for time or place to serve the needs of the present; to bring weight to an argument; to justify a course of action; or to make sense of a knotty problem. For another thing, the past was a store of precious guidance, the true meaning of which the faithful were ever in fear of losing. The further Muslims moved away from the time of the Prophet the greater their fear became. Vigilance was needed to curb deviance or innovation (*bida*) and to preserve their precious gift from God. The most basic impulse was conservative. 'Watch me,' declared Maulana Abdur Razzaq of Firangi Mahal, 'so long as I follow our pious predecessors, follow me; and if I do not follow our pious predecessors, do not follow me. Our predecessors were better than we are, because they lived closer to the time of the Holy Prophet.'[54] Abdur Razzaq reflects the particularly conservative concerns of the learned and holy men. Yet, historians brought up in the manuscript culture of medieval India do not seem to have had a historical consciousness that was substantially more rounded than this. According to K.A. Nizami, they had a poor sense of chronology, a weak conceptual capacity and little idea of causation.[55]

New strands of historical understanding, indeed a strong belief in the importance of history itself, developed as Muslims, concerned to have the strength to cope with the challenge of Europe, came to reappraise their approach to the past. The pioneer in this, as in so many other things, was Saiyid Ahmad Khan. It is now possible, thanks to the research of Christian Troll, to trace the development of Saiyid Ahmad's historical method from the rather primitive techniques of the first edition of *Athar al-Sanadid* of 1847 to his powerful response to Muir's *Life of Mahomed*, the *Khutubat al-Ahmadiyah* of 1870, which, its apologetic purpose apart, was armed with many of the skills of modern historical scholarship.[56] In this development we witness the growth of the understanding that enabled Saiyid Ahmad to argue that the Quran must be interpreted in the light of the circumstances of seventh-century Arabia and that the reliability of Hadiths must be judged in the light of reason and their relationship to Quranic injunctions rather than in that of the soundness of their chain of narrators. Saiyid Ameer Ali, who made similar distinctions between the temporary and permanent injunctions of the Quran, also insisted in his historical writings on the importance of events being understood in the broad context of their time.[57] So too, did Shibli Nomani, the founder of modern Urdu historiography and an admirer of the German historian, Ranke. The substantial introduction to his *Omar the Great*, completed in 1898, is devoted to historical method, emphasizing the importance of context, the examination of sources, the use of reason and the weighing of cause and effect.[58] Part of this approach even seeped into the thinking of traditionally learned man, albeit an exceptionally gifted one. Maulana Abdul Hayy of Firangi Mahal (1848–86) insisted in his work as a mufti that past legal decisions should not be regarded as carrying equal weight for the present; their significance must be weighed in the context of the times in which they were made.[59] This jurisprudential technique no doubt explains in part why his collection of *fatawa* remains widely used in the eastern Islamic world.

Given the new world of understanding which was opened up by history, it is not surprising that emphasis was given to its study. Shibli, for instance, gave it special significance in the curriculum of the Dar ul-Ulum of the Nadwat ul-Ulama. As the twentieth century progressed, it came to be established in the *madrasas* of the *ulema*; as part of the field on which the battle for the future of Islam was being fought, it became too important to ignore.[60] The late Fazlur Rahman, the leading modernist thinker of Pakistan, declared in his last major work, *Islam and Modernity*, that 'the best of the social sciences is history—if done well and objectively ... Macro-history ... is the best service a social scientist can do for mankind. This is the reason the Qur'an invites us again and again "to travel on the earth and see the end of nations".'[61]

This new historical consciousness played a central role in enabling Muslims to bring forward alternative understanding of Islam to set beside those of the *ulema*. Now, against their negative vision of Islamic history as a process of constant effort to hold back the inevitable decline since the time of the Prophet, it was possible to set a positive vision which saw that the essence of Islam could be kept vital and pertinent in each succeeding generation, indeed, it might be possible to see it moving towards stages of higher realization on earth as it travelled through time. History was vital to the techniques which enabled Saiyid Ahmad to bring Quranic revelation into harmony with modern science. It was no less vital to the purpose of Fazlur Rahman in bringing the *sharia* into harmony with modern circumstances, as he demonstrated in a masterly essay on that monument to Pakistani modernism, the Muslim Family Laws Ordinance of 1961.[62] Furthermore, it was central to Iqbal's dynamic vision of the Muslim community in history. For centuries, he argued, the *ulema* and the sufis had concealed the progressive vigour of Islam behind veils of Greek philosophy and pantheistic mysticism. The Quran, on the other hand, taught the ascension of man through higher and higher realms of experience towards perfection. Moreover, just as the capacities of Muslims as individuals would be revealed through time, so too would those of the Muslim community. Iqbal's historical consciousness, alongside his studies of Bergson, Nietzsche, al-Jili and Ibn al-Arabi, helped him to fashion an inspiring idea of progress for his faith.

The Islamic vision of the 'fundamentalist' thinker, Maulana Maududi, is no less dependent on a new historical consciousness than that of the modernists. He was profoundly opposed to the negative historical vision of the *ulema* and to their desperate struggle to emulate the pattern of behaviour established by the Prophet and his companions. He argued that the Prophet and the first two caliphs had realized the underlying principles of the Quranic revelation perfectly, i.e. establishing God's sovereignty on earth. But subsequently the true meaning of the Quran had been lost as caliphate became kingship and even the great renewers of Islamic history failed to understand the proper role of power in Muslim society, i.e. to support revelation. In relating the past to the present, however, Maududi did not argue that the task of Muslims was to recreate the outward forms of the early Islamic community. What had to be translated into the present was the spirit of the Prophet's system and its underlying principles. In this way, like the modernists, Maududi made a very similar distinction between form and essence.[63]

In short, new historical understandings helped both to fashion new visions of Islam and to endow them with extraordinary energies. Although print cannot be regarded as the sufficient cause of these new developments, they could not have emerged and spread without it.

The growth of an understanding of Islam as an object, which might be analysed, conceptualized and even presented as a system, was a second development associated with the distancing effects of print. One illustration of this reification of Islam in the Muslim mind is the growing use of the term not just to describe 'submitting' their relationship to God, but to describe an ideal religious pattern, or a mundane religious system, or even just Islamic civilization.[64] Evidence of this development in the late nineteenth century lies in the titles of books such as the poet Hali's masterwork *Musaddas, Madd-o jazr-i Islam* (1879), or Ameer Ali's *Ethics of Islam* (1893). A second illustration is the increasing emergence in the twentieth century of works designed to explain the nature of Islam whether from the 'fundamentalist' position of Maududi's *Towards Understanding Islam* (1940), or Manzoor Nomani's more traditional *What Islam is* (1964), or Fazlur Rahman's modernist *Islam* (1966), or the anthropologist Akbar Ahmed's *Discovering Islam* (1988). Such uses of the term suggest that these Muslims can stand apart from their faith; they can analyse and conceptualize it. In such circumstances, submitting to God was increasingly a conscious act of will rather than the unquestioning pursuit of the paths in faith followed by one's forefathers.

In its extreme form Islam as an object came to be conceptualized as a system. This was the particular achievement of Maulana

Maududi; it grew out of his concern to establish an Islamic vision of life to set against that of the West. He described Islam as a *nizam*, a system which was comprehensive, complete and covered all aspects of human existence. These aspects, moreover, were integrated, as the human body was integrated, into one homogeneous whole. God, in another image, was the great engineer in his workshop; he had created the world and in the *sharia* had given man a complete set of principles on which to conduct himself in that universe.

It is His explicit Will that the universe—this grand workshop with its multifarious activities—should go on functioning smoothly and graciously so that man—the prize of creation—should make the best and most productive use of all his powers and resources, of everything that has been harnessed for him in the earth and in the high heavens ... The *Shari'ah* is meant to guide the steps of man in this respect.[65]

This vision of Islam as a system meant that the *sharia* must be yoked to power on earth. Such a vision was, of course, the inspiration for the *Nizam-i Islam* that General Zia ul-Haq tried to introduce in Pakistan from February 1979. It should be clear, however, that large numbers of Muslims, and not least among them the eminent Indian scholar Maulana Abul Ḥasan Ali Nadwi, see Islam not as a system but as a message from god to man. The individual is the key building block of society. The battle for power in the world was to be won in the hearts of men and not in the field of politics.[66]

The rise to prominence of a this-worldly understanding of Islam is arguably a third development which can be associated with the distancing effects of print. Many Muslims of the nineteenth and twentieth centuries would argue that a this-worldly understanding of Islam, i.e. one which demands action to put God's will into practice on earth, had always been present in the example of the Prophet but had been concealed by the influence of *ulema* and sufis, particularly the Asharite theologians and sufis influenced by Ibn al-Arabi. Indian Muslims also argue that the re-emergence of an emphasis on action could be dated back to Shaikh Ahmad Sirhindi's development of the idea in the early seventeenth century of the 'unity of witness' (*wahdat al-shuhud*) to place against Ibn al-Arabi's 'unity of being' (*wahdat al-wujud*), a development which meant that reality was not to be found wholly in God but in His word, and therefore demanded action in this world to bring it into harmony with divine order. This emphasis on the need to take action in this world, moreover, suffused the Muslim reform movements of the nineteenth century.

This having been said, it is arguable that the sense of the need for action was sharpened and intensified by the new historical consciousness, the reified understandings of Islam, and the vast expansion of knowledge and information that came with print. Muslims now had a painfully clear view of the decline of their power as compared with the first one thousand years of Islam; it was not for nothing that Hali's *Musaddas*, his elegy on the rise and fall of Islam, was one of the most popular poems of the age. Educated Muslims were now able to have a well-worked out vision of Islam as a whole way of life, as a whole civilization which was threatened both by the Western industrial world and by Hindu India. Furthermore, with every passing day, the workings of the world of print reinforced these facts upon their minds. It is not remarkable therefore that the need for action in this world was a feature as much of modernist thought as it was of the 'fundamentalist'. Saiyid Ahmad Khan's life was a testament to this imperative. Maududi's vision was a blueprint for action now. Consider his view of worship, *ibadat*. Its rituals were not duties to perform so that God will be pleased with you. They were a 'training course' which 'aims at developing so much strength in them [the Muslims] that when they rise with the aim of establishing the caliphate of God on earth, they must prove true to their claim'.[67]

INTERIORIZATION AND RELIGIOUS CHANGE

We now turn to the second major psychological impact of print, the process of interiorization, the opening up of an inner world. One way of charting the path of this process is to note the changing way in which the Quran was read from the early-nineteenth century to the present. Before the advent of print and widespread availability of translations of God's message to man through Muhammad, pondering over the meaning of the Quran was limited to those few who might be able to understand its Arabic and to have access to a commentary either in Arabic or in Persian. The English lady, Mrs Meer Hassan Ali, who lived in northern India from 1816 to 1828, tells of the strong prejudice against the translation of the Quran from Arabic, and of how it was used for incantatory purposes at home or for magical purposes in amulets;[68] sh_ also recounts the family practice in her Shia household in Lucknow, which was no different from that of many contemporary households in London, of reading the scripture aloud to each other and discussing it.[69] The remarkable biography of Bibi Ashraf reveals how, in a similar household of the mid-nineteenth century in Bijnor, women might have known how to read the Quran out loud but without understanding it.[70] Ashraf Ali Thanawi's influential *Bihishti Zewar* urges them to read the Quran out aloud; there is a sense, indeed, that he is concerned to 'discourage ... the privacy of reading silently, of creating a private world of one's own ... .'[71] Thanawi is, moreover, silent as to whether he permitted the reading of the Quran in Urdu, although a commentary on the Quran in Urdu heads his list of recommended books for reading. However, there is no doubt that by this time women were studying the Quran in Urdu. Zubaida Khatun, the young heroine of Hali's *Majalis un Nissa* read the Quran in Urdu after she had learned it in Arabic.[72]

Indeed, the stages of Zubaida Khatun's encounter with the Quran seem to have been an increasingly common pattern for men and women in the late nineteenth century. At least a dozen different translations of the Quran had been published and the government remarked upon how tens of thousands of copies of the books were published in just one year.[73] The Urdu Quran, of course, meant a readily accessible Quran and one which paved the way for its consultation in private by many. The Khilafat leader, Muhammad Ali, offers a charming description in his autobiography of his first serious encounter with Maulvi Nazir Ahmad's colloquial translation of the Quran during his internment by the British during World War One. Up to this point the book had been little more than an icon that, for instance, he had had sumptuously bound and given pride of place on the shelves of his set in Oxford. But now he began to study it in the privacy of his room reading a little each day. He was captivated. 'My brother would call out to me from his room and recite to me a verse, or I would do the same to him pointing out how apposite it was to the question we happened to be debating only little before.'[74] He found his life transformed, and this transformation affected not just his personal life but also his political direction.[75] The *ulema*, too, while continuing to acknowledge the ritual benefits of reciting the Quran, have come to emphasize the importance of reading it with understanding.[76] In the twentieth century the movement is more and more towards a personal and reflective encounter with revelation. Maududi mocked the way in which many Muslims regarded the Quran as a form of magic and insisted upon the importance of their engaging with its meaning.[77] The contemporary religious thinker, Syed Vahiduddin, makes it perfectly clear that the Quran has a constant and vital presence in his inner life:

> Our understanding of the Book is an on-going process, which reveals hidden depths ... For me *al-Qur'an* is primarily the Book to be reflected upon, in silence and in privacy, whose guidance is sought in moments of anguish and its company in times of distress.[78]

A further dimension of interiorization is the expression of a growing sense of self, of the manifold nature of the human individual. As in Europe this is accompanied by the emergence of the novel and the short story, those quintessential forms for the private reader to set alongside the flourishing poetic tradition. There is also the development of autobiography and biography, although rather more vigorously in English than in Urdu.[79] Moreover, even the traditional hagiographical writings of the *ulema* begin to display the humanistic preferences of the age, presenting much more rounded lives to support their didactic purpose.[80] The most powerful expression of this idea in religious terms, however, is the great attention which comes to be paid to the biography of the Prophet. Muhammad had always been a major focus for Muslim love and piety. But a new dimension enters Muslim feeling in the twentieth century. 'Probably more lives of Muhammad appeared between the two World Wars,' according to W.C. Smith, 'than in any one of the centuries between the twelfth and the nineteenth.'[81] In the Punjab, moreover, from the 1920s there was a specific movement, the Sirat movement, to distribute pamphlets and sermons about the Prophet, which had particular success amongst the middle classes.

The new focus on the life of the Prophet was not entirely the consequence of a new sense of the self. Certainly some weight must be given to the need for a new outlet for religious emotion. Reformed Islam had largely discredited the outlets offered by mysticism; the Prophet became the one symbol on which religious imaginations could focus their desire to love and to trust.[82] Certainly, too, the massive assault of much of Christian civilization in general and Christian missionaries in particular on the character of the Prophet would help to explain a desire to assert the virtues of the Prophet both in principle and in contrast to those of Jesus.[83] Furthermore, the whole process of Islamic revival and reform from the beginning of the nineteenth century, with its growing concern to outflank the supposedly deadening influence of the *ulema* and sufis and to take inspiration from the early Islamic community, was bound to bring the example of the Prophet even more to the forefront of Muslim minds. But, when evidence is taken from the content of the biographies, there is a powerful sense that the writers are concerned to project onto him their image of a perfect human self—a perfect, twentieth century, educated Muslim middle-class self: he is no longer the Perfect Man of the sufi tradition but the perfect person.[84] Muhammad is given a wide range of human virtues. He is said to have been 'beloved, charitable, frugal, generous, gentle, honest, lenient, a lover of children, modest, pure, steadfast and successful'[85] and there is plenty in the Islamic tradition to give life to these virtues. For some his quality is summed up in an attitude of love:

What was the keynote of his life? It was nothing but love; love of God; love of mankind; ... love of children; love of the gentler sex; love of friends; love of foe ...[86]

W.C. Smith highlights an emphasis on perseverance under adversity, industry, frugality and seriousness as typical of an early-capitalist society.[87] From our point of view the emphasis on these virtues of the Prophet in expressing the growing sense of the self, reveals the new individualism of a middle-class Muslim world that is acquiring a more and more highly developed awareness of inner resources.

ASSESSMENT

Evidently print, working alongside the great complex of forces brought about by the process of modernization under colonial rule, has helped to work great changes in South Asian Islam. We have seen from our studies of its mass-production effects how it contributed to a range of major developments; the emergence of a protestant or scriptural Islam; the strengthening of the Pan-Islamic layer in the Muslim sense of identity; the levelling of an assault on the *ulema* as sole interpreters of Islam; the outflanking of oral, person-to-person, systems for the transmission of knowledge; the colonizing of Muslim minds with Western knowledge; and the opening of the way towards new understandings of Islam such as those of the modernists and the 'fundamentalists'. We have also seen how the psychological effects of print have played their part in working major developments; the process of distancing, which helped to bring about the new historical consciousness, the reification of religion and the emphasis on this-worldly action; and the process of interiorization which is manifest in an increasingly personal and private encounter with the Quran and a new and yet more powerful focus on the person of the Prophet in Muslim piety.

However, it is important to be aware of the limits to these religious changes. Print and print culture have only achieved a limited penetration of Muslim society in South Asia. Literacy must be a criterion of a basis of susceptibility to such changes; literacy rates in 1980–81 ranged from 20 per cent in Bangladesh, to 24 per cent in Pakistan to 36 per cent in India. It is a sobering thought that the new religious ideas which South Asian Muslims have broadcast throughout the Muslim world in the twentieth century are unlikely to be able to reach even one third of the Muslim peoples of the subcontinent.

Even when there is literacy, patterns of behaviour derived from oral culture can remain very influential, as Amin Sweeney has shown in his studies of Malaysian students.[88] Indeed, print can still be relegated to the status of mere handmaid of oral transmission. One of the most widely followed movements in the Muslim world today, some would say the most widely followed, is the *Tabligh-i Jamaat* or Missionary Society. Members of this society, often highly literate people, learn key texts by heart. They insist on human contact in the transmission of knowledge. This is not to say that members of the *Tabligh* ignore books. Indeed, they contain central parts of the Society's message. There are, moreover, many of them; a recent catalogue of the Society's programme for translating Arabic and Urdu texts into English numbered 645 titles. But these books are all subordinate to the texts which members of the *Tabligh* have learned by heart and teach in person.[89]

Finally, it must be remembered that Muslims in South Asia have experienced barely one hundred years of the wide use of lithography and typography. As print makes its way forward, it is rapidly being caught up by a second revolutionary force in information technology, the electronic media—wireless, telephone, television, sound cassettes, video cassettes etc. ... The electronic media, deceptive though they can be, give a new lease of life to the oral performance of Muslims in the transmission of knowledge. For a long time the Quran has been available on the wireless in Pakistan and Bangladesh, and a host of materials on cassette and now video cassette throughout South Asia. The capacity of such materials to influence public attitudes as well as private piety has been well-demonstrated elsewhere in the Islamic world,[90] in recent years it has been dramatically demonstrated by their role in harnessing Hindu piety to Hindu revivalist politics.[91] The electronic media show every sign of moving up fast to rival the effects of lithography and typography. While print media have revolutionized religious understandings amongst the educated Muslims élites of South Asia, it is unlikely that society as a whole will be as deeply influenced by them as the Christian West.

NOTES

1. The first part of this essay is based on my inaugural lecture as Professor of the History of South Asia in the University of London, which was given at Royal Holloway on 4 March 1992; see Francis Robinson, 'Technology and Religious Change: Islam and the Impact of Print', *Modern Asian Studies*, 27: 1 (February 1993), pp. 229–51. I am particularly grateful to my colleague, Rosalind Thomas, for allowing me to read the typescript of her book, *Literacy and Orality in Ancient Greece* (Cambridge, 1992). She has enabled me to embark upon this essay with greater ease than I expected.
2. The first printing from moveable type was done by Pi Sheng in China during the years AD 1041–49. Because of the vast number of characters required in Chinese, the invention was not widely adopted. Gutenberg's invention was made without the knowledge of the Chinese discovery.
3. Marshall McLuhan, *The Gutenberg Galaxy: The Making of Typographic Man* (London, 1962); George Steiner, *Language and Silence* (London, 1967); much work has also been done on the subtler effects of print on consciousness by Walter J. Ong, *The Presence of the Word: Some Prolegomena for Cultural and Religious History* (New Haven and London, 1967); *Rhetoric, Romance and Technology: Studies in the Interaction of Expression and Culture* (Ithaca, 1971); *Orality and Literacy: The Technologizing of the Word* (London, 1982); 'Writing is a Technology that Restructures Thought' in G. Baumann (ed.), *The Written Word: Literacy in Transition* (Oxford, 1986).

4. Print was, of course, handmaid to an existing oral, and also visual, culture in helping forward the Protestant reformation. See, for instance, Tessa Watt, *Cheap Print and Popular Piety 1550–1640* (Cambridge, 1991).
5. Elizabeth L. Eisenstien, *The Printing Press as an Agent of Change: Communication and Cultural Transformation in Early-Modern Europe* (Cambridge, 1979), vols I and II.
6. Ibid., vol. I, pp. 366–67.
7. Mehmet Kaplan, *Tevfik Fikret ve Siiri* (Istabul, 1946), p. 19, cited in Serif Mardin, *Religion and Social Change in Modern Turkey: The Case of Bediuzzaman Said Nursi* (Albany, 1989), p. 120.
8. Francis Robinson, *Separatism Among Indian Muslims: The Politics of the United Provinces' Muslims 1860–1923* (Cambridge, 1974), pp. 77–8.
9. Thomas F. Carter, 'Islam as a Barrier to Printing', *The Moslem World*, 33, (1943), pp. 213–16; J. Pedersen, *The Arabic Book* (trans. G. French, ed. by R. Hillenbrand) (Princeton, 1984), pp. 131–41; Michael J. Fischer and Mehdi Abedi, *Debating Muslims: Cultural Dialogues in Postmodernity and Tradition* (Madison, 1989), pp. 93–4.
10. An outstanding analysis of the essential orality of the Quran is to be found in William A. Graham, *Beyond the Written Word: Oral Aspects of Scripture in the History of Religion* (Cambridge, 1987), pp. 79–115.
11. Constance E. Padwick, *Muslim Devotions: A Study of Prayer-Manuals in Common Use* (London, 1961), p. 119.
12. See Graham, *Beyond the Written Word*, pp. 96–7.
13. Ibn Khaldun, *The Muqaddimah: An Introduction to History* (trans. Franz Rosenthal, ed. by N.J. Dawood) (Princeton, 1967), p. 421.
14. See Pedersen, *The Arabic Book*, pp. 20–36.
15. Ibid., Timothy Mitchell, *Colonizing Egypt* (Cambridge, 1988), pp. 128–60.
16. See Ibn Khaldun, *The Muqaddimah* p. 431.
17. Ibid., pp, 431–3; see Mitchell, *Colonizing Egypt*, pp. 150–54.
18. An *ijaza* given by al-Mutarriz to his pupil Abu Ja'far al-Tabari, the great historian and commentator on the Quran; see Pedersen, *The Arabic Book*, p. 36.
19. Ibid., p. 35; see Mitchell, *Colonizing Egypt*, pp. 150–54; Sayyed Hossein Nasr 'Oral Transmission and the Book in Islamic Education: The Spoken and the Written Word', *Journal of Islamic Studies*, 3: 1 (January 1992), pp. 1–14.
20. This statement appears in a trenchant exposition of how teachers should be venerated, E.E. Von Grunebaum and T.M. Abel (trans. and eds), *Az-Zarnuji:* Ta'lim al Muta'llim Tariq at-Ta'allum: *Instruction of the Student: The Method of Learning* (New York, 1947), p. 32.
21. Statement by Maulana Abdul Bari, the leading Firangi Mahali scholar of the early twentieth century in Altaf al-Rahman Qidwai, *Qiyam-i Nizam-i Ta'lim* (Lucknow, 1924), p. 86.

22. See Graham, *Beyond the Written Word*, pp. 68, 74–5. To emphasize the oral character of Hindu scripture it is also worth noting that the popular Hindi term for personal worship is *puja-path* or prayer recitation and that the generally accepted categorization of all Vedic texts is *sruti* ('what is heard'). Ibid., pp. 69, 71.
23. Ibid., pp. 75–7.
24. Denis Twitchett, 'Printing and Publishing' in B. Hook (ed.), *Cambridge Encyclopaedia of China* (Cambridge, 1982), pp. 355–57.
25 It should be noted that, when I talk of print in the nineteenth century, I am not talking of Gutenberg moveable type, but of lithography. Moveable type for Islamic cursive scripts was not widely used in South Asia until the twentieth century, and to this day has not succeeded in displacing lithography.
26. For a discussion of the style and content of the first Urdu newspaper published by a Firangi Mahali, Maulvi Muhammad Yaqub, see Iqbal Husain, 'Lucknow between the Annexation and the Mutiny' (unpublished paper, Aligarh Muslim University), which analyses *Tilism-i Lakhnaw*, which came out in 1856 and 1857. *Karnamah* was the second of Maulvi Muhammad Yaqub's papers.
27. Barbara D. Metcalf, *Islamic Revival in British India: Deoband, 1860–1900* (Princeton, 1982), pp. 198–215.
28. Ibid., pp, 203–10; see also a series of articles on the translation of the Quran into Tamil, Telegu, Kannada and Gujarati in Christian W. Troll (ed.), *Islam in India: Studies and Commentaries*, vol. I (New Delhi, 1982), pp. 135–67; and on the translation of the Quran into Malayalam see ibid., vol. II (New Delhi, 1985), pp. 229–36.
29. Metcalf, *Islamic Revival in British India*, pp. 205–6.
30. Barbara D. Metcalf, *Perfecting Women: Maulana Ashraf 'Ali Thanawi's Bihishti Zewar: A Partial Translation with Commentary* (Berkeley & Los Angeles, 1990), p. 376. This advice comes in the first of three essays with which Thanawi ends his book. It is entitled 'On acquiring further knowledge and the names of worthwhile and harmful books' and lists worth-while and, perhaps unwisely, harmful books.
31. See Metcalf, *Islamic Revival in British India*, pp. 46–260.
32. B. Anderson, *Imagined Communities: Reflections on the Origin and Spread of Nationalism* (revised edition) (New York, 1991), pp. 37–46.
33. See Robinson, *Seperatism*, p. 186.
34. The early uniform of Aligarh College included the wearing of a Turkish fez. Abdul Halim Sharar tells how in the late nineteenth century the *ulema* of Firangi Mahal, and also Shibli Nomani, were beginning to adopt the styles of Syria and Egypt. At the same time Shia *ulema* were following Persian fashions. Abdul Halim Sharar, *Lucknow: The Last Phase of an Oriental Culture* (trans. and eds E.S. Harcourt and Fakhir Hussian) (London, 1975), p. 176.

35. From Iqbal's *Rumuz-i-Bekhudi* ('The Mysteries of Selflessness'), in W. Theodore de Bary (ed.), *Sources of Indian Tradition* (New York, 1958), p. 756.
36. Speech of Shibli to the Nadwat-ul-Ulama in 1894. S.M. Ikram, *Modern Muslim India and the Birth of Pakistan (1858–1951)* (Lahore, 1965), pp. 139–40.
37. See Robinson, *Seperatism*, pp. 284–86.
38. Ibid., pp. 289–356; Gail Minault, *The Khilafat Movement: Religious Symbols and Political Mobilization in India* (New York, 1982).
39. See, for instance, Akbar S. Ahmad, *Discovering Islam: Making Sense of Muslim History and Society* (London, 1988).
40. H.A. Walter, *The Ahmadiyya Movement* (London, 1918); Yohannan Friedmann, *Prophecy Continuous: Aspects of Ahmadi Religious Thought and its Medieval Background* (Berkeley & Los Angeles, 1989); and Francis Robinson, 'Ahmad and the Ahmadiyya', *History Today*, 40 (1990), pp. 42–7.
41. Christian W. Troll, *Sayyid Ahmad Khan: A Reinterpretation of Muslim Theology* (New Delhi, 1978), pp. 105–70.
42. Troll emphasizes that Saiyid Ahmad's insistence that the word of God and the work of God could not be in conflict echoes the line taken by the Archdeacon of Calcutta of the time, John Pratt, in his *Scripture and Science not at Variance*, which was first published in 1856. Saiyid Ahmad frequently refers to Pratt's book in his commentary on the Bible. Troll, *Sayyid Ahmad Khan*, p. 155.
43. Emmanuel Sivan, the historian of jihad in the later middle ages, tells us how he was drawn to study the Muslim Brotherhood and its more recent offshoots in Egypt and elsewhere by discovering large quantities of newly published medieval Islamic texts, in particular the works of Ibn Taimiya and Ibn Kathir, in bookshops in East Jerusalem and in Cairo: 'these books, smelling of fresh print, were quickly snatched off the bookstalls by people from all walks of life, but especially by youngsters in modern garb ... I noticed that the introductions and commentaries thereof ... [made] and evident effort ... to reflect upon the meaning these texts could have for a modern and totally different historical situation.' Emmanuel Sivan, *Radical Islam: Medieval Theology and Modern Politics* (New Haven and London, 1985), p. ix–x. For the Nurcular, see Mardin, *Modern Turkey*.
44. See Mardin, *Modern Turkey*, pp. 4, 181–82.
45. A comment by McLuhan on the revolutionary impact of media changes through time: C. McLuhan, 'The TV Image: One of Our Conquerors', in M. Molinaro, C. McLuhan and W. Toye (eds), *Letters of Marshall McLuhan* (Toronto, 1986), pp. 286–87.
46. See Graham, *Beyond the Written Word*, pp. 30–9; W.J. Ong, *Orality and Literacy: The Technologizing of the Word* (Methuen: London, 1982), p. 115.

47. See McLuhan, *Gutenberg Galaxy*, p. 250.
48. See Graham, *Beyond the Written Word*, p. 29.
49. See Ong, *Orality and Literacy*, p. 73.
50. Ibid., pp. 31–77.
51. W.J. Ong, 'Writing Restructures Thought', in G. Baumann (ed.), *Literacy in Transition* (Oxford, 1986), pp. 23–50.
52. See Ong, *Orality and Literacy*, pp. 78–179.
53. See Graham, *Beyond the Written Word*, p. 165.
54. Altaf al-Rahman Qidwai, *Anwar-i Razzaqiyya* (Lucknow, n.d.), p. 61.
55. K.A. Nizami, *On History and Historians of Medieval India* (Delhi, 1983), pp. 39–52.
56. See Troll, *Sayyid Ahmad Khan*, pp. 100–43; the development of Saiyid Ahmad Khan, both in method and in literary presentation has been particularly well demonstrated by Troll in a comparison of the 1847 and 1854 editions of *Athar al-Sanadid*. Troll places the Saiyid's development in the context of his association with the Archaeological Society of Delhi. 'A Note on an Early Topographical Work of Sayyid Ahmad Khan: Athar as Sanadid', *Journal of the Royal Asiatic Society* (1972), pp. 135–46.
57. See, for instance, the preface to the first edition of Ameer Ali's History of the Saracens (1889): Ameer Ali, *A Short History of the Saracens* (Lahore, 1975), pp. vii–x.
58. See chapter 1, 'Introduction: The Element of History' in Shibli Nomani, *Omar the Great* (trans. Maulana Zafar Ali Khan, 2nd ed.) (Lahore, 1975), pp. 1–27.
59. Mufti Reza Ansari, 'Maulana 'Abd al-Hayy Farangi Mahalli un ki tarikhi khudat', *Majallah 'Ulum al-Din* (1971–72), pp. 139–72; and 'Maulana 'Abd al-Hayy Farangi Mahalli ke fuqahi muaqif aur nai Hindustan men uski ma 'niwiyyat', in Ziya al-Hasan Faruqi and Mushir al-Haqq (eds), *Fikr al-Islam ki tashkil-i jadid* (New Delhi, 1978), pp. 291–9.
60. Francis Robinson, 'Problems in the History of the Farangi Mahall Family of Learned and Holy Men' in N.J. Allen et al. (eds), *Oxford University Papers on India*, I: 2 (Delhi, 1987), pp. 21–2; see, for instance, the curricula recommended by the Bihar State Madrasa Education Board and the Central Wakf Board, New Delhi, in Kuldip Kaur, *Madrasa Education in India* (Chandigarh, 1990), Annexures IV and V.
61. Fazlur Rahman, *Islam and Modernity: Transformation of an Intellectual Tradition* (Chicago, 1982), p. 160.
62. Fazlur Rahman, 'The Controversy over the Muslim Family Laws', in D.E. Smith (ed.), *South Asian Politics and Religion* (Princeton, 1966), pp. 414–27.
63. Ahmed Mukarram, 'Some Aspects of Contemporary Islamic Thought: Guidance and Governance in the Work of Mawlana Abul Hassan Ali Nadwi and Maulana Abdul Aala Mawdudi' (D.Phil. thesis, Oxford, 1993), pp. 121–27.

64. Wilfred Cantwell Smith, 'The Historical Development in Islam of the Concept of Islam as an Historical Development', in B. Lewis and P.M. Holt (eds), *Historians of the Middle East* (London, 1962), pp. 484–502.
65. Sayyid Abul A'la Maududi, *Towards Understanding Islam* (trans. and ed. Khurshid Ahmad, 9th edition) (Delhi, 1979), pp. 138–39. Maududi's image of God as the 'great engineer' in his workshop compares well with the way in which eighteenth-century Deists in Europe came to see God not so much as the 'great communicator' who speaks to men but as the 'great architect'. W.J. Ong, *The Presence of the Word: Some Prolegomena for Cultural and Religious History* (New Haven and London, 1967), p. 73. Sheila McDonough has also emphasized Maududi's distinctively modern concept of God the 'engineer'. Sheila McDonough, *Muslim Ethics and Modernity: A Comparative Study of the Ethical Thought of Sayyid Ahmad Khan and Mawlana Mawdudi* (Waterloo, 1984), pp. 92–4.
66. See Mukarram, 'Aspects of Islamic Thought', pp. 213–51. Said Bediuzzaman Nursi, the founder of the Nurcular of Turkey, takes a very similar line to Nadwi. For Nursi the real basis of moral incompatibility between Islam and the West is that the former takes persons as the basic units of social life while the latter makes it society or the nation. See Mardin, *Modern Turkey*, pp. 168–71.
67. Syed Abul A'la Maudoodi, *Fundamentals of Islam* (Delhi, 1979), pp. 250–51.
68. Mrs Meer Hassan Ali, *Observations on the Mussulmauns of India* (W. Crooke, ed., second edition) (London, 1917), pp. 84, 214, 292, 296.
69. Ibid., p. 422.
70. C.M. Naim, 'How Bibi Ashraf Learned to Read and Write', *Annual of Urdu Studies*, 6 (1987), pp. 99–115.
71. Metcalf, *Perfecting Women*, p. 21.
72. Gail Minault (trans.), *Voices of Silence: English Translation of Khwaja Altaf Hussain Hali's Majalis un-Nissa and Chup ki Dad* (Delhi, 1986), p. 50.
73. Metcalf, *Islamic Revival in British India*, pp. 203–4.
74. Mohamed Ali, *My Life: A Fragment* (Afzal Iqbal, ed.) (Lahore, 1942), p. 85.
75. The former Pakistani politician, Altaf Gauhar, recounts a similar discovery of the Quran while in prison in the early 1970s; he was particularly moved by Maududi's interpretation of the Quran in Urdu for the common reader *Tahfim al-Qur'an*. Altaf Gauhar, 'Mawlana Abul A'la Mawdudi—A Personal Account', in Khurshid Ahmad and Zafar Ishaq Ansari (eds), *Islamic Perspectives: Studies in Honour of Mawlana Sayyid Abul A'la Mawdudi* (London, 1979), pp. 265–88.
76. Fatwa 31 'Method of Reading the Quran' and 32 'The Manner of Reading the Quran' in Maulana Mufti Hafiz Qari Saiyid Abdur Rahim Qadri Lajpuri, *Fatawa Rahimiyyah*, vol. I (M.F. Quraishi trans.) (Surat, n.d.), p. 72.

77. 'Our Treatment with the Quran' and following sections in Maudoodi's *Fundamentals of Islam*, pp. 17–23.
78. C. Troll (ed.), *Islam in India: Studies and Commentaries*, vol. III, *Islamic Experience in Contemporary Thought* (by Syed Vahiduddin) (New Delhi, 1986), pp. 120–1.
79. M. Sadiq, *A History of Urdu Literature* (second edition) (Delhi, 1984), p. 601.
80. This development can be sensed by comparing Qidwai's biography of Abdur Razzaq of Firangi Mahal with Sibghatullah Shahid's biography of Inayatullah of Firangi Mahal written some two decades later; Sibghatullah belonged to the next generation. See Qidwai, and Sibghatullah Shahid Ansari, *Sadr al-mudarrisin* (Lucknow, 1941). Ong also points out how, as societies move from orality to literacy, the depiction of character in art becomes less 'flat' and more 'rounded', there is a greater attempt to explore the nature and quality of each individual. See Ong, *Orality and Literacy*, pp. 151–55.
81. Wilfred Cantwell Smith, *Modern Islam in India: A Social Analysis* (London, 1946), p. 65.
82. H.A.R. Gibb, *Modern Trends in Islam* (Chicago, 1947), p. 75.
83. Ibid., pp. 75–6.
84. Annemarie Schimmel, *And Muhammad is His Messenger: The Veneration of the Prophet in Islamic Piety* (Chapel Hill, 1985), p. 231.
85. Smith, *Modern Islam in India*, p. 66.
86. Ibid.
87. Ibid.
88. Amin Sweeney, *A Full Hearing: Orality and Literacy in the Malay World* (Berkeley & Los Angeles, 1987), pp. 267–302.
89. Barbara D. Metcalf, 'Meandering Madrasas: Education, Itinerancy and the Tablighi Jama'at', Nigel Crook (ed.), *The Transmission of Knowledge in South Asia* (New Delhi, 1996), pp. 49–61.
90. Much has been made in recent years of the role played by sound cassettes of Ayatollah Khomeini's sermons in the making of the Iranian revolution. See Peter Chelkowski, 'Popular Entertainment, Media and Social Change in Twentieth-Century Iran' in Peter Avery et al. (eds), *The Cambridge History of Iran*, vol. 7 (Cambridge, 1991), p. 814, and Peter Avery, 'Printing, the Press and Literature in Modern Iran' in ibid., p. 829. Less dramatic, however, but rather more important in a general sense is the way in which electronic media are coming to serve regular habits of piety, whether it be the morning reading of the Quran on the wireless (see Graham, p. 104), or the home use of video-cassettes of leading Middle Eastern preachers in France: Michel Reeber, 'A Study of Muslim Peaching in France', *Islam and Christian Muslim Relations*, 2: 2 (December 1991), pp. 275–94.
91. T. Basu et al. (eds), *Khaki Shorts, Saffron Flags: A Critique of the Hindu Right* (Hyderabad, 1993), pp. 92–110.

Chapter Four

Religious Change and the Self in Muslim South Asia Since 1800[*]

In the nineteenth and twentieth centuries South Asian Muslims, along with Muslims elsewhere in the world, experienced religious change of revolutionary significance. This change involved a shift in the focus of Muslim piety from the next world to this one. It meant the devaluing of a faith of contemplation on God's mysteries and of belief in His capacity to intercede for men on earth. It meant the valuing instead of a faith in which Muslims were increasingly aware that it was they, and only they, who could act to create a just society on earth. The balance which had long existed between the other-worldly and the this-worldly aspects of Islam was moved firmly in favour of the latter.

This process of change has had many expressions: the movements of the Mujahidin, the Faraizis, Deoband, the Ahl-i Hadiths and Aligarh in the nineteenth century; and those of the Nadwat ul Ulama, the Tablighi Jamaat, the Jamaat-i Islami and the Muslim modernists in the twentieth. It has also been expressed in many subtle shifts in behaviour at saints' shrines and in the pious practice of many Muslims. Associated with this process of change was a shift in traditional Islamic knowledge away from the rational towards the revealed sciences, and a more general shift in the sources of inspiration away from the Iranian lands towards the Arab lands. There was also the adoption of print and the translations of authoritative texts into Indian languages with all their subsequent ramifications—among them the emergence of a reflective reading of the

* This paper was first delivered as a keynote lecture at the Biennial Conference of the Asian Studies Association of Australia in July 1996.

scriptures and the development of an increasingly rich inner landscape. Operating at the heart of this process of religious change was the increasing assumption by individual Muslims of responsibility for creating Muslim society on earth—a great and heavy responsibility. Moreover, in the context of British India, where foreign power had colonized much public space, this was a burden of which Muslim women were asked to take a particularly heavy share.

In the scholarship devoted to Christian West, the shift from other-worldly to this-worldly religion, which brought man to stand before the unfettered sovereignty of God, is regarded as a development of momentous importance. Among its many outcomes was helping to shape the modern Western senses of the self, of identity. There is an assumption here, of course, which is that the 'self' is historically defined, that is that the late Roman self might be differently constituted as compared with the twentieth-century Western self. Let us consider some of the shaping processes at work. The new willed religion, which man entered into only of his choice, gave him a sense of his instrumentality in the world, of his capacity to shape it. The new and heavy weight of this responsibility to an all-powerful God led to what has been termed the 'inward turn'—this started with the emergence of spiritual diaries in the Reformation and has continued with an ever deeper exploration of the psyche. Then, this new sense of human instrumentality, aligned to a deepening sense of self, helped to foster a sense of individual personal autonomy. All this tended to affirm the worth of ordinary life, the value of ordinary human experience. There was value in productive work, in marriage, family life, love, sex; there was growing distress at human suffering and a growing sense that good consisted of human activities for the benefit of human welfare.[1]

It is not suggested for one moment that we can look at the impact of the shift to this-worldly religion and somehow read off a series of developments or potential developments among South Asian Muslims. Nothing could be so crass. The particular circumstances of nineteenth- and twentieth-century India, not to mention the ideas and values inculcated by Islam, are different from those of Reformation Europe. Nevertheless, it is worth noting the significance of the shift from other-worldly to this-worldly religion for shaping modern senses of the self in the West. And this should prompt us at least to consider the extent to which a similar change might have helped to shape Muslim senses of the self in South Asia.

Before embarking on this exercise, there are other factors contributing to the shaping of the self which need to be acknowledged. There is the growing influence of Western civilization with its ideas of individualism, personal fulfilment, and the rights of man—with its endorsement of earthly existence and earthly pleasures, and its celebration of individual lives, great and small. Such ideas and values were instinct in much Western literature and in many institutions; they were, of course, embodied by many of the colonial British. There is also growing exposure to other forces which helped to fashion the more autonomous self: there is the spread of capitalist modes of production with their capacity to break down old communal loyalties and empower individuals; there is the emergence of the modern state with its concern to reach down through the thickets of the social order to make contact with each individual; there are the changes in the technology of communication—particularly of print and the shift it helped to bring from orality to literacy—which enabled to individuals to command knowledge as never before and assisted them in the process of exploring their inner selves.[2] There are, or of course, many forces at work in shaping the changing Muslim senses of the self. Our concern is to suggest that the shift from other-worldly to this-worldly religion is worthy of exploration.

Before embarking on our exploration it is necessary to outline the nature and impact of the shift to this-worldly Islam. The nineteenth and twentieth centuries in South Asia saw a growing attack on intercessionary sufism, indeed, at times on all forms of sufism itself. The reformists were determined to rid the world of its enchanted places, that is of anything that might diminish the believers' sense of responsibility. They were determined to assert the principle of *tawhid*, of the oneness of God. This theme ran through all the movements of the age from the Mujahidin of Saiyid Ahmad of Rai Bareli to the Jamaat-i Islami of Maulana Maududi. Not all movements gave quite the same emphasis to this theme. If the Ahl-i Hadiths and Ahl-i Quran were opposed to all forms of institutionlized sufism, the Deobandis on the other hand confined themselves to attacking practices at saints' shrines which presupposed the capacity of the saint to intercede for man with God. There were ironies, too. Maududi, while abhorring the tendency of sufism to compromise the oneness of God, nevertheless found an excellent organizational model in the sufi order which he used for his Jamaat.

(His vision of the role of the Amir of the Jamaat was similar to that of the sufi master to whom all his disciples gave unquestioning submission). This said, we should be aware that there was enormous sensitivity to behaviour at saints' shrines among almost all Muslims. It affected non-reformers as well as reformers. It was an important concern for the *ulama* of the Firangi Mahal family of Lucknow. The research of Claudia Liebeskind on three Awadhi shrines in this period, moreover, has illustrated how behaviour at the shrines changed in order to accommodate some reformist preferences at least.[3] What we need to be aware of is that in the nineteenth and twentieth centuries increasing numbers of India's Muslims from the upper and middle classes were finding the credibility of the friends of God, who had long provided them with comfort, undermined. There could be no intercession for them. They were directly answerable to the Lord, and to Him alone.[4]

There can be no doubt that Reformist Muslims felt the weight of this new responsibility and were meant to feel it. They knew that it was their choice to will the good and forbid the evil. It was their choice as to whether a Muslim society which followed God's wishes existed on earth or not. Moreover, they knew that they were answerable to Him for their actions. Husain Ahmad Madani, principal of Deoband in the mid-twentieth century, often wept at the thought of his shortcomings.[5] Rashid Ahmad Gangohi, one of the founders of the school, when reading the Quran alone at night, would weep and shake and appear terrified at those chapters dealing with God's wrath.[6] The Reformist God was certainly compassionate and merciful, as God always had been, but He was also to be feared. Indeed, 'Fear God' was the very first practice sentence that women in the reformist tradition, who were learning how to read, had to confront.[7] There was a constant sense of guilt that the believer was not doing enough to meet the high standards of this most demanding God. 'Oh God! What am I to do? I am good for nothing', Maulana Muhammad Ilyas, the founder of the Tablighi Jamaat, would exclaim as he paced at night. And when his wife told him to come to bed, he said that if she knew what he knew she would be doing the same. 'I find no comparison between my anxiety, my effort and my voice,' he wrote, 'and the responsibility of *Tabligh* God has placed upon my shoulders. If He shows mercy, He is forgiving, merciful, and if He does justice, there is no escape for me from the consequences of my guilt.'[8]

Nothing brings home more the weight of responsibility with which Reformist Muslims were faced than their visions of Judgement. Consider the picture in Ashraf Ali Thanvi's *Bihishti Zewar*, which has been so ably translated and introduced for us by Barbara Metcalf. Thanvi draws on a vision initially generated by Shah Rafi al-Din, one of the four sons of Shah Wali Allah, and therefore at the heart of the Reformist tradition. *Bihishti Zewar* is one of the most influential books of twentieth-century Muslim South Asia.

The believer is first of all reminded of the Prophet's emotion at the thought of heaven and hell. 'He wept greatly until his blessed beard was wet with tears. Then he declared: "I swear by that Being in whose power is my life that if you know what I know about the afterlife, you would flee to the wilderness and place dust upon your head".'

Then the believer is told the signs of the coming of Judgement. The proper order of the *shari'a* will be reversed; people will think the wealth owed to God is their property: they will seek knowledge of religion not for its own sake but for worldly gain. The natural order will be reversed: stones will rain down from the sky; people will turn into pigs and dogs. The Imam Mahdi will appear to lead the Muslims into battle against the Nazarenes. The one-eyed Dajjal will appear claiming to be the Messiah. Hasrat Isa will descend from the sky with his hands on the shoulders of two angels to kill the Dajjal. The sun will rise in the west. A balmy breeze from the south will produce a fatal growth in the armpits of the believers. Then, on a Friday, the tenth Muharram, in the morning when all people are engaged in their respective work, a trumpet will suddenly be sounded. At first, it will be very, very soft. Then it will grow so much louder that all will die from terror. The heaven and earth will be rent. The world will be extinguished.

Then comes the Day of Judgement. After forty years God will order the trumpet to be blown again. Heaven and earth will again be established. The dead will emerge alive from their graves and will be gathered on the Plain of Judgement. The sun will be very close, and peoples' very brains will begin to cook in its heat. People will sweat in proportion to their sins. Only the Prophet Muhammad's intercession will persuade Almighty God to intervene.

Angels in great number will descend from the heavens and surround everyone on every side. The throne of Almighty God, on which will be the Illumination of Almighty God, will descend. The accounting will begin, and the Book of Deeds will be opened. Of their own accord, the believers will come on the right hand and the unbelievers on the left. The scales for weighing deeds will be set up, and from it everyone's good and bad deeds will be known. Thereupon everyone will be ordered to cross the Bridge of the Way. Anyone whose good deeds weigh more in the balance will cross the bridge and enter into paradise. Anyone whose sins weigh more, unless forgiven by God, will fall into hell. ... When all the inhabitants of heaven and hell are settled in their places, Almighty God will bring forth Death in the shape of a Ram, in between heaven and hell. He will display Death to everyone and have it slaughtered. He will declare: "Now death will come neither to the dwellers in heaven nor to the dwellers in hell. All must dwell for ever in their respective places". There will be no end to the rejoicing of the inhabitants of heaven and no end to the anguish and grief of the inhabitants of hell.[9]

The awfulness of this eschatological vision, the powerlessness of the believer to achieve salvation except through the preponderance of his good deeds on earth, gives real insight into how individual senses of responsibility were likely to be deepened. The penetration of this sense into the individual's inner self, its approach towards the quiddity of the human being, helps to explain the high levels of emotion it generated. It also helps to explain the growth of sectarianism—the many Muslim groups fashioned in nineteenth- and twentieth-century India that exist to this day—as Muslims in different social and intellectual locations strove with great sincerity to find the right way towards salvation. It helps to explain the world of *manazaras*, *fatwa* wars and high combativeness that typifies these groups. This was the price to be paid for the huge release of religious energy generated by what could be called a process of personal religious empowerment.

This sense of responsibility was not just felt among *ulama* of the reformist tradition, and those who followed them, it was felt no less by Muslim modernists, those who wished to build bridges between Western science and Islamic understandings. Listen to that very great man Saiyid Ahmad Khan:

But since I have been the pioneer of Modern Education which, as I have said, is to some extent opposed to Islam, I regard it as my duty to do all I can, right or wrong, to defend my religion and show the people, the true, shining countenance of Islam. This is what my conscience dictates and, unless I do its bidding, I am a sinner before God.[10]

A similar spirit illuminated those other great modernists, Muhammad

Iqbal and Fazlur Rahman, in their endeavours to show the people the shining countenance of Islam.

We should also note that this sense of responsibility has come to be spread more and more widely through the Muslim society of South Asia as the reforming movement has continued to develop, and as it has come to interact with a society where books were more widely available, and literacy was slowly but surely growing. It is one of the ironies of this process that much of this activity was set going by *ulama* who, by translating key works of the Islamic tradition into Indian languages and by printing them large scale, aimed to give Muslim society strength to cope with colonial rule, but in the process they helped to destroy their own monopoly over religious knowledge. If in the nineteenth-century the effort was concentrated on a literate élite, the aristocracy which was attracted to the Ahl-i Hadiths and the Ahl-i Quran, the *sharif* classes which tended to go to Aligarh and the lesser bourgeois of the *qasbas* which tended to go to Deoband, in the twentieth century the effort was taken more widely into society, in part through the publications of the Jamaat-i Islami, which, though élitist itself, spoke to a whole new generation of Western-educated Muslims, but for the most part through the Tablighi Jamaat, or Preaching Society, which aimed, and aims, to involve ordinary Muslims in taking a basic understanding of reformist Islam to the masses. The loss of the *ulama*'s monopoly, this process implied, was a necessary sacrifice in striving to deepen the sense of personal responsibility in society as a whole. This democratization of the possession of religious knowledge and its interpretation, which went hand in hand with the emergence of the concept of the caliphate or vice-regency of man in Muslim thought, is a development of enormous potential and importance for the future of Muslim societies.[11]

There is one final point which needs to be made about the shift towards this-worldly religion and the spread of a new sense of responsibility: it seems to have fallen rather more heavily on women than on men. It is now a commonplace of the literature devoted to gender and identity in South Asia since 1800 that with non-Muslim occupancy of public space women move from their earlier position of being threats to the proper conduct of Muslim society to being the mistresses of private Islamic space, the central transmitters of Islamic values, the symbols of Muslim identity, the guardians of millions of domestic Islamic shrines. Women come, in fact, to bear an awesome responsibility. Thus they had a central role to play in the reformist project. Their education, to the extent, as Ashraf Ali Thanvi declared, of acquiring the learning of a *maulvi*, was crucial to waging war on all those customs which threatened the unity of God and to maintaining fully in place the power of Muslim conscience in fashioning Islamic society. Thanvi also admitted that women would have to struggle harder than men to achieve this outcome.[12]

For Maududi and the Islamists women are expected to acquire knowledge of Islam, just as men do, and to examine their consciences in the same way. On the other hand, they were biologically and psychologically different from men and their place was in *purdah* and in the home. They were to be the rulers of domestic space, sealed off from all those elements of *kufr* which polluted public space. 'The harim,' he declared, 'is the strongest fortress of Islamic civilization, which was built for the reasons that, if it [that civilization] ever suffered a reverse, it [that civilization] may then take refuge in it.'[13] Muslim modernists sent out conflicting messages, on the one hand emphasizing the spiritual and moral superiority of women, which might militate against their education, while on the other, increasingly coming to see their education in Western learning and through the medium of English as the measure of the health and development of society. Wherever women found themselves, a heavy weight of responsibility rested upon them.

This weight is borne down to the present, although the extra burden of political pressures have come to join those of patriarchy and willed religion. Much of the discourse, both about Pakistani identity and about Muslim identity in India, has come to take place around the position and behaviour of women. If there is a correlation between burdens of responsibility and growing senses of the self, there is room for there to be increasingly stressful tension between women's expectations and those of the wider society in which they move.

We now move from the shift towards this-worldly Islam and the new sense of responsibility it fosters to the impact of this responsibility on Muslim senses of the self. There are four themes which should be noted. They are: self instrumentality, the idea of the individual human being as the active, creative agent on the earth; self-affirmation, the autonomy of the individual; to which is connected the affirmation of the ordinary things of the self, the affirmation of ordinary life; and finally, the emphasis on self-consciousness, the reflective self, which in the Western experience is referred to as the 'inward turn'.

SELF-INSTRUMENTALITY

The first outcome of responsibility was that each individual Muslim had to take action to achieve salvation. The theme of individual instrumentality in this world runs through all the manifestation of this-worldly Islam. The life of Saiyid Ahmad Khan was a testament to his belief in self-help, and the need for the individual to take action for the good of his community and of Islam. Ashraf Ali Thanvi, in considering the process of character formation, insists that knowledge of what one should do is itself not enough: 'Knowledge is not true knowledge unless it is acted upon', only thus is the inner self shaped.[14] For his contemporary, Muhammad Ilyas, Tabligh was the concrete manifestation of 'knowing meaning doing' in the light of the Quran's exhortation to Muslims both to acquire and to transmit knowledge.[15] Maududi makes perfectly clear the duty of Muslims to act on their knowledge of God's commandments if they wish to be saved. This world is the ground on which men prepare for the next. But the clearest statement and vision of man's instrumentality comes in the thought of Iqbal who makes the role of the human self, or ego, in the creative activity of shaping and reshaping the world the focus of much of his work. For him the reality of the individual is demonstrated not just in thought but in action in this world—not *cogito ergo sum* but *ago ergo sum*. 'The final act,' he declares in his *Reconstruction of Religious Thought in Islam*, 'is not an intellectual act, but a vital act which deepens the whole being of the ego and sharpens his will with the creative assurance that the world is not just something to be seen and known through concepts, but to be made and remade by continuous action.'[16] Man must not only act but he was the prime mover in God's creation. The new Muslim self is a doing self. Hence the bursts of creative energy released by Indian Muslims during the past two centuries.

SELF-AFFIRMATION

Individuals who will their religion on the basis of their own knowledge have the capacity to be increasingly autonomous and self-affirmative. They make their own choices. Ashraf Ali Thanvi, for instance, aims to give this capacity to women by giving them the learning of a *maulvi* and much practical knowledge as well. Iqbal's moral and religious ideal is of the man who achieves self-affirmation by being more and more individual and more and more unique. In both cases unrestrained individualism is constrained by the godly purposes these authors have in mind for their subjects. There is, however, an essential tension between this-worldly Islam's desire to empower humankind on earth on the one hand and on the other, to continue to focus their attention on godly ends. Once the genie of individualism has been let out of the bottle, there is no guarantee that it will continue to submit to Islam.

AFFIRMATION OF ORDINARY LIFE

With the affirmation of self there also comes the affirmation of the ordinary things of the self, the ordinary things of daily life, which the philosopher, Charles Taylor, terms 'one of the most powerful ideas in modern civilization'.[17] We can see this process at work in the new trends which emerge in the *sirat* literature, in the biographies of the Prophet, whose number increased greatly in the twentieth century. Increasingly Muhammad is depicted not as the 'Perfect Man' of the sufi tradition but as the perfect person. He is said to have been 'beloved, charitable, frugal, generous, gentle, honest, lenient, a lover of children, modest, pure, steadfast and successful'. Less attention, as Cantwell Smith has pointed out, is given to his intelligence, political sagacity and capacity to harness the new social forces in his society and more to his qualities as a good middle-class family man: his sense of duty and his loving nature, and his qualities as a good citizen, his consideration for others and in particular those who are less fortunate.[18] This transition is also mirrored in changes which take place in biographical writing more generally; the concern is less with what the individual might have contributed to Islamic civilization and the transmission of knowledge and more on his life in his time and his human qualities. Even in the writings of the *ulama* it is possible to see them responding to the humanistic preferences of their times and depicting much more rounded lives to support their didactic purpose.[19] Another dimension of this process is the growing discussion of family and domestic issues, and particularly women, in public space. This discourse is begun by men such as Nazir Ahmad, Hali and Mumtaz Ali in the nineteenth century but in the twentieth century it is increasingly taken up by women and not least by the tens of women who aired their views in the pages of those remarkable journals *Ismat* and *Tehzib un Niswan*. All matters are discussed in public from education, diet and dress to love marriages, divorce and the sources of women's inferiority. The writing is often assertive in style, demanding that women and their lives be given respect.[20] Finally, the rise of the short story and the novel is, of course, an indication of the new value given to understanding human character and the many ways of being human. The themes, often shocking in their day, which were taken up by leading practitioners such as Manto and Ismat Chughtai—family life, relationships, feelings, sex—indicate the new arenas of life in which Muslims are finding meaning. Such is the new importance of these profoundly human matters that religious thinkers cannot afford to ignore them. 'The Islamic pattern of inner life,' declares the religious philosopher Syed Vahiduddin, 'finds expression in religious and moral acts, in prayer, in love, in forgiveness, in seemingly mundane activities such as sex and domestic life, which should be radiated by the glow of the world beyond ...'.[21]

The Inward Turn: The Growth of Self-consciousness and Reflection

The final theme is the growth of self-consciousness and reflective habit. A major element of this-worldly Islam in almost all its forms is the requirement for self-examination: a willed Islam had to be a self-conscious one. Muslims had to ask themselves regularly whether they had done all in their power to submit to God and carry out His will in the world. In book Seven of *Bihishti Zewar* Ashraf Ali Thanvi has a rather charming way of illustrating the process of regular self-examination to ensure purity of intentions and avoidance of wrongdoing. He suggests to the believer that she set aside a little time in the morning and in the evening to speak to her lower-self [*nafs*] as follows:

> O Self, you must recognize that in this world you are like a trader, Your stock-in-trade is your life. Its profit is to acquire well-being forever, that is, salvation in the afterlife. This is indeed a profit! If you waste your life and do not gain your salvation, you suffer losses that reach to your

stock-in-trade. That stock-in-trade is so precious that each hour—indeed, each breath—is valuable beyond limit.

O Self, recognize God's kindness that Death has not yet come.

O Self, do not fall into the deception that Almighty God will surely forgive you. [Don't bank on his mercy]

Say to yourself, 'O Self, you are like a sick person. A sick person must follow good regimen. Sinning is a bad regimen ...'

Say to the Self, 'O Self, the world is a place of journeying, and on a journey complete comfort is never available. You must endure all kinds of trouble. Travellers put up with these troubles because they know that when they reach home they will have all comfort ... In the same way, you must endure hard work and distress as long as you dwell in this world. There is work in acts of worship; there is distress in giving up sin; there are all kinds of other troubles. The afterlife is our home. When we arrive there, all trouble will be ended.'[22]

This theme of self-consciousness and self-examination is to be found in many religious thinkers of the late nineteenth and twentieth centuries whether we look at Muhammad Ilyas, Maududi and Vahiduddin or Saiyid Ahmad Khan and Iqbal. In seventeenth-century Europe, as we have noted, this process was accompanied by the emergence of the spiritual diary.[23] Some similar, although not directly comparable, materials exist for twentieth-century Muslim India. There is, for instance, Maulana Mahomed Ali's semi-spiritual *My Life: A Fragment*, which was written while he was interned during World War One. There is also Dr. Syed Mahmud's record of his spiritual reflections while in jail after the non-cooperation movement.[24] Beyond such works there is a great deal of correspondence with sufis which often does contain processes of self-examination. With such evidence for the reflective habit, alongside the widespread exhortation to examine the self, it is arguable that the development of this-worldly religion helped to open up an interior landscape. Whereas in the past the reflective believer, the mystic, might have meditated upon the signs of God, the new type of reflective believer meditated increasingly on the self and the shortcomings of the self. Now the inner landscape became a crucial site where the battle of the pious for the good took place. Doubtless, there had been Muslims in the past—in particular times and contexts—for whom this had been so. The importance of the shift towards this-worldly Islam, however, was that self-consciousness and self-examination were encouraged to become widespread.

The role of reformism in helping to throw open a window on

the inner landscape does not end with the end of belief. Once the original purpose has been lost the window may still remain open for purely secular purposes. The exploration of the inner territory may equally be the quest of one who is purely Muslim by culture. How far the exploration may be a consequence of early religious upbringing, or of values in society widely shared, or of exposure to Western culture will always be hard to judge, even on a case by case basis. That the process of exploration was taking place is evident in books as varied as Ismat Chughtai's remarkable novel of psychological insight *Terhi Lakir* (The Crooked Line) published in 1944 through to K.A. Abbas's *I am not an Island: An Experiment in Autobiography* published in 1977.[25]

Arguably the shift towards this-worldly Islam has emphasized new strands in Muslim selves. There is the sense of empowerment that comes with the knowledge that it is humanity that fashions the world. There is the sense of personal autonomy and individual possibility that comes with the knowledge that the individual makes choices. There is the transfer of the symbols and centres of meaning in life from the signs of God and the friends of God to the mundane things of ordinary life. And there is the development of the extra dimension to the self, the interior space. Arguably the individual has become more complex and the possibilities for human fulfilment have become greater.

We have noted the central role of the human self for the thinkers of this-worldly Islam. The fashioning of a new human self was the central activity of the reformist project. The unlimited capacity of man to create and shape the external world is a central feature of Iqbal's thought exemplified in this challenge he makes man hurl at God:

> You created the night—I lit the lamp.
> Your created the clay—I moulded the cup.
> You made the wilderness, mountains and forests
> I cultivated the flowerbeds, parks and gardens.[26]

We should note, too, that these manifestations of this-worldly Islam empower man but do not give him unlimited freedom. His power is in the service of God's word (Thanvi). His power is to be within the limits set by Him (Maududi). His power, his human potential, can only be fully realized within the framework of the community created by Him (Iqbal).

There remain a few reflections. First, there is an essential tension between the forces of individualism, potential and actual, set loose by this-worldly religion, and the continuity of the Muslim community as the community of all Muslims. We have noted that a central feature of this-worldly Islam is the empowerment of individuals, indeed the requirement placed on individuals to act. What makes sure, for most Muslim thinkers, that these actions are designed to promote Islamic ends is fear of Judgement and faith, or just faith. But, willed Islam would appear to be a two-edged sword. It can release great religious energy and creativity, as it has done in South Asia and elsewhere. But, on the other hand, it opens the door to unbelief. Muslims, who can choose to believe, can also choose not to believe, and become Muslims merely by culture. Once belief goes those mundane areas of life which reformist Muslims cherish in the name of God—work, home, family, relationships, sex—now could become prime theatres of meaning in themselves. With the shift towards this-worldly Islam, and the increasing disenchantment of the world, I wonder, has Islam turned onto a track that, as in the West, leads down a secularizing path? Certainly, here is a package of ideas ready to be powered forward in society by the growth of capitalism and the individual freedoms the modern state can fashion.

Secondly, we have noted how the responsibilities for this-worldly Islam came to bear with especial weight on women. I am not equipped to assess the outcomes of this especial burden, although it seems a subject worthy of investigation. Nevertheless, there is no doubting the tension which exists between ideas of family and community on the one hand and individualism on the other. 'There was a sense of a collective in the lifestyle of this house,' declares Gaythi, the heroine of Altaf Fatima's *Dastak Na Do* [which has been given the English title 'The One who did not ask'], 'the selfish god of individualism had not yet crossed its threshold.'[27] And I wonder if the strident tone of many of the contributions to *Izmat* and *Tehzib un Niswan* in the 1940s was a reflection of the pressure that women were expected to endure. And I wonder, too, if this might not explain the desire of some to test the boundaries of what was acceptable. I think of the erotic novels of Rashid Jahan, of the treatment of sex by Ismat Chughtai which led to her being put on trial in the 1940s, or more recently of Taslima Nasreen's stubborn jousting at the boundaries of the permissible.

Thirdly, if willed self-conscious Islam, leads to a powerful concern to assert and to police the boundaries of difference it surely also leads to a deepening of community affiliation in the psyche. By the same token, it may also form part of the groundwork for the development of a Muslim political identity and responsiveness to Islamic symbols in politics. This said, we should note that leaders of this-worldly Islam have gone in very different directions in the political sphere from Muhammad Ilyas and Abul Hasan Nadvi, who have insisted that Islam is all about fashioning individuals and has nothing to do with the political sphere, to Maulana Maududi, who insisted that mastery of the political sphere is essential to achieve right guidance for society.[28]

More thought needs to be given to the implications of the deep cultural transformation brought about by the shift in Muslim piety firmly towards this-worldly religion. It is important to get a stronger grasp on its role in shaping modern Muslim selves. Among other things it would be useful to have a sense of its contribution, as compared with global processes, to fashioning the greater individualism of some twentieth-century Muslim selves. But we also need a sense of how it may be leading to abrasive interactions between the search for individual fulfilment and the obligations of community, an abrasiveness often felt most particularly by women.[29] Doubtless, as the different paths trodden by Nadvi and Maududi suggest, those travelling down the high road of this-worldly Islam can branch off in different directions. Among them may be that of a well-developed ethical self and largely private faith.

NOTES

1. Charles Taylor, *Sources of the Self: The Making of Modern Identity* (Cambridge, 1989), pp. 1–24.
2. For the significance of the role of print and the shift from orality to literacy, see Francis Robinson, 'Islam and the Impact of Print in South Asia' in Nigel Crook (ed.), *The Transmission of Knowledge in South Asia: Essays in Education, Religion, History and Politics* (New Delhi, 1996), pp. 62–97.
3. The shrines concerned were those of Takiya Sharif, Kakori, Khanqah Karimiya, Salon, and Haji Waris Ali Ahah, Deva. Claudia Liebeskind, *Piety on Its Knees: Three Sufi Traditions in South Asia in Modern Times* (Delhi, 1998).
4. For the attack on intercession, and the new religious states of mind it was

fashioning, see Barbara D. Metcalf, *Islamic Revival in British India: Deoband, 1860–1900* (Princeton, NJ, 1982).

5. Ibid., p. 163.
6. Ibid., p. 166.
7. Barbara D. Metcalf, *Perfecting Women: Maulana Ashraf 'Ali Thanawi's Bihishti Zewar: A Partial Translation with Commentary* (Berkeley, 1990), p. 63.
8. S. Abul Hasan Ali Nadwi, *Life and Mission of Maulana Muhammad Ilyas*, trans. by Mohammad Asif Kidwai (Lucknow, 1979), p. 108.
9. Metcalf, *Perfecting Women*, pp. 222–30.
10. Speech of Saiyid Ahmad Khan quoted in *Altaf Husain Hali*, trans. by K.H. Qadiri and David J. Matthews (New Delhi, 1979), p. 172.
11. For these developments see Robinson, 'Islam and the Impact of Print'; Barbara D. Metcalf, 'Meandering Madrasas: Knowledge and Short-term Itinerancy in the Tablighi Jama'at', in Crook (ed.), *Transmission*, pp. 49–61; and Christian W. Troll, 'Five Letters of Maulana Ilyas (1885–1944), the Founder of the Tablighi Jama'at', translated, annotated, and introduced, in C.W. Troll (ed.), *Islam in India: Studies and Commentaries 2: Religion and Religious Education* (Delhi, 1985), pp. 138–76.
12. Metcalf, *Perfecting Women*, pp. 1–38.
13. Cited in Faisal Fatehali Devji, 'Gender and the Politics of Space: The Movement of Women's Reform, 1857–1900' in Z. Hasan (ed.), *Forging Identities: Gender, Communities and the State* (New Delhi, 1994), pp. 35–6. The whole point is summed up in a classic text: Abul A'la Maududi, *Purdah and the Status of Women in Islam* (New Delhi, 1974).
14. Metcalf, *Perfecting Women*, p. 107.
15. Troll, 'Five Letters', p. 143.
16. M. Iqbal, *The Reconstruction of Religious Thought in Islam* (Lahore, 1954), p. 198.
17. Taylor, *Sources*, p. 14.
18. Wilfred Cantwell Smith, *Modern Islam in India: A Social Analysis* (London, 1946), pp. 64–7.
19. Robinson, 'Islam and the Impact of Print', n. 80, pp. 96–7.
20. See, Gail Minault, *Secluded Scholars* (Delhi: OUP, 1998) and Azra Asghar Ali, 'The Emergence of Feminism Among Indian Muslim Women, 1920–47' (PhD dissertation, Univ. of London, 1996), especially, pp. 319–81.
21. Christian W. Troll (ed.), *Islam in India: Studies and Commentaries, 3: The Islamic Experience in Contemporary Thought* (New Delhi, 1986), p. 153.
22. Metcalf, *Perfecting Women*, pp. 235–36.
23. See, for instance, Tom Webster, 'Writing to Redundancy: Approaches to Spiritual Journals and Early Modern Spirituality', *The Historical Journal*, vol. 31, no. 1 (1996), pp. 35–56. But, it remains important to realize that the rise of self-consciousness was not restricted to one time or one culture.

Peter Burke, 'Representations of the Self from Petrarch to Descartes', in Roy Porter (ed.), *Rewriting the Self: Histories from the Renaissance to the Present* (London, 1997), pp. 17–28.

24. Mohamed Ali, Afzal Iqbal (ed.), *My Life: A Fragment: An Autobiographical Sketch* (Lahore, 1942). Syed Mahmud's spiritual reflections may be found in the Firangi Mahal Papers, Karachi.
25. Abbas' father was known for his strict reforming principles, K.A. Abbas, *I Am Not An Island: An Experiment in Autobiography* (New Delhi, 1974), p. 35 and K.H. Ansari, *The Emergence of Socialist Thought Among North Indian Muslims (1917–1947)* (Lahore, 1990), pp. 288–89. Ismat Chughtai's background was notably liberal but in her early religious background she was exposed to a strict *maulvi*, ibid., pp. 316–17.
26. Translation of part of Iqbal's poem 'God's Talk with Man' in N.P. Ankiyev, 'The Doctrine of Personality', H. Malik (ed.), *Iqbal: Poet–Philosopher of Pakistan* (New York, 1971), p. 274.
27. Altaf Fatima, Ruksana Ahmad (trans.), *The One Who Did Not Ask* (London, 1993), pp. 62–4.
28. The point is well made in Ahmed Mukarram, 'Some Aspects of Contemporary Islamic Thought: Guidance and Governance in the World of Maulana Abul Hasan Ali Nadwi and Mawlana Abul Aala Mawdudi' (D.Phil. dissertation, University of Oxford, 1993).
29. Precisely the kind of study to elucidate this issue, even though it is on a Hindu rather than a Muslim community has recently been completed by Mines in the context of Madras city. Mattison Mines, *Public Faces, Private Voices: Community and Individuality in South India* (Berkeley, 1994).

Chapter Five

Secularization, Weber and Islam[1]

For the hundred years preceding the Muslim revival of the late twentieth century, the Islamic world seemed to be following a path of secularization similar to that on which the Western Christian world embarked some centuries before. Law derived from revelation had been increasingly removed from public life; religious knowledge had steadily lost ground in education; more and more Muslims who were Islamic by culture but made 'rational' calculations about their lives—in much the same way as Christians formed in the secular West might do—had come forward. The development of this 'rationality' and rationalization within Christianity, according to Max Weber, brought the secular world into being. This essay is concerned to explore how far Weber's theory of secularization, which is derived specifically from the experience of western Europe, can help us both to make sense of this process in Islamic society and, perhaps, to reach some understanding of what the measure of secularization might be in an Islamic environment.[2]

Weber's process of secularization is a unique Western development, with its roots deep in ancient Judaism, and its trunk in Protestantism and the growth of capitalism. At the heart of the process lie the concepts of rationality and rationalization. We discern the growth of rationality in increasing human capacity to calculate and to control all aspects of life without appeals either to traditional norms or to charismatic enthusiasm. As bureaucracies come to embrace all the activities of the economy and of the state, opportunities for individual initiative, and dependence on traditional loyalties, are reduced. Social relationships are rendered steadily more impersonal. As rational legal systems, in which lawyers make the law, come to be adopted more widely, the hold of sacred traditions an all forms of arbitrariness in law is loosened, and individuals contemplate their prospects with greater precision. Society grows more like a machine, the individual like a cog in that machine, and human actions come more and more to be rationally calculated. The individual gains a growing sense of control over life.[3] There flow from this substantial consequences for religious understanding.

There is that famous 'disenchantment of the world'; Weber uses Schiller's term '*entzauberung*', meaning literally 'the driving out of magic from things'. The human being no longer dwells in a great enchanted garden. To find direction, and to win security in this world and the next, the human being no longer needs either to revere or to coerce the spirits; there is no longer need to seek salvation through ritualistic, idolatrous or sacramental procedures.[4] Human beings lose their sense of providence in life. 'Once upon a time,' declares Owen Chadwick in surveying the secularization of the European mind, 'the wood was bewitched, and goblins and fair spirits dwelt in the trunks of trees and among the roots. But now the wood is administered by the Forestry Commission, and although romantic men may still hear a goblin running in the undergrowth and glimpse beauty behind a bush, they know when a subjective experience is subjective.'[5]

Closely associated with disenchantment there is a fragmentation of human understanding of the world. The development of science reveals how the world consists of natural and cultural processes; humans learn that a religious understanding of it is partial, indeed, subjective. The growth of a functionally differentiated society leads to the steady relegation of religion from public life; it is forced out of the realms of economic, political and even social conduct, and into the further recesses of private life in which its function is merely to interpret and to organize the relationship of the individual human being to the sacred. Thus, the unified vision, in which all human experience was understood through Christian revelation, is replaced by a fragmented vision in which no one set of values either embraces both public and private life, or is shared by citizens in their individual existences.[6]

This is Weber's path of secularization. From his sociology of the great religions he takes us down a path of disenchantment which culminates in the sociology of the intelligentsia, amongst whom, like as not, each human is a god unto himself or herself.[7] We should note, nevertheless, that Weber's theory is regarded as offering only one possible perspective over secularization in the West. It does not explain, so Turner claims, the American case of immigration, religious revival and the secularization of theological content; nor does it account for the East European path of secularization from above.[8] Then, again, it does not satisfy those heirs of Comte and Durkheim who find religion deep-seated in humanity and in the consensus which makes up human society. They suspect those who talk of secularization of presupposing some golden age in the past as compared with an over-secularized present; they feel they ignore a continuing interaction between Christian revelation and Western civilization, a continual working and reworking of the Christian message through the lives and minds, the societies and institutions of Western man.[9]

These reservations noted, let us see what Weber's theory can tell us about secularization in the Islamic world. Our evidence will be derived mainly from the Islamic world of South Asia, although we shall reach out, where appropriate, to seek parallels and comparisons elsewhere. In exploring Weber's perspectives of disenchantment and fragmentation, we shall use Peter Berger's distinction between structural secularization, that is the evacuation of religion from society's institutions and its consequences, and subjective secularization, that is the evacuation of the religious from the consciousness of man and its consequences.[10]

First, we consider structural secularization, the driving out of Islam from the frameworks of law, of knowledge, and of power in British India. In the case of law, we find that in the century which followed the 1770s the Islamic criminal and civil law was first encroached upon, and then replaced outright, by British codes of law. By the 1870s the Muslims of British India found that their Islamic law, the *shari'a*, accounted for no more than their personal law, that is the law relating to matters such as marriage, divorce and inheritance. Moreover, that law was no longer strictly Islamic in its rules of procedure but slowly being reshaped, as Islamic doctrines of strict adherence to established authorities were set aside in favour of English doctrines of equity and binding precedent, by the procedures of that limited form of Weberian *qadi-justice*, the Anglo-Muhammadan law.[11] We can discern fragmentation in at least two senses. There was fragmentation between public and private worlds, between a public world ruled by law derived from the West, and a private world ruled by law derived from Islamic sources. There was also fragmentation between the world of the British courts, whether they applied the British codes of public law or the Anglo-Muhammadan personal law, and the world of the *ulama*, the traditionally learned men of Islam, who strove to offer as full guidance in the ways of the *shari'a* they could. Beneath the framework of British justice the *ulama* sustained a limited system of Islamic legal guidance represented by institutions such as the *Dar al-Ifta* of the Deoband School and the *Amir-i Shari'at* organization of Phulwari Sharif, Bihar.[12]

In the case of learning, an entirely new system was erected, which owed nothing to Islam. The knowledge taught would enable men to work modern bureaucracy, it was not knowledge which would make God's revelation through Muhammad work more successfully in the world. The peaks of achievement in the new system were in Western scholarship and science, usually reached in British universities, not in *tafsir* (Quran commentary) or *fiqh* (jurisprudence) to be scaled in Cairo or an-Najaf. Education in Islamic knowledge was increasingly relegated to a minor position and increasingly became less relevant to the broad purposes of society and state. Here, too, we can discern fragmentation. There were differences between government educational institutions, which taught Western knowledge in an anglicized environment, and Muslim institutions, like Aligarh College, which to some degree at least wished to hold Western knowledge within a Muslim cultural frame. There were greater differences between all such colleges, which produced swelling streams of trousered graduates able, by and large, to think in Western terms and to serve the purposes of Western civilization and Islamic *madrasas*, which produced a dwindling stream, relatively at least, of turbaned graduates able to see the world only through the prism of revelation.[13]

In the case of power, the only association between Islam and power which remained after the British abolished Muslim judges, or *qadis*, in the 1860s was the Anglo-Muhammadan law. Nevertheless, there did develop an association between Muslims and power. At each stage, as the British gradually devolved power on Indians between 1909 and 1947, a separate Muslim political identity was further entrenched in the modern political framework they were fashioning for India. Muslims gained separate electorates; they gained guaranteed numbers of seats in the legislatures; and ultimately some won an Islamic state of Pakistan. We seem to witness in the first fifty years of twentieth-century British India the somewhat paradoxical process, which also took place in Victorian Britain, that while the disenchantment of learning and other institutions goes on apace the political importance of religion remains strong.[14] Of course, we can also find fragmentation in the wake of disenchantment. There was the development of both a secular and a communal framework for politics within the colonial state. More significantly, there was the growth of a fundamental distinction between Muslims for whom freedom meant removing the British and taking over the framework of the colonial state and its law, either in a secular India or in a Muslim Pakistan, and Muslims for whom the only real form of freedom was the imposition of the *shari'a*, a true marriage between law derived from revelation and the machinery of the modern state.[15]

British India, therefore, reveals a moderate structural secularization; Islam was, to various degrees, disentangled from the frameworks of law, of learning and of power. Indeed, we might understand the situation best in terms of a kind of structural dualism. On the one hand, there was the developing fabric of the modern colonial state onto which, admittedly, some Muslim preferences had been imposed. On the other, there were the residual Islamic institutions of law and learning and the political vision which they fostered. By comparison, Turkey between the nineteenth-century reform period of the *Tanzimat* and the death of Ataturk had achieved a total disentangling of Islam from the frameworks of law, learning and power. But in Iran, up to the abdication of Riza Shah in 1941, or in Egypt, up to the Free Officers Revolution of 1952, we must talk more in terms of structural dualism along the lines of British India. Indeed, by the mid-twentieth century this was the pattern in most of the Islamic world.[16]

We now turn to consider subjective secularization, the disentangling of the religious vision from the consciousness of human beings. Here, too, we seem to be able to see the realization of a Weberian perspective. There seem to be processes of disenchantment in the emergence of a protestant or puritan Islam. This had its immediate origins in the great movement of revival and reform which swept through the Islamic world in the eighteenth and nineteenth centuries.[17] Barbara Metcalf analyses one of its Indian manifestations in her study of the context and the emergence of the Deoband school in the second half of the nineteenth century. She notes the growth of Islamic practice based more firmly on the Quran, the *Hadiths* and the *Shari'a*. It is an Islam based on scripture; it is one which is rationalizing in the sense of making religion self-conscious, systematic and based on abstract principles. Groups of Muslims come forward who, while they do not in the main reject saints and Islamic mysticism (sufism), increasingly see themselves as following religious practice which is different from that of the *sufi* shrines, indeed, they often define their Islam in contrast to the parochial forms of the shrines. Theirs is a universal form in which Muslims all over India, indeed, all over the Muslim world, could share. It is one, moreover, whose growth and development is closely interwoven, as in the emergence of European protestantism, with the translation of scripture into the vernacular languages and the harnessing of the printing press to the spreading of religious knowledge.[18]

Thus, there came to be established among the forms of Indian Islam a puritan form, which in its extreme manifestation of the *Ahl-i Hadiths* (People of the Traditions) was stripped to the bare essentials of Quran and Hadiths. These puritan Muslims began to dispense with the great network of saints and ancestors through whom they once came close to God. They came to live less in a world penetrated through and through by sacred beings and forces. God was firmly transcendent and humans had no comfort, no guidance except God's revelation through Muhammad to help them live in this world so that they might be judged favourably in the next. These Muslims increasingly seemed to find the world a cold, bleak, disenchanted place. It is a process which in protestant Christianity many see to be preparing the way for secularization. Once the channels between humankind and God had been narrowed down to His Word, belief in God became dependent on the credibility of that Word. Once that credibility was undermined, the floodgates of secularization were open.[19]

We do not wish to suggest that the outcome for Islam will be the same, only that there are some similarities in the path travelled. For the moment, we would note that the emergence of a puritan Islam is not confined to India but is also to be found in other parts of the Islamic World. The closest parallel is probably the Muhammadiyah of Indonesia. A less close one is that of the Salafiyah of North Africa, whose assertion of the ideal or a reformed Islam as against that of a saintly Islam in the context of urbanization of Algeria has been set out by Ernest Gellner in his somewhat misleadingly entitled essay, 'The Unknown Apollo of Biskra'. Some of the same drives and concerns, on the other hand, have also been expressed through the framework of a sufi order as in the case of the Nurcular of Turkey.[20]

If we can see disenchantment in the processes of subjective secularization, we can also see fragmentation and growing conflict of world views. The very emergence of the new puritan Islam in the towns and *qasbahs* of nineteenth-century India led to bitter conflict with those for whom the world was still enchanted; it led to those endless battles over behaviour at saints' shrines which Deobandis and Barelvis have carried with them from India to Pakistan to the towns and cities of midland and northern Britain.[21] It also led to conflict, often no less bitter, in letter, tract, newspaper and debate, among the reforming sects themselves. Then, there was further conflict between the various traditonalist groups and those called Islamic modernists. Islamic modernists grew from the same stock as the puritan traditionalists but strove somehow to hold elements of Western knowledge and understanding within an Islamic frame. Their line began with the great theological and historiographical efforts of Sayyid Ahmad Khan and the Aligarh movement. It moved through the crises of pan-Islamism from the late nineteenth century to the great Indian movement of 1919–24 to preserve the Turkish caliphate. Then it came to a peak, on the one hand in Abul Kalam Azad and the genesis of the idea of a composite Hindu–Muslim Indian nationalism as the political counterpart to a continuing Islamic universalism, and on the other hand in Muhammad Iqbal and the genesis of the idea of the Islamic state of Pakistan as the realistic answer to the answer to the political failure of Islamic universalism.[22] The further elaboration of Islamic modernist thought by Fazlur Rahman, that most creative of Pakistani thinkers, who was once head of the Islamic Research Institute established under his country's constitution, led to his being driven into exile to die on the shores of Lake Michigan.[23]

All these thinkers, whether traditionalist or modernist, understood the world within an Islamic frame. Their vision of world history was bound by Islam: the Quran was their starting point. But, there also came those who espoused visions which challenged Islam as an all-inclusive moral, social and political system, men whose understandings of the world were distinctly secular in a

Western sense. There are those, like K.M. Ashraf and Sajjad Zaheer and other supporters of the Progressive Writers Movement of the 1930s and 1940s, who espoused a primarily socialist vision of progress.[24] There are also those, both in India and in Pakistan, who have espoused a nationalist vision of past and future: there is Zulfiqar Ali Bhutto's transient vision of five thousand years of Pakistani history; there is also Mushirul Hasan's vigorous advocacy of a secular nationalist future for India in general and India's Muslims in particular. For such men Islam is no longer the explanation of the beginning and end of things; it is just another form of culture.[25]

This process of fragmentation and conflict, of the emergence of multiplying strands of conflicting thought among Muslims, which come eventually to include those that challenge Islam as total ideology, can be seen yet more distinctly in the world outside South Asia. Here the nationalism of Ataturk and Riza Shah Pahlavi stood both more confident and better developed. Here the socialism of Nasserite Egypt and Baathist Iraq was more fully thought through and realized. But here, of course, Islam was only threatened by Western domination from without, as opposed to the South Asian Muslim's fear of the pincer threat of Western domination from without and Hindu domination from within.

Thus, we find within the Islamic world much evidence of the growth of secularization along the lines that Weber traced in Christian Europe. Disenchantment and fragmentation takes place in structural terms; it also takes place in subjective terms. From almost any Western point of view the signs of secularization are plentiful. Yet, one reflection gives pause for thought about just how much weight we should attach to what we find. This secularization was a consequence of the projection of Western capital and power into the Islamic world from 1800 onwards. The steady disenchantment and fragmentation of the structures of law, learning and power was either the direct result of the impact of Western imperialism, as in British India, or as in Turkey and Iran the result of deliberate attempts to copy European ways and institutions to make the state strong enough to keep the foreigner out. These processes were in large part forced on Muslim societies from outside or imposed from above; they were only to a limited extent the result of new economic and social formations within these societies. We could, moreover, argue along similar lines in dealing with those Muslims who espouse secular ideologies which deny the all-inclusive vision of Islam. That they were able to espouse these ideologies seems mainly a function of the extent to which they were caught up within a web of Western economic influence, power and thought. They embraced a Western secularism rather than developing an Islamic one.

Some might counter this argument by pointing to those processes of religious change in the recent Islamic past which bear comparison with similar processes in Christian history. We think of that development of a Muslim puritanism out of the internal dynamics of Islamic civilization which developed a modernist aspect as it came into contact with the West. There are certainly aspects of rationalization here, aspects of Weberian disenchantment and fragmentation. But they do not, as yet, threaten to undermine the Islamic world view from within. Indeed, these processes seem more aspects of religious change, a reduction in the sufi element in Islam and an increasing emphasis on the law. They seem as much spurs to find a new relationship between revelation and history as a notable manifestation of secularization within an Islamic environment. It may be that this is in large part because Muslims have contemplated the meaning of Western knowledge in the context of overwhelming Western power, which has made it particularly difficult to critically explore their own world and to risk turning it upside down. More time, perhaps, is needed. On the other hand, there may be limits to what a theory of secularization derived from the experience of the Christian world can tell us about religious change in the Islamic world.

So we turn from exploring the potential of Weber's theory of secularization in the Islamic context to considering the problem of secularization in Islamic terms, in fact, to considering the problem as Weber might have done, in terms of the unique 'developmental history' of Islam, that is, in terms of the development of Islam as a form of rationlization of world views.[26] We start from the position that the orientation of Islam to the world is different from that of Christianity, and thus its pattern of development will be so too. As Weber suggests, Islam is particularly concerned with this world.[27] It is much more concerned with how men behave than with what they believe, in fact, all that they need believe is contained in the one sentence of the *shahada*, the confession of faith. In most of its fundamental rituals Islam concentrates on the creation and support of a community of believers on earth. There is to be communal prayer, communal fasting, alms-giving to support the community, and pilgrimage to affirm the community. Indeed, a Muslim life is primarily significant as being lived as part of the community, that best community, as the Quran declares, raised up for men.[28] A prime function of the community is to support the power which will enforce the *shari'a*. This is ideally, though not wholly, the distilled essence of the Quran and the life of the Prophet which offers guidance for every aspect of human life. It is ideally, and certainly, the constitution of the Muslim community, as Gibb describes it, which stands 'for all that the Constitution stands for the United States of America and more'.[29] It embodies both the patterns of behaviour which the Muslim should strive to realize in his own life and the patterns of behaviour which the state should try to impose upon him. Muslim society is Islamic to the extent that it follows the *shari'a*. Muslim states are Islamic to the extent that they support the *shari'a*. Here we have a possible criterion of secularization in Islamic societies and states; if they are Islamic to the extent to which the *shari'a* is followed and applied then they are secular to the extent that it is not followed and applied.

Let us see what we can learn if we use this criterion in the case of South Asia. We have already noted that by the 1870s the application of the *shari'a* in British India had been reduced to the personal law, and that in its distorted Anglo–Muhammadan form. Nevertheless, there were important developments in its shape and in its support up to the mid-twentieth century. Throughout the history of Islam in South Asia, as in that of other Muslim societies, the *shari'a* had tolerated the continuing existence of customary laws, the non-Islamic laws of new, and not so new, entrants to the Islamic milieu. But, by the time of the Shariat Application Act of 1937, almost all toleration of these customary laws came to an end. As far as their personal lives were concerned, Indian Muslims lived under the *shari'a* alone.[30] Then, in the past, the reach of the state, particularly into rural communities, had always been limited; so had been its capacity to apply the law. But the superior machinery of the colonial state, and later of the national states of India and Pakistan, was able to bring the *shari'a* much closer to the lives of each individual Muslim. By the mid-twentieth century Muslim personal law, that point where the Quran is most explicit, that point Muslims feel, in Anderson's telling phrase, that the *shari'a* partakes most intimately in the very warp and woof of their lives,[31] had come to be more completely applied than ever before in South Asia. Similar developments can be traced in Malaysia and Indonesia, for instance, and even in Saudi Arabia.[32]

If we now turn to examine how the *shari'a* might have been followed, it seems that, up to the eighteenth century, although many knew they were Muslims, not so many knew how to behave as the holy law might direct. Islamic knowledge, knowledge of what Muslims should and should not do, was hard to come by.[33] We know, as Bulliet, Geertz, Eaton and many others have demonstrated, that through much of the Islamic world the process of Islamization, the patterning of society after some version of the *shari'a*, has been painfully slow. Many centuries divide the first confession of faith from the wide mastery of the scriptural tradition.[34] We also know that the early nineteenth-century movements of revival and reform in Kerala, in Bengal, and in Northern India, all suggest that there was a large gap between the practice of rural and even *qasbah* society and preference of an alert, reforming Islam. But the nineteenth and twentieth centuries have seen unprecedented drives, fuelled by continuing movements of reform, by vast increases in the availability of Islamic knowledge, and by favourable economic and social changes, which have brought Muslims to live lives closer to the *shari'a*.[35] Just as the application of the personal law by the state is more rigorous and more widespread than before, so is knowledge of the *shari'a*, and perhaps the following of it, in Indo–Muslim society at large. This, too, is not a development confined to South Asia. It is also expressed, for instance, in the popularity of the Muslim Brotherhood throughout much of the Middle East, and, in spite of the determinedly secular face of the Turkish state, or perhaps because of it, in the extraordinary thirst for Islamic knowledge among the Turkish people in recent times. It is, in fact, a feature of the late twentieth-century revival of Islam that has touched every Muslim society.[36]

We are left with contrasting perspectives. If we take that derived from Weber's theory of secularization, it does seem that Indo–Muslim society, indeed Muslim societies in general, has advanced some way down the path of disenchantment and fragmentation, the path of secularization. But, if we respect the integrity of the 'developmental history' of Islam as a rationalization of world views, we have a picture which is more complex. Certainly, the exercise of European power in the nineteenth and twentieth centuries drove the *shari'a* out of the public and the private sphere of Muslim life. Certainly, it undermined the Islamic world view of Muslim elites. Yet, on the other hand, the modern state and the modern technology, which the Europeans brought, helped to draw many Muslims closer to the *shari'a* than before. In recent times, moreover, the retreat of the European, and some failures of the state machinery they left behind, have often been accompanied by a reassertion of Islamic world view and a reinstatement of the *shari'a* in public life. A continuing process of islamization, following Weber's understanding of developmental history, seems as notable a feature of recent Islamic developments, as one of the secularization, following Weber's theory of secularization.

Reviewing the argument of this essay some thirteen years after it was first written, and in the light of recent developments in the Muslim world, there is an additional reflection. We have noted above that in terms of the unique developmental history of Islam the faith was particularly concerned with this world. This is, of course, true if it is approached in a sense that veers in an orientalist/essentialist direction. But, if we consider the effective practice of Islam in many societies over much of the past 1400 years, it has had powerful other-worldly dimensions. Most believers have attended saints' shrines and implored the saint to intercede for them with God.

The great event of Islamic history over the past two hundred years has been the attack by the movement of revival and reform on all ideas of saintly intercession for humankind with God and the new emphasis on the this-worldly dimension of the faith. The many movements of Islamic reassertion have been, and are, impelled by the consciousness of the need to act in this world to achieve salvation. There is evidence that these manifestations of 'willed Islam' have come to develop new strands in Muslim consciousness that bear resemblance to similar outgrowths of European protestantism. There is a new sense of empowerment that comes with the knowledge that it is humanity that fashions the world. There is a new sense of personal autonomy and individual possibility that comes with the knowledge that individuals are able to make choices. There is a steady transfer of the symbols and centres of meaning in life from the signs of God and the friends of God to the mundane things of life—family, home, love, sex, food.

There is the 'inward turn' as the individual comes to examine and to reflect upon the self. In sum the individual becomes more and more focussed on earthly activity and earthly fulfilment.

If we take Islam as widely practised through time as the basis of our understanding of the developmental history of Islam, strands are emerging which would appear to point in similar directions to those of protestant Christianity. We recognize, of course, that the new individualism derives some of its impetus from the influence of the West as well as having firm roots in this-worldly Islam. This said, there is growing tension between demands for individual fulfilment and the requirements of obligation to community, a tension felt most acutely in many Muslim societies by women. It is worth considering whether this tension may not be at the cusp of a process of secularization in Muslim societies.[37]

NOTES

1. The first draft of this paper was given at the conference on Weber and Islam held under the auspices of the Werner–Reimers–Stiftung, Bad Homburg, in June 1984. I am particularly grateful for comments made then and later by Professors Guenther Roth and Wolfgang Schluchter. This version of the paper is in large part the same as that originally published in German, except for minor changes in the text to bring it up-to-date and some additions to the supporting notes.
2. It is important to emphasize that Weber's theory of secularization sees the process as an historical one. It is not a model, or ideal type, like patrimonialism, feudalism, or charismatic domination, which is meant to be applicable in different places and at many times.
3. Bryan S. Turner, *Weber and Islam: A Critical Study* (London: Routledge and Kegan Paul, 1974), pp. 151–52.
4. Guenther Roth and Claus Wittick (eds), *Max Weber: Economy and Society: An Outline of Interpretive Sociology* (Berkeley: University of California Press, 1978), I, p. 630.
5. Owen Chadwick, *The Secularization of the European Mind in the Nineteenth Century* (Cambridge: Cambridge University Press, 1975), p. 258.
6. This perspective, with a particular emphasis on the role of functional differentiation, is discussed by Wolfgang Schluchter in 'The Future of Religion' in Mary Douglas and Steven M. Tipton (eds), *Religion and America* (Boston: Beacon Press, 1983), pp. 64–78. Strikingly, although he mentions Weber not once, the controversial, but also moving, work by the Anglican theologian Don Cupitt, *The Sea of Faith: Christianity in Change* (London: British Broadcasting Corporation, 1984), seems much in harmony with Schluchter's Weberian perspective.

7. This broad sweep is outlined by Guenther Roth in 'Religion and Revolutionary Beliefs' in Guenther Roth and Wolfgang Schluchter, *Max Weber's Vison of History: Ethics and Methods* (Berkeley: University of California Press, 1979), p. 166.
8. Turner, *Weber*, pp. 158–59.
9. See, for instance, David Martin, 'Towards Eliminating the Concept of Secularization' in Julius Gould (ed.), *The Penguin Survey of the Social Sciences* (Harmondsworth: Penguin Books, 1965), pp. 169–82; this position would also seem to underpin Chadwick, and especially his concluding statement in *Secularization*, pp. 264–66.
10. See the chapter entitled 'The Process of Secularization' in Peter L. Berger, *The Social Reality of Religion* (Harmondswoth: Penguin Books, 1973), pp. 111–30.
11. Qadi-justice is justice which knows no rational rules of decision. It is one of Weber's ideal types. See, Weber, *Economy and Society*, II, pp. 976–78. For the Anglo–Muhammadan law and the impact of its rules procedure see, N.J. Coulson, A History of Islamic Law (Edinburgh: Edinburgh University Press, 1978), pp. 165–71.
12. Tahir Mahmood, *Muslim Personal Law: Role of the State in the Subcontinent* (New Delhi: Vikas, 1977) pp. 67–9; at the end of its first one hundred years the *Dar al-Ifta* of Deoband reckoned that it had issued 269, 215 legal decisions—the work of this office and the nature of its decisions are discussed in Barbara Daly Metcalf, *Islamic Revival in British India: Deoband, 1860–1900* (New Jersey: Princeton University Press, 1982), pp. 146–54.
13. Two excellent books enable us to enter these very different worlds under British rule: David S. Lelyveld, *Aligarh's First Generation: Muslim Solidarity in British India* (New Jersey: Princeton University Press, 1978), and Metcalf, *Islamic Revival.*
14. Alan D. Gilbert, *The Making of Post-Christian Britain: A History of the Secularization of Modern Society* (London: Longman, 1980), especially chapter 4.
15. Aspects of these attitudes are dealt by Francis Robinson 'Islam and Muslim Separatism' in David Taylor and Malcolm Yapp (eds), *Political Identity in South Asia* (London: Curzon Press, 1979), pp. 78–112; Peter Hardy, *Partners in Freedom — and True Muslims: The Political Thought of Some Muslim Scholars in British India 1912*–1947 (Lund: Scandinavian Institute of Asian Studies, 1971); Aziz Ahmad, *Islamic Modernism in India and Pakistan 1857–1964* (Oxford: Oxford University Press, 1967).
16. For a general survey of these processes see, Francis Robinson, *Atlas of the Islamic World since 1500* (Oxford: Phaidon, 1982), pp. 130–56.
17. Ibid., pp. 118–29.
18. Francis Robinson, 'Islam and the Impact of Print in South Asia' in Nigel Crook (ed.), *The Transmission of Knowledge in South Asia: Essays on*

Education, Religion, History and Politics (Delhi: Oxford University Press, 1996), pp. 62–97; Metcalf, *Islamic Revival*, especially chapters 4 and 5.

19. A sense of this more demanding, disenchanted, world is expressed in the famous guide for women, but whose advice was equally applicable to men, published by the Deobandi scholar, Ashraf Ali Thanawi, at the beginning of the twentieth century, Barbara D. Metcalf, *Perfecting Women: Maulana Ashraf 'Ali Thanawi's Bishishti Zewar: A Partial Translation with Commentary* (Berkeley: University of California Press, 1990).
20. For a local study of this development in Indonesia see, Mitsuo Nakamura, *The Crescent Arises over the Banyan Tree: A Study of the Muhammadiyah Movement in a Central Javanese Town* (Yogyakarta: Gadjah Mada University Press, 1983); for Algeria, Ernest Gellner, 'The Unknown Apollo of Biskra: The Social Base of Algerian Puritanism' in his *Muslim Society* (Cambridge: Cambridge University Press, 1981), pp. 149–73; for the Nurcular, Serif Mardin, *Religion and Social Change in Modern Turkey: The Case of Bediuzzaman Said Nursi* (Albany: State University of New York Press, 1989).
21. Metcalf, *Islamic Revival*, pp. 232–34, 309–11, 355–60; Philip Lewis, *Islamic Britain: Religion, Politics and Identity among British Muslims* (London: I.B. Tauris, 1994).
22. Ahmad, *Islamic Modernism*, pp. 141–94.
23. Fazlur Rahman was professor of Islamic Thought in the Department of Near Eastern Languages and Civilization at the University of Chicago. The final statement of his thinking was *Islam and Modernity: Transformation of an Intellectual Tradition* (Chicago: University of Chicago Press, 1982).
24. For a detailed study of this group and their ideas see, Khizar Humayun Ansari, *The Emergence of Socialist Thought Among North Indian Muslims (1917–1947)* (Lahore: Book Traders, 1990).
25. One attempt to develop Bhutto's vision was Ahmad Abdulla, *The Historical Background of Pakistan and its People* (Karachi: Tanzeem Publishers, 1973); Hasan's advocacy appears most powerfully in Mushirul Hasan, *Legacy of a Divided Nation: India's Muslims since Independence* (Delhi: Oxford University Press, 1997).
26. Guenther Roth has shown how fruitful it is to see Max Weber as a 'developmental' historian working amongst other German developmental historians who competed hotly with each other. '"Developmental History" in Max Weber's Time and Work', unpublished paper.
27. Weber, *Economy and Society*, I, pp. 623–27.
28. Maulana Muhammad Ali, *The Holy Qur'an*, 6th ed. (Lahore: 'Ahmadiyyah Anjuman Isha'at Islam 1973), chapter 3, verse 109.
29. 'Structure of Religious Thought in Islam' in Hamilton A.R. Gibb, *Studies on the Civilization of Islam* (New Jersey: Princeton University Press, 1962), p. 200.
30. Mahmood, *Muslim Personal Law*, pp. 20–33.

31. Norman Anderson, *Law Reform in the Muslim World* (London: Athlone Press, 1976), p. 17.
32. See, for instance, Daniel S. Lev, *Islamic Courts in Indonesia: A Study in the Political Bases of Legal Institutions* (Berkeley: University of California Press, 1972); Moshe Yegar, *Islam and Islamic Institutions in British Malaya*; Donald Powell Cole, *Nomads of the Nomads: The Al Murrah Bedouin of the Empty Quarter* (Illinois: AHM Publishing Corporation, 1975), pp. 123–25.
33. Metcalf emphasizes the difficulties which even *ulama* experienced in finding books in the days when they were reproduced by hand and consequently the great change made by the introduction of the lithographic printing press in the first half of the nineteenth century, *Islamic Revival*, pp. 198–215.
34. Richard W. Bulliet, *Conversion to Islam in the Medieval Period: An Essay in Quantitative History* (Cambridge Mass.: Harvard University Press, 1979); Clifford Geertz, 'Modernization in a Muslim Society: The Indonesian Case' in R.N. Bellah (ed.), *Religion and Progress in Modern Asia* (New York: The Free Press, 1965), especially pp. 96–7; Richard M. Eaton, *Sufis of Bijapur 1300–1700: Social Roles of Sufis in Medieval India* (New Jersey: Princeton University Press, 1978) and *The Rise of Islam and the Bengal Frontier, 1204–1760* (Berkeley: University of California Press, 1996). A general argument regarding islamization is advanced in Francis Robinson 'Islam and Muslim Society in South Asia', *Contributions to Indian Sociology* (n.s.), 17, 2, 1983, pp. 185–203.
35. See, Stephen F. Dale, *Islamic Society on the South Asian Frontier: The Mappilas of Malabar 1498–1922* (Oxford: Clarendon Press, 1980); Rafiuddin Ahmed, *The Bengal Muslims 1871–1906: A Quest for Identity* (Delhi: Oxford University Press, 1981); Metcalf, *Islamic Revival*; S.A.H.A. Nadwi, *Life and Mission of Maulana Muhammad Ilyas* (Lucknow: Academy of Islamic Research and Publications, Nadwat-ul Ulama, 1993) and M. Anwarul Haq, *The Faith Movement of Mawlana Muhammad Ilyas* (London: George Allen & Unwin, 1972).
36. For a recent assessment of the popularity and influence of the Muslim Brotherhood see, John Obert Voll, *Islam: Continuity and Change in the Mod-ern World* (Boulder, Colorado: Westview Press, 1982), pp. 174–76, 251–52, 314–15, 318–19, 339–40; and for developments in Turkey, see, Annemarie Schimmel, 'Islam in Turkey' in A.J. Arberry (ed.), *Religion in the Middle East* (Cambridge: Cambridge University Press, 1969), II, pp. 68–95; Jacob M. Landau, *Radical Politics in Modern Turkey* (Leiden: E.J. Brill, 1974), pp. 171–93; Hamid Algar, 'Said Nursi and the Risala-i Nur: An Aspect of Islam in Contemporary Turkey' in Khurshid Ahmad and Zafar Ishaq Ansari (eds), *Islamic Perspectives: Studies in Honour of Mawlana Sayyid Abul A'la Mawdudi* (Liecester: The Islamic Foundation, 1979).
37. This argument is developed in Francis Robinson, 'Religious Change, the Self and Community in Muslim South Asia since 1800', *South Asia*, vol. XX, no. 1 (1997), pp. 1–15.

Chapter Six

The Muslims of Upper India and the Shock of the Mutiny[1]

RUSTKHEZ-I BEJA

'In our ancient capitals once so well-known, so rich, so great and so flourishing', declared Saiyid Ahmad Khan to the Muhammadan Literary Society of Calcutta in 1863, 'nothing is now to be seen or heard save a few bones strewn amongst the ruins of the human-like cry of the jackal.'[2] He was reminding the Muslims assembled at the house of Nawab Abdul-Latif that, five years after the end of the Mutiny uprising, Delhi and Lucknow, the two great centres of Muslim culture in Upper India, the London and Paris of their milieu, were, in large part, deserted. In doing so, he draws our attention to the protracted shock which the uprising and its brutal suppression brought to the Muslims of Upper India.

The impact of the Mutiny uprising on the British is well understood. No other event in British imperial history has attracted as much attention, and certainly, for the hundred years that followed, discussion of it might begin 'as every schoolboy knows ...'. The meaning of the event for British policy is also widely understood. Dalhousian self-confidence was replaced by caution and conciliation; policies towards the army, finance, the States and the landlords were changed; it was recognized that the government could not transform India willy-nilly in the light of Western values and that it must make a point of listening to, indeed, taking the advice of, the powerful in Indian society.

The impact of the events of the Mutiny years on Muslims is not quite so well understood. Among the reasons for this must be counted, some notable exceptions apart, the silence on the subject which many contemporaries observed, some for fear of further British retribution, others because they sought refuge from the trauma of the times in a collective amnesia. This said, it is widely accepted that the Mutiny uprising and its aftermath forms a watershed in the development of the ideas and attitudes of the Muslims of Upper India in the nineteenth century. Before the great upheaval they did not appear to take seriously into account either the challenge of Western civilization or the meaning of British power. After it they were increasingly concerned to discover how best they could be Muslim under the new dispensation, whether it meant building ideological and institutional bridges between Islam and West, or developing systems which could enable them largely to ignore Western civilization and the colonial state, or making a point of defending Islam wherever it was threatened in India and the world.

We have some knowledge of the Mutiny experiences of those who were to take the lead in these initiatives in Muslim life. There is value in drawing together these experiences and the wider contexts in which they took place. For it is in their shattering nature that we find some of the origins both of the realization that new Muslim approaches were needed and of the urgency which lay behind the great outpouring of Muslim creativity that resulted. In this light we shall examine three sets of people; the 'modernists' who coalesced around the Muhammadan Anglo-Oriental College at Aligarh, the 'reformers', a somewhat more disparate group whose most notable institution was the *Dar al-ulum* at Deoband, and the learned and holy men of the great Lucknow family of Firangi Mahal.

It is striking how many of those who were to play leading roles in the attempts to build bridges between north Indian Muslims and the West were caught up amongst the events of 1857 in and around Delhi. Of the leaders of the Aligarh movement, only Chiragh Ali (1844–95) and Nawab Mushtaq Husain (1841–1917) do not appear to have been involved in any way.

Saiyid Ahmad Khan is, of course, the outstanding figure in the group. Scion of a distinguished Mughal service family, noted writer on religious, historical and archaeological matters, when the Mutiny broke out he had served the British for nineteen years. Because he wrote his own history of the rebellion in Bijnor and because the period is well-covered in Hali's great biography of the Saiyid we know more of his experiences than those of anyone else apart from the poet, Ghalib. There is his rescue of the European population of

Bijnor district and his assumption of its administration until he was forced to flee to Meerut by the forces of Nawab Mahmud Khan. There is his journey to Delhi, after hearing that his family property had been ransacked by government troops and his uncle and cousin murdered, to find his mother and her companion in desperate straits. There is the death of his mother a few days later in Meerut, which meant the premature passing of the woman who had almost total charge of his upbringing and education, on whose behalf he had lived in Delhi from 1846 to 1856, and for whom he had enormous respect. Looking back on these years in 1889, Saiyid Ahmad declared that he contemplated leaving India: 'for some time I wrestled with my grief and, believe me, it made an old man of me. My hair turned white.' He grieved in part over his personal losses and in large part over the appalling condition of his community.[3]

Khwaja Altaf Husain (1837–1914), who is better known under his *takhullus* 'Hali', poet and biographer of the Aligarh movement, came from the famed Ansari family of the *qasbah* Panipat on the banks of the Yamuna, some fifty-five miles north of Delhi. In 1854 he had run away from the limited opportunities and stifling atmosphere of the *qasbah* to seek his fortune in the Mughal capital. It was not long before his exploits in the *mushairas* drew his family's attention to where he was and he was brought back to meet his obligations in Panipat and to find a job as a clerk in a government office in Hissar. On the outbreak of the Mutiny he fled back to Panipat being robbed of all he had on the way save a Quran tied in a scarf around his neck. The experience left him physically ill and in a state of shock. He did not work again until he took up a position in 1861 as tutor to the sons of Nawab Mustafa Khan 'Shefta'.[4]

The ancestors of Munshi Zakaullah (1832–1910) were, for many generations, tutors to the Mughal royal family. The Munshi himself was the schoolteacher of the Aligarh movement; he taught at Agra College, Muir Central College, Allahabad, and was the headmaster of Delhi Normal School. His great achievement was the writing and also the translation into Urdu of many textbooks in mathematics, physics, history, geography and ethics. During the Mutiny uprising he was deeply affected when English friends, and notably Mr Taylor, the principal of Delhi College, were killed by the rebels. But he was particularly affected when the man 'whom he loved and revered most in the world', Maulvi Imam Baksh Sahbai, saintly cherisher of the learning of the Delhi renaissance and assistant to

Saiyid Ahmad Khan in his work for *Asar us-Sanadid*, was murdered along with his family by government troops. 'This deed of blood,' he told C.F. Andrews half a century later, 'can never be forgotten.'[5] After the capture of Delhi he and his family were forced out of their house and had to seek refuge among the tombs of Nizamuddin Auliya, some three miles from the city wall. The family property, which lay between the Jama Masjid and the royal palace, was demolished and no compensation was ever paid. 'For a long time,' Zakaullah told Andrews, 'the shock of those last Mutiny days was beyond all bearing. The torturing thoughts of his mind drove him at last to a melancholy that bordered on despair.'[6]

Three further figures in the Aligarh movement were caught up in the events of the uprising. Saiyid Mehdi Ali Khan (1837–1907), who succeeded Saiyid Ahmad as the effective leader of the movement, apparently performed useful services during the disturbances as an officer under A.O. Hume in the Etawah collectorate. Maulvi Nazir Ahmad (1830–1912), who came from Bijnor, was a contemporary of Zakaullah at Delhi College and later British government servant and novelist of the movement. He was appointed a deputy-inspector of schools for saving the life of an English woman during the disturbance in Delhi. Then, there was Maulvi Samiullah Khan (1834–1908), Zakaullah's closest childhood friend and scion of a scholarly and noble family of Delhi. A successful government servant on the judicial side, he was Saiyid Ahmad's right-hand man in the early development of Aligarh. During the British sack of Delhi he saved Saiyid Ahmad's wife and family, escorting them to Nizamuddin; afterwards, like so many others, he suffered from shock.[7]

One further individual deserves at least partial inclusion in this group, the editor and literary critic, Muhammad Husain Azad (1830–1910). A contemporary of Zakaullah and Nazir Ahmad at Delhi College, his father was a pioneer of Urdu journalism. He was a devoted pupil of Zauq, the penultimate Mughal poet laureate, and much of his working life was spent in the Punjab education service where he wrote textbooks for schools. In the aftermath of the Mutiny his father, although he had tried to give shelter to the principal of Delhi College, was executed for treason and his property confiscated. Azad only succeeded in escaping from Delhi in disguise, his one comfort being that he managed to take with him, as he was being driven from his home, the unpublished ghazals of

Zauq. In 1885, he began to show signs of mental disturbance; by 1890 he had lost his mind.[8]

With regard to our second group, the 'reformers', we have details of their experience in the Mutiny uprising, but less personal ones. We do not know how they thought about the great upheaval, either at the time or subsequently; we must judge them by their actions. Five out of six of the group had been educated in Delhi: some in the ambience of Delhi College, and they shared teachers and acquaintances with Aligarh 'modernists' such as Saiyid Ahmad Khan, Nazir Ahmad, Zakaullah and Samiullah Khan. Three of the group, Haji Imdadullah (1817–99), both the spiritual director of Islamic reform and the spiritual guide of hundreds of South Asian Muslims in the second half of the nineteenth century, Muhammad Qasim Nanautawi (1833–77) and Rashid Ahmad Gangohi (1829–1905), the developers of the key institutional frameworks of Islamic reform in the *Dar al-ulum* at Deoband and its offshoots, were all educated in the traditions of the great eighteenth-century reformer, Shah Waliullah of Delhi. Haji Imdadullah studied briefly under Maulana Mamluk Ali of Delhi College, a great sustainer of the Waliullahi tradition until his death in 1851, and then found his vocation as a sufi. Muhammad Qasim and Rashid Ahmad, on the other hand, were star pupils both of Mamluk Ali and Maulvi Abdul Ghani Naqshbandi, the successor of Shah Muhammad Ishaq, the great grandson of Shah Waliullah.[9] A direct contemporary of these two young tyros, Siddiq Hasan Khan (1832–90), a leading figure amongst the Ahl-i Hadith and the husband of the Begum of Bhopal, studied under Sadruddin Azurdah, a much respected scholar of mid-nineteenth-century Delhi and the leading pupil of Shah Abdul-Aziz, son of Shah Waliullah.[10] Rahmatullah Kairanawi (1818–90), the major force in the first Muslim defence in modern times against Christianity at Agra in 1854, and later the author of an attack upon it, studied in Delhi under Imam Baksh Sahbai at Maulana Muhammad Hayat's *madrasa* by the Red Fort. And finally there is the odd man out, Dr Wazir Khan, the key supporter of Kairanawi in his controversies with Christian missionaries, who was very active in the Mutiny uprising. Kairanawi's background is relatively unknown but for his birth in Bihar, his attending an English-medium school in Murshidabad, his further education at the Medical College in Calcutta and subsequently his further studies in London in the 1830s.[11]

It has been suggested that at least some of this group had actually formed an organization to rid India of the British. According to the Deobandi, Ubaidullah-Sindhi, who wrote in the twentieth century, there had been a continuous *jehad* movement in India going back to the time of Shah Abdul-Aziz. This had reached its peak in the *jehad* of Saiyid Ahmad Shahid (d. 1831) but continued in a organized form after his death, first under the leadership of Shah Muhammad Ishaq, a great-grandson of Shah Waliullah, and, after his departure for the Hijaz in 1841, under Maulana Mamluk Ali, and, after his death ten years later, under Haji Imdadullah. Indeed, we are given the impression that the 1840s and 1850s there was a full-fledged organization in existence with committees and so on. However, the claims of Sindhi apart, there is no hard evidence for this level of organization, and Farhan Nizami sums up the probabilities well when he suggests that the case for ideological continuity is reasonable but that for organizational continuity rather far-fetched.[12]

It has also been suggested that some of these same 'reformers' played a major role in one of the more important incidents of the Mutiny uprising, the *jehad* raised in the *qasbah* of Thana Bhawan (Muzaffarnagar district) in the early autumn of 1857. The story goes that Haji Imdadullah was the Amir of the *jehadis*; Muhammad Qasim, the commander-in-chief; Rashid Ahmad, the qazi; and Rahmatullah, a leading figure. There are detailed descriptions of how Rahmatullah went twice to Delhi to assess developments, of how the decision to launch the *jehad* was taken, of how the tahsil at Shamli was captured, of how Thana Bhawan was defended, and indeed of how Muhammad Qasim used a school playground trick to enable him to cut a Sikh sepoy in two, and of how Rahmatullah felt the pebbles which spurted up from the hooves of his pursuers' horses as he hid in a field to escape capture.[13] The one problem with this story is that there is no evidence for much of it before the 'reformist' tradition entered its nationalist phase in 1920. Indeed, earlier descriptions of events in Muzaffarnagar, one of which is by an eyewitness and friend of Muhammad Qasim, Muhammad Yaqub Nanautawi, are concerned to indicate how small the involvement of Muhammad Qasim in these events had been. Defenders of the post-1920 version, however, urge that theirs is the oral tradition of the 'reformers' and that, if publication of this was suppressed for sixty years, it was to avoid the attention of the colonial powers.[14]

Fortunately, we do not have to adjudicate the truth of these matters. It is enough that the 'reformers' were caught up in events to some extent. Of the following facts there is little doubt: that Haji Imdadullah was in Thana Bhawan when the *jehad* was declared and thereafter migrated to Mecca; that Muhammad Qasim and Rashid Ahmad were in Thana Bhawan with their spiritual director in August and September 1857; that Rahmatullah made at least one visit to Delhi to see how the uprising fared and later migrated to Mecca; that Muhammad Qasim lived in hiding until the general amnesty of 1859; and that in the same year Rashid Ahmad was arrested on suspicion of involvement in the uprising but released six months later for lack of evidence.[15]

Turning to our two remaining 'reformers', Rahmatullah's partner in the Agra debates, Dr Wazir Khan became governor of Agra for a brief moment while the British were driven into its fort, and later seems to have been active in several places: with the Maulvi of Fyzabad, Feroz Shah, son of the last Mughal Emperor, and in supervising the casting of a cannon in Bareilly. Afterwards he migrated to the Hijaz.[16] Then, finally, there is Siddiq Hasan Khan who, when the uprising took place, returned to his family in Kanauj only to have his entire village razed to the ground. For nearly two years he and his family lived the life of nomads, sheltering in the houses of friends, until the Begum of Bhopal asked him to write the history of her state and he was set on the road of becoming one of nineteenth-century India's more upwardly mobile Muslims.[17]

For the 'reformers', whether they were active participants, sucked into events unwillingly, or just victims of the moment, the uprising and its aftermath could have been nothing less than a time of loss, of shattered dreams, and of harsh lessons. Three of the six in our group chose to leave India permanently, either for fear of British retribution or because they could no longer bear to live under British domination: they were not the only Muslims to take this path. Two lived lives of some uncertainty in the years after the uprising and had to do so without the comforting presence of their sufi shaikh, which was no mean loss for pious mystics. One saw his home destroyed, all possessions lost, and lived a life of much privation. In the suppression of the uprising the weight of British power had been made abundantly clear, not to mention their willingness to use it without mercy. It was now evident that a *jehad* of a military kind had no real chance of success.

Our third group, the learned and holy men of Firangi Mahal, is somewhat different. It is less a group formed by one common ideological theme than by blood and memory. The family dates its existence in Lucknow back to the early 1690s when emperor Aurangzeb granted the Firangi Mahal, the confiscated property of a European indigo merchant, to the four sons of Mulla Qutbuddin Sihalwi, a prominent scholar who had been murdered in a squabble over land. The descendants of the Mulla made Firangi Mahal into the leading centre of learning in Upper India. They created a new Islamic syllabus, the *Dars-i Nizamiyya*, and spread it throughout the subcontinent and beyond, its popularity deriving not least from the fact that it both strengthened students' intellectual faculties and enabled them to learn more quickly. They were also devout sufis, moderate supporters of Ibn al-Arabi's *wahdat al-wujud* and three affiliations passed down the family generations—Chishti-Nizami, Chishti-Sabiri and Qadri-Razzaqi. Quintessentially representatives of an Islamic culture which had developed under the wings of Muslim power, they stood apart from the Waliullahi reforming tradition which was designed to help Muslims survive without power. As Sunnis, their relations with the Shia government of Awadh had not always been easy; one of the most gifted members of the family was forced to leave Lucknow because of the Shia-Sunni strife, while the biography of a noted family saint records several brushes with the Court over religious matters. The years immediately before the Mutiny uprising, nevertheless, find the family well-placed: Maulvi Waliullah had recently retired from Awadh service loaded with honours, Mufti Muhammad Yusuf was the Sunni *mufti* at the Court, Maulana Hafizullah was *darogah* of Fyzabad, Maulanas Naimatullah and Naimullah were well-placed in the Awadh administration. More generally the family continued its work of teaching, scholarship and spiritual leadership in Lucknow and beyond. Firangi Mahalis were to be found throughout northern India from Panipat to Calcutta, and in outposts further south such as Hyderabad and Madras. Wherever possible they served Muslim princes and Muslim institutions.[18]

In the Firangi Mahali mind the Mutiny disaster began two years before the events of May 1857 with what has come to be known as the Hanumangarhi *jehad*, and earlier round in the 'Babri Masjid' affair of the 1980s, in which Muslims campaigned to protect a supposed mosque at Ayodhya, which they claimed dated from Babur's time, against Hindu insistence that the building was the birthplace of Rama. The affair began in February 1855 when one Shah Ghulam Husain tried to oust a group of Hindu mahants who had taken possession of the building. A battle took place between large groups of Hindus and Muslims in which the latter were outnumbered and defeated. The Awadh court set up a three-man commission to investigate the matter which reported that no mosque had ever existed on the site. The king, Wajid Ali, tried to reach a compromise on the findings of the commission by suggesting that a mosque be built along the wall of the building. The Hindus refused to compromise. The Muslims, Sunnis almost to a man and now led by Amir Ali of Amethi, declared *jehad* against the occupiers of the 'mosque'. Wajid Ali warned Amir Ali to stop, his Shia *mujtahid* and Sunni *mufti* issued *fatawa* denying that *jehad* was appropriate in this case, and they also went out to preach to the *jehadis*. Amir Ali, although he lost much support as a result of the king's action, persisted in his course; on 7 November nearly 400 *jehadis* died in front of the guns of the Awadh army.[19]

Firangi Mahalis were involved in most stages of this affair. Maulana Hafizullah, as *darogah* of Fyzabad, provided evidence for the three-man commission regarding the history of the alleged mosque, although it was dismissed as too strongly supporting the Muslim cause. Maulana Abdur-Razzaq, the leading spiritual force in Firangi Mahal at the time, supported Amir Ali's declaration of *jehad* along with his cousin Burhan ul-Haq, and then left Lucknow to join the *jehadis* with Hisam ul-Haq and Amin ul-Haq. However, because Amir Ali deputed him to negotiate a compromise with the Court in October, he missed the fateful battle of 7 November. Then, it was Mufti Muhammad Yusuf who gave the *fatawa* against the *jehad*, and both Maulvi Khadim Ahmad of Firangi Mahal and the *Mufti* reached out to the *jehadis* at different times to dissuade them. Other leading members of the family, such as Naimatullah and the saintly Abdul Wali, were expected, by government at least, to play a similar role. It is clear that the affair divided the family; it was not forgotten how Muhammad Yusuf and Khadim Ahmad had worked against the cause.[20] Abdur-Razzaq, on the other hand, had to live with the memory that when the critical moment of the *jehad* came he was absent, a fact which his biographer in the 1920s worked hard to explain. There was also the belief, which was in part correct, that the *jehad* precipitated Britain's annexation of Awadh in the following year, an event which, amongst other disadvantages, had a crippling impact on the fortunes of all the Firangi Mahalis in the Awadh administration.[21]

The Mutiny uprising, therefore, came on top of two disastrous years for the family. Moreover, it brought further family division. Abdur-Razzaq presented his turban to the 'mutineers' as a banner, and found support in the family for his determination to crush the infidel.[22] Others, however, saw the affair, in retrospect at least, as lawlessness in which not only did the Europeans suffer at the hands of Indians, but Hindus at the hands of Hindus and Muslims at those of Muslims.[23] In July 1857 the family was driven out of its *mohullah* in the Chauk by the fighting to Saadatganj on the outskirts of the city, and later to the *qasbahs* beyond. Lives were lost; houses and possessions destroyed. All were forced to face, what most had hitherto managed to avoid, the fact of British domination in their world. 'Up to now,' declared Muhammad Yusuf as, in tears, he explained why he had left the job of registrar found for him by the Chief Commissioner of Awadh, 'I have been signing *fatawa* relating to God and His Prophet, and now I am expected to sign *fatawa* relating to interest.'[24] 'Although his feet tread the ground' said Abdur-Razzaq of a disciple who came to him wearing English boots, 'I feel they tread on my heart.'[25]

On top of what were often ghastly personal experiences, there was the fate of Delhi and of Lucknow, for so many the acme of cultivation, the centres of their civilized existence. Both cities were sacked. In Delhi, according to one estimate, almost 30,000 were killed, most of them indiscriminately. Those left alive were herded out of the city, the Muslims amongst them not being permitted to return till many months had passed. Much of their property was auctioned off by prize agents. Meanwhile the British set about reshaping the cities in the best interest of colonial control, stamping on them the imprint of their industrial civilization.

For those who go through troubled times it helps if loved homes, comfortable streets, accustomed vistas remain, as reminders at least, of the folkways in which they were brought up, and of the values they were taught to cherish. At the same time, it helps if great buildings, symbols of their community's achievements in the past, and of the possibility of the continuance of its thread of existence into the future, are regarded with respect, indeed survive. The citizens of Delhi and Lucknow found no such comfort. The bricks and mortar, stone and marble, carapace of Indo-Persian civilization, which had so long stood proud against the oncoming tide from Britain, was either blown up or abused.

The British revenge on Delhi was terrible. Indeed, for a time they considered demolishing the city altogether. Fortunately, less drastic counsel prevailed. In June 1858 Hindus were permitted to return and in August 1859 Muslims, although the overall numbers of inhabitants within the walled city did not reach the 1857 mark until 1900. Poets, most notably Ghalib, took to composing elegies on the death of the city, a genre of Urdu verse known as *Shahr-e-Ashub*. His letters recount week by week the humiliation and the destruction of the Mughal capital. For five years the Jama Masjid was used as a barrack for Sikh soldiers. The greater part of the second largest mosque, Fatehpuri, was sold to a Hindu, and was restored by Viceroy Lytton only twenty years later. The Zeenatul Masjid, the 'Ornament of Mosques' was used as a bakery until restored by Viceroy Curzon almost fifty years later. Most of the structures within the Red Fort were flattened, and of those that survived, the Mughal hall of Public Audience became a hospital and the buildings to the south of the Hall of Private Audience a barrack. All houses, mosques and bazars within 448 yards of the walls of the Fort were razed. 'Here it seems the whole city is being demolished', wrote Ghalib to a friend in September 1860, 'some of the biggest and most famous bazars—Khas Bazar, Urdu Bazar—each of which was practically a small town, have gone without trace. You cannot even tell where they were. Householders and shopkeepers cannot point out to you where their houses and shops used to stand.'[26] Further demolitions took place to make way for the cantonment which was to cover the eastern third of the city, its parade ground placed insolently between the Red Fort and the Jama Masjid. Then, the railway line from Calcutta was punched through the northern walls of the old Mughal palace and a path nearly four hundred yards wide was laid waste as it made its way through the city to the Lahore Gate. By means of the confiscation of land from those who could not prove their innocence there was a great transfer of property from Muslim into the hands of Hindu bankers. The character of the citizens also changed: '"Delhi People" now means Hindus, or artisans, or soldiers, or Panjabis or Englishmen'—Mughal Delhi was gone. 'By God,' wailed Ghalib in 1861, 'Delhi is no more a city, but a camp, a cantonment. No Fort, no city, no bazars, no water-courses ...'[27]

Muslims who returned to Delhi after the general amnesty of 1859 entered a nightmarish world. For all those in our first two groups, whether they were to become 'modernists' or 'reformers', the places of their youth, of their learning, of their spiritual development—the very nurseries of their civilization were gone. Saiyid Ahmad Khan, who had lived close to the world of the Red Fort, will have noted how complete was the assertion of British over Mughal past down to the renaming of the palace gates after Victoria and Alexandria. Saiyid Ahmad Khan, the historian, will have seen just how many of the monuments he had recorded in his *Asar us-Sanadid* had been wiped away. Zakaullah, the scholar, will have bemoaned the loss, as we all do, of the city's great libraries, that of the Imperial household, of Shah Waliullah's descendants, of Shaikh Abdul Haq Muhaddith's descendants, of Mufti Sadruddin, and of Nawab Ziauddin Ahmad Khan of Loharu which had supplied the manuscripts from which Sir Henry Elliot had compiled his eight volumes of translated excerpts on the history of India. Zakaullah, the man, as he visited the site of his Kuchah-i Chilan Mohalla around which many of the intellectual and cultivated families traditionally lived, must have shivered at the memory of the 1400 people who were butchered there as British bloodlust ran wild. Those 'reformers' who stayed in India, Rashid Ahmad Gangohi or Siddiq Hasan Khan, if they picked their way through the ruins which were strewn through their old haunts from Kashmiri Gate to Daryaganj, will have noted the palaces of the nobility destroyed, for instance Jhajjar, Ballabgarh, Farrucknagar and Bahadurgarh, the palaces of the mind that had gone, for instance, the Akbarabadi Mosque where the reforming tradition had been long sustained by the descendants of Shah Waliullah, and the palaces of the spirit that were no more, for instance, the *Khanqah* of the progenitor of the Chishti revival, Shah Kalimullah, and that of the sustainer of the Naqshbandi revival, Mirza Jan-i Janan. 'Harken to me,' Hali told his *mushaira* audience in 1874 'do not go into the ruins of Delhi. At every step priceless pearls lie buried beneath the dust ... times have changed as they can never change again.'[28]

The fate of Lucknow was little better. It was the largest pre-colonial city in South Asia with population of 400,000, the 'Baghdad of India' as Ghalib called it,[29] whose buildings were much admired by European visitors. Bishop Heber on seeing the Rumi Darwaza and Asaf al-Daula Imambarah in October 1825 compared it to the Kremlin, but thought it was better.[30] W.H. Russell, correspondent of the *Times*, wrote in March 1858 of 'a vision of palaces, minars, domes azure and golden, cupolas, colonnades, long facades of fair perspective in pillar and column terraced roofs—all rising up amid a calm still ocean of the brightest verdure. Look for miles and miles away, and still the ocean spreads, and the towers of the fairy-city gleam in its midst.'[31] Within weeks of Russell sending this despatch from the newly conquered city the demolition squads had set to work. Two-fifths of the city buildings were razed as a great swathe four miles long and half a mile wide was cleared along the river Gomti from Ghaziuddin Haidar's canal to well beyond the Jama Masjid, and wide straight roads were driven through the city, as Haussman had done in Paris, to enable troops to move easily to curb a turbulent citizenry. The Jama Masjid was turned into a barrack, as was Asaf al-Daula's Imambarah, and fifty or so *mohulla* mosques were seized and for two decades put to other purposes, some most demeaning. Fifteen years after the Mutiny uprising the population of the city was little more than 280,000.[32]

In the 1860s, as the Firangi Mahalis began to raise their heads to look about them, the magnitude of the changes and the shape of the new colonial world must have been clear. One wide straight road, Victoria Street, swept by the edge of their *mohulla*; if they thought about it they were fortunate to hang on to Aurangzeb's gift at all. Should they wish to pray in the Jama Masjid they now had to cross an open plateau full of rubble to do so; the focal point of the Islamic city was now an island on the outskirts. To the southeast, where once there had been the country residences of the king and the nobility, there was now the cantonment and the civil station, a world of straight-lined sameness so different from the *mohulla* arabesques of the city. As in Delhi, moreover, the railway was driven through the tight-packed *mohullas* until it reached a station, in this case fortified, on the far side of the city.[33] The few words we hear the Firangi Mahalis utter in these years, whether in *Karnamah*, the newspaper edited by Muhammad Yaqub, a member of the family, or in the *malfuzat* recorded in the biography of Abdur-Razzaq, are ones of suppressed rage.[34]

The extent of the shock of the Mutiny uprising and its aftermath is clear. To the 'modernists', who came from or were associated with the old elite of Delhi, it was evident that there was no future in the Mughal way; it was in a phrase Saiyid Ahmad used of the emperor himself 'a mouldering skin stuffed with straw'.[35] The events of these years had given a sharp and dramatic demonstration of how the basis of power had changed; to repeat the words of Hali, 'times have changed as they can never change again'. It was evident too to these men of the *sharif* class, who felt that power and privilege was theirs by right, that they must build a bridge between their world and that of British power if they were to maintain their status. The Aligarh movement, the fervour for things Europeans it meant, the cultural sacrifices it represented, the sense of urgency which accompanied it, had their psychological origins in these years. 'I could not even bear to contemplate the miserable state of my people,' Saiyid Ahmad told the Muslim Educational Conference in 1889 as it celebrated the anniversary of the founding of Aligarh College: 'it was my duty to share its misfortunes and do all in my power to dispel them.'[36]

To the 'reformers', conscious sustainers of the Waliullahi tradition of Delhi, the lessons of these years, at least to those who remained in India, were no less clear. Dreams of a military *jehad* must be abandoned. Now was the time for a *jehad* of the pen and the tongue. Moreover, because British power seemed so durable and so transforming, and because the *qasbahs* to which they had retreated were so evidently in decline, it became a matter of the utmost urgency to find ways of sustaining Islamic life outside the framework of the colonial state. It is against this background that the creativity of the Deoband movement, of which Muhammad Qasim and Rashid Ahmad were the founders, should be understood. We think of the new bureaucratically organized *madrasa* with the capacity both to survive its founders and to give birth to fresh *madrasas*, of the dependence of the organization on the subscriptions of the community at large rather than on grants from the government or the nobility, of the missionary impulse to spread Islamic knowledge as widely as possible both by printed word and by word of mouth. We also think of the 'protestant' style of Islam it helped to fashion, in which the sanctions which brought Muslims to follow the *sharia* were not those of the law, in part at least imposed by the state, but those of the individual Muslim conscience. The personal responsibility for sustaining Islamic society was taken yet further by the 'reformer' of our group who stayed in India, Siddiq Hasan Khan, a leading figure in the Ahl-i Hadith movement. Furthermore, the crucial role of personal responsibility in religion must be understood. It explains, for instance, the intensity of the 'reformers' quarrels with the followers of Ahmad Reza Khan Barelwi; whose beliefs in the intercessionary powers of the Prophet and of saints undermined that very foundation of human will on which the 'reformers' aimed to sustain Islamic society under British rule.[37]

To the learned and holy men of Firangi Mahal, the events of the Mutiny era brought division. Some freely cast in their lot with the colonial government. Others, particularly those in the circle of Maulana Abdur Razzaq, who was, it should be noted a Chishti Shaikh, did not. The Hanumangarhi *jehad* and the Mutiny uprising, it was felt, had been great tests for Muslims and they had been found wanting. 'The weakness displayed by the Muslims in the Mutiny,' Abdur Razzaq declared at the time of Russo-Turkish war of 1878, 'resulted in the calamities that followed. If you want to compensate for these and to be rescued from the calamities, you should help Islam and an Islamic country. Thus it is possible that Allah will forgive your past mistakes.'[38] So he founded the *Majlis Muid ul-Islam* in order to support the Ottoman Empire, toured India to raise funds, wrote articles and issued *fatawa* urging donations to the cause as a *jehad*. This same organization contributed to the early stages of the family's striking efforts for the defence of Islam from 1911 through to the early 1920s; this same spirit was present throughout. Family members worked for Islam at home in matters such as the Kanpur mosque affair and Council reform, and abroad, as the Ottoman empire went into terminal stages, the holy places were threatened and the Khilafat moved towards its end.[39] To place all this remarkable activity at the door of the family's Mutiny experiences would be going too far, but it had certainly helped to spur Abdur Razzaq into establishing their tradition of public effort for Islamic causes which reached a peak in those twentieth-century organizations it either founded or played a part in founding: the Anjuman-i Khuddam-i Kaaba, the Khilafat Committee, the Jamiyat al-Ulama-i Hind and the Anjuman-i Khuddam-i Haramain. Maulana Abdul-Bari, Abdur-Razzaq's grandson, was the leading Firangi Mahali involved in all these ventures, and it was he too who, in dictating his grandfather's biography to Altafur Rahman Qidwai, drew the connection between their work for Islam in the twentieth century and the shock of the Mutiny years.[40]

NOTES

1. 'Unseasonable tumult', chronogram by Ghalib—1273 AH/1857. Ghalib produced this chronogram in *Dastanbuy*, his diary of the events of the Mutiny which was published in Agra in November 1858. See Khwaja Ahmad Faruqi (trans.), *Dastanbuy: A Diary of the Indian Revolt of 1857* (London, 1970), pp. 30–1. The translation offered here is that of Ralph Russell and Khurshidul Islam. They note that 'rustkhez' means 'Judgement Day' as well as any great tumult or upheaval such as that caused by the stunning impact of a woman's beauty or the news of a friend's sudden death. Ralph Russell and Khurshidul Islam, *Ghalib: Life and Letters* (London, 1969), p. 247.
2. Quoted in the introduction to Hafeez Malik and Morris Dembo (trans.), *Sir Sayyid Ahmad Khan's History of the Bijnor Rebellion* (East Lansing, 1972), p. x.
3. Altaf Husain Hali, *Hayat-i Javed*, K.H. Qadri and David J. Matthews (trans.) (Delhi, 1979), p. 56.
4. For the life and work of Hali see: Gail Minault (trans.), *Voices of Silence* (Delhi, 1986), pp. 3–30, and Laurel Steele, 'Hali and his *Muqaddamah*: The Creation of a Literary Attitude in Nineteenth Century India' in *Annual of Urdu Studies*, I, 1981, pp. 1–45.
5. C.F. Andrews, *Zakaullah of Delhi* (Lahore, 1976), p. 60.
6. Ibid., p. 75.
7. S. Moinul Haq, 'Samiullah Khan and Mohsin-ul-Mulk' in *A History of the Freedom Movement*, vol. II, part II (Karachi, 1961), pp. 533–43.
8. Muhammad Sadiq, *A History of Urdu Literature*, (2nd edition, Delhi, 1984), pp. 375–78.
9. For the Delhi world of the 'reformers' see Barbara Daly Metcalf, *Islamic Revival in British India: Deoband, 1860–1900* (Princeton NJ, 1982), pp. 46–86.
10. For the life of Siddiq Hasan Khan see: Saeedullah, *The Life and Works of Muhammad Siddiq Hasan Khan Nawab of Bhopal (1248–1307/1832–1890)* (Lahore, 1973), pp. 21–53.
11. A.A. Powell, 'Maulana Rahmat Allah Kairanawi and Muslim–Christian Controversy in India in the Mid-19th Century' in *Journal of the Royal Asiatic Society*, no. 1 (1976), pp. 42–63.
12. Farhan Ahmad Nizami, 'Madrasahs, Scholars and Saints: Muslim Response to the British Presence in Delhi and the Upper Doab 1803–1857', unpublished D.Phil., Oxford University, 1983, p. 214.
13. Among the main promoters of this account are: Muhammad Mian in his *Ulama-i Hind Ka Shandar Maazi* (Delhi, 1963), whose argument is reflected in I.H. Qureshi, *Ulama in Politics* (Karachi, 1972), pp. 200–2. The most recent discussion along these lines is in Saiyid Tahzibul Hasnain Rizvi, 'Life and Works of Haji Imdadullah Muhajir-i Makki', Thesis

submitted for the degree of Ph.D. in the University of Calcutta, 1984, pp. 101–53.

14. The most thorough critique of the twentieth-century historiography of the Deoband school is in Mushir U. Haq, *Muslim Politics in Modern India 1857–1947* (Meerut, 1970), pp. 4–19. Metcalf, *Islamic Revival*, pp. 82–3, is also sceptical of the claims made by twentieth-century writers, as is Powell, 'Maulana Rahmatullah', pp. 58–61.
15. *Idem.*
16. S.A.A. Rizvi, *Freedom Struggle in Uttar Pradesh*, vols I–IV (Lucknow, 1957–61), II, pp. 145–49; V, pp. 381, 437; Nizami, 'Madrasahs', p. 218.
17. Saeedullah, *Siddiq Hasan Khan*, pp. 38–53.
18. Francis Robinson, 'The Ulama of Farangi Mahall and their Adab' in B. Metcalf (ed.), *Moral Conduct and Authority: The Place of Adab in South Asian Islam* (Berkeley, 1984), pp. 152–83; 'Problems in the History of the Firangi Mahall Family of Learned and Holy Men' in N.J. Allen, et al. (eds), *Oxford University Papers on India*, vol. I, part 2 (Delhi, 1987), pp. 1–27; 'Firangi Mahall' in B. Lewis, et al. (eds), *Encyclopaedia of Islam*, 2nd ed, supplement, pp. 292–94.
19. For a clear description of the complicated development of this affair see Michael H. Fisher, *A Clash of Cultures: Awadh, the British and the Mughals* (Delhi, 1987), pp. 227–34. From the government point of view it is covered in a remarkable file, Foreign & Political Consultations, 28 December 1855, National Archives of India; and from the Firangi Mahal point of view a version is offered in Altafur Rahman Qidwai, *Anwar-i Razzaqiyya*(Lucknow, n.d.), pp. 23–9.
20. For Firangi Mahal involvement in the affair see: Foreign & Political Consultations, 28 December 1855, nos 355–56, 389, 422, 429–34; Qidwai, *Anwar-i Razzaqiyya*, pp. 23–9; Maulvi Rahman Ali, *Tazkira-i Ulama-i Hind*, edited by Muhammad Ayub Qadri (Karachi, 1961), pp. 74, 177–78, 485–86,; Maulvi Inayatullah, *Tazkira-i Ulama-i Farangi Mahall* (Lucknow, 1928), pp. 53–4, 96–9. For criticism of the actions of Mufti Muhammad Yusuf and Khadim Ahmad see: Qidwai, *Anwar-i Razzaqiyya*, p. 27 and Rahman Ali, *Tazkira*, pp. 177–78, 485–86.
21. Qidwai, *Anwar-i Razzaqiyya*, pp. 27–8.
22. Ibid., pp. 29–30.
23. Muhammad Abdul Khaliq, *Salah Falah* (Lucknow, 1909), pp. 26–9.
24. Inayatullah, *Tazkira*, p. 209.
25. Qidwai, *Anwar-i Razzaqiyya*, p. 59.
26. Russell and Islam, *Ghalib*, p. 244.
27. Ibid., p. 252; the fullest analysis of the post-Mutiny changes in Delhi is to be found in Narayani Gupta, *Delhi Between Two Empires 1803–1931: Society, Government and Urban Growth* (Delhi, 1981), pp. 1–69; there is further coverage in Percival Spear, *Twilight of the Mughals: Studies in Late Mughal Delhi* (Cambridge, 1951), pp. 218–28.

28. From a *marsiya* entitled 'The Devastation of Delhi' recited by Hali at a mushaira in Lahore in 1874, Gupta, *Delhi*, pp. xviii–xix.
29. This falls in a passage by Ghalib bemoaning the fate of Lucknow: 'What praise was too high for Lucknow? It was the Baghdad of India, and its court—may God be praised!—a mint of rich men. A man could come there penniless and become wealthy. Alas the autumn should come to such a Garden.' Russell and Islam, *Ghalib*, p. 241.
30. Reginald Heber, *Narrative of a Journey through the Upper Provinces of India from Calcutta to Bombay, 1824–1825* (London, 1828), vol. I, p. 386.
31. W.H. Russell, *My Indian Mutiny Diary*, Michael Edwardes (ed.), (London, 1957), pp. 57–8.
32. For an analysis of the post-Mutiny changes made by the British in Lucknow see Veena Talwar Oldenburg, *The Making of Colonial Lucknow, 1856*–1877 (Princeton NJ, 1984).
33. Ibid., especially pp. 27–61.
34. Ibid., pp. 34, 111, 114, 121, 145; Qidwai, *Anwar-i Razzaqiyya*, p. 59.
35. Hali, *Hayat-i Javed*, p. 61.
36. Ibid., p. 56.
37. Metcalf, *Islamic Revival*, pp. 87–260.
38. Qidwai, *Anwar-i Razzaqiyya*, p. 30.
39. Francis Robinson, *Separatism Among Indian Muslims: The Politics of the United Provinces' Muslims 1860–1923* (Cambridge, 1974), pp. 262–356, 419–20; and Inayatullah's biography of Abdul-Bari, Maulana Maulvi Muhammad Inayatullah, *Risala-i Hasrat al-afaq ba wafat majmua al-akhlaq* (Lucknow, 1348/1929–30).
40. Qidwai, *Anwar-i Razzaqiyya*, p. 30. Lest it appear that we argue nineteenth-century action from twentieth-century sources, it should be clear that our understanding of Firangi Mahali attitudes during the Mutiny and afterwards does not rest purely on the Abdul-Bari/Qidwai biography of Abdur-Razzaq but amongst other sources, on the file Foreign and Political Consultations, 28 December 1855, the records of the Majlis Muid ul-Islam for the late nineteenth-century, Rahman Ali's *Tazkira*, and the vernacular newspaper reports.

Chapter Seven

Nation-formation: The Brass Thesis and Muslim Separatism[1]

For the student of nationalism the Indian subcontinent offers an enthralling prospect. Here lie a myriad nationalisms: some proudly embracing the framework of a nation state, some proclaiming their intention to do so, and others waiting in the wings. In his recent book, *Language, Religion and Politics in North India,*[2] Paul Brass has investigated the role of language and religion, two of the major symbols around which movements have coalesced in the making of nations. His primary concern has been to reveal 'the dynamic processes by which people come to identify their interests with their language or their religion, to build associations to pursue those interests, and to form bonds strong enough to build or to destroy states.'[3]

Brass focuses his analysis on the four areas on which students of emerging nationalism concentrate; the importance of objective differences between groups of people; the values of these groups and social changes taking place within them; the relations between these groups, and the different rates at which they mobilize socially; and the impact of government and politics. He sums up his argument thus: 'the process of nationality-formation is one in which objective differences between peoples acquire subjective and symbolic significance, are translated into group consciousness, and become the basis for political demands.[4] He discerns two stages in the process. The first involves the transformation of an objectively different group of people into a subjectively conscious community. An elite takes the lead, infuses certain objective characteristics of a group with symbolic value, defines its boundaries, creates a myth of group history and group destiny, and tries to communicate this myth to the group, particularly to its socially mobilizing segments. Essential to the success of this process is the existence of a 'pool of symbols' of distinctiveness to draw upon; an elite willing to select, transmit, and standardize these symbols for the group; a socially mobilizing population to whom the symbols of group identity can be transmitted; and the existence of one or more other groups from whom the group is to be differentiated. 'Of central importance at this stage,' declares Brass, 'is the relationship between rates of social mobilization and assimilation of an ethnic group in relation to another, dominant or competitive group.' When a group is mobilizing socially more rapidly than it is being assimilated to other groups with which it traditionally interacts, the ground is being prepared for the emergence of a new nation.[5]

The second stage in the formation of a nation involves the move from consciousness of community to political action. The group makes political demands and takes political action. Two conditions dictate the group's ability to do so successfully: it must perceive that the distribution of and competition for scarce values and material rewards is unequal and it must develop political organization to make demands. 'Government policies may intensify or moderate group conflicts, but the kinds of political demands made are likely to depend more upon calculations relating to the relative power of competing elites and competing groups in a political system than to the adequacy or inadequacy of government policies in satisfying group demands.' Political action lies at the heart of the process: 'the only proof of the existence of a nationality,' emphasizes Brass, 'is the achievement and maintenance of group rights through political activity and political mobilization.'[6]

Several points of theoretical significance emerge from Brass' argument. For instance, his concern to show that 'objective marks of group identity, such as language or religion, are not "givens" from which group identities naturally spring, but are themselves subject to variation', and his demonstration that nationalist elites, in developing identities, 'tend to emphasize one symbol above others and strive to bring others symbols into congruence with the primary symbol.'[7] Two points, however, stand out. First, the central importance which Brass gives in the first stage of his model both to levels of social mobilization and to the function of differences between rates of social mobilization and social assimilation in creating a consciousness of community. This means, of course, the central importance which Brass gives to the thesis of Karl Deutsch. He is concerned to test this thesis in an Asian environment. So, much of his argument is devoted to assessing levels of social mobilization, assimilation, and differentiation; and there are conclusions suggesting qualifications to the Deutsch thesis.[8] The second aspect is Brass' pronounced concern to indicate the influence of the political process itself in the business of nation formation. 'Political organizations', he asserts, 'do not simply reflect or transmit communal demands. They shape group consciousness by manipulating symbols of group identity to achieve power for their group. Moreover, the character of the political arena and the outcome of struggles for political power between competing elites within it may determine whether a communal group is mobilized for political action or not.'[9] Politics is not just the process in which nations are made, politics itself makes nations.

Brass' model is based on what are really four, though he regards them as three, case-studies of political movements centred on language and religion. The Maithili language movement in Bihar—a failure; the Sikh demand for a Punjabi-speaking state—a success; the rather unsuccessful attempts of Muslims in Uttar Pradesh (UP) to organize after Independence around the symbol of Urdu; and their extremely successful attempt in that state (then United Provinces) before Independence to organize around the symbol of Islam. The Muslims in UP who organized around the symbol of Islam were the heart of one of the most striking examples of nation formation the world has seen. It has stimulated wide study; its early stages also form the focus of my recent work as an historian, *Separatism Among Indian Muslims*.[10] It is an important as well as a convenient point to test Brass' model.

When he analyses the case of Muslim separatism in UP before 1947, Brass declares that his aim is 'to reveal the process by which the pre-existing differences separating Muslims from Hindus were emphasized, communicated, and translated into a political movement; the groups which took the lead in that process; and the choices which they made.'[11] He argues that there was little in the objective differences between Hindus and Muslims, and not much more in their revivalist movements to make their separation inevitable. What was crucial was the process of 'symbol selection'; and the fact that the Muslim elite chose divisive rather than composite symbols. 'Muslim leaders in north India in the late nineteenth century did not recognize a common destiny with the Hindus, because they saw themselves in danger of losing their privileges as a dominant community ...' So they chose to emphasize 'a special sense of history incompatible with Hindu aspirations and a myth of Muslim decline into backwardness'.[12] They were able to develop a Muslim political identity with success because they were well-placed in the social structure of the province, because they communicated the myths they selected to a socially well-mobilized population, and because they were able to create the political organization to do so. Brass sums up his argument thus:

> The course of Muslim separatism in north India suggests the importance of four factors in determining the success of a nationalist movement—the ability of a people to draw upon cultural and historical symbols to create a myth and to cultivate a sense of grievance capable of appealing to the sentiments of the entire community; the importance of a socially mobilized population to whom the sense of communal identification can be communicated; the existence of one or more elite groups in positions of economic and political power willing to take the lead in promoting communal identity; and the need for political organization. The history of Muslim separatism in the UP suggests several additional conclusions. The first is that the objective differences between Muslims and Hindus and the objective circumstances of the Muslims in the north were less important in creating Muslim solidarity than the objective process of symbol manipulation and myth creation ... The second conclusion is that, from the point of view of social science, what stands out in the history of Muslim separatism in not the ineluctable movement of events on an historically predetermined course, but the process of conscious choice by which men decide, because it suits their interests to do so, to emphasize the differences rather than the similarities between people ... The third conclusion ... is that, although there was considerable internal differentiation among the Muslim elites (as well as between elite and mass), which expressed itself in a competition for leadership within the Muslim community and in political differentiation among the elite groups, the three major Muslim elite groups did not differ significantly in their determination to defend and protect the separate rights and interests of the Muslim community ... Finally, the importance of politics and political choice as an independent variable must be stressed. If history does not exclusively determine the relationships between peoples, neither is it inevitable that objectively different peoples must choose to separate when they reach a certain stage of social mobilization. There must be, ultimately, political organization — and not only political organization, but political polarization.[13]

There are several points where my work endorses that of Brass. For instance, the ability of UP Muslims to draw on cultural and historical symbols with an appeal to a large part of the community was important. So too was the existence of powerful elites willing to promote a communal identity. That objective differences between Hindus and Muslims in northern India were not themselves great enough to fuel a separatist movement is also a point of agreement. So too is the argument that, though there was considerable internal differentiation among UP Muslims, there was a general concern to defend Muslim interests. On the other hand there are two aspects of Brass' formulation which seem fundamentally weak. They are the importance he gives to social mobilization and the failure of a group to assimilate other groups as rapidly as they are socially mobilized, and the extent to which he elevates the political process to being an independent variable in the business of nation formation.

Let us consider the significance of social mobilization. The course of the Muslim separatist movement in the UP, according to Brass, suggests 'the importance of a socially mobilized population';[14] and much of his examination of Muslims in UP is devoted to showing that up to the third decade of the twentieth century they were urbanizing, learning, and getting jobs in the modern sectors of the economy faster than the Hindus. He stressed that 'it was only through the social mobilization of the Muslim population' that the differences between Islam and Hinduism 'could be communicated and stressed to the mass of Muslims, whose religious practices and language did not differ as significantly from the mass of Hindus as did the religious practices and languages of the elite Muslim groups from the Hindu'.[15] Brass implies that the Muslim League, the organization of Muslim separatism, would not have had the success it did but for the support it received from a socially well-mobilized Muslim population. There is, of course, some truth in this, but it would be unwise to accept without question the idea that the League would not have been successful if it had not been supported by a socially well-mobilized population. Our knowledge of how the League won support between 1937, when it won a mere twenty-seven of sixty-four seats reserved for Muslims in the UP legislative assembly elections, and 1946, when it won fifty-one seats, is limited.[16] We know enough, however, to know that there were factors at work quite independent of levels of social mobilization. There were the loyalties built up by schools and families of *ulama* (religious teachers) down the centuries by teaching and writing;[17]

there were also those powerful allegiances, though slippery ones for the historian to deal with, built up through the mystic orders of Islam and the practice of *pirimuridi*.[18] Since 1947 there has been a tendency to play down the role of religious leaders and religious connections in winning support for the Muslim League,[19] and Brass is content to follow this tendency. But a preliminary investigation suggests that the networks influenced by religious leaders could be of considerable importance in winning votes whether it was a matter of fighting the Jhansi by-election of 1937 or the general election of 1946.[20]

A second factor on which levels of social mobilization have little bearing is the pervasiveness of the values inculcated by Islam. According to Brass 'it was only through the social mobilization of the Muslim population' that the differences between Islam and Hinduism would be communicated and stressed to the mass of Muslims.[21] The suggestion is that only urban, educated Muslims responded to Islamic symbols in politics while the illiterate masses of the countryside remained unresponsive. One difficulty with this suggestion is that the rather mechanistic urban-rural, great tradition-little tradition dichotomy is not wholly satisfactory in the context of Muslim settlement patterns in northern India. Large numbers of Muslims, of course, lived in the towns, but large numbers also lived in the myriad *qasbahs* and large villages where great Muslim families had been established for generations and which often surrounded former centres of Muslim rule. The seats of some of the great Sheikh families around Lucknow—Sihali, Juggaur, Masauli, Gadia—are excellent examples. These settlements were too small to be included under the heading 'town' in the census returns but their inhabitants, some of whom claimed descent from the followers of the first Muslims to enter Oudh, were as conscious of the 'great tradition' as any Muslim town-dweller. A second difficulty is that there are good reasons for believing that the Muslim masses, as Brass terms them, were aware of important differences between Islam and Hinduism and were not moved by the same symbols as Hindus. They had, in fact, a sense of Muslim identity, and they had it largely independently of levels of social mobilization in their society, although increased levels of social mobilization might make them more conscious of it. So the fact that rural Muslims took part in festivals which acknowledged the interdependence of the peasant community and celebrated the stages of the cultivating year did not mean that they were not also strongly susceptible to the sense of community bred by such Muslim observances as communal prayer, communal fasting in the month of *Ramazan*, and the shared experience of the Haj.[22] That rural Muslims worshipped at saints' tombs and observed caste practices, that their religious life revealed much of a syncretism associated with the 'little tradition', though so did the religious life of the Muslim elite, did not mean that they needed a member of this elite from the towns to tell them to fall in behind the green flag when the cry 'Allah-o-Akbar' was raised. Moreover, there is evidence that the consciousness of former rule, of 'we Muslims' who once governed the whole country, exists among the masses as it exists among the elite.[23] It is a mistake to assume that a sense of Muslim identity did not exist among the followers of the 'little tradition'.

These factors, the networks commanded by religious leaders, and the sense of Muslim identity shared by Muslims at all levels, were going to be powerful factors in mobilizing support for the Muslim League, whatever the levels of social mobilization. That some 'socially mobilized' Muslims were necessary is evident; that we should attach significance to whether their numbers were large or small is less evident. This conclusion moreover, is supported by the success of the Muslim League in the 1940s in mobilizing support in Bengal and the Punjab, where the proportions of 'socially-mobilized' Muslims were much smaller than in the UP.[24] Indeed, the fact that there was a large well-mobilized Muslim population in the UP might do something to explain the UP Muslim elite's early interest in Muslim separatism but it does less to explain how large numbers of Muslims came to vote for the Muslim League.

In deploying the Deutsch thesis, Brass is also concerned to demonstrate that nations are likely to be formed when a group is mobilizing socially more quickly than it is being assimilated to other groups with which it normally interacts—a suggestive hypothesis. In the case of Muslim separatism in the UP the argument works out thus: that, although Hindus were less socially mobilized in the nineteenth century than Muslims, they were nevertheless mobilizing more quickly than they could be assimilated to Muslim elite culture, and this helped to create the situation of conflict in which Muslim separatist ideas and institutions were bred.[25] But the argument rests on two questionable assumptions: that all Hindus could conceivably be absorbed by this Muslim culture, and that, even if they were, the powerful strands of identity in Hinduism could somehow be subordinated to this non-Hindu culture.

Take the first assumption. Muslim elite culture did not at any stage embrace all aspects of elite life; it was the product of a specific milieu—the government office.[26] It flourished in towns which were, or had been, administrative centres. Those whose work required only occasional contact with government, Hindu traders for instance, had no pressing reason to absorb Muslim culture. Moreover, they had down the centuries been the foremost protagonist of Hindu culture; founders of religious trusts, builders of temples, and supporters of Brahminical scholarship. Though leading Hindu traders and bankers were occasionally absorbed into the Muslim cultural world, the *bania Mohullas* of any north Indian town were sturdy bastions of a Hindu cultural world, and, however slowly they mobilized socially, Hindus such as these were unlikely ever to be assimilated to the Muslim culture of those involved in government.[27] But, turning to the second assumption, what if they were assimilated? Would they subordinate their Hindu identity to a greater Muslim cultural elite identity? The actions of those who were assimilated suggest that they would not. One of the foremost Hindu revivalists from the 1860s was a distinguished government servant and Urdu poet, Raja Siva Prasad.[28] Another was Jai Kishen Das, government servant, friend of Sir Syed Ahmed Khan, Secretary of the Aligarh Scientific Society—a man who moved with the stars of the Muslim firmament. It was he who in the late 1860s insisted that there should be Sanskrit *pundits* at Aligarh schools, supported the cause of the Nagri script, and attempted to set up a Sanskrit College.[29] When Hindus entered the government offices of northern India, when they mastered Urdu's rich and flowery tongue so full of Arabian and Persian resonances they did not leave their Hinduism behind them.

The Deutsch thesis, as deployed in this context, is a distorting mirror through which to see the processes at work in the UP society. Its emphasis on the socially mobilized sections of the population, its treatment of the non-mobilized sections as so much clay, exaggerates the role played by the elite in winning support for Muslim separatism and conceals the part played both by religious institutions which might link all levels of society and by religious values which were widely shared. There is much the same problem in the second element of the Deutsch thesis; the argument that the conditions for Muslim separatism were created when Hindus mobilized socially faster than Muslim elite culture could absorb them. This process did exacerbate relations between Hindu and Muslim. But the idea that Hindus could ever be totally assimilated into Muslim elite culture outside conversion to Islam is misleading. There were distinct differences between Hindus and Muslims and these were potential strands in two different national identities whatever the levels of social, cultural, and political assimilation in the nineteenth century.

The second area where Brass' formulation has weaknesses is in his attempt to elevate the political process to being an independent variable in the business of nation formation. They are evident in the very strong emphasis placed on symbol selection, symbol manipulation and myth creation—the image that is given of the UP Muslim elite from 1860 to 1947 largely detached from the values, the history, and the immediate concerns of their society, making political decisions purely in the light of their (elite) interests. They are also evidence of the small value Brass accords to the context in which Muslims and their politicians existed. Little significance in the development of a Muslim political identity is attributed either to the influence of Hindu revivalism, which infused nationalist organizations throughout the period, or to the framework for politics created by the imperial system of political control which was particularly concerned with Muslims.

Let us first examine the problems centering around Brass' argument regarding symbol manipulation. He claims that UP Muslims deliberately emphasized symbols of disunity as opposed to those of unity. 'Muslim leaders in north India in the late nineteenth century did not recognize a common destiny with the Hindus, because they saw themselves in danger of losing their privileges as a dominant community as the Hindus rose to self-assertion, and so they searched their past to find inspiration for retaining their privileges. Out of this search rose a special sense of history incompatible with Hindu aspirations and a myth of Muslim decline into backwardness.'[30]

The first problem is that the 'special sense of history' did not arise to inspire UP Muslims to counter the emergence of 'the Hindus', and though once in existence it did gain a purpose of this kind it was by no means its only purpose. The primary object of the historical and literary strands in Muslim revivalism was to give UP Muslims the strength to confront the British, and all that

British domination meant in terms of a new questioning of Islam, a dilution of the Islamic quality of life and a reduction of their political importance. All Syed Ahmed Khan's efforts should be seen in this light from the publication of *Asar-i-Sanadid* in 1847, though the Bible commentary and education projects of the 1860s (though these latter were designed to help not just Muslims but Hindus as well meet the challenges of the modern world),[31] to the foundation of Aligarh College and the publication of *Tahzib-ul-Akhlaq* in the 1870s. A similar concern is evident in the work of the Lucknow writer Abdul Halim Sharar. His historical romances were the works with the greatest impact, and the best known were produced between 1887 and 1907. They all have a single theme—'the portrayal of the glorious past of Islam and of the great superiority of Islamic civilization in its heyday over contemporary non-Muslim (especially Christian) powers'.[32] *Flora Florinda* set in ninth-century Spain is a classic example. Even as late as the second decade of the twentieth century when Sharar came to write of Lucknow in *Dil Gudaz* his over-riding purpose was to emphasize the superiority of the civilization of Muslim Lucknow at its zenith over the Westernized life of present.[33] Moreover this emphasis on an Islamic civilization in conflict with a Christian civilization persisted as a major strand in Muslim revivalism at least up to the end of the Khilafat movement. It is, of course, true that the historical perspective created to confront the British came also to be used as inspiration and justification for non-cooperation with the Indian nationalist movement. But it should be noted that the aim to resist Indian nationalism followed the development of Muslim revivalism and was at no stage its sole concern.

The second problem concerns Brass' insistence that UP Muslims emphasized Islamic historical symbols of disunity in preference of Indian historical symbols of unity purely because they coincided with their power interests. The assumption is that the UP Muslim elite were somehow a *tabula rasa* when they entered the political arena, and able to make decisions unfettered by religious or cultural preferences. Such an assumption is highly questionable. For many of the Muslim elite to look back to an Islamic past was instinctive rather than a matter of deliberate choice. Much of their lives they perceived and lived in Islamic terms. Some moved on the Muslim job-circuit within India—Hyderabad, Bhopal, Rampur. Many knew, or liked to think, that they were descended from Muslims who had come to India from outside. Many too looked forward to performing the pilgrimage to Mecca. Some had travelled the Islamic world outside India to study or to seek employment. For hundreds of years the Muslim elite of north India had received a constant flow of inspiration from the Islamic world outside, and their great interest in this world is illustrated by the explosions in newspaper circulation whenever it was troubled by crises.[34] As Muslim revivalism developed, the instinctive tendency of many of the UP Muslim elite to seek inspiration outside India was reinforced, and this no doubt helps to explain the speed with which so many were, in the first instance, swept into the Khilafat movement. Only part of the heart of the UP Muslim elite lay in Hindustan.

A third problem emanates from the 'myth of Muslim backwardness'. Brass produces proof, superficially convincing, that UP Muslims claimed that they were a backward community when knowing full well that their situation was quite the reverse. The argument centres on the Muslim position in education and employment. Examining the school and college attendance figure, Brass shows that in the late nineteenth century Muslims sent a greater proportion of children to government schools, and colleges than their proportion of the provincial population.[35] Brass concludes that Muslims who said that they were educationally backward were fabricating political myths. In doing so he misunderstands, or misrepresents, the UP Muslim elite's perception of their traditional function, their perception of the purpose of the government educational system, and the significance of the overall Muslim education figures as opposed to those relating to Muslims in government educational institutions alone. He assumes, for instance, that the UP Muslim elite, and indeed all in north India, would accept that their fair proportion of educational places would be the same as their proportion of the population. But he ignores the fact that the primary occupation of the UP Muslim elite was service in government offices and so they expected to be markedly more educated than the rest of the community. He also ignores the fact that the governmental educational system was thought to exist mainly to train government servants. If no more than 15 per cent of UP Muslims attended government schools and colleges it was not unreasonable for them to claim that they were backward in acquiring the skills which would enable them to occupy their traditional role in UP society, particularly as in the late nineteenth century government was regularly raising the qualifications required to enter its services. Further support is given to the Muslim claim by the overall figures for education. In 1881, 17.7 per cent of Hindus and 43.7 per cent of Muslims attending school went to private schools. In 1901 the figures were 13.2 per cent and 39.7 per cent. Evidently Muslims were slow to transfer from the traditional educational system to the government one, and this was likely to affect their chances getting into government service. Syed Ahmed Khan was not propagating myth but asserting the truth when he told the Hunter Education Commission that Muslims were backward in entering government educational institutions.[36]

Turning to the Muslim position in employment, Brass shows that between 1881 and 1921 the proportions of Muslims in all kinds of state employment went up from 34.8 per cent to 47.7 per cent, and of course the suggestion is that any claim made by Muslims that they were backward in this field is arrant nonsense.[37] Unfortunately Brass' blanket figures conceal wide variations of experience. The lesser service classes, most of whom would not fit Brass' definition of the UP Muslim elite, according to Brass' figures, improved their position, but the elite, Brass' 'symbol manipulating' group, fared badly. Their proportion of top government jobs, i.e. posts in the subordinate judicial and executive service, fell from 63.9 per cent in 1857 to 34.7 per cent in 1913, while in the elite's major alternative occupation of the law their proportion fell from 52.6 per cent in 1873 to 22.1 per cent in 1919. In comparison with their traditional expectations in employment the UP Muslim elite were by the second decade of the twentieth century very backward.[38]

A fourth problem centres on the extent to which the Muslim elite's choice of symbols may have been influenced by developments in the Muslim community as a whole. The picture which Brass paints of the elite selecting symbols not only in isolation from their values and their immediate circumstances but also without apparently taking into account the audience for which they were designed, does not ring true. Surely no elite is so insensitive to the society in which it lives. It certainly seems unlikely that the Muslim elite of northern India were. Those who edited newspapers, for instance, soon discovered that nothing sold their journalism more effectively than news about Islam and their fellow Muslims throughout the world.[39] Those who were concerned to work with or to influence the Muslim masses came to look more like orthodox

Muslims. Thus Shaukat Ali on becoming a pilgrim broker in 1913 put off his dandified silk shirts and donned a long green coat and 'on the erstwhile smooth cheeks and chin was now to be seen a shaggy beard ...'[40] This was something of a general trend. Were it possible to make an inventory of the wardrobes of leading Muslim politicians between 1900 and 1947 we would discover an increasing proportion of 'Muslim' as opposed to 'Western' style clothes. From Mahatma Gandhi to Mrs Indira Gandhi sensitive Indian leaders have reflected in their dress, the expectations of the groups they wished to lead. Even Jinnah was, from time to time, prised out of his Savile Row suits into a *sherwani*. Of course, the elite did frequently fill the columns of their newspapers with the language of Muslim revivalism as well as responding to the demands of the market. Of course the changes in the dress of men such as Shaukat Ali and his brother Mahomed were also part of their personal evolution from men who were Muslims primarily by upbringing to men who became Muslims by faith. But the point to note is that this was a two-way-process. Muslim leaders were not just trying to impose specific symbols on Muslim society, they were also responding to its preferences. They sensed that they were part of a society which was becoming increasingly conscious of its Muslim identity as Muslims from different spheres and different places came into contact with each other more frequently through the All-India Muslim Education Conference or the All-India Muslim League, through the Nadwat-ul-ulama or the Jamiat-ul-ulama, through the press which told them more about each other, and through the political system which encouraged the development of fresh vertical connections between elite and mass both by establishing separate electorates which created the need to win votes along communal lines and by driving politicians to experiment with mass agitation. Mahomed Ali described how the outlook of his generation changed in the first twenty years of the century: 'their mental and spiritual horizon has suddenly expanded and they have been brought into the closest touch, on the one side, with the old world conservatism and orthodoxy and on the other with the masses whose troubles they now begin to share as comrades in arms ...'[41]

There is, however, evidence for the Muslim elite not only being influenced by the preferences of Muslim society in selecting symbols but also having them to some great extent imposed upon them.

The Khilafat symbol is a good example. Though the Khilafat issue was adopted by some Muslim politicians and quickly exploited by others, with vast popular support it quickly outgrew the expectations of all, and many Muslim politicians were forced to adopt a religious political agitation that was opposed to their better judgement and to their political interests. Thus men such as Syed Riza Ali and Syed Ali Nabi mouthed Khilafat rhetoric and at the same time campaigned for seats on the UP legislative council in 1920, thus Wilayat Hussain, the government's major ally in Allahabad, was swept into the Khilafat non-cooperation movement in 1919–20, and only resurfaced in his traditional role in 1921, and thus myriads of local leaders stepped on to the Khilafat bandwagon in order to preserve their local position. Moreover, one imagines, though little is known about the way in which Muslim politicians jumped between 1937 and 1947, that many politicians were again forced to follow the herd against their better judgement. It is a naïve assumption that political leaders lead all the time.

These four problems associated with the way in which the UP Muslim elite selected and deployed myth and symbol makes them seem less free to choose than Brass suggests. That they emphasized the factors which divided them from Hindus seems much less a decision, much less a process of conscious choice, and much more product of forces beyond their control than Brass makes out. They stressed the myth of backwardness not because they were aiming to strengthen an already strong position but because they wished to shore up one which was rapidly deteriorating. They argued less with the deliberation of the strong than with the desperation of once strong whose strength was fast draining. They did not generate Islamic historical symbols to fight rising Hindu power but found them already forged and ready for use as a result of the process of coping with British domination and countering Christian civilization. If they emphasized these symbols of disunity, they did so in part because their values as conscious members of the world of Islam encouraged them to do so, in part because they were responding to social change among Indian Muslims, and in part because they sometimes followed rather than led their community. They were certainly able to make political choices but their range of choice was mightily hedged about by what Brass terms 'ineluctable forces of history'.

This was not all. The political choices made by the UP Muslim elite were not just constrained by forces within Muslim society, they were also limited by forces playing on it from outside—notably Hindu revivalism and British imperialism. The importance of these Brass also largely ignores. Hindu revivalism, for instance, Brass finds significant in the nineteenth century as a force which intensified the existing bases of religious differentiation and he quite rightly emphasizes in a sentence or so that its symbols were taken up by nationalist organizations.[42] But having made this tantalizing statement he allows the matter to drop; Hindu revivalism plays no further part in the development of Muslim separatism. This is surprising. An awakened Hindu consciousness was a prominent feature of north Indian life and politics in the twentieth century. Few Muslims in the towns and cities of the UP from the 1880s can have been unaware of Hindu attempts to impose their preferences on local religious practice. Few cannot have known of the Hindu University movement of the second decade of the twentieth century and the *Shuddhi* and *Sangathan* movements of the third. Few can have missed the flash of saffron under the skirts of the Indian National Congress. None will have missed the increasing 'Hinduization' of public life from the growing dominance of the Hindi press to the mainly Hindu idiom of nationalist politics. Did not developments such as these make it harder for Muslims to opt for unifying political symbols? Did not the presence in north Indian society of an increasingly clearly defined Hinduism assist in sharpening a sense of Muslim identity? It seems likely.

A further force playing on Muslim society from outside was British rule and the framework it provided for political development. Brass' attitude here seems somewhat inconsistent. In his chapter on Muslim separatism, government policy and the political system have no part to play in the development of a Muslim political identity. Yet in his concluding passage on nationality formation it suddenly emerges as a factor to be taken into account; separate electorates provided a framework within which Muslims could mobilize for politics as Muslims, and government policy was important in that it was prepared to endorse Muslim demand for separate electorates.[43] This rates the significance of government far too low. Government played a continuing role in enhancing a sense of Muslim identity and on occasion a crucial role in making Muslim political initiatives succeed, as a brief glance at the British system of political control and its working will reveal. This system is usefully seen as a gigantic web of patronage designed to win all who were powerful rulers of native states, landholders, social and religious groupings, trade and professional groupings—to government's side. Government identified those groups which were powerful and asked them to help in the business of ruling in return for which their interests would be given consideration. In this system Muslims as Muslims played an important part. Just why this should have been so is a problem which, unfortunately, has so far eluded thorough scholarly attention. Among the causes I would suggest are: the image the British had of Indian society, which was seen to consist primarily of religious groupings; the image of Muslims which the British carried with them from Europe—Muslims were described, on occasion by the most intelligent and tolerant of men, in language which seemed to date from the crusades; the abiding British fear in the second half of the nineteenth century that Muslims as Muslims represented the greatest threat to the Raj, and therefore had to be squared as Muslims; and then towards the end of the nineteenth century and at the beginning of the twentieth century there was the striking vigour of Muslim revivalism centred around Aligarh College.[44] But, whatever the reasons for British attitudes to Muslims, they meant that even before the development of elected bodies, Muslims formed with various landlords' groups the twin pillars of British control of the UP. As a result they received government patronage both official and unofficial, and without it, it is doubtful whether Aligarh College would have survived its early years, whether it would have grown so great, or its leaders so influential.[45] After the development of elected bodies Muslims with reserved numbers of seats in municipal, district, and provincial councils frequently maintained the balance which enabled the British to stay in control despite the apparent devolution of power.[46]

That Muslims played a vital role in helping the British rule the UP, as indeed they helped them rule India, was a fact of major importance in encouraging Muslims to organize on a religious basis in politics. First, if government, which was year by year interfering more and more in Indian life and controlling and redistributing a greater part of society's resources, handed out patronage to Muslims as Muslims, the odds were that this would encourage men to assume a Muslim identity in politics. It made the Muslim platform a useful one to adopt. This did not mean that the same men adopted the Muslim platform all the time; different groups did so at different times, when it suited their interests. But the fact that the Muslim platform was always a good one to use, that it evoked sympathy rather than resistance from government, gave the development of the Muslim political identity a momentum it would not otherwise have had. Second, as Muslims knew that their support was important to government, this gave them extra leverage in bargaining for protection of their interests, a fact which was always well-demonstrated when the British came to devolve further power on Indians. In the making of the Morley–Minto reforms of 1909, for instance, UP Muslims who controlled the Muslim League bargained their continued support for government against the concession of separate electorates and a reserved share of power. A similar bargaining can be seen at work in the making of the Communal Award of 1932, though UP Muslims were much less involved here. Indeed the Viceroy was driven to threatening to resign if the home government did not give in to Muslim pressure.[47] Third, because government took so much account of Muslims as Muslims the Congress had to do so too. After 1909 it knew that the best way of gaining further devolution from the British was to present a joint Hindu–Muslim front. Such a front could only be made by recognizing the Muslim League demand for separate electorates, which for instance Congressmen did in the third reading of the UP Municipalities Bill of March 1916 and the Lucknow Pact of December 1916.[48] So gov- ernment's attitude to Indian society led to the seeming paradox of the organization of Indian nationalism endorsing the demands of the organization of Muslim separatism.

The process of nationality formation is complex but in this context the role of government should not be underestimated. Government has traditionally bulked large in the minds of Indians and commanded greater respect than in many other societies.[49] The growth in the range and intensity of government activity has played a great part in working change in Indian society over the last hundred years. It has played no less a part, certainly not less than in many other colonial societies, in jerking Indian society into political activity. It is to be expected, then, that the framework government created for political development should have had some considerable influence on the way in which politics developed. When government was particularly concerned about Muslims before 1909, it played an important part in developing the

Muslim identity in UP politics. When government became less concerned to woo Muslims after 1909, and was indeed more concerned to woo landed groups instead, the Muslim identity lost force in politics, as was evident from the great weakness of Muslim League in the 1920s and the early 1930s.

Brass' work is an important attempt to build a model in which the processes involved in nation-formation can be understood. Those interested in nationalism, whatever the context, would do well to give it their attention. They should note in particular his attempt to establish politics as an independent variable. Brass' aim is to show that men who seek power can make nations. In a society where over the last hundred and fifty years the pace of modernization has been slow, and where it still has markedly little impact on most of the population, this inevitably means an emphasis on elites. The use of the Deutsch thesis with its focus on the modernizing sectors of the population plays an important part in sustaining this emphasis.

The endeavour is interesting. There may well be a level at which it is fruitful to see the political process as a force working largely independently of its social and ideological context. But Brass' model, considered in the light of admittedly only one but the most important of his case studies, needs modification. The political activity he depicts is too independent of the world in which it takes place. The example of Muslim separatism in the UP suggests that Muslim leaders were not just manipulators of their society but were also formed by their society as they interacted with it, that they were not just makers of social and ideological change but were also influenced by changes taking place in their community. It also suggests that more emphasis should be placed on the way in which the choices of elites were restricted both by their relationships with other protonationalities and by the framework for political development created by an increasingly active and pervasive government. The problem is that the relationship between the politicians and the world in which they operated has been too crudely drawn. If politics is to be discerned as an independent variable, it is not in the unwieldy categories deployed by Brass and the Indian census, it is not through the use of a thesis which appears to give so little weight to institutions and values shared by society as a whole, but in a sphere which is more closely defined and more minutely observed.

NOTES

1. An earlier version of this paper was given to the seminar on 'Language, Religion and Political Identity' at the School of Oriental and African Studies, London University. I am grateful to the seminar for its comments; I am also particularly grateful for comments made by Ralph Russell.
2. P.R. Brass, *Language, Religion and Politics in North India* (Cambridge, 1974).
3. Ibid., p.3.
4. Ibid., p. 43.
5. Ibid., p. 44.
6. Ibid., pp. 44–5.
7. Ibid., p. 45.
8. K. Deutsch, *Nationalism and Social Communication: An Inquiry into the Foundations of Nationality* (Cambridge, Mass. Second edition, 1966). Brass explains his approach to social mobilization and how he intends to use the Deutsch thesis in Brass, op. cit., pp. 32–6, and he sets out his qualifications to the thesis in Ibid. pp. 422–23.
9. Ibid., pp. 45–6.
10. F. Robinson, *Separatism Among Indian Muslims: The Politics of the United Provinces' Muslims 1860–1923* (Cambridge, 1974).
11. Brass, op. cit., p. 124.
12. Ibid., p. 140.
13. Ibid., pp. 178–80.
14. Ibid., p. 178.
15. Ibid., p. 179.
16. P.D. Reeves, B.D. Graham and J.M. Goodman, *A Handbook to Elections in Uttar Pradesh 1920–1951* (Delhi, 1975), pp. 246–47, 250–51. In fact, the Muslim League won overall twenty-eight seats in 1937 and fifty-two in 1946.
17. For instance, the connections built up since the early eighteenth century by the Firangi Mahal family of Lucknow. These connections played an important part in mobilizing support in both the Khilafat movement and probably the Muslim League campaigns from 1937 to 1947.
18. Many Muslims followed one or more of the sufi paths, and acknowledged a particular individual as their *pir*, or spiritual guide. The *murid* (follower) in the hands of the *pir* is supposed to be like a corpse in the hands of the washer of the dead. If the *pir* took an interest in public issues, as many did for instance in the Khilafat movement, he could bring many men and women with him. Moreover, a *murid* who took a different line to that of his *pir* had some explaining to do as Mohamed Ali had when he found himself supporting Ibn Saud between 1924 and 1926 against his *pir*, Maulana Abdul Bari's, powerful support for Sharif Husain of Mecca. A. Iqbal, *The Life and Times of Mohamed Ali* (Lahore, 1974), pp. 336–41.

19. Among the reasons for this tendency are the fact that Muslims in India have a powerful interest in stressing the loyalty of most of the Deobandi *ulama* and the Jamiat-ul-ulama-i-Hind to the Indian Nationalist movement, while leading Muslims in Pakistan, where the relationship between Islam and the state is a perennial subject of controversy, have had less of an interest in demonstrating the role which *ulama* and *pirs* played in winning support for the Muslim League, although religious leaders, particularly of the Firangi Mahal family, were prominently connected with the League's activities.
20. C. Khaliquzzaman, *Pathway to Pakistan* (Lahore, 1961), p. 159; K.B. Sayeed, *Pakistan: The Formative Phase 1857–1948* (London, second edition, 1968), pp. 202–6; I.A. Talbot, 'The Rise of the Muslim League in the Punjab 1937–46', unpublished paper delivered at Royal Holloway College, University of London, June 1977.
21. Brass, op. cit., p. 179.
22. The force with which a sense of Muslim identity was left at lower levels of society is stressed by Ralph Russell, 'Strands of Muslim Identity in South Asia', 6 *South Asian Review* (1972), pp. 21–32.
23. Ibid., p. 22.
24. Of course volunteers from the UP were involved in the League's campaigns in the Punjab and Bengal, but the bulk of the work had to be done by local men.
24. Brass, op. cit., p. 158.
26. The nature of the government office milieu is brilliantly analysed by D. Lelyveld, 'Aligarh's First Generation: Muslim Solidarity and English Education in Northern India, 1875–1900' (unpublished Ph.D. Thesis, University of Chicago, 1975).
27. For the world of the Hindu merchant and banker and their patronage of Hindu culture see C.A. Bayly, 'Patrons and Politics in Northern India' in J. Gallagher, G. Johnson and A. Seal (eds), *Locality, Province and Nation: Essays on Indian Politics 1870 to 1940* (Cambridge, 1973), pp. 36–48.
28. Robinson, op. cit., p. 434.
29. J.H. Garcin de Tassy, *La Langue et la Litterature Hindoustanies en 1874* (Paris, 1875), p. 90.
30. Brass, op. cit., p. 140.
31. Robinson, op. cit., pp. 84–98.
32. R. Russell, 'The Development of the Modern Novel in Urdu' in T.W. Clark (ed.), *The Novel in India: Its Birth and Development* (London, 1970), p. 123.
33. Abdul Halim Sharar, *Lucknow: The Last Phase of an Oriental Culture* translated and edited by E.S. Harcourt and Fakhir Hussain (London, 1975). In an article introducing the first number of *Dil Gudaz* Sharar stated his aim as being 'to stir people through the imagination by an effective description of their historic past and present-day conditions', ibid., p. 19.

34. Robinson, op. cit., p. 186.
35. Brass, op. cit., p. 145.
36. Robinson, op. cit., pp. 37–9.
37. Brass, op. cit., pp. 150–51.
38. For changes in the UP Muslim elite's position in government service see, Robinson, op. cit., 46, Table V, and for changes in the proportion of Muslims in those practising law see, ibid., p. 182, Table X.
39. Ibid., p. 186.
40. A. Iqbal (ed.), *My Life a Fragment: An Autobiographical Sketch of Maulana Mohamed Ali* (Lahore, 1942), p. 49.
41. Ibid., pp. 47–8.
42. Brass, op. cit., p. 127.
43. Ibid., pp. 425–27.
44. Robinson, op. cit., especially pp. 98–105.
45. Ibid., especially pp. 126–32.
46. For an excellent analysis of this process in the 1920s see D.J.A. Page, 'Prelude to Partition: All India Moslem Politics 1920–1932' (Unpublished D.Phil thesis, Oxford University, 1974).
47. In July 1932, in the midst of negotiating the Communal Award, the Viceroy wrote to the Secretary of State: 'What we propose is, I think, fair and equitable. Anything else would spell disaster and I can only add that if owing to your decision I lost their (i.e. Muslim) support as well, I should probably have to ask you to send out someone else to take up the role of Akbar ...' Willingdon to Hoare, 10 July 1932, Ibid., p. 260.
48. Robinson, op. cit., pp. 248–56.
49. W.H. Morris-Jones, *The Government and Politics of India* (London, 1964), pp. 15–16.

Chapter Eight

Islam and Muslim Separatism

There would appear to be a tendency amongst Muslims to organize in politics on the basis of their faith. Where Muslims predominate, organizations take the form of Islamic political parties such as the Muslim Brotherhood of Egypt or the Jama'at-i-Islami of Pakistan, whose aim has been to ensure that state and society run as far as possible along what they consider to be Islamic lines. Where Muslims form a minority, there frequently springs up a demand that Muslims should be organized as a separate political community, either as a separate nation state or as a state within a state. One excellent example outside South Asia is the Moro liberation movement of the Muslim Filipinos, but there is no shortage of examples within South Asia: there is the demand of the Moplah community of Kerala in 1947 for the foundation of a Moplastan within the Indian Union;[1] there is the formal request made by the Majlis-e-Ittehadul-Muslimeen of Andhra Pradesh to the Indian government in the late 1960s that a separate state for all Indian Muslims should be carved out on the east coast between Vishakhapatnam and Madras;[2] and there is the most striking example of this phenomenon, the campaign of the All-India Muslim League which led to the foundation of Pakistan as an Islamic state in 1947. Of course, the formation of religious political parties is not restricted to Muslim societies; it is a feature of societies whose faiths have a strong ideological content. So alongside the Jama'at and the Muslim Brotherhood we must set the Christian Democratic parties of Europe and Latin America. But the formation of separatist movements on the basis of religious confession, the assertion of a political identity on the basis of religion, which on occasion in modern times threatens to become a national identity, does seem to be an especial characteristic of Muslims. It is a characteristic which requires explanation.

One example of Muslim separatism, that of the Muslims of the United Provinces who were at the heart of the drive to create Pakistan, has received more scholarly attention than most examples. In his book *Language, Religion and Politics in North India*, Paul Brass has explained the phenomenon thus: there was little in the objective differences between Hindus and Muslims, and not much more in their revivalist movements to make their separation inevitable. What was crucial was the process of 'symbol selection'; and the fact that Muslim elites chose divisive rather than composite symbols. 'Muslim leaders in north India in the late nineteenth century', Brass writes, 'did not recognize a common destiny with the Hindus, because they saw themselves in danger of losing their privileges as a dominant community ...' So they chose to emphasize 'a special sense of history incompatible with Hindu aspirations and a myth of Muslim decline into backwardness'.[3] According to Brass, if Muslims organize on the basis of their faith in Politics, it is because Muslim elites perceive it to be the most effective way of keeping or gaining political power.

If this somewhat baldly stated argument, which implies that Islam is epiphenomenal, stands up in the case of the UP Muslims, we should have a useful starting point from which to examine other examples of Muslim separatism. But it does not. Brass, in his important attempt to elevate the political process to the status of an independent variable in the fashioning of political identity, has made his Muslim elites far too free to choose a separatist path deliberately as the best way of protecting their material interests. When UP Muslims emphasize Islamic historical symbols of disunity as opposed to Indian historical symbols of unity, he does not allow that these may have been symbols they preferred. When they parade the so-called myth of Muslim backwardness, he does not make room for the element of truth in the claim. Similarly he gives little weight to the way in which the choices of Muslim politicians may have been restricted by the preference of Muslim society, by competition from an increasingly assertive Hindu revivalism, and by the moulding influence of the imperial system of political control and the framework it created for political action. The realm in which politics is autonomous has been made far too large.[4]

In a separate essay Brass seems to have gone some way to meet this criticism. He acknowledges the role of the colonial government in encouraging Muslims to organize as Muslims in politics: the

British always being prepared to accept rather than to ignore the divisions of the societies they ruled.[5] Implicit in his analysis of the use of the cow as a symbol is an acceptance of the way in which Hindu revivalism not only limited the options of the UP Muslim elite but also those of Hindu elites.[6] Then Brass, in distancing himself from those he terms the 'extreme instrumentalists' who hold that cultures are infinitely malleable and manipulable by elites, suggests a further constraint of sorts. He recognizes that 'cultural groups differ in the strength and richness of their cultural traditions and even more importantly in the strength of traditional institutions and social structure' so 'the persistence ... of religiously-based communal institutions among Jews and Muslims wherever they are found means that these cultural groups always form potential bases for ethnic movements.' This means 'it is likely that the groups can be mobilized on the basis of specific appeals and not others and that, when ethnic appeals are made, the pre-existing communal and educational institutions of the groups will, if made available for the purpose, provide an effective means of political mobilization. In short, the values and institutions of a persisting cultural group will suggest what appeals and symbols will be effective and what will not be and may also provide traditional avenues for the mobilization and organization of the group in new directions.'[7] We may conclude, though Brass does not, that the rich resources for mobilization and organization which existed amongst the Muslims of north India may well have acted as an incentive to Muslim elites to organize on the basis of religion in politics. And an incentive to take one form of action as opposed to another is usually regarded as something of a restriction on an individual's freedom to choose.

The prime purpose of Brass's essay, however, is to analyse a further constraint on the freedom of elites to select and manipulate symbols. He is concerned to consider 'to what extent and in what ways the pre-existing values, institutions and practices of cultural groups with long and rich cultural heritages constitute primordial attachments that constrain elites who manipulate symbols of group identity for political purposes'.[8] And after analysing elite use of the symbols of the cow, the Sharia and the Hindi and Urdu languages over the last hundred years, he concludes that 'elites are indeed limited and constrained by the cultures of the groups they hope to represent'.[9] So implicitly as well as explicitly considerable constraints on the freedom of elites to manipulate symbols are acknowledged. The realm in which politics is autonomous has been greatly reduced. This is an important step forward.

However, when he concludes that elites are constrained by the cultures of the groups they wish to represent, Brass admits much more than he seems to realize. The argument which he uses with respect to symbols surely applies no less to all the ideas which might go to form the culture of a group. These represent the range of possible actions. And thus Brass's argument falls into line with Quentin Skinner's recent contribution on the role of ideas in political action. Concerned to demonstrate the dynamic relationship between professed principles and actual practice in seventeenth- and eighteenth-century English politics, Skinner argues that men in pursuing their interests are limited by the range of concepts available to legitimize their actions, and that this range of concepts is in turn limited by the prevailing morality of society.[10] Thus, in explaining Muslim separatism, account must be taken of the ideological framework within which the Muslim elites of north India operated. This would seem to make Brass's development of his original thesis a stride rather than a step forward.

Nevertheless, there is yet one more constraint of central importance which Brass does not seem to take into account. His elites seem to stand apart from their societies and their cultural traditions. They manipulate, they choose within their cultural framework apparently at will and only according to their political interests. Their rational pursuit of power is constrained only by the cultures of the groups they hope to lead and not by their own culturally determined preferences and beliefs. That this approach is unsatisfactory has already been indicated,[11] but the point would appear to need emphasizing. It is not just the masses but the elite who understand and pursue their interests within the frameworks of ideas they possess for understanding the world. Moreover, on occasion these ideas may act as a motivating force; in the mysterious dialectic between ideas and reality there are times when ideas are not just legitimizers of action taken for other reasons but also a prime force in directing the deeds of men. In our context, of course, it is Islamic ideas and values in their particular north Indian form which inform the assumptions and penetrate the consciousness of the UP Muslim elite. Nor does it matter whether we deal with the acknowledged holy man whose life consists of learning, prayer and fasting or the man in a suit whose visits to the mosque are rare; few, if any, will escape something of the moulding force of their culture's religious base. If for the holy man the Islamic vision of the world will be all-embracing, its power is often still strong in apparently secular men who have often merely made the transition from 'religiousness' to 'religious-mindedness',[12] while even the highly secularized usually carry with them some of the assumptions and preferences of the particular religious culture from which they have sprung.[13] Islamic ideas and values, then, both provide a large part of the framework of norms and desirable ends within which the UP Muslim elite take their rational political decisions, and act on occasion as a motivating force. Here is a further constraint on the autonomy of politics.

This essay will examine the Islamic tradition for ideas which might encourage political separatism; it will see, necessarily somewhat impressionistically, what parts of this body of ideas were received in northern India and how they developed there; it will then consider their role in influencing the politics of the Muslim elite of the UP. This last endeavour involves problems of method. Using the Skinnerian or Brass technique, all we need do is to show that the Muslim elite profess particular ideas in order to suggest their impact on political action. As necessary legitimizers of action they will place limits on the range of possible actions elites can perform. Thus far matters are relatively uncontentious. The problems arise when we confront the question of ideas as a motivating force. It is hard to know the springs of human action. All the historian can do is to suggest what might have been the case and stand by his judgement, which is no doubt an unsatisfactory method for the political scientist, but it is part of the historian's craft and he should uphold it. The best method of investigating motive forces is through extensive exercises in biography. We do not have room for such exercises here, assuming that enough information was available in the first place; all we can do is to use our judgement, based on what we know of the lives of the men concerned and of what others thought of them. Frequently we shall give weight to a man's reputation for faith. It seems reasonable to do so when in Islam no distinction is made between religion and politics and when, indeed, religio-political ideas are derived from the very word of God to whose guidance the believer submits in all things. For the faithful such ideas will have something of a commanding force. This is not to say that the faithful will be moved in all things and at all times by Islam. They are after all human. Nevertheless, their strivings as humans will be motivated in part at least by their desire to fulfil their vision of the world of God.

The particular aspect of the Islamic tradition which bears on the tendency of Muslims to organize on the basis of their faith in politics is the emphasis it places on the idea of community. Being part of the Muslim community is a central part of being a Muslim. The Islamic era begins not with the birth of Muhammad, or with the first revelation of the Quran, but with the *Hijrah*, the point when Muhammad and the Muslims left Mecca for Medina. This was the point when the Muslims of the Quraish tribe opted to place their loyalty to Allah before the ties of kinship. Now the *umma*, the community of believers, was advanced as the best of all communities. It was an especial favour granted by God to the Muslims, a charismatic community. The charisma can be seen at work in the major role of *ijma*, or consensus of the community, in the maintenance and development of the *Sharia*; 'my community', declared Muhammad, 'will never agree on error'. Muslims believe that it is through belonging to this community that their lives become significant.[14]

However, in forsaking the lesser community of the tribe for the greater community of the Islamic *umma*, Muslims did not leave all their tribal values behind. Some came to play a part in the new solidarity, most notably the tribal sense of *asabiyya*, or the brotherhood of those who belong,[15] which has been a value most strikingly manifest in Islamic history. We see it continually underpinning the idea of the equality of all believers. We see it in the career of the fourteenth-century traveller Ibn Battuta who was able to cross the world from Tangier to China, from Sumatra to Mali, be received as a brother by Muslims wherever he went, and frequently gain employment. We see it now in the immense interest of Muslims in Indonesia, in the break-up of Pakistan,[16] and in the partisan support for the Arab states from Muslim Filipinos,[17] or for that matter from Muslims throughout the world, whenever the Arab states go to war with Israel.

This sense of community is fostered by the key rituals of Islam. All confess their faith with the same formula. They acknowledge one book, and with minor differences follow one law. All pray in basically the same way and are urged to pray communally whenever possible, while the last act of prayer itself commemorates the community as the Muslim turns to his neighbour on either side in performing the salam. When Muslims give alms, and the mandatory requirement is often about one-fortieth of his income a year, it is to support the community. No one who has lived with Muslims in the month of Ramadan can fail to feel the powerful sense of community generated in the joint experience of hardship. The performance of the *Haj*, the fifth pillar of the faith, represents the ultimate celebration of the community. All focus on Mecca and the Ka'aba. All on reaching the land of pilgrimage don two white sheets, the *ihram*, in recognition of the equality of all men before Allah. They camp in their hundreds of thousands on the Plain of Arafat, and though they speak with many different tongues, and come from all corners of the earth, as they live through the first thirteen days of the month of Zu'l-Hijja they experience the reality of the community as never before. Of course, only a fraction of the Muslims perform the Haj in their lifetimes, but there are many who wish to, and know its meaning.

The sense of community is also fostered by the distinctive qualities of Islamic society and culture derived at various removes from the central requirements of the faith. There is, for instance, the custom of keeping women in strict social segregation from men. There is the use of the Arabic script for writing whatever local language the Muslim uses, a practice which has helped create 'Islamic' languages out of almost identical 'non-Islamic' ones. There are the typically Islamic decorative patterns, most notably the arabesque. Then there is the classical literature ranging from devotional and legal works through to belles lettres in prose and verse 'which have been carried wherever Muslims have gone, and transmitted from generation to generation, have formed the common background of literary culture shared among all Muslims of cultivation, those who maintained the norms of Islamic society'. Everywhere Islam went, writes Marshall Hodgson, 'there has been a continuous pressure toward persuading all Muslims to adopt like standards, like ways of living based on the Islamic ideals prevailing at a given time ... everywhere Muslims are noted for their keen consciousness of the world Muslim community ... and maintain in the most diverse geography not only the essential distinctive Islamic rites ... but also, to some degree, a sense of a common cultural heritage.'[18]

Further insights into the meaning of the community are offered by Muslim attitudes to non-Muslims. The latter were divided into two categories. There were *kafirs*, pagans, polytheists, atheists, who must be brought by holy war under the authority of the true faith. There were *dhimmis*, Jews and Christians, peoples of the book, who were allowed to live as tolerated minorities within the *umma*. Of course, they suffered disabilities. They were not, for instance, allowed to play a part in the running of the community, or to convert others to their faiths. But they were allowed to keep their religion, and they could if they wished become Muslims. In time the distinctions between *dhimmi* and Muslim became stronger. The *dhimmi* communities who contributed so much to the working of the early Islamic state and the intellectual development of Islam came increasingly to be seen in a hostile light, being recognized only to be rejected and their beliefs refuted. This process, which also signified the increasing mental isolation of the *umma*, reached its peak in the *millet* system of the Ottoman state. The *millet* was any religious group of *dhimmi* status. They were allowed to administer their own personal law and to manage their own education. Copts, Greeks, Armenians, etc. thus had their own identity under the law. Fundamental attitudes to non-Muslims seemed to lead inexorably to the creation of separate legal and social orders, and hence to suggest a separate political order as well.[19]

More flows from the Muslim attitude to non-Muslims than their desire to assert and maintain their distinctiveness. Also implicit is their sense of superiority. When they made themselves a separate community, as they fled from Mecca to Medina, the Muslims did so in the knowledge that theirs was God's path and that their fellow-tribesmen turned away from it. 'You are the best nation raised up for men,' Muhammad told them, 'you enjoin good and forbid evil and you believe in Allah.'[20] This sense of superiority was further boosted by the consciousness that Islam was historically final amongst religions. Muhammad's revelation was perfect because it brought to mankind the principles which made further revelation unnecessary. This feeling should never be forgotten either in assessing Muslim responses to the challenges of history or in understanding their relationships with men of other faiths.

Clearly associated with the superiority of the community has been its relationship with political power. It has been forged in the successful assertion of power, and the exercise of power brought a large part of the civilized world to submit within its first hundred years. 'Islam did not speak from catacombs ... it saw the way of truth as passing always through thrones.'[21] And reasonably so, because from the earliest days the possession of power had ensured that Muslims would be able to follow their faith. Moreover, the use of this power was as much a matter for God's concern as the observance of the fundamentals of the faith. 'To Allah belongs whatever is in the heavens and whatever is in the earth' declared the Prophet.[22] Church and state in the charismatic community were indivisible. So history and belief encouraged men to feel that Islam could be Islam properly only in conjunction with political power.

The symbol of the charismatic community was the Caliph (*Khalifa*), or successor of Muhammad. He was believed, for long in practice and always in theory, to be the divinely ordained head of the community. His task was on the one hand to lead the community in submission to God, to be the Imam, the model whom Muslims should follow. Thus he acknowledged his subservience to God's law, the *Sharia*. On the other hand, he was to use his power to create the conditions in which the *Sharia* would be preserved and put into effect, which in the long run meant enabling the *ulema* to guard and interpret the law. Until the end of the Ummayyad Caliphate in 750 AD, the political sway of the Caliphs of Islam matched the spread of the community of believers. But from this time onwards power in the Islamic world was dispersed amongst many rival Caliphs and Sultans. Yet 'The Caliphate did not cease to symbolize what it failed to embrace. It stood for the fundamental axiom of Islamic existence, namely that the state is the sign and surety of the faith and faith is the ground and seal of the state.'[23] That the *umma* and power should go hand in hand has always been a belief with astonishing emotive appeal for Muslims. 'Might', declared Muhammad, 'belongs to Allah and His Messenger, and the believers.'[24]

This was the ideal. Our purpose is to assess the impact of the ideal on north Indian Muslims. We need to see it flowing into their minds, interacting with reality and forming their actions. In doing so it is important to remember that, although we can comprehend the ideal in its entirety, intellectually, that is though not emotionally, it is unlikely to have been perceived thus by most Muslims. Theirs will have been an understanding, and perhaps an emphasis, on part of this body of ideas: on relations with non-Muslims perhaps, or the sense of brotherhood, or the feeling of superiority; some sort of understanding of the whole will have been reserved for few. Nevertheless, whether understanding was fragmentary or more complete, it helped to shape the Muslim's apprehension of the real world contributing both to the framework within which he made his rational political decisions and indicating the ends which he ought to pursue. In South Asia one of the hardest aspects of the real world which Muslims had to take into account was the fact that they formed a small minority in a population that was Hindu and polytheistic, *kafir* by the strictest tenets of their faith. This fact should never be forgotten because it raised in an acute fashion the problem of the relationship between the community of believers and power. Muslim attempts to cope with this problem offer us continuing insight into the enduring appeal of the ideal of the charismatic community.

Our primary concern is to assess the influence of the ideal that Muslims should form a distinct religio-political community during the rapid political mobilization of north India over the last hundred years. Nevertheless, we should understand the potency of this ideal somewhat better if we learn something of its impact on Indian Muslims in earlier centuries, and how it had varied with Muslim fortunes. Clearly, almost from the time that Muslims first entered India it had not been possible for them to live as true members of the *umma*; that possibility had finally disappeared with the loss of effective control by the Abbasid Caliphate in the ninth and tenth centuries and the rise of regional rulers. All the same, the writings of Indo-Muslim historians from the thirteenth to the eighteenth centuries make it clear that they saw the history of Islam in India as a direct continuation of universal Islamic history. The ideal was reconciled with reality by means of the 'pious sultan' theory. The *ulema* agreed that the central test of whether Muslims were living as Muslims ought to live was not whether they lived beneath the writ of the Caliph of Islam but whether they lived beneath the law of Islam. The local sultan was to fulfil the role of the Caliph, and, providing that he enforced the *Sharia* through *qazis*, or merely providing that he did not commit apostasy or force Muslims to go against the *Sharia*, he was not forcibly to be resisted. Thus the 'pious sultan' theory coped with the problem of the unity of the *umma*. But there was a second and rather more serious problem, that of the relationship between Muslims and non-Muslims, which in India bore so heavily on the relationship between Islam and power. Medieval Muslim regimes in India could not survive without Hindu support; they needed Hindu taxes, manpower and political authority. The problem of reconciling ideal with fact, of bending the Islamic vision of the *umma* to embrace a tolerance of, if not the equality of, the polytheistic Hindu, was hard. Sometimes the problem seems just to have been ignored; at others, Hindus were given the status of *dhimmis* and subjected to the *jizya* tax; while at others, and most notably under Akbar, whose expanding empire came to depend so much on Rajput support, they were treated as equals. The ideal was distorted greatly beneath the weighty logic of power.[25]

Not all were prepared to accept such a distortion. There was a fairly continuous undercurrent of dissent, particularly from members of the *ulema*. Most notable was the Mahdawi movement of Syed Muhammad of Jaunpur which, beginning in the Lodi period, laid upon each individual Muslim the duty of seeing that the *Sharia* was put into effect in its entirety. There was also the Naqshbandi Sufi order which came to have widespread influence under the Mughals and propagated a hostile attitude to Hindus. Indeed, whenever Muslim rulers found themselves in difficulties there seems to have been a demand for the strict application of the *Sharia* to Hindu–Muslim relationships. It was almost as though Muslims felt that it was because their rulers had lapsed in this respect that they were in trouble. It was to this sentiment that Aurangzeb appealed when, confronted by his rebellious Hindu subjects, he reimposed the *jizya* in 1679. By the beginning of the eighteenth century, Muslim writers who a hundred years before had written of rebellious Hindus as *mardud* or rejected of God, now wrote of them as *kafirs*.[26]

As Muslim power declined in the eighteenth century, as Hindus, Sikhs and Christians acquired increasing sway and Muslims found themselves cut off from the foundations of their culture in the central Islamic lands, the Muslims began to fear for the future of Islam in India. Their reaction was to distinguish between Muslim and non-Muslim yet more rigorously, to purify Islam of its Hindu accretions, and if necessary to use force to achieve these ends. When possible, and sometimes when impossible, Muslims tried to unite their vision of Islam with power. Shah Waliullah dominated this process in the eighteenth century. He aimed both to consolidate

Islam intellectually within India and to free it from Hindu accretions. Moreover, he was a man of action, inviting, first, petty Muslim princes to wage *jihad* against the Hindu powers to save the *Dar al-Islam*, and when they failed, turning to Ahmad Shah of Afghanistan for aid. For Waliullah, Indian Muslims were a community within India, but one in need of a Sultan because it was in danger of becoming 'a people without any knowledge of Islam or paganism'.[27]

The movement of Sayyid Ahmad Shahid (Barelvi) drew inspiration directly from Waliullah just is it drew support directly from his grandchildren. Sayyid Ahmad aimed to create an ideal Muslim community where individual and social life could follow the tenets of Islam unhindered. So in 1826–27 following the example of the Prophet, he fled from pagan-dominated India to establish his ideal state on the North-West Frontier. His followers waged *jihad* first against the Sikhs and, after the annexation of the Punjab, against the British, being active right down to World War One. In the same vein there sprang simultaneously in Bengal the peasant rising of Dudu Miyan, inspired by Barelvi, and the Fara'izi movement of Haji Shariatullah, inspired by Arabian Wahhabism. Both Bengali movements gained much support from peasant economic grievances, but the important point was that they strived to realize their vision of the Islamic ideal. There were similar strivings elsewhere, ranging from the scholarly movement of the Ahl-i Hadiths with its austere interpretation of the *Sharia* to the extraordinary *jihad* waged by some Sunni *ulema* of Awadh in 1855 against the Shia government with the object of putting a stop to the large concessions which had been made to Hindus and Hinduism.[28]

Thus, whenever the protective umbrella of Muslim power was lifted, or Muslim rulers obeying the exigencies of power in a largely Hindu society appeared to betray the Islamic ideal, there were Muslims who retreated to first principles. Their examination of these was likely, almost paradoxically, to drive them to try and reunite Islam with power. Not all Muslims subject to the growing influence of what has been termed 'shariat-mindedness' were likely to follow its directions to their conclusion. Such an outlook had obvious limitations for those who wished to survive somehow under the British, or in Hyderabad, or in Awadh up to 1856 where a universalistic Persian Shi'i culture arguably reached its peak in India. Nevertheless, versions of the ideal, much stimulated by increasing contact with Wahhabi Arabia and much circulated by those members of the *ulema* who were quick to seize the opportunities offered by the Raj's religious neutrality and the growth of the press, had been powerfully asserted since the mid-eighteenth century. The Muslim elite knew of them, and knew their import.

It would appear that Brass wishes us to believe that these ideas had no force amongst the UP Muslim elite as they led their community into modern politics. Their thoughts, all of a sudden, owe nothing to their past. Versions of the Islamic ideal, or the fragments of it they receive, carry no weight. The elite, we are asked to accept, have disentangled their faith, and the political values it generates, from their political thinking. As they select and manipulate symbols, if this is what they do, their prime consideration is how best to serve their material interests. Islam does not help to mould their apprehension of their interests and commands no end they wish to seek. It is merely a tool, and nothing more. Thus Muslims who write about the history of Islamic civilization rather than that of the Mughals, who move to defend Urdu rather than let its cause go by default, who direct their thoughts to men of their faith rather than to the Indian nation, are made to do so not because it might have been religious instinct, or cultural preference, but because, from a choice of possibilities, they saw these policies as the best mobilizers of support for their interests. Of course, it is improbable that we shall ever have the privilege of entering the minds of the UP Muslim elite which existed during the one hundred years before 1947, but it seems unlikely that Islamic ideas and values which were so significant in the past played no part in influencing the direction of their thoughts and in motivating particular actions.

Take, for instance, Sayyid Ahmad Khan. His role as the protagonist of Muslim elite interests, as the founder of Muslim separatist politics is well known. There is his attempt to rehabilitate the Muslims in British eyes after the Mutiny; there are his educational projects designed initially to benefit the Urdu-speaking elite but after the language question was raised quickly re-directed to benefit primarily Muslims; there is his political leadership which during the last thirty years of the nineteenth century taught Muslims that their best chance of preserving their strong position in north India lay in allying with the British. Throughout he fought hard to preserve the Muslim elite position in education, in jobs, and in the developing of a representative system of government. Nor did he allow any pan-Islamic loyalties to hinder this purpose. Though he, like most Indian Muslims, was sensitive to the international brotherhood of Islam, when it seemed that Indian Muslims might make much of their loyalty to the Turkish Caliph after the Russo–Turkish war of 1877–78, he was adamant that loyalty was owed to the British first of all.[29] The British filled the role of 'pious sultan'. Considering Muslims in India, he seemed at first to regard them as a *qaum* or nation within the Indian *qaum*,[30] but faced with the realities of Indian nationalist politics from the mid-1880s he made it clear that the Muslim *qaum* was the *qaum*.[31]

It is tempting to interpret, as many have done, Sayyid Ahmad's politics, his concern for the Indian Muslim *qaum* before all other considerations; entirely in terms of the material interests of the north Indian Muslim elite. But if we place his politics in the context of his whole life and work, the picture seems somewhat different. Though many detested his approach to Islam, no one who knew him seems to have doubted his faith. They could not because it was awe-inspiring. 'Man cannot forget God,' he declared, 'God himself pursues us so tenaciously that if we want to leave him, He does not leave us.'[32] Before the Mutiny, when his biographer Hali described his piety as 'terrifying', most of his writing was on religious subjects. After the Mutiny almost all his intellectual energy, greatly informed by the insights of the Naqshbandis, of Shah Waliullah and of Sayyid Ahmad Barelvi, was devoted to trying to resolve the conflict between religion and science,[33] indeed his endeavour to reinterpret Islam in the light of Western learning played a central role in his life.[34] 'Today,' he told an audience in Lahore in 1884, 'we are, as before [i.e. when Islam came into close contact with the world of Greek ideas] in need of a modern *'ilm al-kalam* by which we should either refute doctrines of modern sciences or undermine their foundations, or show that they are in conformity with the articles of Islamic faith.' If we did not 'reveal to the people the original bright face of Islam. My conscience tells me ... I would stand as a sinner before God.'[35] Islam had to be defended against the prejudiced ignorance of Western orientalists; but, much more important, it had to be interpreted so that young Muslims could imbibe modern science and remain Muslims. Sayyid Ahmad saw the world as a Muslim. This fact defined for him his nation, his first allegiance. And he was, according to Nazir Ahmad, 'intoxicated with love of his nation'.[36] As a Muslim, the conditioning of his

Mughal heritage apart, he believed it was his duty to make his people strong. 'The more worldly progress we make, the more glory Islam gains' was his motto according to one student of his ideas.[37] If he thought primarily in terms of the Indian Muslim nation, it was because it was his life's work to persuade Muslims to come to terms with the realities of the present, two of which were the political fragmentation of the *umma* and British power in India.

Most of Sayyid Ahmad's supporters were also men of deep faith. And for the most part they supported him in spite of what they regarded as his dangerous innovations in attempting to accommodate Islam to Western rationalism. Two of these whom, no doubt, Brass has in mind when he talks of he UP Muslims emphasizing 'a special sense of history incompatible with Hindu aspirations' were Altaf Husain Hali and Shibli Nu'mani. Hali's *Musaddas*, an epic poem describing the rise and splendour of Muslim achievement and its decline, was first published in 1879. So great was its impact that it became a kind of Muslim national anthem, parts of it usually being recited to inaugurate sessions of Muslim social and political organizations. And, although the work was commissioned by Sayyid Ahmad and had an impact which was far greater than anyone could have imagined, it was an outpouring of faith as much as it was calculated and successful propaganda. 'I was wholly given to religious fanaticism,' says Hali of himself in the early 1870s, 'and was prey to dogmas and orthodoxy. I considered the Muslims the very cream of creation ...'[38] Moreover the poem was in harmony with the Indo-Muslim historical tradition which saw the history of Islam in India as a continuation of universal Islamic history, and suggested too that the only history fit for study was that of Muslims. Shibli Nu'mani, poet, theologian, but primarily historian, shared this outlook, which was bolstered in his case by wide travel in the Ottoman empire and, despite all his professions of detachment, a desire to demonstrate the superiority of Islam.[39] Turning to Sayyid Ahmad's political successors we have a similar picture. Viqar al-Mulk, who played a leading part in Muslim separatist politics from 1901 till his retirement from the secretaryship of Aligarh College in 1913, greatly increased the Islamic content of education and daily life at the College, and according to Shaukat Ali, 'his example inspired us with respect for the grandeur of the Muslim life ...'.[40] Muhsin al-Mulk, the leading figure in the 1906 Muslim deputation to the Viceroy and in the foundation of the All-India Muslim

League, was profoundly interested in religious questions,[41] and declared his distinctly Islamic attitude to earthly matters in *Tahzib al-Akhlaq*: 'our worldly affairs cannot be independent of our religion. This applies to our politics as well.'[42]

For the *ulema*, of course, the indivisibility of politics and religion was an axiom. Although many seem tacitly to have accepted that the 'pious sultan' theory might apply to the British, the penetration of the modern state into their world and their growing realization that the control of that state was being devolved on Indians raised for them, in new form, the problems of the relationship between Islam and power and their relations with Hindus. They needed a new theory to reconcile ideal with fact. Shibli outlined the direction the *ulema* should take in his opening address to the *Nadwah al-ulama* in 1894. He attacked the idea that religion could be separated from the rest of the community's affairs. The concerns of the *ulema*, the guardians and interpreters of the *Sharia* were not just regulations concerning prayer and fasting but every aspect of Muslim life. 'The national life,' he declared, 'is in the *ulema*'s right of owenership ... and they alone have or can have absolute sway ... over it.'[43] Shibli's hopes for the reassertion of the control of the *ulema* over Muslim affairs, which of course meant that Muslims would be subject to the *Sharia*, came to nothing. The idea, however, lived on. It was the object of two associations founded by the *ulema* of Firangi Mahal in 1910, the *Majlis-i-Islah* and the *Majlis Muid-al-Islam*.[44] It was most powerfully expressed in the addresses of the *ulema* of Deoband and of the *Muid-al-Islam* to Montagu and Chelmsford in 1917, which government described as 'a nakedly impracticable demand for the predomination of priestly influence'.[45] Moreover, it was actually given concrete form during the Khilafat movement, through which the *ulema* came to have for three years great influence on Muslim and even on Congress politics.[46] By 1921 some of them were setting up organizations to administer the *Sharia*. In Bihar, for example, a system of religious courts was established in the districts, each headed by an Amir-i-Sharia, which were subject to a provincial court headed by an Amir for the province,[47] and this organization was still working in 1924.[48] Thus both in word and deed the *ulema* demonstrated their view of the kind of community in which Muslims should live: the only true 'Home Rule' for Muslims, declared Abd al-Bari of Firangi Mahal, would be the enforcement of the Sharia.[49] This did not necessarily mean that

Muslims need fall out with non-Muslims, but as power was being redistributed in India in the years before 1947 there was an attraction in the thought that the *Sharia* might be supported by the full force of state power.

For almost all the *ulema*, the ideal source of power of Muslims lay in the Caliph of Islam. During the modern Ottoman period, the Sultans had arrogated this position to themselves. Of course, that they should provide the conditions in which the *Sharia* could be enforced throughout the Islamic world was impossible. Nevertheless, the Indian *ulema*, in common with Muslims in other countries where they were in minority, tended to be powerful supporters of the Ottoman claim to the universal Islamic Caliphate and were concerned that the Sultans should have the power to maintain the claim; and in offering their support, expressed their sense both of Muslim brotherhood and of the significance of the Islamic *umma* of which the Caliph was the symbol and focus. Such ideas were strong in the Shah Waliullah school, particularly after his grandson Muhammad Ishaq migrated to the Hijaz, and they became strongly associated with the *ulema* of Deoband and the *Nadwah al-ulama*.[50] But such ideas or sympathies seemed to be no less strong amongst those members of the *ulema* who owed little to Shah Waliullah, like the Firangi Mahalis, who were in the forefront of the Khilafat movement.[51] In the late nineteenth century the pan-Islamic sentiments of the *ulema* were stimulated, as the Christian powers encroached increasingly on the central Islamic lands, as learned Indian Muslims travelled more frequently in the Ottoman territories, as Sultan Abd al-Hamid's sedulous propaganda had some effect, and as Jamal al-din al-Afghani's ideas began to hit their mark. These feelings reached a new intensity as the Ottoman empire came under the final assault before and during World War One. They launched Abu'l Kalam Azad's *Al-Ḥilal*, instinct with the ideas of Afghani. They spurred the foundation of organizations such as the Anjuman-i-Khuddam-i-Ka'aba to protect the Holy Places of Islam, and the attempts of Mahmud al-Hasan of Deoband and his followers to persuade Ottoman armies and frontier tribesmen to attack British India through the Khyber Pass. These feelings reached their peak in the Khilafat movement which was primarily designed to prevent the allied dismemberment of Turkey after World War One. British India was declared *Dar al-harb* and thousands of poor Muslims fled to Afghanistan. Many of the *ulema* launched themselves into the mainstream of Indian politics and for some years diverted them in their direction. And all was reinforced by Abu'l Kalam Azad's caliphal theory which insisted that 'no nation or community lives ... without a political centre .... The only possible political centre for Islam in the twentieth century is the Ottoman Caliphate with all its imperfections. ... The Ottoman Caliphate possesses the only sword which Muslims have for the protection of the Religion of God ... and it is not only the sense of brotherhood of Muslims but also the recognition that the Ottoman Caliphate is the last independent Muslim power that inspires the devotion of Indian Muslims to it.'[52]

The pan-Islamic vision of the *ulema*, and their concern actively to defend the institutions of their faith beyond the frontiers of India, found an echo amongst many young Western-educated Muslims. Two strands seemed to be uppermost in their minds: one was the sense of *asabiyya*, the sense of fellow-feeling with all those who bore the impress of Islamic civilization; and the second was the lingering concern that Islam should have power, and if an Islamic empire bounding the *umma* was impossible in contemporary conditions, the Turkish Caliph should at least wield enough power to protect the heartlands and holy places of the faith. When the young men were first moved in the years before World War One, the sense of *asabiyya* seems to have been the predominant strand. For instance, Hasrat Mohani was imprisoned for a newspaper article criticizing British educational reforms in Egypt. Iqbal, sailing past Sicily, bemoaned the end of Muslim civilization in that island many centuries before. Muhammad Ali made clear his concern over the fate of Moroco, Tripoli, Persia as well as Turkey. And his feelings were extraordinarily strong; when in 1912 he heard that 'the Bulgarians were only 25 miles from the walls of Constantinople—from Constantinople, a name that had for five centuries been sacred to every Muslim as the centre of his highest hopes', he contemplated suicide.[53] After World War One the pan-Islamic feeling of the Western-educated came to focus on preserving the Ottoman Caliphate, and the emotive concern that Islam should be linked with some kind of temporal power came uppermost. By this time changes had taken place in some at least of the Western-educated. They grew beards, replaced their Western suits with more 'Islamic' dress, began to read the Quran and discovered Islam. Thus the pursuit of a secularized pan-Islam drew men back to their faith. At the same time they built up close relations with the *ulema*, leading to the foundation of the Khilafat organization, which ran the greatest mass movement India had yet seen. After Ataturk's abolition of the Turkish Caliphate in 1924, which brought the movement in large part to an end, the pan-Islamic vision remained with some at least of the Western-educated, most notably the Ali brothers. As there was no longer any element on which their lingering desire to unite Islam and power could focus, their sense of *asabiyya* came to the fore again. They supported the Arabs against the Jews during 1929–30 over the Wailing Wall affair. They supported a plan to establish a pan-Islamic university in Jerusalem, which they envisaged perhaps as an Aligarh for the *umma*. And so it was in symbolic tribute to the sacrifices of Indian Muslims for pan-Islamic causes that the Grand Mufti of Jerusalem arranged in January 1931 for Muhammad Ali to be buried in the enclosure of the Aqsa mosque. Thus the pan-Islamic drives of Indian Muslims came to focus on Zionist settlement in Palestine which to this day they see not only as a stake thrust by the West into the Islamic heartland but also as a symbol of the shadow cast by the West over the Islamic vision of history.

The pan-Islamic feeling, which for some years was prominent in Indian politics and for a moment engulfed them, illustrates the latent force amongst Indian Muslims of Islamic ideas, and the emotional drives they derived from them. The material interests of various leaders were to some extent served by the pan-Islamic movement: they found occupations commensurate with their self-esteem, they found an income, their newspapers paid, they became the greatly admired leaders of their people, they acquired power. But it was not primarily for reasons such as these, and in some cases it was not at all, that men like Hasrat Mohani, Muhammad Ali, Abu'l Kalam Azad or Mahmud al-Hasan gave of themselves so freely and spent years in captivity. It was not for these reasons that they indulged in politics which had little bearing on the fate of Indian Muslims. Above all things they wanted to do something for Islam; they wanted to assert their visions of Islam. Common to most of their visions were the various key ideas associated with the Muslim sense of community. There was a belief in the reality of the *umma* and in the importance of Islamic brotherhood and the obligations it brought with it. There was belief in the superiority of Islam, which caused an uproar when Muhammad Ali announced that a Muslim of low character was superior to any non-Muslim be he Mahatma Gandhi himself.[54] And there was an overwhelming feeling that the Ottoman Caliphate should have power, that the *umma* should have a powerful political centre which was the nearest even these visionaries could come to unifying Islam with power in the modern world. If ever Islamic ideas created the frame within which men apprehended reality and acted on it, it was here. Pan-Islamism ignored the realities of great power conflicts, the conflicting ambitions of Turks and Arabs, the existence of nation states, but most of all the situation of Muslims in India.

Considering the UP Muslim elite in the years between the end of the Khilfat movement and the creation of Pakistan we are hampered, somewhat surprisingly, by a lack of biographical evidence about many leading men. No one can be placed quite so completely in the context of his life as Sayyid Ahmad Khan or Muhammad Ali, while even where there is evidence it is often of a secondary kind and, one senses, subject to the requirements of the polemic which surrounds the emergence of Pakistan.

Let us turn first to the *ulema*, who are conventionally, but quite incorrectly, regarded as opposing Muslim separatist politics as a group. Those of the *ulema* who did so were primarily those of the Deoband school closely associated with the Jami'yat-al-ulama-i-Hind. Until the 1937 elections they followed a course largely parallel with that of the Muslim League, being concerned to protect Muslim interests as they saw them against the power of the majority, by which they meant protecting the *Sharia*. And they were prepared to support the League, and other Muslim organizations so long as they worked in harmony with the Congress. But, when the League refused to cooperate with the first Congress government formed in the UP after the 1937 elections, the Jami'yat opposed it, and the *ulema* from the Jami'yat were prominent in Congress battles for Muslim seats from the Jhansi by-election of June 1937 to the memorable struggle for Liaqat Ali Khan's Muzaffarnagar constituency in 1946. They were implacable enemies of the League in word and deed.

The point which concerns us is how did the *ulema* of the Jami'yat reconcile their support for Indian nationalism with the tendencies to political separatism inherent in basic Islamic ideas? The answer is that they did not in any realistic sense. They were nationalist only in so far as they wanted to rid India of the British.

They saw the Hindus as a force given by God to help them in this task.[55] In everything else they followed the separatist tendencies of their faith. In independent India they were not going to be subject to the Indian Penal Code, but to the *Sharia*; they were not going to participate in an Indian education which might breed a sense of a common culture and common purpose, but they were going to continue to educate and be educated in Islam.[56] In the laws they observed and the values they cherished Muslims were to be a separate people in the Indian nation, or, as Husain Ahmad Madani put it, a *millat* in the Indian *qaum*.[57] The sense of Muslim distnictiveness persisted as strongly as ever. If they had to accept, temporarily, that they would have to deal with Hindus on an equal footing, their sense of the superiority of Islam, of its historical destiny, came through in their belief that, although the non-Muslim could no longer be made to submit by force, nevertheless, when he saw the quality of life lived by Muslims, he would freely choose the way of Islam.[58] This represented some considerable feat of reinterpretation, but it was nothing to the change they envisaged in the relationship between Islam and power. Whatever happened in independent India, they could not expect the state machinery automatically to enforce the *Sharia*. They knew that the Sharia would only be observed if Muslims wished it to be, if they saw it as a moral imperative—without state sanctions.[59] Thus the community lost some of its charisma. It existed less because God commanded it than because Muslims willed it. Muslims submitted no longer because of His awfulness and the power of His earthly authorities but through internal struggle and feats of will. God was no longer above but in the heart. It is tempting to suggest that the *Jami'yat* made it possible for Muslims to live in a Hindu-dominated India by pulling God out of the heavens and placing him within man. The final meaning of accepting the political weakness of Muslims seemed to be acknowledging the weakness of God to command.

It is not hard to see why so many Muslims should have found the position of the nationalist *ulema* unattractive. Their use of the principle of *ijtihad* seemed to deny so much of what many Muslims thought central to their faith. Fighting for a community which seemed to depend less upon the will of God than upon the will of Muslims had none of the appeal of the struggle for the Caliphate, and, as events turned out, none of the emotive appeal of Pakistan for all the attempts of the nationalist *ulema* to show how little the Western-educated leadership of the Muslim League would respect the *Sharia*. Large numbers of the *ulema* supported the Muslim League, indeed we may well learn, when more work is done and our understanding of the period is less shrouded by the mists of propaganda, that the balance of opinion amongst the learned men of Islam favoured the Muslim League and Pakistan.[60] Certainly, members of the *ulema* from a wide range of schools gave the League active support. Foremost, from the extremely influential Firangi Mahal family, were Maulana Inayatullah, principal of the Madrassa Nizamiyya, and Maulana Jamal Miyan, son of Abd al-Bari, leading member of the family and eventually Joint Secretary of the Muslim League. There were many influential Deobandis. Maulana Mazhar al-din, for instance, who helped to found the organization which broke away from the Jami'yat-al-ulama-i-Hind, the Jami'yat-al-ulama-i-Hind (Kanpur).[61] There was Mufti Muhammad Shafi,[62] the chief Mufti of Deoband, and Shabbir Ahmad Usmani,[63] a leading scholar or *hadith* and Zafar Ahmad Thanvi who, it would appear, practically single-handed, wrested Sylhet from the Congress in the referendum of 1947.[64] But most important was Maulana Ashraf Ali Thanvi, a leading Sufi with many followers and a scholar whose handbook on the requisites of Islam, *Bihishti Zewar*, was and remains an exceptionally popular guide to correct behaviour. He resigned from the management committee of Deoband over its pro-Congress stance and eventually came out publicly in support of the League.[65] A third school, the Barelvis, gave itself entirely to the idea of Pakistan from the early 1940s; its organization, the *Jamhuriyya-i-Islamiyya*, spread more widely throughout north India and devoted itself to propagating the necessity of Pakistan.[66] Indeed, the group was so committed to Pakistan that its leader, Maulana Na'im al-din, declared in 1946 that, regardless of what Mr Jinnah made of the Cabinet Mission proposals, it could 'in no circumstance give up the demand for Pakistan'.[67]

The reasons why so many of the *ulema* from these different schools supported the demand for Pakistan were, no doubt, mixed. For some, the Barelvis, for example, it was often almost a reflex action to take a line opposed to Deoband. Not all would have been exposed to the overwhelming hostility to the British which was so powerful an aspect of the Deobandi tradition, and thus would have been open to solutions other than the nationalist one. Personality clashes will have played a part with some; patronage will have influenced others. But it is hard to see why for most of these scholars of Islam the prime motive was not ideological. Not all who fought for Pakistan migrated there, while those who did often did so at great cost. Many were Sufis, and as they went to Pakistan they severed contact with the shrines from which they and their ancestors down the centuries had received spiritual sustenance and from their connections with which they frequently gained status.[68] When the *ulema* came to consider the idea of Pakistan, not all, like Maulana Maududi, who was not a UP man nor strictly an *alim*, but nevertheless a religious thinker of great influence among the *ulema*, were happy about the intentions of the Western-educated leadership of the League.[69] On the other hand, Pakistan did seem the better of two poor alternatives, and two strands seem prominent in the thought of those prepared to support the idea. One, which appeared to dominate the thinking of all, was fear of Hindu domination, fear that without power Muslims would not be able to survive as proper Muslims. Some had been horrified by the lengths to which Muslims has gone to win Hindu support in the Khilafat movement.[70] It was the same for the renegade Deobandis, the Barelvis and the Firangi Mahalis. Maulana Inayatullah of Firangi Mahal, a Congressman and a founder member of the Jami'yat-al-ulama-i-Hind, summed up the position when in the late 1930s he came to the conclusion that the salvation of Indian Muslims lay in the Muslim League and that the means to preserve the *Sharia* lay in supporting the League.[71] The sophistries of the nationalist *ulema* had an appeal for these men. Muslims must have power to protect their way of life even if the pan-Islamic idea of the *umma* might be compromised in the process. But frequently this desire to defend the *Sharia* was accompanied by the emotionally appealing concern to demonstrate the superiority of Islam, to restore its glory, which represents a second prominent strand in the thought of the learned men. 'Our attitude', Maulana Na'im al-din Barelvi told a conference of 5000 *ulema* in April 1946, 'was always governed by the dictates of Islam. At no time did we trust non-Muslims: now that the League took a step in the direction of the propagation of the ordinances of Islam, we opposed the opponents of the Muslim League for the glory of Islam.'[72]

During the 1920s and early 1930s Muslim separatism as a political force reached a low ebb. Western-educated UP Muslims were scattered through several organizations: the Khilafat Committee, the Congress, landlord political organizations, a shrunken Muslim League. Some dropped out of politics altogether. It was not till they understood the consequences of Congress power in the province after its victory in the 1937 elections that they came together in large numbers to support Muslim separatist politics again. From this moment till the emergence of Pakistan they were at the heart of the League's activities, dominating many of its committees and holding many of its top offices. Among them were: Nawabzada Liaqat Ali Khan of Muzaffarnagar, League Secretary and in effect Jinnah's deputy; Nawab Ismail Khan of Meerut, Chairman of the Committee of Action; the wily Choudhry Khaliquzzaman, a very influential member of the Working Committee, as was the young Raja of Mahmudabad, who gave the League the weight of his family name and much financial support. When it came to campaigning, students from Aligarh Muslim University played a major role going out in their hundreds, even in their thousands, to win the support of Muslims in towns and villages in Punjab, Sind and Bengal.[73]

Without the leadership and devotion of these Western-educated Muslims there would have been no Pakistan. Their motives are usually summed up as entirely self-interested. Religious ideology, we are told, can have played no part in moving them. On the one hand, many were not practising Muslims, so were unlikely to be impelled by a desire to realize an Islamic state even if they knew what such a state should be.[74] While, on the other hand, they had good reasons to create a separate Muslim homeland. Congress power revealed to them after 1937 what might happen to their culture and to their jobs and to their chances of ever being influential in an independent India, and so they fought for Pakistan to maintain their status and their power.[75] Much research needs to be done before we can be convinced by such an explanation, though the opinions of such acute, though committed, observers as Muhammad Mujeeb and W.C. Smith demand respect. Nevertheless, it need not be denied that an uneasiness about culture, jobs and influence in a Hindu-dominated India was an important strand in the thinking of many UP Muslims: Choudhry Khaliquzzaman is a good example of such men. But to see this as explaining all is unsatisfactory. There were, for instance, practising Muslims amongst the UP leadership. The Raja of Mahmudabad put his faith first throughout his life; he was a member of the Islami Jama'at, and as a believer in Pakistan as an Islamic state disagreed with Jinnah in the 1940s.[76] Even Liaqat Ali Khan, whose style and clothes always seemed so Westernized, is remembered by a contemporary as a devout Muslim.[77] Then, for many of these leaders, advocacy of Pakistan seemed to involve more sacrifice and selflessness than gain. Nawab Ismail Khan never went to Pakistan; it took the Raja of Mahmudabad some years to do so, while although Liaqat Ali may have been sated by the power he gained as Pakistan's first premier, he also lost his large estates in west UP and died a poor man.[78] But to discover religious conviction in a man or to point to apparently selfless action is not all we can do to suggest the influence of ideology. As we have stated above, it is a commonplace of secularizing societies that religious values still penetrate the consciousnesses, still form part of the subjective orientation to the world, of men who may no longer practise their faith. Such men may well hold with the conviction of deeply religious men secular values derived from the culture's religious base.[79] Thus a man may no longer pray five times a day, or look forward to the Haj or observe the *Sharia*, but he may still be moved by the sense of Muslim brotherhood, by a belief in the superiority of Muslims and their culture, by the feeling that Muslims live their lives best in association with power, and by the feeling that, although Islam and politics may be divisible, nevertheless, Muslim peoples ought to have Muslim governments. Such considerations help explain why the Muslim League was supported in its demand for Pakistan by Muslim minorities in both north and south India who could derive little benefit from it. Such considerations should also be thrown into the balance before the UP Muslim elite can be dismissed as crude manipulators of Islamic symbols, and their actions robbed of any emotional authenticity.

The ideas associated with creating and sustaining 'the best nation raised up for men' contained in the Islamic tradition (that Muslims form part of a community; that the laws of the community are God-given; that it is the duty of the ruler to put them into effect; that he must have the power to do so; that all Muslims are brothers; and that they are distinct from and superior to non-Muslims) have continually influenced many north Indian Muslims towards trying to realize the ideal religio-political community. Moreover, as a minority in the midst of idolaters, abiding concerns were both to draw sharp distinctions between the idolaters and themselves and to ensure that Islam lived hand in hand with power. Understandably, these were concerns which grew in force with the decline of Mughal power and the emergence of the modern state in non-Muslim hands. Their action is evident amongst the *ulema* whose very *raison d'etre* was to strive to create the *Sharia* community, and for whom ideas must frequently have operated as a motivating force. Even when the influence of these drove members of the Indian *ulema* in opposite political directions in the twentieth century, there is no doubting their separatist force. If those of the *ulema* who supported the League saw the creation of an Islamic state as the only way of protecting the *Sharia* when the British left, those who supported the Congress envisaged a Muslim future in India which was not much less separate and in which the sense of Muslim identity would always be made to compete strongly with that of Indian nationality. Turning to the secular, or secularizing elite, the influence of these ideas, though less direct and harder to assess, is still strong. Even without powerful religious sanction, which is not to say that many who were not members of the *ulema* were not deeply committed Muslims, they still underlaid men's assumption about the world and helped to form what were emotionally the most satisfying ends.

If this understanding of the formative influence of the ideal of the Islamic community on Muslim political behaviour is correct, it must be seen to work more widely than just amongst the UP Muslims, and so it does. Take, for instance, the Moplahs of Kerala who have shown for eight centuries that it is possible to survive as a Muslim community under non-Muslim rule. They have asserted with a practice of suicidal *jihad* the distinction between the Muslim community and the Hindus and Christians who lived around them;[80] in recent years they have demonstrated a powerful sense of *asabiyya* with Muslims elsewhere on the subcontinent; while the essentially separatist tendencies in their outlook are revealed in their strong preference to act politically through an exclusively Muslim party whose demand for the creation of a Moplah-dominated district of Mallapuram was granted in 1969.[81] This achievement, we are told, 'met an important psychological need';[82] within the limits of what was possible some of the Moplahs of Kerala had at last succeeded in combining Islam with power. We know enough about the Moplahs to sense with some confidence the way in which their vision of the world has been shaped by Islam, and how this has influenced their politics. We do not as yet know enough to assert the same of the Deccani Muslims who support the Majlis-e-Ittehadul-Muslimeen which demands to establish a separate Muslim state in Andhra Pradesh,[83] or of the Labbais of Tamil Nadu who identified strongly with the movement for Pakistan,[84] or of the Maharashtrian Muslims who in recent years have joined the Muslim League in increasing numbers.[85] But it seems likely that the ideal of the Islamic community did shape and still shapes their apprehension of what is legitimate, desirable and satisfactory political action.

Considering Muslim minorities in Asia more generally, a similar relationship between ideas associated with creating and sustaining the Muslim community and political separatism is evident. In the Philippines close connections have been drawn between the resurgence of Islam since World War Two, with a consequent deepening of religious consciousness and the growth of more orthodox religious practice, and the movement of Muslim Filipinos to set up a separate Muslim state.[86] In China, for centuries, large numbers of Muslims have resisted absorption into the dominant culture. Muslims have preserved their sense of superiority and distinctiveness; they have built strong communal organizations; and throughout they have enhanced their consciousness of the *umma* 'by cultivating in the Muslim the centrality of Arabia, Islam, the Islamic Empire, and Islamic traditions and values'.[87] Not surprisingly, they have not been able to identify with the unitarian Confucian and Communist states, and have followed a politically separate path as far as possible. 'China is not the fatherland of the Hui nationality,' they declared during the Hundred Flowers relaxation of 1956, 'Arabic is the language of the Hui people ... all the Hui people of the world belong to one family.'[88]

If the Islamic ideal of the religio-political community has such influence amongst Muslim minorities, it would appear also to have influence in states where the population is largely or entirely Muslim. Indeed, there is hardly a Muslim state in the world which does not have a party whose professed aim is to impose its vision of the Islamic ideal on contemporary politics and society. And whatever the motives of the leaders and followers of the Muslim Brotherhood of Egypt, the Jama'at-i-Islami of Pakistan, or the Fadayan-i Islam of Iran, there can be no doubt that their vision is formed, and limited, by the Islamic tradition. Nowhere has this process been more minutely observed in recent years than in Kessler's study of the rise of the pan-Malaysian Islamic party to power in the Kelantan province of eastern Malaysia. Here an anthropologist with an historian's perspective shows how in the 1950s and 1960s Islamic social theory continuously impinged upon and shaped political developments.[89] The experience of Muslim-majority societies confirms our understanding of the pervasive influence of the Islamic ideal, the one difference being that whereas in minority communities a primary problem is uniting power to Islam, in majority communities it is uniting Islam to power.

The fundamental connection between Islam and political separatism suggests further modifications to Brass's theory of nation-formation. To those factors that are already agreed to be significant:[90] the ability of UP Muslims to draw on cultural and historical symbols with an appeal to a large part of the community; the existence of powerful elites willing to promote a communal identity; the fact that objective differences between Hindus and Muslims were not great enough of themselves to fuel a separatist movement; the determination of Muslims to defend Muslim interests; the importance of competition from an increasingly assertive Hindu revivalism and the significance of the imperial system of political control, we must add the religio-political ideas of Islam, in particular those that stress the importance of the existence of a Muslim community. We see these ideas not only limiting the range of legitimate actions for the elite, which is the process implied (though not specifically expanded) in Brass's article for this volume, but also forming their own apprehensions of what was possible and of what they ought to be trying to achieve. Brass has made a bold attempt to delineate the realm in which the laws of competition for power are absolute. But the example of Muslim separatism would suggest that the area in which we can see politics as autonomous must be cut down yet further than he has been prepared to admit.

This conclusion has broader theoretical implications. Brass hints at its significance for political science in the discussion at the beginning of his article when he points to the fundamental conceptual differences that exist among scholars over the processes by which nations are formed. Some, the 'primordialists', argue that every man carries with him through life attachments (to birthplace, kin, religion, language etc.) that are the 'givens' of the human condition, that are rooted in the non-rational foundations of the personality, and that provide the basis for an easy affinity with other people from the same background. Others, the 'instrumentalists', argue, as Brass seemed to do in *Language, Religion and Politics*, that ethnicity is to be seen 'as the pursuit of interest and advantage for members of groups whose cultures are infinitely malleable and manipulable by elites'.[91] These are extreme positions; the answer, as Brass himself now suggests, lies somewhere between the two. He veers towards the 'instrumentalists' position in which the autonomy of politics is considerable. Nation formation, he says, is 'the process by which elites and counter-elites within ethnic groups select aspects of the group's culture, attach new value and meaning to them, and use them as symbols to mobilize the group, to defend its interests, and to compete with other groups'.[92] These elites are fancy-free and constrained only by the cultures of the groups they wish to lead. We propose that Islamic ideas had a moulding and on occasion a motivating role to play amongst the elites of the UP, that they seem to have played a similar role amongst the elites in other Muslim societies, and that the continuing power of these ideas suggests that the balance of the argument should shift more towards the position of the primordialists.

NOTES

1. R.E. Miller, *Mappila Muslims of Kerala: A Study in Islamic Trends* (Bombay, 1976), pp. 162–65.
2. G. Ram Reddy, 'Language, Religion and Political Identity: The Case of the Majlis-e-Ittehadul-Muslimeen in Andhra Pradesh' in David Taylor and Malcolm Yapp (eds), *Political Identity in South Asia* (London: Curzon Press, 1979), pp. 125–26.
3. P.R. Brass, *Language, Religion and Politics in North India* (London, 1974), p. 124.
4. F. Robinson, 'Nation Formation: The Brass Thesis and Muslim Separatism', *Journal of Commonwealth & Comparative Politics*, 15, 3 (November 1977), pp. 215–30.
5. P.R. Brass, 'Elite Groups, Symbol Manipulation and Ethnic Identity Among the Muslims of South Asia' in Taylor and Yapp (eds), *Political Identity*, p. 54.
6. Ibid., pp. 43–6.
7. Ibid., p. 40.
8. Ibid., p. 43.
9. Ibid., p. 67.
10. Q. Skinner, 'Some Problems in the Analysis of Political Thought and Action', *Political Theory* 2, 3 (August 1974), pp. 277–303. I am very

grateful to my colleague, John Dinwiddy, for drawing my attention to this article. Moreover, it should be noted that Skinner's argument goes further than stated: he points out that once a political actor has accepted the need to legitimize his behaviour, and has adopted a particular set of principles, his actions to be effective must be to some extent in harmony with the sources of legitimation he has chosen. This represents a further way in which ideas influence action.

11. Robinson, 'Nation Formation', p. 222.
12. This development is powerfully analysed and evoked in C. Geertz, *Islam Observed: Religious Development in Morocco and Indonesia* (Chicago, 1971), pp. 18, 102–7, 114–17. See also, D.E. Smith's more general assertion of the power of religious values among the populations of secularizing societies in D.E. Smith, *Religion and Political Development* (Boston, 1970), pp. 169–71.
13. D.E. Smith, op. cit., pp. 169–200.
14. W. Montgomery Watt, *Islam and the Integration of Society* (London, 1961), p. 204.
15. Ibid., pp. 174–75.
16. C.P. Woodcroft-Lee, 'From Morocco to Merauke: Some Observations in the Shifting Pattern of Relationships between Indonesian Muslims and the World Muslim Community as Revealed in the Writings of Muslim Intellectuals in Indonesia', paper delivered at the International Conference on Asian Islam, Hebrew University of Jerusalem, 1977.
17. P.G. Gowing, 'How Muslim are the Muslim Filipinos?', in P.G. Gowing and R.D. McAmis (eds), *The Muslim Filipinos: Their History, Society and Contemporary Problems* (Manila, 1974), pp. 284–94. Riazul Islam considers this sense of *asabiyya* to have been the most powerful force working amongst those Muslims who supported the Pakistan movement: Riazul Islam, 'The Religious Factor in the Pakistan Movement: A Study in Motivation' in *Proceedings of the First Congress on the History and Culture of Pakistan*, vol. III, Islamabad, 1974.
18. M.G.S. Hodgson, *The Venture of Islam: Conscience and History in a World Civilization*, vol. I, (Chicago, 1974), pp. 75–8.
19. K. Cragg, *The House of Islam*, 2nd ed., (Encino and Belmont, California, 1975), pp. 82–4.
20. Maulana Muhammad Ali, *The Holy Qur'an*, 6th ed., (Lahore, 1973), III, p. 109.
21. Cragg, op. cit., p. 76.
22. *The Holy Qur'an*, III, p. 108.
23. Cragg, op. cit., p. 78.
24. *The Holy Qur'an*, LXIII, p. 8.
25. P. Hardy, 'Islam and Muslims in South Asia', unpublished paper, p. 12; Hodgson, *Venture of Islam*, vol. III, pp. 59–73.
26. Hardy, op. cit., p. 13.

27. A. Ahmad, *Studies in Islamic Culture in the Indian Environment* (Oxford, 1964), p. 208.
28. Full descriptions of this extraordinary *jihad* may be found in G.D. Bhatnagar, *Awadh Under Wajid 'Ali Shah* (Benares, 1968), pp. 117–40, and in a diary of the *jihad*, Mirza Jan, *Hadikat us-Shuhada*, 1856.
29. Ahmad, op. cit., pp. 60–1; F. Robinson, *Separatism Among Indian Muslims: The Politics of the United Provinces' Muslims 1860–1923* (London, 1974), pp. 112–13.
30. See, for instance, the supra-communal emphasis of Sayyid Ahmad's political activities in the 1860s, Robinson, *Separatism*, pp. 84–98; and the wording of a circular written by Sayyid Ahmad around 1872 which talks of the Muslims forming 'an important section of the community', 'Circular from The Mahammedan Anglo-Oriental College Fund Committee' Tract 969, India Office Library.
31. A. Ahmad, *Islamic Modernism in India and Pakistan 1857–1964* (London, 1967), pp. 33–4.
32. Altaf Husain Hali, *Hayat-i-Jawid*, quoted in J.M.S. Baljon Jr., *The Reforms and Religious Ideas of Sir Sayyid Ahmad Khan* (Leiden, 1949), p. 86.
33. Ahmad, *Islamic Modernism*, p. 32.
34. C.W. Troll, *Sayyid Ahmad Khan: A Reinterpretation of Muslim Theology* (New Delhi, 1978), p. 223.
35. M. Siraj al-Din (ed.), *Lectures ka Majmu'a*, p. 210, quoted in Baljon, op. cit., p. 87.
36. Ibid., p. 12 n. 38.
37. Ibid., p. 88.
38. M. Sadiq, *A History of Urdu Literature* (London, 1964), p. 264.
39. Ibid., pp. 279–80.
40. S.M. Ikram, *Modern Muslim India and the Birth of Pakistan (1858–1951)*, 2nd ed., (Lahore, 1965), p. 120.
41. Muhsin al-Mulk was most powerfully opposed to Sayyid Ahmad's attempts to reformulate Islam, and emerges from his writings as a man for whom matters of faith were of the first importance, which was perhaps not surprising for a convert from Shiism. Baljon, op. cit., p. 74 and especially n.24.
42. Ahmad, *Modernism*, p. 71.
43. Ikram, op. cit., p. 140.
44. Robinson, *Separatism*, p. 276.
45. Ibid., p. 286.
46. Ibid., pp. 289–337.
47. Ibid., pp. 328–30.
48. Fortnightly Report (Bihar) for the second fortnight of September 1924, Home Poll. 25 of 1924, National Archives of India.
49. *Jadu* (Jaunpur), 21 May 1918, United Provinces Native Newspaper Reports, 1918.

50. Ahmad, *Modernism*, pp. 123–24.
51. Robinson, *Separatism*, pp. 289–325 and especially p. 325.
52. P. Hardy, *Partners in Freedom—and True Muslims: The Political Thought of Some Muslim Scholars in British India 1912–1947* (Lund, 1971), p. 22.
53. A. Iqbal (ed.), *My Life: A Fragment: An Autobiographical Sketch of Maulana Mohammed Ali* (Lahore, 1942), p. 35; the English novelist, E.M. Forster, witnessed this moment in Muhammad Ali's life. P.N. Furbank, *E.M. Forster: A Life*, vol. I, (London, 1977), pp. 228–29.
54. A. Iqbal, *Life and Times of Mohamed Ali: An Analysis of the Hopes, Fears and Aspirations of Muslim India from 1778 to 1931* (Lahore, 1974), p. 313.
55. Hardy, *Partners*, p. 32.
56. Ibid., p. 41.
57. Ibid., pp. 37–8.
58. Ibid., p. 35.
59. Ibid., pp. 40–1.
60. I.H. Qureshi, *Ulema in Politics: A Study Relating to the Political Activities of the Ulema in the South-Asian Subcontinent from 1556 to 1947* (Karachi, 1972), p. 360.
61. Ibid., p. 357
62. Ibid., pp. 362–63.
63. Ibid., pp. 360–62.
64. Ibid., p. 362.
65. Ibid., pp.358–59; Z. Faruqi, *The Deoband School and the Demand for Pakistan* (Bombay, 1963), p. 102 n.4.
66. Qureshi, op. cit., pp. 365–66.
67. Ibid., p. 366.
68. For instance, those Firangi Mahalis who migrated to Pakistan, for the greater part, severed connections with the Qadiri shrine of Shah Abd al-Razzaq of Bansa which for 200 years had both supplied them with spiritual resources and, by giving them great prominence at the Urs, added status. They also lost contact with another important spiritual resource which was derived from Bagh Maulana Anwar in Lucknow where most of their ancestors, some of whom were saints, were buried. Together with these spiritual losses, deeply felt, they cut themselves off from a family tradition built up over 250 years, and sacrificed the benefits derived from an eminent position founded on spiritual and intellectual leadership over that period.
69. L. Binder, *Religion and Politics in Pakistan* (Berkeley, 1963), pp. 94–5.
70. Qureshi, op. cit., pp. 358–59.
71. Sibghat Allah Shahid Ansari, *Sadr al-Mudarrisin* (Lucknow, 1941), p. 73.
72. Qureshi, op. cit., p. 366.
73. K.B. Sayeed, *Pakistan: The Formative Phase 1857–1948*, 2nd ed., (London, 1968), p. 200; I.A. Talbot, 'The 1946 Punjab Provincial Elections', paper delivered at Royal Holloway College, University of London, June 1978.

74. M. Mujeeb, 'The Partition of India in Retrospect' in C.H. Philips and M.D. Wainwright (eds), *The Partition of India: Policies and Perspectives 1935–1947* (London, 1970), p. 408.
75. Ibid., p. 410 and W.C. Smith, *Modern Islam in India* (London, 1946), especially pp. 246–92.
76. The Raja of Mahmudabad, 'Some Memories' in Philips and Wainwright, op. cit., pp. 388–89.
77. I.H. Qureshi, 'Liaquat—The Ideal Muslim' in Z. Ahmad (ed.), *Liaquat Ali Khan: Leader and Statesman* (Karachi, 1970), pp. 80–3.
78. Ibid., p. 82.
79. D.E. Smith, op. cit., pp. 169–200.
80. S.F. Dale, 'The Islamic Frontier in Southwest India: The Shahid as a Cultural Ideal among the Mappillas of Malabar', *Modern Asian Studies* 11, 1, pp. 41–56.
81. Miller, op. cit., pp. 176–83.
82. Ibid., p. 183.
83. Ram Reddy, op. cit.
84. M. Mines, 'Labbai' in R.V. Weekes (ed.), *Muslim People: A world Ethnographic Survey* (Connecticut, 1978), pp. 227–31.
85. M. Shakir and U.B. Bhoite, 'Maharashtrians', ibid., pp. 246–50.
86. C.L. Reimer, 'Maranao', ibid., pp. 267–72 and P.G. Gowing, 'The Muslim Filipinos' in Gowing and McAmis, op. cit., pp. 288–90.
87. R. Israeli, 'Muslims in China: The Incompatibility between Islam and the Chinese Order', paper delivered at the International Conference on Asian Islam, Hebrew University of Jerusalem, 1977, pp. 25–6.
88. Ibid., p. 29.
89. C.S. Kessler, *Islam and Politics in a Malay State: Kelantan 1838–1969* (Ithaca, 1978), especially pp. 208–34.
90. I must reiterate that I cannot accept the significance Brass gives to social mobilization, Robinson, 'Nation Formation', op. cit., pp. 218–21, and this position has recently been further emphasized by the detailed research of Ian Talbot on the Muslim League's rise to power in the Punjab in the 1940s: Talbot, op. cit.
91. Brass, above, p. 39.
92. Above, p. 41.

Chapter Nine

The Congress and the Muslims

The achievement of no colonial nationalist movement is as striking as that of the Indian National Congress: it led the most diverse peoples of the world against the greatest of the imperial powers; it developed new forms of protest which limited the number of lives lost in action against the colonial state; it concluded its struggle with the colonial power in a manner which was both gracious and statesmanlike; it went on to form a constitution which tempered idealism with a sound sense of political reality; it then proceeded to work this framework for political development in a way which seemed to offer a greater degree of constitutional government and a greater degree of respect for the rule of law than most post-colonial societies have experienced. On the other hand, no colonial nationalist movement had to submit, at the moment of victory, to such a grievous partition of its territories and peoples: the loss of more than one fifth of the population, of half of the army, of the substantial resources which went to form the new Muslim state of Pakistan. It is clear that the failure of the Indian National Congress either to cherish within its fold substantial numbers of Indian Muslims, or to make deals with Muslim separatist groups which would encourage them to work within the Indian Nationalist movement, must remain the greatest question mark, beside its achievement.

The main lines of argument, which have been deployed to explain why Congress dealings with Muslims were in general unsuccessful, are well known; they are, of course, those used to explain the obverse of the coin, Muslim separatism and its success. We rehearse them briefly now as they form our point of departure.

One argument was put forward long ago by W.W. Hunter. He

argued that Muslims had been discriminated against by the British, that they had been slow in taking advantage of Western education, and as a result had fallen behind in the competition for jobs and economic advancement. This theory of Muslim backwardness was loudly repeated by Muslims in the late nineteenth century. It subsequently found favour both with Marxist and with Muslim historians in explaining why Muslims should not be keen to join the Congress.[1] Undoubtedly true when applied, for instance, to the Muslims of Bengal, or those of Sind, the argument was distinctly dubious when applied to the Muslims of the UP, who for much of the time were both the leaders of all-India Muslim politics and the loudest in making the claim. Over the last two decades the position of the UP Muslims has been examined with some care, and it quickly emerged that, far from being backward, they were, if anything, forward in matters of education and employment and that the reasons why they might be unwilling to join the Congress might derive more from a desire to protect a strong position than to improve a weak one—it was, furthermore, an argument as true for their responses to the Congress between 1937 and 1939 as it was for their responses between 1885 and 1906.[2]

A second line of argument has been that the British deliberately created division in Indian society for their own imperial purpose, and this led to Muslims being discouraged from joining the nationalist movement. More sophisticated versions of this argument see less the deliberate fomenting of division on the part of the British than a desperate search for allies in Indian society which meant, as political circumstances changed, that the imperial power would throw its weight first behind one group, and then behind another, as it sought to prop up its rule. Whatever the level of sophistication, this is an argument which the early Indian nationalist historians found particularly attractive; they were able to play down the shortcomings of their own movement and to blame the imperial overlord for having destroyed an evolving synthesis of Hindu–Muslim politics and culture.[3] More recently this line of argument has, in part at least, received some support from Britain itself. One major concern of the so-called Cambridge School of South Asian historians has been to show that the assumptions that the British made about Indian society, their vision of it, influenced the way in which they approached it, and thus provided the channels along which their patronage flowed. Instinct in this approach is the belief that the developing form of the colonial state helped to fashion the growing shape of nationalist politics.[4]

A third line of argument focuses on Hindu communalism. If Muslims did not want to join the Indian National Congress, the argument goes, it was in part at least because the Congress never truly developed a secular ethos; its symbols, its idiom, its inspiration were all Hindu; it was frequently associated with aggressive Hindu revivalism. In the same way, if the All-India Muslim League and the Congress found it increasingly difficult to reach compromises over the future structure of power, and their individual shares of it, it was because of the influence of Hindu communalists in the nationalist movement. This position had strong support at the time from Congress Muslims and Congress socialists; it still has today.[5]

The fourth line of argument is, of course, what the Indian nationalist would term Muslim communalism, and what in Pakistan has come to be known as the two-nation theory. 'It is extremely difficult,' declared Jinnah in his presidential address to the Lahore session of the All-India Muslim League in 1940,

> to appreciate why our Hindu friends fail to understand the real nature of Islam and Hinduism. They are not religions in the strict sense of the word, but are, in fact, different and distinct social orders, and it is a dream that the Hindus and Muslims can ever evolve a common nationality ... They neither intermarry nor interdine together and, indeed, belong to two different civilisations which are based mainly on conflicting ideas and conceptions. Their aspects on life and of life are different ... their inspiration from different sources of history. They have different epics, different heroes, different episodes. Very often the hero of one is a foe of the other and, likewise, their victories and defeats overlap. To yoke together two such nations under a single state, one as a numerical minority and the other a majority, must lead to growing discontent and final destruction of any fabric that may be so built up for the government of such a state.[6]

The historiography which has flowed from this point of view has found little chance that Muslims might have sought common political ends with the Indian National Congress. It is a position which, while taking a severe knock from the emergence of Bangladesh in 1971, has derived some support from recent work on processes of Islamization in pre-colonial and colonial South Asia.[7] Its possibilities, moreover, have been further explored by recent attempts to examine the ways in which Muslim elites might both have been influenced in their political vision and have been constrained in their political choices by the Islamic, or, as Marshall Hodgson would have us say, the Islamicate value systems to which they adhered.[8]

These, then, are the four main ways in which the failure of the Congress to hold the bulk of British India's Muslims within the nationalist movement has been explained. They have variants and refinements, and most are not restricted to one approach but present a blend of several in which one ingredient is predominant, that ingredient usually depending on where the scholar is 'coming from'. We propose to examine the contributions of recent research to these four lines of explanation, and to do so primarily in the context of the UP, for long the heartland of Muslim separatism. We shall organize these new contributions around the answers to two key questions: Why did relatively few Muslims support the Congress? And why did the Congress become increasingly less inclined, or less able, to reach compromises with most Muslim political organizations, in particular the All-India Muslim League?

WHY DID RELATIVELY FEW MUSLIMS SUPPORT THE CONGRESS?

Taking the attendance at the annual December sessions of Congress as a criterion, we note that, although they counted for more than twenty per cent of the population of British India, between 1892 and 1909 Muslims amounted to less than six and a half per cent of the yearly gathering of nationalist forces. Their involvement reached a peak during the Khilafat–Non-cooperation movement when they formed nearly eleven per cent of those attending the Ahmedabad session. But by 1923 Muslim attendance had fallen to just over three and a half per cent, and subsequently it is unlikely that it rose significantly above that figure.[9] Indeed, from the late 1920s the Muslim presence in the Congress was embraced almost entirely by a small but courageous band of nationalist Muslims—for instance, Mukhtar Ahmad Ansari, Abul Kalam Azad, Tassaduq Ahmad Khan Sherwani, Rafi Ahmad Kidwai, Syed Mahmud—men of enormous importance to the Congress because their adherence to the organization supported its claim to represent the whole Indian nation, but also men increasingly separated from old friends, even reviled by them. The personal correspondence of Ansari, the leading Muslim nationalist in the Congress until his death in 1936, makes sad reading. As he stands up for national rather than communal action between 1927 and 1929, he receives sickening letters of disapproval from his Muslim friends: 'in your blind adherence to Motilal Nehru,' wrote one, 'you betrayed Muslims, your friends and co-workers.'[10] By the mid-1930s Ansari's political circle, to judge by surviving correspondence, has narrowed to become a largely Hindu one; his Nationalist Muslim Party existed mainly in the Press; while Jawaharlal Nehru dismissed his group as 'divested of any shred of principle or practice'.[11] A similarly embittered isolation was the fate of others, for instance, Syed Mahmud, who right down to his death in 1971 trod a difficult path, and it was a difficult path not just for him but also for his family, between the attacks his support for the nationalist cause brought from fellow Muslims and the need to defend the very same Muslims against what he increasingly perceived to be the arrogant unfairness of the majority community.[12] The message is that few Muslims joined the Congress, for as time went on it could require guts to do so, and that from the late 1920s they were increasingly a token presence in the organization of Indian nationalism.

This point established, let us turn to the explanations of why Muslims fought shy of the Congress. C.A. Bayly has brought one substantial new dimension to our understanding of the whole context of Muslim responses to the emergence of the nationalist movement in northern India. In explaining the ways in which the ideologies and institutions of the pre-colonial period contributed to the social formations of the colonial and post-colonial periods Bayly has shown how the commercialization of royal power in the seventeenth and eighteenth centuries helped to bring about the development of a rooted Islamic service gentry and a unified Hindu merchant class. These were distinct social formations, expressing themselves in different cultural idioms and operating in sharply differentiated economic contexts—the one was to become increasingly the sustainer of an Islamic high culture, the other of a Hindu high culture; they were, Bayly declares, the most significant social formations to emerge from the decline of the Mughal empire.

The Islamic service gentry perpetuated its sense of identity and its economic domination through the institution of the rural *qasbah* town. The largely Hindu merchant class, although formally divided by caste and by function, expressed common interests and values through the organization of markets, the systems of credit, and the Hindu and Jain religions, all of which transcended their ascriptive and functional divisions. This class and its culture flourished in market towns which were often known as *ganjs*. In the eighteenth century these two forms of town grew and prospered along parallel tracks. From the early nineteenth century, however, their fortunes began to diverge: the impact of British rule brought economic decline to the *qasbah*, while the commercialization of agriculture and the growth of long distance and local trade brought continuing prosperity to the Hindu *ganj*.[13]

The people of the *qasbahs* and the people of the *ganjs*, these two distinct social formations of Islamic service gentry and Hindu merchant class, have much to do with the fact that Muslim and Congress politics developed along different lines in northern India. The ideologues and the leaders of Muslim separatism, the men of Aligarh College and the All-India Muslim League, were deeply rooted in the *qasbah*. On the other hand, much of the leadership and much of the support for the Congress in northern India came from the *ganjs*, as well as larger trading centres, where an assertive Hindu revivalism, carried into national politics from 1915 by the Hindu Mahasabha, was never far away. We are struck by the enduring separateness of the worlds of the *qasbah* and of the *ganj* as they entered the wider political arenas which developed under the colonial state. Consider how few of the gifted Muslim products of the *qasbah* world joined the Congress. Even by the 1930s and 1940s, when many had developed a substantial secular dimension to their thinking, they tended not to do so. If they did not join Muslim organizations, they joined left-wing orgnizations like the Progressive Writers Movement in which socialism might range from magnolia through pink to a kind of red. Many supported the Moscow party line, as opposed to that of the Congress, during World War II, and, when partition came, many opted for Pakistan.[14] Consider, again, the response of one *qasbah* product as he surveyed the new intake into the UP Legislative Council after the Government of India Act of 1935, which brought Hindus from the *ganjs* in large numbers to the provincial council:

> I felt extremely uncomfortable. I could not spot anyone dressed like me, the language spoken around me was not the Urdu which I thought was the language of Lucknow and there seemed to be no one in sight worth talking to. I left the Assembly building with a feeling of mingled panic and disgust.[15]

Bayly's insights suggest that we should find some of the social and economic reasons why Muslims were unwilling to join the Congress much further back in time than we have been accustomed to look. More particularly they suggest that at the level of the distinctively different worlds of the north Indian *qasbah* and *ganj* there was some material substance in Jinnah's two-nation theory.

A second area in which our knowledge has deepened recently is in that of Muslim revivalism, where we owe a debt to, among others, S.A.A. Rizvi, Christian Troll and Barbara Metcalf.[16] For long it has been argued that in the late nineteenth century north Indian Muslims, under the pressure of Hindu and Muslim revivalist movements and the need to defend their interests, 'broke away' coming to emphasize what differentiated them from Hindus rather than what united them to them.[17] At the back of this argument there seems to lie the assumption that Hindus and Muslims belong to some seamless fabric of Indian society which was just now beginning to tear apart. Certainly, at one level there is truth in this; as the 1860s became the 1870s Saiyid Ahmad Khan's efforts did shift from working primarily for the interests of a Hindu–Muslim Urdu-speaking elite to working primarily for those of Urdu-speaking Muslims.[18] Moreover, the Aligarh movement which he set going in the 1870s was to be the womb from which several modern organizations of separate Muslim activity were to be born. But to suggest that it was only in the late nineteenth century that Muslims began to emphasize what differentiated them from the rest of Indian society is to ignore the long history of the Muslim revivalist movement and its separatist tendencies. Indeed, if there is a real starting point for this revival, it is arguably not even in the eighteenth century but at the height of Mughal power in the late sixteenth century when *ulama* and sufis, concerned about the compromises made by the Mughals with the Hindu world in which they ruled, began to emphasize the study of the *Hadiths* and to oppose pantheistic thought.[19] This strand of Indian Islam began to gain significant numbers of supporters in the eighteenth century as Muslims developed strategies to cope with their declining power. Moreover, it both contributed to similar attempts to cope with the loss of power elsewhere in the eighteenth century Islamic world and took inspiration from them. It meant an assertive sense of difference from things Indian. 'We are an Arab people,' declared Shah Wali Allah, the outstanding leader of the eighteenth century Islamic revival in India, 'whose fathers have fallen in exile in the country of Hindustan, and

Arabic genealogy and Arabic language are our pride.'[20] 'We must repudiate,' declared his early nineteenth century successor, Saiyid Ahmad Barelvi, 'all those Indian, Persian and "Roman" customs which are contrary to the Prophet's teaching.'[21]

The early nineteenth century saw a determined attempt to give this Muslim revivalist movement a broader base. The feeling went that now there was no state power to support Islamic revelation in this world, Islamic knowledge must be spread as widely as possible through the Muslim community so that Muslims should know more clearly themselves how to behave as Muslims; the Quran was translated into the vernacular—Urdu; many other religious works were translated, all of which published large-scale as the process coincided with the introduction of the lithographic printing press; at the same time public lectures came to be introduced to instruct Muslims in correct behaviour, and sufi teaching increasingly came to be one long lesson in the practice of the Prophet. Such developments, with their Islamizing effect, were not restricted to northern India. We can see them, for instance, in Bengal as Asim Roy and Rafiuddin Ahmed have shown; we can see them in Malabar as Stephen Dale and Roland Miller have shown;[22] we can see them in many places elsewhere in the Islamic world. Indeed, on the eve of the European conquest there was throughout much of this world new consciousness and new definitions of what it was to be a Muslim.[23]

Thus, in northern India in the early nineteenth century, there was a vigorous revivalist movement which was concerned to emphasize the distinctions between the Muslim and the Hindu worlds. It was entangled with a Perso-Islamic cultural tradition which always tried to live in the Islamic world beyond India and to refuse to recognize anything specifically Indian as a fit subject for literary inspiration.[24] Moreover, it kept company with the prejudices of the Islamic *qasbah* gentry class which always liked to stress its origins outside India and the fact that it was to power born. Out of this milieu sprang two strands of thought and action which were both, although in rather different ways, to limit Muslim support for Indian nationalism.

The first strand, which sprang from the environment of early nineteenth-century Delhi, was that of Islamic reformism. This development came to be focused on the Deoband School, now one of the leading 'traditional' universities of the Islamic world. It offered a distinct response to the problems of the loss of Muslim power, the threats presented by Hindu society, and the difficulties of being a good Muslim in the colonial state. It created a form of Islam in which the state was irrelevant and in which any form of contact with Hindu religious practices were avoided. It concentrated on spreading Islamic knowledge as widely as possible and on teaching that it was the individual conscience, primed by the awful awareness that there could be not intercession for man with God, which would now be the sanction which would bring men to follow the holy law. It was a protestant, willed Islam. Highly selfconscious, it envisaged no merging of its Islamic world with Indian national life, no merging with the institutions of the modern state.[25] Admittedly many Muslim reformists supported the Congress in the last few years of British rule, but this was more because they feared to live in a modern state run by the British or by Islamic modernists, whose policies could verge on the purely secular, than because they had any wide-ranging identity of purpose with the Congress.

The second strand was, of course, that of Muslim modernism, that of Saiyid Ahmad Khan, the Aligarh movement and the Muslim League. It is here that the crucial acts of separation from the stream of Indian national life are discovered in Saiyid Ahmad Khan's foundation of Aligarh College, his opposition to the elective principle, or his opposition to the Congress. But to focus purely on these important political developments as starting points of Muslim separatism, or crucial breaking points of national unity, without taking into account Saiyid Ahmad Khan's background or his fundamental concerns is to present a distorted picture. Saiyid Ahmad's family, indeed the milieu in which he was brought up, was redolent with the spirit of the eighteenth-century movement of revival and reform. His life's mission, like that of the Deobandis, was to find the best way forward for Islam in a world in which Muslims had little power and were threatened by other civilizations. He was a deeply religious man for whom Islam could never be an instrument, only the best path along which mankind could progress. He used similar techniques to those of his predecessors in the Wali Allah tradition, going back to the Quran and the *Hadiths* for guidance; he used the same legal principle as they did—*ijtihad*. This great man, who built bridges between revelation and modern science, was quintessentially a product of the eighteenth-century revival. We should think less of his leading of a Muslim breakaway, than of his participation in an already established trajectory which he came further to elaborate in ideas, actions and institutions.[26]

A third, and also a new, area in which we have been given significant food for thought belongs in particular to the work of Farzana Shaikh. She has been concerned to demonstrate how the political values of the north Indian Muslim elite, derived in large part from their Islamic background, were profoundly opposed to those of Western liberalism. At the heart of what distinguishes the Muslim from the Western liberal concept of representation was an emphasis on the community as opposed to the individual as the prime building block of political society. The Muslim community had been created by God's revelation to man; it was only by living in it that a man's life became significant; it was by doing so that men trod the path towards salvation. Muslims, therefore, tended to focus on the communal group as the basic unit of representation rather than the individual, who only had rights within the framework of the Muslim community. There was a feeling that only Muslims could represent Muslims; this meant that religion and politics, however secular the light in which the latter was perceived, should not be divided, which was in stark contrast to the Western liberal view which was coming to have a horror of associating political commitment and religious affiliation. There was also a sense that representative bodies should consist of an evenly balanced arrangement of the ascriptive communal groups which made up society rather than the relatively fluid associations of individuals that could form majorities which might tyrannize minorities.

Such political values, whatever weight we should give other factors such as the interests of particular Muslim groups or the moulding influence of imperial policies, were bound to make it difficult for Muslims to join the Congress. They were likely to prefer some form of separate representation as opposed to seeing their identity absorbed within a greater Indian political community. They were likely to believe that only Muslims could truly represent Muslims, which meant that they found it difficult to imagine that a heterogeneous Congress could fully represent their interests. Moreover, they were unlikely to feel comfortable with a devolution of power from the British which at the all-India level, and that of the Muslim minority provinces, promised the subordination of a Muslim minority to a Hindu Majority. Political values, the understandings and the prejudices with which north Indian

Muslims considered the Congress and its policies, ought to be thrown into the balance.[27]

A fourth area in which our knowledge has deepened is that of Hindu revivalism and the barriers it presented Muslims who might have considered joining the Congress. Of course, we have long known of the association between Hindu revivalism and the Congress in Bengal and Maharashtra, and its specifically anti-Muslim content. We have long known, too, of the association between forms of Hindu revivalism and specific demands in Upper India whether for the abandonment of cow-slaughter, or for the imposition of the Nagri script on the government machine, or for the conversion of Christians and Muslims back to Hinduism. Recent work, however, has given us a richer sense of the Janus-faced quality of nationalism in northern India. Study of the writers and journalists in the circle of Bharatendu Harischandra, who were involved in the early promotion of national issues, reveals on the one hand an awareness of national interests and of how Hindu–Muslim unity might contribute to their progress, but on the other hand a hatred of Muslims the depth of which still takes us aback: British rule is hailed for supplanting Muslim tyranny; Muslims are accused of robbing Hindus of religion, wealth and women; they are outsiders in India; they are not Hindustanis; only Hindus are Indian; while relics of Muslim power are presented as 'wounds in the heart' kept fresh by the sight of a mosque by the holy temple of Vishwanath.[28] In the same way Kenneth Jones has revealed the development by the Arya Samaj of an aggressive Hindu consciousness which was often openly communal and anti-Muslim, and which by the end of the first decade of the twentieth century led some to demand the replacement of the Congress organization, which appeased Muslims far too readily, by Hindu Sabhas, a Hindu press, and a Hindu Defence Fund.[29] We now have a richer sense of the background of Hindu feeling which so often in the localities was hard to distinguish from Congress feeling. It forms a further aspect of the context in which Muslims decided whether to join the nationalist movement or not.

WHY DID THE CONGRESS HAVE GROWING DIFFICULTY IN MAKING DEALS WITH MUSLIM POLITICAL ORGANIZATIONS?

Evidently, if significant numbers of Muslims could not be drawn into the Congress, then the Congress, if it was to hold together some form of Indian Nationalist movement, ought to be able to come to effective working arrangements with Muslim political organizations. If the Congress failed to do so, one great danger was that the nationalist movement would have decisions regarding the distribution of power among groups in Indian politics imposed upon it by the British; a second was that Muslims might come to feel that a nationalist movement which was unwilling to respect their worries—their concern for safeguards as a minority—would be even less likely to do so when it came to govern an independent India..

Let us book briefly at five occasions when the Congress made, or attempted to make, deals with major Muslim political organizations. They are: (1) the Lucknow Pact of 1916 when the Congress agreed to a formula with the Muslim League giving Muslim separate electorates and extra seats over and above their proportion of the population in those provinces where Muslims formed a minority of the population—this arrangement came into operation in the Montagu–Chelmsford constitution of 1919; (2) the period from 1920 to 1922 when the Congress coordinated a movement of non-cooperation with government in harmony with the Muslim Khilafat organization; (3) the period from 1927 to 1929 when the Congress refused to agree to any formula for the distribution of power between itself and the Muslims which accepted the principle of separate electorates—in consequence, there was no agreement with any of the various Muslim organizations and the British eventually imposed a settlement; (4) the refusal of the Congress to form a coalition government with the Muslim League in the UP after the 1937 election unless the League disbanded in the province and its members joined the Congress; and (5) the uncompromising stance of the Congress in June and July 1946, after Jinnah and the Muslim League had accepted the Cabinet Mission plan for the constitution of an independent India, towards the League's terms for entering the interim government, and towards its understanding of how the provinces of the North East and the North West should be grouped.

Clearly, early on, in 1916 and 1920, the Congress was able to make deals with Muslim organizations. That of 1920 was an agreement over political action which owed much to the ascendancy of Gandhi within both the Congress and the Khilafat organization and the fact that India's Muslims were agitated less about their political position within India than about the decline of Muslim power in the world at large. That of 1916 was the first and the only major agreement over power-sharing. It was possible, among other reasons, because the political world at this stage still belonged more to the clubroom than the crowd and because both Congress and League were strongly influenced by groups from the UP who worked together, knew each other well, and enjoyed a mutual trust.

From the mid-1920s, however, the situation was no longer thus. One reason was the growing influence of Hindu revivalism within the Congress. Whenever the Congress seemed to come close to the Muslims, there was a Hindu backlash. It happened after the Lucknow Pact; it was even stronger after the prominence of Muslims during the Khilafat/non-cooperation period of 1920–22, which was followed by a bitter assault on the Muslim leadership and by communal rioting throughout much of India. By the late 1920s Hindu Mahasabha influence over Congress 'high command' reached its peak, raising Congress demands to an unrealistic level as it negotiated with Muslim organizations over the future distribution of power. When Jinnah, in a last ditch attempt to reach an agreement, offered terms which envisaged the eventual phasing out of many Muslim safeguards in return for some immediate protection, a leading Mahasabhaite remarked.

> No compromise is possible for the purpose of tampering [sic] nationalism with communalism. It is in this sense that if the Muslims cannot trust and remain in the Congress and give up their separate mentality, let us leave them alone to go to the Government for whatever it may grant them.[30]

Intransigence of this kind meant that Hindu revivalists were left with the greater part of the blame both by contemporaries and by posterity for the failure to reach some form of Hindu–Muslim agreement at this crucial stage in the devolution of power. It also meant that Muslims did eventually 'go to the Government' for whatever it would grant them, meaning in this case the Communal Award of 1932 which established much of the structure of interests on which the subsequent emergence of Pakistan was to be based.[31]

Hindu revivalism had no such direct influence on the failure of 1937 and 1946. Nevertheless, throughout the 1930s and 1940s, however much the Congress 'high command' came to insist on a secular approach, for instance, declaring membership of the Hindu Mahasabha a disqualification for membership of the Congress in

December 1938, at the local level Muslims found it difficult to distinguish between Hindu leadership and Congress leadership, Hindu populism and Indian nationalism. By the late 1930s the new president of an increasingly strong Mahasabha was declaring 'we Hindus are a Nation by ourselves ... Hindu nationalists should not be at all apologetic to being called Hindu Communalists',[32] and fellow sympathizers had succeeded in putting an end to the Congress's last attempt to draw the Muslim masses into the nationalist movement.[33]

The question remains why Hindu revivalist influences should have come to be as considerable as they were in the Congress. In one sense Hindu influences were bound to grow in the Congress as it sought a mass base and its centre of gravity moved away from the secular and Western-educated, at home in the society of the Bar, university and club, and towards the caste-conscious Hindu, at home in *ganj*, temple and *math*. Similar developments were bound to take place in the League as its support moved from being purely that of the Muslim landed and service classes, whose Islamic understanding might have a strong secular dimension, to embrace the Muslim masses whose political vision was primarily religious. What distinguished the two organizations was that whereas the former began seriously to widen the base of its support in the 1920s the latter did not do so until the 1940s.

The tendency of politics to become communal, however, was not simply a function of the extension of the franchise. We should also note, as David Page has so clearly instructed us to do, how the framework for modern politics, which was gradually developed under British rule, tended to reinforce communal divisions, a tendency which stemmed in part, of course, from the British need to maintain control over a framework in which more and more Indians participated. One aspect of the framework was separate electorates with reserved numbers of seats. These meant that at no stage did either Hindus or Muslims have to consider constituents from the other community and, as more power was devolved in particular provinces, communal bastions came to be established. Furthermore, separate electorates, and the substantial Muslim interest groups they came to embrace after 1920, enabled government to work a system of political control which in large part could ignore the Congress. Thus, if the Congress in the late 1920s seemed to talk with the voice of the Hindu Mahasabha, it was in part because the political framework had forced it to depend on these communal elements.[34]

A second divisive aspect of the political framework involved the way in which it brought conflict between Muslim and Hindu communities to mingle with conflict between provincial and central levels of government. The Montagu–Chelmsford reforms created a powerful Muslim bloc in the Punjab which had little interest in a strong centre. In the discussions leading up to the Government of India Act of 1935 this bloc came to dominate the Muslim point of view, working for arrangements in the reformed federal system which would give Muslims the possibility of controlling the Punjab and Bengal while the British still controlled the centre. By means of the Communal Award of 1932, a situation was entrenched in India's multi-level political system by which the most powerful Muslim forces in the land had an interest in either a British or a weak centre while the Congress had an equally powerful interest in both a nationalist and a strong centre. The conflict built into the system was to come to a head as the British tried to leave India. It surfaced in the Cabinet Mission negotiations of May–June 1946 in the League's demand for an equal voice to that of Congress in the interim government, and therefore a weak centre, and Congress's demand that its support in the country should be reflected in the composition of this government, and therefore that there should be a strong centre. The working of the structure of politics had established irreconcilable interests at the peak of the federal system. The Congress could not accede to the League's demands without sacrificing effective control of the interim government and perhaps the subsequent government of India; the League could not back down without surrendering Muslim control over the bulwarks of provincial advantage established over the previous two decades.[35]

Finally, there is the ideological dimension. Here there can be little doubt that whatever might have been the most effective strategy to defend particular Muslim interests in British India's multilevel political system, Islamically derived political values—the communitarian basis of politics, the belief that only Muslims could represent Muslims, the concern that religion and politics should not be placed in separate compartments—underpinned the Muslim League's two-nation theory and the steady development of its claim in the last decade of British rule 'from simple *political parity* between League and Congress to *communal parity* between Muslims and Hindus ... (to) *ideological parity* between Muslims and non-Muslims.'[36] The working out of what these values might mean, how they might be expressed as Muslim League, Congress and the British negotiated over the devolution of power, represented a continuing obstacle to Congress's attempts to reach some kind of agreement with the League.

Similarly Congress had its own ideological positions which limited its capacity to deal effectively with the League. They were most eloquently expressed by Jawaharlal Nehru. 'The tremendous and fundamental fact of India,' he told an American audience in January 1938, 'is her essential unity through the ages.' Innumerable peoples have entered India 'but always they have been absorbed and assimilated'. British rule gave political expression to the enduring and fundamental unity of India. 'It was a unity of common subjection, but it gave rise to a unity of common nationalism.' This national movement is represented by the National Congress which is the manifestation of the political unity of India.

> In India today no one, whatever his political views or religious persuasions, thinks in terms other than those of national unity. There are separatist tendencies, but even these do not oppose national freedom or unity. ...There is no religious or cultural conflict in India. What is called the religious or communal problem is really a dispute among upper-class people for a division of the spoils of office or of representation in a legislature.[37]

Men with such a vision were always likely to see the Muslim League as an affront: a betrayal of India's real self, a bastion of feudal privilege which stood in the way of socially radical reform, an organization of place-seekers who in pursuing their selfish ends helped to keep the imperialists in power and to sabotage the sacrifices of the nationalists. They were likely to feel either on good nationalist grounds, or on good socialist grounds, or perhaps on both, that it ought not to exist, indeed that it ought to be destroyed at the first opportunity. In this light it is hardly surprising that in July 1937 the Congress 'high command' insisted that, despite their earlier collaboration in fighting the elections, the price that UP Muslim Leaguers must pay to join the Congress ministry was to leave the League and join the Congress. There is, of course, nothing new in drawing the connection between the 'one nation, one party' approach of the Congress and the rough treatment of the League at this juncture.[38] Nevertheless, it remains a significant point at which we can see ideology helping to limit the capacity of the Congress to make a deal with the League. It is, moreover, a point which many have come to see as crucial in the development of the movement for Pakistan.

Recent research, therefore, contributes to three of the four main lines of argument traditionally deployed in explaining the failure of the Congress either to win significant Muslim support or to persuade Muslim organizations, notably the Muslim League, to work with the nationalist movement. The old Muslim backwardness argument as far as the UP is concerned remains as dead a duck as before, although Bayly's work has shown how those Muslims from northern India who rejected Congress came in the main from a *qasbah* world which had been in decline for nearly a century and which had reason to feel threatened by the rise of the people of the *ganjs*. On the other hand, the equally hoary divide and rule argument, which was the mainstay of nationalist explanations of Muslim separatism, has gained significant new force from Page's demonstration of how the framework for politics created by the Montagu–Chelmsford reforms tended to push Hindus and Muslims into communal positions and how the British, short of room for manoeuvre, were not slow to use the leverage offered. Furthermore, our understanding of the baleful influence of Hindu communalism, which Nehru found so much less excusable than Muslim communalism, has also been increased. And this is as evident in the specific attention of Mushirul Hasan to the events of the late 1920s as it is in Sumit Sarkar's survey of the whole nationalist period.[39] There is also much new light shed on aspects of Muslim separatism from Bayly's work on its social, economic and cultural underpinnings in Upper India to the considerable amount of recent research revealing the divisive impact of Muslim movements of revival and reform, to Farzana Shaikh's wholly fresh perspective regarding the influence of Islamically derived political values.

To these lines of explanations we should add the constraints offered by the nationalist vision of the fundamental unity of India and the nationalist concern that if the independent state was both to survive and to work a socio-economic revolution for the people it must have a strong political centre. This vision and this most reasonable concern reduced the willingness of Congress to make those compromises which might have enabled its leaders to shepherd British India's largest minority from its religious or communal understanding of politics towards some kind of acceptance of the political ways of a modern Indian state.

Recent research seems to offer no more clear cut explanation of the Congress failure to win the Muslims than we had before, although we do have a stronger idea of the deep-rootedness of the sense of difference amongst much of the Muslim elite. Overall, however, we are left in the main with a richer understanding of the obstacles with which the Congress contended as it strove to win Muslims for the nationalist movement and to hold them within it. While at no stage would we wish to suggest that the division of India was inevitable, the odds against Congress success in sustaining its one-nation theory in practice do now seem higher than before.

NOTES

1. W.W. Hunter, *The Indian Musalmans*, 2nd ed. (London: Trubner and Co. 1872). For a Marxist perspective taking up the Muslim backwardness theory see W.C. Smith, *Modern Islam in India* (London: Victor Gollancz, 1946) and for a Muslim one see Abdul Hamid, *Muslim Separatism in India: A Brief Survey 1858–1947* (Lahore: Oxford University Press, 1967).
2. Francis Robinson, *Separatism among Indian Muslims: The Politics of the United Provinces' Muslims 1860–1923* (Cambridge: Cambridge University Press, 1974), chapters 2 and 3; Paul R. Brass, *Language, Religion and Politics in North India* (Cambridge: Cambridge University Press, 1974), chapter 3.
3. The classic formulation of the divide and rule thesis can be found in A. Mehta and A. Patwardhan, *The Communal Triangle in India* (Allahabad: Kitabistan, 1942). The argument regarding the destruction of an evolving Hindu–Muslim synthesis was frequently put forward by Jawaharlal Nehru, see, for instance, *An Autobiography* (London: Bodley Head, 1936).
4. This position is explicit in Anil Seal's keynote essay 'Imperialism and Nationalism in India' in John Gallagher, Gordon Johnson and Anil Seal (eds), *Locality, Province and Nation: Essays on Indian Politics 1870–1940* (Cambridge: Cambridge University Press, 1973), pp. 1–27.
5. See, for instance, Bipan Chandra, 'Communalism and the National Movement' and Mushirul Hasan, 'Communal and Revivalist Trends in Congress' in Mushirul Hasan (ed.), *Communal and Pan-Islamic Trends in Colonial India* (New Delhi: Manohar, 1981), pp. 186–98 and 199–223.
6. Jamil-ud-Din Ahmad (ed.), *Some Recent Speeches and Writings of Mr. Jinnah* (Lahore: Sh. Muhammad Ashraf, 1943), p. 153.
7. See, for instance, David Gilmartin, 'Religious Leadership and the Pakistan Movement in the Punjab', *Modern Asian Studies*, XIII, part 3 (1979),

pp. 485–517 and Stephen Frederic Dale, *Islamic Society on the South Asian Frontier: The Mappilas of Malabar 1498–1922* (Oxford: Clarendon Press, 1980). For an attempt to provide an overall context in which the relationship between Islam and Indian society might be understood see Francis Robinson, 'Islam and Muslim Society in South Asia' in *Contributions to Indian Sociology* (n.s.) XVII, part 2 (1983), pp. 185–203.

8. Francis Robinson, 'Islam and Muslim Separatism' in David Taylor and Malcolm Yapp (eds), *Political Identity in South Asia* (London: Curzon Press, 1979), pp. 78–112.
9. Judith M. Brown, *Modern India: The Origins of an Asian Democracy* (Oxford: Oxford University Press, 1985), pp. 178, 228.
10. Shaukat Ali to Mukhtar Ahmad Ansari, 19 May 1929, in Mushirul Hasan (ed.), *Muslims and the Congress: Select Correspondence of Dr M.A. Anasari 1912–1935* (New Delhi: Manohar, 1979), p. 70.
11. Ibid., p. xxxiv.
12. This is evident from the correspondence of Syed Mahmud from the mid-1930s onwards. See V.N. Datta and B.E. Cleghorn (eds), *A Nationalist Muslim and Indian Politics; Being the Selected Correspondence of the Late Dr Syed Mahmud* (Delhi: Macmillan, 1974), parts 4–6.
13. C.A. Bayly, *Rulers, Townsmen and Bazaars: North Indian Society in the Age of British Expansion, 1770–1870* (Cambridge: Cambridge University Press, 1983), especially pp. 449–57.
14. Khizar Humayun Ansari, 'The Emergence of Muslim Socialists and their Ideas in India between 1917 and 1947' (Unpublished Ph.D. thesis, University of London, 1985), chapters 4 and 5.
15. So Spake Muhammad Mujeeb, historian and later Vice-Chancellor of the Jamia Millia Islamia, as he reflected in later life on the partition of India, quoted in Brown, *Modern India*, p. 302.
16. Among notable recent books shedding light on this phenomenon are: Saiyid Athar Abbas Rizvi, *Shah Wali-Allah and His Times: A Study of Eighteenth Century Politics and Society in India* (Canberra: Ma'rifat Publishing House, 1980) and *Shah Abd al Aziz: Puritanism, Sectarian Polemics and Jihad* (Canberra: Ma'rifat Publishing House, 1982): Christian W. Troll, *Sayyid Ahmad Khan: A Reinterpretation of Muslim Theology* (New Delhi: Vikas, 1978): Barbara Daly Metcalf, *Islamic Revival in British India: Deoband, 1860–1900* (Princeton NJ: Princeton University Press, 1982).
17. Anil Seal, *The Emergence of Indian Nationalism: Competition and Collaboration in the Later Nineteenth Century* (Cambridge: Cambridge University Press, 1968) chapter 7, and Brass, *Language, Religion and Politics*, chapter 3.
18. Robinson, *Separatism*, pp. 92–8.
19. Francis Robinson, *Atlas of the Islamic World since 1500* (Oxford: Phaidon, 1982), pp. 61–3.

20. Annemarie Schimmel, *Islam in the Indian Subcontinent* (Leiden-Koln: E.J. Brill, 1980), p. 157.
21. Barelvi's *Sirat-i Mustaqim* quoted in Aziz Ahmad, *Studies in Islamic Culture in the Indian Environment* (Oxford: Clarendon Press, 1964), p. 210.
22. Asim Roy, *The Islamic Syncretistic Tradition in Bengal* (Princeton NJ: Princeton University Press, 1983); Rafiuddin Ahmed, *The Bengal Muslims 1871–1906: A Quest for Identity* (Delhi: Oxford University Press, 1981); Roland E. Miller, *Mappila Muslims of Kerala: A Study in Islamic Trends* (Bombay: Orient Longmen, 1976): Dale, *Islamic Society*.
23. Robinson, *Atlas*, chapter 4.
24. Ahmad, *Islamic Culture*, pp. 252–53. We do not forget, of course, that there were exceptions to this rule like Nazir Akbarabadi (d: 1830), although he was virtually unknown in his time.
25. Metcalf, *Islamic Revival*, pp. 87–260, and Peter Hardy, *Partners in Freedom—and True Muslims; the Political Thought of Some Muslim Scholars in British 1912–1947* (Lund: Scandinavian Institute of Asian Studies, 1971), pp. 37–9.
26. Troll, *Sayyid Ahmad Khan*, pp. 28–56.
27. Farzana Shaikh, 'Islam: Ideology or Instrument? Muslims and Political Representation in British India, 1860–1946' (Unpublished Ph.D. thesis, Columbia, 1983), and 'Muslims and Political Representation in Colonial India: The Making of Pakistan', *Modern Asian Studies*, XX, part 3 (1986), 539–58.
28. Sudhir Chandra, 'Communal Consciousness in Late 19th Century Hindial [sic] Literature' in Hasan (ed.), *Communal and Pan-Islamic Trends*, pp. 170–86.
29. Kenneth W. Jones, *Arya Dharm: Hindu Consciousness in 19th Century Punjab* (New Delhi: Manohar, 1976), especially chapter 10.
30. Mushirul Hasan, *Nationalism and Communal Politics in India, 1916–1928* (New Delhi: Manohar, 1979), p. 305.
31. David Page, *Prelude to Partition: The Indian Muslims and the Imperial System of Control 1920–1932* (Delhi: Oxford University Press, 1982), chapter 4.
32. Statement of V.D. Savarkar, President of the Hindu Mahasabha, at the Nagpur Session of the Congress in December 1938 quoted in Sumit Sarkar, *Modern India 1885–1947* (Delhi: Macmillan, 1983), pp. 356–57.
33. For an analysis of the failure of this last attempt see Mushriul Hasan, 'The Muslim Mass Contact Campaign: An Attempt at Political Mobilisation', *Occasional Papers on History and Society*, Number XIV (New Delhi: Nehru Memorial Museum and Library, 1983).
34. Page, *Prelude to Partition*.
35. For this development of Page's insights into the 1940s see, Ayesha Jalal, *The Sole Spokesman: Jinnah, the Muslim League and the Demand for Pakistan* (Cambridge: Cambridge University Press, 1985).

36. Shaikh, 'Muslims and Political Representation', p. 550.
37. Jawaharlal Nehru, 'The Unity of India', a lecture address to an American audience, January 1938, in Dorothy Norman (ed.), *Nehru: The First Sixty Years* (London: Bodley Head, 1965) vol. I, pp. 554–60.
38. R. Coupland, *Indian Politics 1936–1942*, part II, (Oxford: Oxford University Press, 1943), chapter 10 'The Character and the Policy of the Congress'.
39. Hasan, *Nationalism and Communal Politics*, pp. 263–305 and Sarkar, *Modern India*, pp. 235–37, 262–63, 356–57.

Responses
to
Major Contributions
to
Indo–Muslim History

Chapter Ten

Sufis and Islamization*

There was a time when, seduced by Fitzgerald and gorged upon the translations of Nicholson and Arberry, we fondly believed that the most important point about sufis was that they taught Muslims how to know God. Of course some went rather far: they drank, they sang, they danced, they whirled. Nevertheless, they did seem to be the prime mediators of religious experience to the faithful, and for generations of Westerners Islam seemed accessible, even sympathetic, in their beautiful devotional poetry. Sufis were mystics whose achievement Christians might find it hard to equal. Enter the sociologist: Evans Pritchard and the Sanusiya of Libya, Ernest Gellner and the Saints of the Atlas, Michael Gilsenan and the Hamidiya Shadhiliya of Cairo and Dale Eickelman and the Sherqawa of western Morocco. We learn that the sufi might be important less for his role in mediating between man and God than for mediating between man and society. He offers a framework greater than the fissile lineage group within which the east Saharan Bedouin can act; he mediates between the transhumant Berber tribe and the settled areas; he eases the lower middle classes of Cairo through the transition into modern city life; for three hundred years he protects caravans, guards markets, provides sanctuary and deals with the sultan in western Morocco. Out of Africa, as the Romans used to say, always something new.

It was about time the message reached India, and Richard Eaton has brought it. He investigates sufis in Bijapur from 1300, when they first began to arrive in the Deccan plateau, to the last decade of the seventeenth century, when after Aurangzeb's capture of the

* Richard Maxwell Eaton, *Sufis of Bijapur 1300–1700: Social Roles of Sufis in Medieval India* (New Jersey: Princeton University Press, 1978), pp. xxii, 358.

city in 1686, followed by plague and famine, it quickly became a place of desolation. Part of the study covers the arrival of the sufis and the establishment of the great Chishti and Qadiri shrines in Gulbarga and Bidar under the Bahmani sultanate, but the bulk examines sufis at the height of Bijapuri power from 1580 to 1656 under the Adil Shahi sultanate. Bearing in mind three key questions—how do sufis relate to the *ulama*, to the Court, and to the non-Muslim population—Eaton's prime concern is to demonstrate the interaction between the social roles of sufis and the changing historical context. So the first sufis, who accompanied the Muslim invasions of the Deccan and helped to legitimize the war against the Hindus, are identified as 'warrior sufis', and interesting comparisons are made with the Ghazi-babas of fourteenth-century Anatolia and the Safawi murids of fifteenth-century Azerbaijan. Two and a half centuries later, as the Adil Shahi sultans at the summit of their power displayed increasingly syncretic tendencies, not unlike their Mughal contemporaries, there emerged 'reformist sufis' eager to keep the court upon the sure path. Then, as the power of the Bijapur court began to decline in the second half of the seventeenth century, sufis came to perform two new roles. There were the 'landed sufis' created by the sultan's *inam* and *muafi* grants which were designed to harness to the state interest these Muslims who wielded great influence at the lower levels of society, Hindu and Muslim alike. There were also the 'dervish sufis' who appeared, so we are told, as a direct response to the court's attempts to bind the religious establishment to its side. Many of the latter were Chishtis, as one would expect, and they enjoyed thumbing their noses in every possible way at the '"worldly men" who had sold out to the structured and confining world of the city's orthodox establishment'. Finally, spanning the whole two-hundred-year period of Adil Shahi rule and always standing apart from the court, there were the 'literati sufis' who both played a pioneering role in developing the Dakhni language and in creating a popular literature which mediated Islamic mysticism to the common man. While identifying these five sufi types, Eaton also demonstrates the evolution of sufism in Bijapur over 400 years through the three main phases suggested by Trimingham in his *Sufi Orders of Islam*. We move from the Khanqah stage, apparently the age of the 'warrior sufis', to the tariqa stage, when sufis began to form orders and mystic practice became institutionalized and socially differentiated.

Many Bijapur sufis were at this second stage. Then in the sixteenth and seventeenth centuries we find some moving to the third or ta'ifa stage when devotion to a spiritual discipline promoted by an order was replaced by devotion to a saint exercised in the veneration of his tomb and his descendants.

It should be clear, first of all, that Eaton's achievement is considerable. He has worked on a large number of sources, manuscript and lithograph, in Persian, Dakhni and Urdu, and in the case of many he must be the first to see them. He demonstrates the rich potential, for those who wish to study Islam in South Asia, of two classic genres of religious writing—the *tazkirat* or collection of biographies, and the *malfuzat* or the sayings of a sufi as recorded by one of his disciples. He does so, moreover, alert to the traps which such sources hold for the unwary. Then, joining to his skills as a linguist, and no doubt something of a palaeographer, further skills as a social scientist and a historian, he brings a new dimension to our understanding of Indian sufis. They are no longer just reflections, sometimes rather pallid, of those who strove to know God in the high Persian tradition, but now agencies through which Hindus were drawn into a Muslim religious culture, men who negotiated jobs for their followers with the court, men who could help consolidate the court's hold on the lower classes of the countryside. Furthermore, as society changed, so did sufi functions. Now we can begin to develop an image of Indian sufis and their significance as broad as that we already have for their African brethren.

Among the several areas in which Eaton enlarges our knowledge is that of conversion to Islam, or better put, the slow drawing of peoples into an Islamic cultural milieu. For some time it has been suggested that sufis were important agents in converting Hindus, particularly of the lower castes, to Islam, but it has not been made clear how this happened. Eaton suggests three ways. Hindus made *bai'at* with a pir which meant they recited the Muslim creed, became a spiritual disciple and submitted themselves body and soul to the directions of the pir. They came to believe in the intercessory power of the many saints buried in and around Bijapur, making pilgrimages to their shrines and attending the annual celebrations of the saints' Urs. Most important, they came to use the poems written by sufis specifically to accompany the common round of life: the *chakki-nama* sung while grinding food grains, the *charkha-nama* sung while spinning thread, the *lori-nama* or lullaby etc. In one of the most striking parts of his work, Eaton demonstrates how these poems, using the metaphor of the task in hand, draw connections between Allah, the Prophet, the pir and the reciter, and how at times they even use the stages of the *zikr* to regulate the phases of work. These poems, he asserts, in Bijapur at least, were the prime agents of Islamization. Here lies the kernel of an idea rich in possibilities. The poems are all associated with women's work, and were transmitted by women from generation to generation. So it was in the Hindu women of the Deccan that sufis planted the seed which would eventually bring forth a 'Muslim community'.

As one would expect, Eaton reveals much of how Islam has interacted with Hindu influences. The Chishti sufis of Bijapur conceived of God in the final stage of the sufi path as a lover or friend (*muhibb*), which apparently finds a parallel in the bhakti ideal of a personal deity actively concerned with his devotees characteristic of both the Lingayat and Vithoba traditions of the Deccan. Burhan al-Din, the great Chishti of the sixteenth century, borrowed from the lore of Krishna to discuss the importance of asceticism and used Sanskrit terms to express sufi concepts. This point made, however, Eaton issues timely warning to those eager to find the heart of religious feeling in Hinduism rather than Islam. 'For one thing,' he declares, 'the central ideas expressed by these Sufis remained thoroughly within the framework of the Islamic mystical tradition, and such Hindu influences as those cited above seem to have been selectively borrowed only when they could serve as supporting buttresses for this framework ... .'

If there was nothing fundamentally syncretic about how these particular sufis conceived their faith, there was much that was syncretic about the court culture of Bijapur under Sultan Adil Shahi II (1580–1627). Hindu influences grew more and more prominent. Dakhni and Perso-Marathi began to rival, if not to replace, Persian as the court language. Painting reflected the Vijayanagar artistic tradition, while architecture which had been Persian or Turkish in style since Muslims came to the Deccan was infected by a vigorous Hindu spirit. This lively cultural syncretism is to be explained, it seems, in part in the rise of the Portuguese on the sea and the Mughals on the land which broke contact with Safavid Iran, in part in the growing numbers of Hindus in Bijapur service—Marathas in the army and revenue bureaucracy, and artists and craftsmen dispersed after the destruction of the Vijayanagar empire—and in part in the leadership of Sultan Adil Shahi II himself. The sultan knew Sanskrit better than Persian; he composed one of the landmarks of Dakhni literature, the *Kitab-i Nauras*, on Hindu aesthetics, and began it not with the Bismillah but with a hymn in praise of Ganapati; he encouraged devotion to Hindu deities. Like his great contemporary the emperor Akbar, he travelled a long way up the road of religious eclecticism.

No Muslim monarch could take such a path without risking opposition from his learned and holy men. In Bijapur it came from sufis, 'reformist sufis': for the responses of the *ulama*, apparently, there is no evidence. In the early seventeenth century, Qadiri and Shattari sufis adopted various tactics from physical assault to 'ostentatious disdain' to bring the lives of Bijapuris and their court closer to the *sharia*. These sufis were Arabs and had recently arrived. Some filtered up from Arab settlements long established on the Konkan coast, but most, particularly after Portuguese control of the sea slackened in Sultan Muhammad II's reign (1627–56), came directly from Arabia. They wrote and spoke Arabic, retained Arab customs, often performed pilgrimage to Mecca and were looked up to, understandably, as models of correct Islamic behaviour. They probably played a part in shifting the court towards more orthodox Islamic behaviour; they probably helped to foster the atmosphere in which the Bijapuri general, Afzal Khan, pursed the mistaken policy of devastating the holy places of Deccani Hinduism in 1659.

Thus Eaton demonstrates a central theme at work in Islamic history. It is the conflict between the powerful in Muslim societies, who because power is their first concern must usually make compromises which involve ignoring the orthodox ideal, and the pious whose concern is to realize on earth their vision of the ideal community as set down in the *sharia* and their vision of the ideal Muslim life as exemplified in the life of the Prophet. We see this conflict manifest in Muslim states from the Ummayyad Caliphate to the present day. In seventeenth-century Bijapur it takes a form typical of the further Islamic lands. Muslim rulers, whose power and resources are rooted in a society the culture and faith of which are quite different from theirs, slip from the high religio-cultural ideal of the orthodox, in part from necessity and in part because they have been charmed by those amongst whom they dwell. They are confronted by the pious, in contact with the Islamic heartland and in this instance Arab in blood, who are supported by, and travel along, a Muslim controlled international trade network. They are confronted by men who still make real in their own lives the supranational Muslim community. They are confronted by that combination of bazar and mosque, or in this case bazar and *dargah*, which has so often worked as the conscience of the Sultan.

There are just one or two areas of niggling doubt. A rigid distinction is made between *alim* and sufi. We are given the impression that there are *ulama* and there are sufis—different people, embodying distinct traditions, and the only hint that they might mingle in one person comes when we learn that some sufi children were taught by an *alim*. It is as though al-Ghazzali never lived and the *Ihya ulum al-Din* was never written. It may be that Bijapuri's *ulama* would suffer no taint of mysticism, but that they should apparently be so free of it, especially in an area exposed to Iranian influence for at least 200 years, seems unlikely—though if true, worthy of comment.

A more serious doubt flows from the leading assumption of the book which is that, if we understand the socio-historical context in which sufis live, and the changes that take place in it, we have all we need to know to understand their changing responses to their environment. Study society, Eaton seems to say, and you will unlock the springs of human action. Ideas have no power of their own; they are mere products of man's necessity; a dependent variable in the argument. Perhaps Eaton did not intend that his attempt to reveal the social dimensions of sufi existences should appear thus. But if historians wish to know why Bijapur sufis moved as they did, they must realize that the story is not yet fully told. Their world of ideas and the movements within it are still to be explored. We need, for instance, to be able to consider the possibility, if only to be able to dismiss it, that the growth of the 'reformist sufis' may have owed as must to intellectual developments in Mecca and Medina as to some mechanistic response to the syncretism of the Bijapur court.

These reservations apart, there should be no doubt that this is one of the best of those mature first books which now come in increasing numbers from American South Asianists. Rich in skill and fact, suggestive, stimulating, it lays bare a whole new subject; the publishers, perhaps, sensed this as they have made it a most beautiful book. Imitators it is bound to have, and they will be tribute to its achievement.

Chapter Eleven

*Nineteenth-Century Indian Islam**

Some day someone will have to take on Sir Sayyid Ahmad Khan. This is no mean task. Consider the distances he travelled in his lifetime: from the Persianate sophistication of the Mughal court to the drab purposefulness of British mofussil station, from a Ptolemean to a Copernican understanding of the place of the earth in the universe, from a traditional Islamic faith to one which went hand in hand with modern science. Consider the spread of his interests: poetry, prose, theology, history, education, politics; he was a man of Baconian, even Jeffersonian range. Consider his impact on Indian Muslims: the most radical theologian of his time—and ours; the reconciler of the Muslim élite to Western things, the starting point of modern Urdu historiography, the Imam and Mujaddid according to Shibli of modern Urdu prose, the founder in spirit and in organizations of Muslim separatism; but above all things, a leader of men standing head and shoulders above his fellows yet able to command the energies and the respect of the best of them. Among those who led their people against the political, intellectual and spiritual challenges of the West in modern times, he has few peers. 'The biography of this extraordinary man,' declared his outstanding biographer Altaf Husain Hali, 'is not the kind of work that can be duly effected just by one or two authors.' Today, with at least fifteen books and 150 articles devoted to Sir Sayyid's achievement, Hali would appear to be right. Yet it is also true that, in spite of the many studies of aspects of Sir Sayyid's life, we are the poorer for

* David Lelyveld, *Aligarh's First Generation: Muslim Solidarity in British India* (Princeton: Princeton University Press, 1978), pp. xxii, 380; Christian W. Troll, *Sayyid Ahmad Khan: A Reinterpretation of Muslim Theology* (New Delhi: Vikas Publishing House, 1978), pp. xxii, 384.

the want of a successful attempt in recent times to embrace the whole.

Sir Sayyid is the central figure in Lelyveld's study, which aims first both to analyse the world from which Aligarh College sprang and to examine the first twenty-five years of its existence, and second, to explore how an Indian Muslim cultural identity may have changed as Muslims moved from the world of the Mughal cultural élite to the carefully orchestrated Victorian public school environment of Aligarh College. Lelyveld begins by presenting the cultural and institutional context in which the College was founded. He interprets the meaning of the word 'Muslim' as a group identity in what he terms the 'Colonial', 'Liberal', 'Mughal' and 'Islamic' models of Indian society; he examines the life patterns of the Mughal service élite and demonstrates how these patterns had to adapt for the élite to survive as the British introduced the bureaucratic institutions of the modern state. After describing the campaign to establish Aligarh College, the élite's route to survival under the British, he moves to the 'heart of work' which explores what Aligarh's first generation of students experienced—the knowledge they were given, the intellectual style they were taught, the especial sense of Muslim solidarity they came to feel. Finally, and somewhat reluctantly, one senses, he looks at the world beyond Aligarh to assess the impact of its old boys, most particularly in the growth of a separate Muslim political movement alongside Indian nationalism.

It should be clear from the beginning that this book contains jewels. There is the long chapter 'Sharif Culture and British Rule' in which, drawing on a wide range of sources—biographies, fiction and feel, Lelyveld guides us along the path taken by the well-born Muslim from mother's breast to government office. He demonstrates, as never before, the shock which the institutional changes of British rule administered to a whole system of family culture, of upbringing, of getting on in life; and in doing so helps to explain why Muslims had difficulty in entering the British educational system. Then there is that 'heart of the work' in which Lelyveld, using in particular materials from the Aligarh Archives which to my knowledge no scholar has been privileged to use before though many have supplicated, explores student life and the world of learning. Cut off from the rest of his society the young sprig of the Mughal élite was given a training unique in India. He did not just pick up English learning according to the Calcutta or Allahabad syllabus, but also English ways and English style. It did not do to be a swot, or a 'smug' as they were called: the Aligarh man had to speak well in public and to talk well in private; he was to play games, or at least to enjoy the idea of them, and he was expected to do everything with a degree of *savoir faire*. Shaukat Ali was the archetype, captain of cricket, popular, a swell, yet bright enough to do little work and not be ploughed. This style was transmitted by the English staff, amongst the ablest undergraduates of their generation, whose attempts to recreate with missionary zeal a Cambridge in India is sympathetically described. As time passed their grip on the College strengthened, which amongst other things led to a tightening up of student religious observance. There were prayer monitors, daily readings of the Quran, while a maulvi from Deoband was appointed religious Dean. It was compulsory chapel all over again, except it was not 'muscular Christians' in the making but 'muscular Muslims'. Sir Sayyid was delighted by such successful cultural imperialism: the aim of the College, he told the Education Commission in 1882, no doubt consciously echoing Macaulay, was 'to form a class of persons, Muhammedan in religion, Indian in blood and colour, but English in taste, in opinions, and in intellect'.

Out of the contrast between sharif upbringing and Aligarh College education flows the answer to Lelyveld's second major question concerning the way in which cultural identity, perceptions of what it was to be Muslim, may have changed in the context of the restructuring of social and political institutions under colonial rule. So we move from a 'Mughal' society of the early nineteenth century in which Muslims identified primarily with family and lineage, and through these with the Mughal political system, to the late nineteenth century product of colonial rule, Aligarh College, in whose hothouse atmosphere young Muslims discovered a common identity as Muslim students. This new affiliation was stronger than the old ties of lineage, it was powerfully manifest in the first Aligarh student strike in which the young showed remarkable cohesion in braving the displeasure of their elders, and was projected later into the activities of the Educational Conference, the Muslim League and politics generally—not by chance did Muhammad Ali's quintessentially Aligarh newspaper come to be called the *Comrade*. 'As the political system shifted from Mughal to British patterns, the cultural meaning of a group identity' also changed. With changes in the socio-political context, being a Muslim came to have political connotation; a simple point, well-made, which adds another dimension to our understanding of how the Muslim political identity emerged.

In the end, however, Lelyveld makes no more than this simple point. Of course he tells the story of Aligarh as never before, and does so with a sensitivity to his subject and a command of literary artifice which is unusual—his book will live long and deservedly, but he does not take his argument any further than this simple point. Yet it cries out to be played in context, and not just in the context of Aligarh in Indian politics up to the First World War which he gives us, but also in that of the theory on which it clearly bears. Lelyveld has described a process which increases our understanding of the development of Muslim separatism but gives little idea of how important it might be: in his very last paragraph he merely sets it down beside other factors like British imperialism and the 'anti-Muslim' acts of others. Then again, Lelyveld's description of the growth of peer-group loyalties to displace older loyalties to family and to elders surely deserves some wider Indian airing. Is it not full of possibilities? And might it not have been related, moreover, to the modernization theory from which it would seem to derive? But no. 'Here is my mite,' he seems to say, 'make of it what you will.'

Then there is a question about the 'simple point', the central argument itself, which needs to be raised because Lelyveld does not make himself clear. He seems to allow no fragment of autonomy to Islamic ideas in the Muslims' changing perceptions of themselves; the spirit which drives men in every generation to explore the fundamentals of their faith is given no weight. What it was to be a Muslim is made to seem entirely a function of the changing socio-political context; there is no core of perception or experience which is not subject to the moment and the place. Ponder over what Lelyveld thinks it important to tell us about the sharif Muslims of nineteenth-century India and this impression is reinforced. Theirs is a Mughal world of complaisant *ulama* and dynastic allegiance, a world in which the logic of power is greater than the faith in dictating a man's identity. The significance of men, who like Shah Waliullah reacted to the decline of Muslim power in the eighteenth century by purifying Islamic practice of Hindu accretions, by distinguishing between Muslim and non-Muslim more rigorously, and indeed, by inviting Ahmad Shah of Afghanistan to invade to protect the dar ul-Islam, is discounted. The many *ulama* and religious families in the sharif class, their position at the heart of intellectual life especially in early nineteenth-century Delhi, their preaching of a reformist message, their religious debating both with other Muslims and with Christians, the heightened religious consciousness which was generated and surely permeated the Muslim's vision of himself, is ignored. Lelyveld draws heavily on the life of Sir Sayyid to illustrate his argument, but one would not guess from what he writes that Sir Sayyid wrote religious tracts and reflected the heightened religious atmosphere of his time. Indeed we are given the opposite impression, Sir Sayyid being represented as the kind of man who knew how to be pious 'when appropriate'. Yet Hali described his piety as 'terrifying': 'Man cannot forget God,' declared Sir Sayyid, 'God himself pursues us to tenaciously that if we want to leave him, he does not leave us!' It is hard to believe that the religious concerns which Sir Sayyid pursued from the beginning to the end of his life did not influence the formation of the Muslim political identity he came to have, just as it is hard to accept that the growing religious awareness of the nineteenth century did not resound amongst the sharif Muslims and alter their perceptions of themselves. Of course, it did not of itself dictate the development of a Muslim political identity, but it did interact with the socio-political context and thus helped to form one.

Christian Troll understands the relationship between ideas and their context in precisely this light. Sir Sayyid's life, he declares, 'exemplifies that change of ideas, rather than being a mere epiphenomenon or ideological superstructure of changes in the economic, social and political field, is in fact related to all of them by way of mutual interaction.' This, moreover, was how Sir Sayyid saw things himself: 'his religious thought developed for intrinsic reasons. ... He does not think that his ideas had altered simply in consequence of a radically changing social and cultural pattern.' On this assumption Troll bases his study of the development of Sir Sayyid's theology. He looks for the origins of Sir Sayyid's theological vision of Islam; examines how that vision was influenced by the challenges of Christian preaching, of historical criticism and of the natural sciences, and shows how these challenges came to modify his per- ception of Muslim religious thought. In addition Troll places Sir Sayyid in his intellectual context, assesses his contribution to Muslim theology and expounds and analyses his beliefs. He supports this last endeavour with 130 pages of Sir Sayyid's writings, most of which are translated for the first time.

Troll enriches our understanding of Sir Sayyid in several ways. He shows, for instance, how distorted our vision of him has become because it has focused primarily on the post-Mutiny period of his life when he was absorbed by the religious challenges of Western science and the political challenges of British rule. Sir Sayyid did, after all, live as much of his life before 1857 as after, and his early days in the vibrant intellectual atmosphere of pre-Mutiny Delhi left a powerful impress upon him. Here his mind was formed, and here he became firmly rooted in the religious traditions of Indian Islam. He was steeped in its formative influences, as-Suyuti, Ibn al-Arabi and al-Ghazali for instance; indeed, once he attempted to translate the great sage of Tus into Urdu. Though not a maulvi, he wrote works which any able *alim* of his day might well have written: a biography of the Prophet for mawlid recitation, a piece on the dead and tombs, a piece on visualizing within the image of one's spiritual guide, and a piece on piri-muridi which adopts the position popular amongst nineteenth-century Indian *ulama* that tariqat and shariat should go hand in hand. All that he wrote in the religious field—for he wrote much history too—betrayed the mark of major strands in contemporary Indo-Islamic thought: the restrained sufism of the Naqshbandi–Mujaddidi tradition with which his family was closely associated, the flexible approach to *sharia* interpretation which typified Shah Waliullah and his descendants, and the driving desire to purify Indian Islam of all non-Muslim practices which characterized the Mujahidin movement of Sayyid Ahmad Shahid.

What Troll is particularly keen to demonstrate is the inner coherence of Sir Sayyid's religious thought. From the beginning of his life, as the Sayyid himself declares when he introduces his collected religious writings in 1883, he sought to establish a 'pure' or 'true' Islam, an Islam unencumbered by the accretions of later development and fit to meet the challenges of the age. If in the 1830s and 1840s this meant removing Hindu elements from Islamic practice and bringing forward the Prophet as the model of the perfect Muslim life, in the 1860s and 1870s it meant reconciling modern science with revealed truth in the way in which one thousand years before Muslims had reconciled Greek Philosophy with Quranic revelation. Sir Sayyid's concern with theology was not merely a response to the challenges of British rule but a product of 'a long-existing commitment to, and an ever-widening knowledge of, the theological tradition of Islam'. It may be fashionable to diminish the impact of European rule on colonial societies but Troll's argument, and the evidence he brings to bear, carries overwhelming weight.

A similar continuity in Sir Sayyid's life emerges from the writings which Troll so illuminatingly appends to the book. One does not read for long, whether the piece be written at the beginning or towards the end of his life, before being struck by the power of his faith. Listen to these verses in praise of the Prophet written when he was twenty-four: 'My heart and soul, may they be a sacrifice to you, O Muhammad! My head, be it the dust for your feet to rest upon! Bless Muhammad and the family of Muhammad, Oh God! Praise be to God!' Listen again to the final sentence of a trenchant statement of his credo given to the Anjuman-i Himayat-i Islam when he was sixty-seven: 'After considerable reflection and thought I became deeply convinced that if there is any true religion it is Islam alone, and I reaffirm Islam on the basis of this heartfelt certainty, not because I was born in a Muslim home and because I am a Muslim.' One wonders that such burning faith did not release Sir Sayyid from the necessity of pursuing scientific truth in the way that his English contemporary Philip Gosse FRS, when he found that his own research and that of Darwin challenged the book of Genesis, abandoned science and chose Genesis. Such conflicts caused Sir Sayyid, some of whose family had been experimental scientists within the traditional Islamic frame, few problems at least from the 1860s: if scripture and scientific fact appeared to be in conflict, either science was wrong or he had failed to understand God's message.

Troll's writing makes the magnitude of Sir Sayyid's intellectual achievement more clear. He realized before anyone else in the world of Islam, except perhaps Shihabeddin Marjani (1818–89) the Tartar mulla, theologian and historian of Kazan, that Muslims must prepare to face the challenges of Western science and philosophy. More than twenty years before Muhammad Abduh, who is generally regarded as the first proponent of Islamic modernism, published the essentials of his reformed theology, Sir Sayyid had published and demonstrated his theological principles. And this was achieved without, perhaps because he was without, a maulvi's education, like the great twentieth-century Indo-Muslim thinker Maulana Maududi. One part of his work remains unique in modern Muslim theological scholarship, the evaluation of the Christian and Jewish scriptures and dogma till the coming of Muhammad. Another part, his promotion of the historical study of Muslim religious thought is widely accepted by Indian Muslims today. He markedly influenced Shibli, Iqbal and Azad, while the contents of *madrasa* libraries reveal that he remains a challenge to the modern *ulama*. But a full understanding of his influence awaits, as Troll says, the much needed detailed study of the development of theological thought in India from the 1870s.

It is a pity that Troll himself could not have placed Sir Sayyid more illuminatingly in the context of modern Islamic thought, but like Lelyveld he limits his scope with that endemic thesis-writer's caution. This may rob him of the wider audience he deserves, as will the lack of a glossary which is demanded by the many Arabic technical terms he uses. On the other hand the book remains a remarkable feat of scholarship in Arabic, Persian and Urdu; there are not many Western scholars who can pick up faint resonances of Shah Waliullah or Imam Ghazali in an Urdu text. There are not many too whose understanding remains so little clouded by secularism and materialism. Troll should be read with Lelyveld to gain some balance of interpretation. Together the two books mark the greatest single advance in our appreciation of Sir Sayyid's achievement since Hali published *Hayat-i Jawid* in 1901. They also suggest what might be learned should one scholar devote himself to studying in depth every aspect of this remarkable human being.

Chapter Twelve

Islam in Malabar*

Muslims first settled on India's southwestern shore a century or so after the death of the Prophet Muhammad. For nearly eight hundred years they traded peacefully. Then, in 1498, the Portuguese arrived, and these Muslims, Mappilas as they were known, became the first to experience what all South Asian Muslims were eventually to suffer: the fate of being caught between the hammer of European pressure and the anvil of Hindu society. The Mappilas responded by developing a tradition of holy war and martyrdom. The tradition is enshrined in an epic work, the *Gift to the Holy Warriors in Respect to Some Deeds of the Portuguese*; it is celebrated in the body of Mappila literature, nine-tenths of which is devoted to martial songs; it has been manifest in outbreaks of religious violence—there were thirty-two, for instance, between 1836 and 1919, in which 319 Mappilas were killed, and the process reached its climax in the rebellion of 1921–22, in which, according to the Mappilas, up to 10,000 lives were lost.

Stephen Dale explains how Portuguese assaults on Muslim control of the Kerala spice trade led both to the growth of Mappila traditions of violence and to the breakdown of the good relations between the Mappilas and dominant Hindu castes. The European intrusion brought competition between the Mappilas, the Malayali Rajas and the Nayar aristocracy for territorial control and for social and economic influence. By the early eighteenth century the competition was flaring into bloody incidents between the Mappilas and the Nayars; by the late eighteenth century, when Mysorean

* Stephen Frederic Dale, *Islamic Society on the South Asian Frontier: The Mappilas of Malabar 1498–1922* (Oxford: Clarendon Press, 1980), pp. xvii, 290. 7 plates, 8 maps.

influence had tipped the balance in favour of the Mappilas, it had developed into civil war. The British conquest shifted the balance back in favour of the Hindu landed castes who were given new powers of coercion and eviction over their Mappila tenants by British attempts to regulate Malabar land tenure. The Mappilas found themselves boxed in; they had finally lost their struggle against the European, the odds were yet more firmly stacked in favour of the Hindu. They responded with a long series of attacks on the Hindu landed castes which 'represented a continuation of the Mappila challenge to the economic and social power of the upper castes and by extension a challenge to the political authority of the British'. These attacks were carried out as ritual acts in which the Mappilas sought martyrdom. Dale emphasizes, moreover, that they were not just religious expressions of social and economic grievances but, on occasion, the expression of religious drive alone. The climax to the attacks was the rebellion of 1921–22 in which the Mappilas strove to bring Islamic ideology to an advanced state of practice on earth by establishing an Islamic state.

It should be said straightaway that this is a good monograph. There is a challenging argument about Islamic traditions of holy war and martyrdom, and Muslim behaviour in frontier situations, which is developed through the text. The changing economic and social background to Mappila religious violence is set out, although a simple economic determinism is very properly eschewed. The details of actual outbreaks are described with all the care that an Asa Briggs, an Eric Hobsbawm, or a George Rudé might once have devoted to chartists, grain rioters or the political mob. Important evidence, moreover, is brought forward to show how the Mappilas were driven to further levels of violence by Islamic inputs from outside—the new fundamentalism brought by Sayyid Fadl from Arabia in the early nineteenth century, for instance—and the Islamic anxieties generated by the last throes of the Ottoman empire and caliphate in the twentieth century. There is an exhaustive bibliography; eight most informative maps chart Malabar and its Mappilas; black-and-white plates of storied mosques hint at how the Mappilas might have more in common with the Muslims of Sumatra and Java than with those of northern India. Materials in six languages have been studied. Archives in India, Portugal and Britain have been consulted. The air of Mappila villages, bazars and festivals has been sniffed and flavours absorbed; we can savour for the first time the special and different worlds of Ponnani, Kondotti and Tirurangadi. This work of deep and careful scholarship deserves prominent notice.

This said, there is one reservation to be made: for a scholar whose subject is the Islamic dimension of Mappila life, Dale seems to have ignored, almost wilfully, some of its Islamic possibilities. For instance, he makes only one reference, his very last, to R.E. Miller's *Mappila Muslims of Kerala: A Study of Islamic Trends*, which was published in 1976. Miller is a historian and missionary who has worked in Kerala for nearly thirty years. His book says some of the same things as Dale's but without the latter's concern to develop an overall argument; his book also offers much information about the nature of Islam in Kerala and several important observations.

Miller notes, for example, that the Mappila outbreaks of the mid-nineteenth century coincided with an extraordinarily high rate of population growth in the Mappila community, which was derived in the main from the conversion of Hindu depressed castes. For the period 1831–51, the increase was estimated at 42.8 per cent; large increases were also noted for later in the century. The period of growing violence, Miller suggests, coincided with a period in which Mappila society was under considerable demographic pressure, a time when its Arab-blooded elements were beginning to feel overwhelmed by converted Hindus, indeed Mappila society itself was being redefined.[1] There seem to be interesting possibilities in this observation, which surely deserved consideration, if only to be dismissed.

There is a more substantial point which flows from Miller's extensive analysis of Islamic organization in Malabar society.[2] He tells us that today there are 5,350 mosques in the region, which is one for every 500 Mappilas, or one for every seventy Mappila homes. There are 2,500 *madrasas*, 25,000 religious teachers, and every mawlvi is assigned a particular number of families for whom he is responsible. All are supported by donations, fees and *waqf* income. This is a remarkable level of organization for any Islamic community, in particular one which is primarily rural. Are we to assume that it has suddenly sprung into existence? Certainly, in the first half of this century, there was considerable revivalist and fundamentalist activity, which was led by Wakkom Mawlvi and the Nadwat al-Mujahidin. But there is indication that the Mappilas may have been almost as well organized in the mid-nineteenth century as they are now. In 1851, according to government records, there were 1,058 Mappila mosques for a population which was probably rather less than the 630,000 counted in the 1871 census; indeed the ratio of mosques to Mappilas was probably not dissimilar to the present. There is the distinct possibility that the Mappilas had an unusually high level of communal organization as compared with other Muslim communities. Dale's explanation of Mappila behaviour in terms of the interactions of their Islamic ideologies of holy war and martyrdom and their economic and social position seems insufficient. Such ideologies flourished because there was a high level of Islamic consciousness. Doubtless this was stimulated by contact with the Hindu and British enemy on the frontier, but it was also nourished from within by the *ulama* in an extensive network of mosques and schools.

Mention of the *ulama* and their leadership represents another Islamic area which, had it been investigated further, might well have brought some shift of emphasis in Dale's argument. He emphasizes that at the heart of Mappila behaviour is a long-remembered and long-adopted tradition of *jihad* and martyrdom, and that, when this tradition is adopted more and more frequently in the nineteenth century as a course of action, it is in part because the *ulama* from abroad gave it fresh leadership and fresh vigour. These *ulama* were the Mambram Tannals of Tirurangadi. There was Sayyid Alawi, who came from the Hadramawt in the 1760s; he taught a strict adherence to the Quran and the *hadiths*, encouraged the building of mosques, the opposing of the British, and won widespread reverence amongst the Mappilas. There was Alawi's son, Sayyid Fadl; he also encouraged the building of mosques (between 1831 and 1851 the number in Malabar rose from 637 to 1,058), taught a strict adherence to Quran and *hadiths*, declared the murder of oppressive Hindus lawful, and in 1852 was expelled for his pains by the British. Dale tells us that violent action in the nineteenth century was not the way of all Mappilas but of those who 'mobilized around an ideology which was articulated by a specific and limited group of individuals, the Mambram Tannals and their disciples'. Nevertheless, they 'really only gave new content to a long tradition of religiously expressed violence'.

Here, perhaps, a point has been stretched too far. In the light of the Arabian background and education of the Mambram Tannals, and the emphasis in their teaching; in the light, too, of the restriction of violent outbursts to their followers and those of their disciples, we might not unreasonably argue that nineteenth-century Mappila violence had less to do with 'a long tradition of religiously expressed violence' interacting with economic and social conditions, than with the great movement of Islamic revival and reform. The latter gained much stimulus, though not exclusive stimulus, from teaching and spiritual leadership available in seventeenth and eighteenth-century Arabia, and in the eighteenth and nineteenth centuries was manifest in holy wars from West Africa to China, and from the Caucasus to island Southeast Asia. The nineteenth-century Mappila outbreaks, in fact, might just as well have been the result primarily of the interactions between the new wave of Islamic revival and conditions in the region. Unfortunately, Dale does not tell us quite enough about the Arabian origins and the intellectual history of the Mambram Tannals for us to form a judgement. Work on Middle Eastern materials like that of John Voll on the great cosmopolitan teaching centres of Mecca and Medina, where leading revivalists and reformers were taught,[3] and that of Anthony Johns on the connection between a leading teacher in Medina and the movement of Islamic thought and practice in northern Sumatra is needed.[4] Work might also be done on the Makhdum Tannals of Ponnani, who were generally regarded as the heads of the Mappila *ulama*, and to whom Dale refers but once. Indeed, with one exception, he uses no materials relating to them, or records emanating from them. Yet, the Ponnani Makhdum college is said to have been founded in the twelfth century, to have had dealings with at least one Mambram Tannal in the early nineteenth century, and for many hundreds of years down to the twentieth century, to have taught almost all the Mappila *ulama*. Moreover, the author of the *Gift to the Holy Warriors*, Zayn al-Din (1498–1581) who we are told encapsulated the Mappila *jihad* tradition and who was known as the 'junior Makhdum', was the college's greatest figure; his writings were standard Mappila textbooks. One senses that in the reasons why the Ponnani Makhdums surrendered effective leadership to the Mambram Tannals, there might lie the answer to the larger question of whether the Mambram Tannals represent a decisively new input into Malabar, or just new energy for an old tradition. Moreover, it is hard to believe that a group with a long history of Islamic teaching, which reaches right down to the present, has left no trace. We should hope to find in their records, as we can in those of other established groups of *ulama* for the late eighteenth and nineteenth centuries, accounts of their reactions to the incursion into the region of revivalist *ulema*, whose teachings were probably a threat to their authority. But this, too, might be stretching a point!

With regard to his work's wider significance, Dale points to the evidence that he offers of the European powers heavily influencing the development of Asian society long before they assumed political control, and certainly long before they experienced industrial revolutions; he thus modifies the arguments of Van Leur, Smail and others. This is fine. But, if the rather different interpretation of his evidence which we have suggested is correct, and it is better to talk of the impact of the world-wide movement of Islamic revival and reform rather than a fresh outbreak of a long-established local tradition, then it would seem that, while Dale certainly tells us about the traumatic effect of early European expansion, he also gives us another example of the unusual vigour of the Islamic world on the eve of the great expansion of European power. Indeed, he charts the beginning of a process of renewed and assertive Islamization which may prove to be of more long-term significance to the history of Kerala, perhaps of Asia, than the interlude of Western dominance.

The problem of Islamization draws us to the way in which Dale's work bears on one further matter of scholarly concern. In recent years a school of anthropologists have come to assert, as their leader Imtiaz Ahmad declares, that in India high Islamic and custom-centred traditions peacefully 'co-exist as complementary and integral parts of a single common religious system', and that they do so, and have done so, because of 'the constraints of Islam's own struggle for survival in an alien environment'.[5] Dale tells us of Muslims who have been by no means intimidated by the 'struggle for survival in an alien environment'; he reveals a continuing process of Islamization in Malabar. On the one hand there is conversion from Hinduism, which Miller tells us continues down to the present,[6] on the other, and more important, there is a continuing concern to model Mappila life more closely on the perfect pattern laid out in the Quran, the *hadiths* and the *sharia*. Sayyid Fadl told Mappila women that they should cover their breasts, and they did so. When a Hindu landlord ordered them to walk bare-breasted once more, he was killed. That Mappilas continue to make progress towards the pattern of perfection is suggested by the facts that their children begin their education at Islamic schools, that they support an unusually high level of Islamic organization, and that they have struggled to win political autonomy, which they achieved in part when the Muslim majority district of Mallappuram was formed in 1969. Far from wanting to coexist with what they perceive to be the high Islamic tradition, the Mappilas would seem to have striven down the centuries to realize it in their lives and in the organization of their society.

NOTES

1. R.E. Miller, *Mappila Muslims of Kerala; A Study in Islamic Trends* (Madras, 1976), pp. 121–22.
2. Ibid., esp. pp. 223–303.
3. J.O. Voll, *Islam: Continuity and Change in the Modern World* (Boulder, Colorado, 1982), pp. 56–9.
4. A.H. Johns, 'Friends in Grace: Ibrahim al-Kurani and Abd al-Rauf al-Singkeli' in S. Udin (ed.), *Spectrum: Essays Presented to Sultan Takdir Alisjahbana on his Seventieth Birthday* (Jakarta, 1978), pp. 485–95.
5. I. Ahmad (ed.), *Ritual and Religion among Muslims in India* (New Delhi, 1981), p. 15. For a general discussion of this issue see Francis Robinson, 'Islam and Muslim Society in South Asia' in *Contributions to Indian Sociology*, 1983, see chapter 2.
6. Miller, *Mappila Muslims*, pp. 240–41.

Chapter Thirteen

Islamic Revival[*]

For far too long, in Western eyes, the *'ulama* have appeared to be the obscurantist and uncreative opponents of 'progress'. For far too long, as well, non-Western societies have been thought fated to follow the Western path forward in the world; Western patterns would mould the organization of their public lives as they would also come to shape the movement of their hearts and minds; it was the inevitable result at first of civilization's onward march, and then of the world system's inexorable growth. The *'ulama* were little studied as compared with those few Muslims who reached out to learn their lessons from the West. The transmitters of the central messages of the beaten Islamic civilization were of little interest as compared with the Muslim evangelists for the European and American revelation. In consequence the great vitality of the purely Islamic world in the eighteenth and nineteenth centuries was ignored.

In the early 1970s the tide began to turn, and scholarly attention began to focus more strongly on the world of Islamic leadership and thought in recent times. The famous volume of essays in memory of von Grunebaum, *Scholars, Saints and Sufis: Muslim Religious Institutions since 1500* (California UP, 1972), edited by Nikkie Keddie, in which Hamid Algar made his prophetic analysis both of the strength of the *'ulama* in Iran and of the unique standing of Ayatollah Khomeini, was the first major indication that something new was stirring. Since then important work has appeared on *'ulama* and on their responses to modernization. There is, for instance, the work of Arnold Green on the Tunisian *'ulama* from 1873 to 1915, and that of Edmund Burke III on the Moroccan *'ulama* from 1860

[*] Barbara Daly Metcalf, *Islamic Revival in British India: Deoband, 1860–1900* (Princeton, New Jersey: Princeton University Press, 1982), pp. xiv, 386. Seven maps.

to 1912; there is the substantial work of Hamid Algar, Michael Fischer and Shahrough Akhavi on the Iranian *'ulama*; then for the cognoscenti there are the highly suggestive writings of John Voll on the world of the *'ulama* from the eighteenth century and the finely etched pieces of Anthony Johns on the *'ulama* of northern Sumatra. South Asia, so far, has seen little of this new movement of scholarship: Z.H. Faruqi's pioneering *The Deoband School and the Demand for Pakistan* (Bombay, 1963) and I.H. Qureshi's *Ulema in Politics* (Karachi, 1972) are chronicles too influenced by the political concerns of Muslims in India and Pakistan, S.A.A. Rizvi's *Shah Wali-Allah and his Times* (Canberra, 1980) and *Shah Abd al-Aziz: Puritanism, Sectarian Polemics and Jihad* (Canberra, 1982) are huge and somewhat ill-digested compilations in which others will quarry with profit. But now Barbara Metcalf has transformed the scene. Combining the highest standards of Western scholarship with both an unusual sympathy for her subject and an extensive knowledge of the Urdu sources, she has achieved a considerable advance in our understanding of the workings and the changing shape of nineteenth-century Islam. She has also written a book which sets a new standard for those who wish to comprehend the variety of Islamic reactions to modernization in an era of Western domination.

At its simplest level, Metcalf's book analyses the responses of *'ulama* to the collapse of Muslim political power and the rise of British power. A thoughtful introduction considers the pattern of Islamic reform as a worldwide phenomenon, and directs our attention, as Marshall Hodgson has also done, to the value of studying South Asian Muslim behaviour as a guide to that of Muslims in the world as a whole. In chapters one and two the *'ulama* in eighteenth-century India are described, the strands in the nineteenth-century movements of revival and reform are laid out, major activities and important figures in the last years of Mughal Delhi are identified, the psychological blow of the Mutiny and its suppression is made plain. Then we move to the heart of the book in which the Deoband movement, the most constructive and most important Islamic movement of the past century is examined. We see how the Deoband *madrasa* came to be founded, how it was organized, how it taught, and how it spawned new *madrasas* so that by the centenary year of 1967 they were said to number 8,934. We learn of the emphases in the work of the Deobandi *'ulama*, we discover their particular quality as sufi shaikhs, we are allowed to peep into the world of the pupil and of the disciple. We follow the activities of Deobandis in nineteenth-century India at large, their achievement as champions in prose and in debate, the nature of their Islamic vision. We examine the regions and the families from which they came, their background and their social standing as *'ulama* is established. This done, the movement is set in the context of the main Islamic movements and responses to the West in northern India; the radical Ahl-i-Hadiths and the latitudinarian Barelwis, the Nadwah which wanted to make *'ulama* into the political leaders of all Muslims, and Aligarh College whose graduates sought leadership too, but on Western terms. Then the book concludes by assessing how much came to be different in Indian Islam, and how much remained the same.

Metcalf develops her argument from the perspective of the *'ulama* themselves. Indeed, the whole book is underpinned by the belief, which I endorse, that there is an Islamic reality and that the historian must accept this before genuinely profitable study can begin. We are dealing with people, reformers and revivalists in the main, whose vision was shaped by their participation in a great religious tradition, who lived in the company of the Prophet, great Muslims and great sufi shaikhs of yore, who had a clear view of life and how it ought to be lived, who stood for a standard which was quite different from that of their imperial overloads, who used the technical advances of modernization to seek Islamic ends, and who embraced the great changes of modern times, political, economic and social within an Islamic frame. None of this is stridently put, and the overall tone is one of rigour and judicious understatement, although a distinct preference for the *'ulama* as opposed to the British is barely concealed. Indeed, plenty of sympathy and feel is expressed for the world of the Islamic learned, whether it is an evocative description of Deoband, from whose very ground, according to Saiyid Ahmad Shahid, came an 'odor of learning', or it is the story of a supportive sufis shaikh as he counsels a disciple through his infatuation with a beautiful boy. Moreover, there are also discreet moments of humour. It is good to know that early nineteenth-century reformers eager to encourage widow remarriage went in for 'widow-rustling' (p. 59), how rowdy Afghan students shot up Deoband station (p.135), and how God became an Urdu speaker (p. 198).

Among Metcalf's notable achievements is the study of the various reactions amongst the *'ulama* of northern India to Muslim decline and British dominance, which offers new information and many insights regarding the Barelwis, the Ahl-i-Hadiths, the Nadwah and the Deoband school. The Barelwis, who call themselves the Ahl-i sunnat wa jama'at, are now a considerable group in Pakistan and in recent years have begun to make themselves felt in Britain. For the first time their background is traced in terms of people and ideas, the remarkable personality and particular Islamic orientation of their founder, Ahmad Riza Khan, is described at length. The social origins and widespread influence of the Ahl-i-Hadiths is examined so that now can we can understand them as a radical intellectual leaven, comprising many of the best educated and best born Muslims of the time, which worked amongst northern India's learned men and which stressed in particular the responsibility of the individual for the Islamic standard of his life. The high ambition and the failure of the Nadwat al-ulama is made clear, as is the unusual psychology of its leading figure, Maulana Shibli. But Metcalf's greatest feat is the study of Deoband, a study which reaches far beyond the simple outline drawn by Faruqi two decades ago, and challenges some of the assumptions on which the school has taken its place in Indian nationalist mythology. Now we can share in the life and the workings of an Indian *madrasa*, the world of the nineteenth-century *'alim* and sufi loses some of its mystery, and the men themselves emerge as men of flesh and blood. We also have a sharper understanding of how they fitted into their social milieu. They were not, as Peter Hardy once suggested, a lesser bourgeoisie cut off from the 'collaborating class' of government officials and big landlords, but by and large men of high social standing, ashraf, and if a man were not ashraf such was the perceived status of the *'ulama* that by becoming an *'alim* he might begin to assert ashraf status. Moreover, analysis of the 2,658 listed as donors to Deoband in its first thirty years (Metcalf made a card for each) suggests that most of the *madrasa*'s supporters were ashraf too.

Metcalf's second notable achievement is to demonstrate the vitality of eighteenth and nineteenth-century Indian Islam and the new religious forms which it generated. She reminds us, as Albert Hourani once suggested, that, seen from the point of view of Islamic history overall, the eighteenth century might be considered Islam's Indian century. This was the time when India was a centre of new spirit and new ideas which were felt elsewhere. There is the wide range of responses to the decline of Muslim power, the new patterns for the *'ulama* revealed by the Firangi Mahal family of Lucknow and Shah Wali Allah's family of Delhi, the new vigour amongst the pirs of Sind, the Chishtiya in the Punjab and the Naqshbandiya in Delhi. Out of these strands there grew the nineteenth-century revival which worked in various ways amongst most north Indian *'ulama* and saw its greatest realization in the movement of the Deobandi *'ulama*. Two distinct but connected results emerge, although Metcalf, it should be said, would never state them quite so baldly. On the one hand, there is the growth of Islamic practice based more firmly on the Quran, the Hadiths and the Shari'a—scripturalist Islam. It is 'rationalizing in the Weberian sense of making religion self-conscious, systematic, and based on abstract principles'. Groups of Muslims come forward who, while they do not in the main reject sufism, increasingly see themselves as following religious practice which is different from that of the sufi shrines, indeed they often define their practice in contrast to the parochial forms of the shrines. For theirs was a universal form, in which Muslims all over India, indeed all over the world could share; they no longer accepted the compromises with local customs and other religious communities which the sufi pioneers and Muslim princes had been prepared to make. On the other hand, *'ulama* strove to build machinery both for transmitting the central messages of Islam and for fashioning an Islamic community in a world in which there was no Islamic power. As they could no longer rely on the authority of Muslim sultans, they must now turn to the efforts of Muslims themselves. All kinds of techniques for broadcasting Islamic knowledge were developed: new emphasis was given to the nurturing of personalities who so embodied Islam that they would be models for the community; the Quran, and important works of Islamic scholarship, were translated into the vernaculars; legal opinions were issued directly to believers and later published in collections for popular guidance; religious works were written for public consumption; public debates were held to discuss disputed points of law; schools were founded, which were paid for by the people rather than by rulers, and which depended on the working of a bureaucratic system rather than the survival of individuals. At the same time attitudes were encouraged which would smooth the working of the new techniques and underpin the new Islamic forms. Most important was the emphasis on personal responsibility in religious observance. As right conduct could no longer be imposed on Muslims from without, they must now learn how to discipline themselves from within.

Thus the outcome of the *'ulama*'s response to the decline of Mughal power and the rise of British rule was the fashioning of a distinct religious style, which the Deobandis came to recognize self-consciously as their own *maslak* or way, supported by new forms of organization quite independent of the state. This came to exist side by side with India's other Islamic styles but hoped as time went by to mould them all in its likeness. It was a new and exciting Islamic development, but in their creativity the Deobandis were also 'firmly based in the long tradition of the faith and fulfilled rather than disowned their cherished heritage'. There were, of course, similar developments elsewhere in the Islamic world, to which parallels might be drawn. There is the heightend concern to develop personalities which embody Islamic knowledge which is represented by that increasing emphasis throughout the nineteenth-century Muslim world on the Prophet as a model, which Anne-Marie Schimmel has noted. There is the assertion of the right of the *'ulama* to lead society at large, represented, for instance, in eighteenth-century Iran by the ideological victory of the Usuli *'ulama* over the Akhbari *'ulama*. There is the spreading of Islamic knowledge through the use of the vernacular, as did 'Abd al-Qayyum Nasiri in Czarist Russia. There is the founding of great networks of schools, privately funded and apart from the state, as did the Muhammadiya in Dutch South East Asia. No movement outside South Asia shared the precise orientation of the Deobandi way, but many had similar aims and employed similar techniques in their pursuit. Nevertheless, amongst the range of fertile responses to the threat of losing control of Muslim society and the Muslim future, that of Deoband seems amongst the most creative and the most dynamic, just as it has also come to be amongst the most enduring.

Metcalf's third notable achievement is to tell us why the Deobandi way should have been so successful. She shows how it struck a powerful psychological chord amongst the Muslim ashraf whose world was contained by British rule and whose Muslim pride was greatly bruised. *'Ulama* of learning and humility, who manifest Islamic learning in their outward lives and who submitted to no earthly powers, were 'particularly valued in a period that lacked

Muslim political institutions to affirm communal unity'. Indeed, the prime expression of Islamic being seemed to move from the community to the individual. But there was also a more concrete appeal to the ashraf, whose path to government service under British rule the Deobandis eased. No *jihad* need be performed, no economic sacrifice made. Such a strategy was made possible by reformist doctrine which emphasized correct religious behaviour after an authentic text and so fostered a sense of cultural self-esteem. A Saiyid might work for the politically dominant British so long as he was sure that he was morally superior. The implications went further. Muslims often feel that, if their fortunes fail, it is because they live imperfect Muslim lives. The Deobandi strategy meant that the ashraf might feel that if they lived better Muslim lives, not only would they have fresh spiritual and cultural strength as individuals, but the political fortunes of the community would be transformed as well. It was, as Metcalf points out, a very Gandhian vision of the road to independence.

Metcalf's fourth notable achievement, although it is not one to which she explicitly refers, is to offer plentiful evidence for what one might term the vulgarization of Islamic learning. She tells us how in the nineteenth century, Indian *'ulama* developed a wide range of new methods for the transmission and broadcasting of Islamic knowledge. To add to the networks of schools founded, the new emphasis in sufism, and the work of translation mentioned above, there was the harnessing of this effort to the lithographic printing press, which at last made it possible mechanically to produce large editions of works in Islamic scripts in the way that it had been possible to reproduce European Christian works since the fifteenth century. *'Ulama* leapt at the opportunities provided by the lithographic press; some turned them into big business. Everything was published from Islamic classics to the simplest textbooks, from significant achievements of seventeenth and eighteenth-century Indian scholarship to the biographies of holy men and the collections of *fatawa* through which *'ulama* hoped to provide new guidance for the community. 'Now God has been gracious in providing books,' one learned man rejoiced in 1895, 'books which one could not see in dreams or conceive of in imagination are now available for cowries.' In fact, Metcalf describes for us a revolution in the availability of Islamic knowledge in India. What had previously been the monopoly of learned and holy men, what even they had struggled to command, because books were so rare and so costly, was now readily available to all those members of the community who could read. Of course, what was happening in India was also happening elsewhere in the Islamic world, though rarely so early and to such a full extent. It is one of the greatest transitions in Islamic history, the fullness of whose historical significance has still to be worked out no less than its meaning for contemporary Muslim affairs has still to be appreciated.

There are few errors, indeed, so few that one is tempted to suggest that Metcalf might have slipped in the few there are on purpose, like the maker of a carpet, so as not to pretend to that perfection which belongs to God alone: Sambhal becomes Sanbhal (p. 31n. 104), Saiyid Ahmad Shahid's *Taqwiyatu'l-Iman* is attacked by some Shia bug and becomes *Taqwiyatu'l-Imam*, she fails to realize that 'Abd al-Hayy Firangi Mahalli and 'Abd al-Hayy Lakhnawi are the same person (pp. 282–83), the odd Americanism, which might confuse, has crept in as when Saiyid Ahmad Khan places 'his son in school in Cambridge' (p. 321).

Nevertheless, there are several points of emphasis and interpretation which should be questioned. There are some regarding the Firangi Mahallis, the family of Lucknow *'ulama* who did so much to sustain the Indian tradition of Islamic learning from the decline of the Mughal Empire to the great surge in the nineteenth century of revival and reform. We are told, for instance, that 'wherever there was a prince Firangi Mahallis sought positions under him' (p. 32). Certainly, there were many Firangi Mahallis associated with princely courts, but the sources do not support the assertion that all members of the family were running after princes for posts in the way that the poet Ghalib pestered the British about his pension. They tend to speak of distinguished scholars 'being called' to a certain court. Then, amongst several lines in the family, association with princes was always thought undesirable, and especially so from the mid-nineteenth century onwards; teaching, scholarship and spiritual leadership were the only occupations to be followed. Secondly, there is the suggestion that the Firangi Mahallis failed to respond to the decline of Muslim power by addressing a more widely based audience, preferring to focus on abstruse and technical kinds of scholarship (p. 33). Again, there is some truth in this, but the emphasis is wrong. There were initiatives as scholars and as teachers to meet the situation. There was, moreover, an attempt to reach out to that more widely based audience through the introduction of maulud ceremonies in Lucknow, Allahabad and Madras, which were designed to be a form of public education. Finally, there is the photograph on p. 34 which purports to depict 'a group of scholars at Firangi Mahall today'. It depicts in fact my good friend Maulana Faqir Mian who had just retired as a minor government servant to succeed Maulana Nasir Mian, his father, as sajjada in the silsila which flows from the great eighteenth-century scholar, Maulana 'Abd al-'Ali Bahr al-Ulum. But no scholar was he, or those about him, just a hereditary holy man, and one only beginning to learn his calling at that.

A further question must be raised regarding the level of organization which Metcalf finds amongst the *'ulama*. She makes the important point that the various groups are all beginning to experiment with new forms of organization. But to suggest that 'formal educational institutions, annual conferences, and deputations for proselytisation were standard by the beginning of this century' (p. 314) is to go too far. If this were true of the Deobandis, and to a lesser extent of the Ahl-i-Hadiths, it gives a false impression of the levels of organization amongst the Barelwis. There was still much about them of the old-style one-man-band focused around the personality of Ahmad Riza Khan; their first real *madrasa*, the Jami'at-i Manzir-i Islam, was not founded until 1905. One feels that Metcalf may have succumbed to the temptation of ascribing too much of the Deobandi achievement to other groups of *'ulama*. This is misleading, because to lump all these groups together as having acquired 'modern' institutional forms by 1900 blurs the very real distinction of the Deobandis, which was to have created an organization with a very high level of bureaucratic efficiency, an organization greater than individuals or families, one with a momentum of its own, and one which to this day stands out amongst the organization of the *'ulama*.

But the most important question concerns just how much weight we should give to the changes in Indian Islam which Metcalf has set before us. In concluding she draws together the strands in her argument. That Indian Islam was not transformed in some Western image is made clear from the start. Change was largely stimulated and constrained by Western expansion, but the changes themselves were long characteristic of the Islamic tradition. 'Religious change in this period primarily entailed self-conscious reassessment of what was deemed authentic religion—it was not syncretism, not acculturation to western patterns, not conversion.' While useful Western knowledge was not disdained, Islam remained the only frame of reference, the only source of inspiration. There were changes in religious thought: Islamic teaching 'was presented increasingly on the basis of systematic assessment against an ideal of the original sources', the Quran and Hadiths were emphasized as never in the recent past, there was a 'shift in emphasis and meaning of central symbols of the faith'. There were changes in institutions: the variety of *'ulama*, the worldly, the orthodox, the righteous disappeared, and now there were only the righteous; sufis became less of a law unto themselves and placed increasing emphasis on the holy law; there emerged a religious specialist, typically both *'alim* and shaikh, whose prime concern was not the organization of state and society but the moral qualities of individual Muslims, and whose main field of action was the school. These changes were expressed through a diversity of religious styles and interpretations, which revealed overall a move away from local cults to formulations found in written tradition. As Muslims made the move, and came to espouse a particular vision of the true path, they came increasingly to quarrel with Muslims who took other paths. Nevertheless, the result of religious change was 'for all the bitterness of conflict among sectarian groups ... not that a previously united community was divided but that there was now substantial homogeneity amongst Muslims'. There was a new level of concern with religious life: more mosques were built, more schools founded, more religious books published, more pilgrimages undertaken, Urdu more widely shared than ever before. There was in fact a new form of religious awareness in which 'Muslims were ever more self-conscious, their religion not taken for granted but espoused deliberately'. The leaders of the movement saw little of this, they thought only in terms of renewal of old ways. To understand this, Metcalf urges, 'is crucial if one is not to be misled into seeing "modernity" where the participants would see Islam'.

Metcalf remains unclear as to how much weight we should give to this process of religious change, as to how widely it was felt by 1900. At one moment she talks of Indian Muslims, at another of north Indian Muslims, yet one senses it may be the former she has in mind. If true, objection must be raised. No one questions the vitality and the impact of the nineteenth-century revival, what we do question is quite how widely and how early that impact was felt in Sind, in the South, in Bengal, even in parts of the UP itself. Old religious styles persisted alongside the new. How else to explain, for instance, the rise of the old-style saint cult in the late nineteenth century of Hajji Waris Ali Shah of Deva, vastly popular till recent times? How else to explain the twentieth-century efforts of Maulana 'Abd al-Bari of Firangi Mahall to bring knowledge of the holy law to many pirs of northern India, simply because they were old-style sufi leaders? There were limits to the impact of this process of religious change. Such limits, of course, are hard to gauge; changes in man's perception of God are not amenable to the crude precision of percentages. Nevertheless, historians will need a clearer idea of where these limits might be found. They need it to be able to assess the movement's intrinsic significance. They need it, too, because the overall impact of the process of change will have to be weighed by those seeking to explain, for instance, how colonial rule interacted with Indian society, how a Muslim political identity came to be formed, or how Muslims came to move in the politics of twentieth-century South Asia.

These reservations, however, are of minor account as compared with Metcalf's formidable achievement. Her work is original, technically skilled, and full of ideas; she both introduces a whole new subject and places an elegant framework of argument over it. But most important is her approach. She knows that Islam is not marginal to the lives of the men she studies, but central to what they think and do. We are in the hands of a scholar who has sympathy for ways of understanding human experience other than her own, and passionately believes in the importance of approaching these ways of understanding on their own terms. These are good hands to be in. The approach helps us both to sympathize with, and to be moved by, the feat of the *'ulama* of nineteenth-century South Asia in preserving and in strengthening their religious tradition in the face of the greatest material and intellectual challenge they had yet encountered. The outcome is not just an important book for scholars of Islam and of South Asia, but one which all who deal with other societies should consider reading.

Chapter Fourteen

The Jinnah Story*

The life of no man, not that of Mahatma Gandhi, not that of Jawaharlal Nehru, is so entangled with the nationalist politics of British India as that of Muhammad Ali Jinnah. Consider its span. In the 1890s he was helping Dadabhai Naoroji in his campaign to become the first Indian Member of the British Parliament. In the 1900s he entered the Imperial Legislative Council as the representative of Bombay's Muslims. In the 1910s he was a member of both National Congress and Muslim League and principal negotiator of the Lucknow Pact for Hindu–Muslim unity. In the 1920s, 1930s and 1940s he was involved in promoting the Muslim League interest at all stages of constitutional reform, becoming its Quaid-i Azam or Great Leader, who alone commanded the Muslim platform throughout the transfer of power negotiations. Consider his impact. He was regarded by all concerned as the man primarily responsible for the division of British India into two sovereign states at independence. Then, consider the extent to which his career is beset by seeming paradox. He is the ambassador of Hindu–Muslim unity who ends up dividing India. He is the man of avowed secular habit who presides over the realization of a religious ideal. He is the advocate of Pakistan who leaves open to the end the possibility of a united India, indeed, shows interest in being its first prime minister.

For much of the time since Jinnah's death in 1948 we have had little fresh evidence to help us unravel these paradoxes. Unlike Gandhi and Nehru, he wrote no autobiography. He left no intimate

* Stanley Wolpert, *Jinnah of Pakistan* (New York: Oxford University Press, 1984), pp. xii, 421; Ayesha Jalal, *The Sole Spokesman: Jinnah, the Muslim League and the Demand for Pakistan* (Cambridge: Cambridge University Press, 1985), pp. xvii, 310, maps.

diaries. There were no confidences from close friends; they were so few. There were no indiscretions from members of his family; they remained tight-lipped. The assumed needs of state-making, moreover, conspired to preserve and to project a cardboard image of the man. For India he had to be the malevolent force, as played in the Attenborough film *Gandhi*,[1] who seduced Muslims into rending the sacred fabric of the motherland. For Pakistan he had to be the leader of genius and increasingly the good Muslim, who, almost as the Prophet had done thirteen centuries before, led the faithful to the promised land where they might live under the holy law. It has not been easy to gain a satisfactory idea of what Jinnah was trying to do, or why he was trying to do it.

In recent years, however, enough new evidence has become available to make possible a major reassessment of his career, indeed, to enable us to resolve some of its paradoxes: there are the twelve volumes of British documents relating to the transfer of power which were published between 1970 and 1982, the 80,000 pages of Quaid-i Azam papers which are deposited in the National Archives of Pakistan, and the archives of the All-India Muslim League which are slowly being made available. Stanley Wolpert and Ayesha Jalal are the first to attempt major reassessments. Wolpert examines the whole life, Jalal the last most important part.

Wolpert draws together much detail about Jinnah's life which makes him, in his earlier years at least, seem more human than he has done. The boy was a young rip who cut school to gallop his father's Arab stallions in the desert. The young man was still enough of a rip to get arrested for pushing his friends around in a cart on the Oxford–Cambridge boat race night. Like many barristers he was a thwarted thespian who was good enough to sign a contract with a Manchester repertory company and dreamed of starring in Romeo and Juliet at the Old Vic. When he did get to play Romeo it was opposite Ruttie, the spirited and precocious daughter of a Parsee millionaire twenty-five years his junior. Wolpert makes us constantly aware of how the fortunes of this ill-fated match and those of Jinnah's political career were intertwined, from the high point of its announcement after his triumph of the Lucknow Pact, through its deterioration in the early 1920s together with that of his political life, to Ruttie's death at the end of the decade and his complete withdrawal from politics. In the same way he keeps us continually alert to the progress of Jinnah's degenerative lung-disease from the late 1930s, the toll it took of his resources, the effort it demanded to keep up appearances, until the very struggle itself seemed to fuel his concentration of effort and to focus his will to win. Thus Wolpert paints a life which moves from hope in youth, to brilliant success in middle age, to declining years spent striving to salvage some kind of victory out of defeat on several fronts, personal and physical as well as political.

Wolpert's vision of Jinnah's political progress is strictly conventional. The paradoxes of the Quaid's career are not serious enough to make him pause for thought. So Jinnah begins as the Muslim Gokhale, opposing the Muslim League and separate electorates and working for Hindu–Muslim unity. Although harried from the centre of the political stage at Nagpur in 1920, he continues to strive for some form of Hindu–Muslim agreement, most notably as Indians begin to negotiate the next stage in the devolution of power from 1926 to 1928, and as they face up to the meaning of the new rules for politics between 1934 and 1937. This endeavour, however, is wrecked by the Congress victory in the general elections of 1937; now the Congress is strong enough to ignore both him and his League. Jinnah must revive the League or die. At the Lucknow session of 1937, therefore, he devotes himself completely to the Muslim cause. At Patna in the following year he declares Congress to be nothing but a 'Hindu body'. Then, sixteen months later, at the famous Lahore session of March 1940 he makes clear, so Wolpert tells us, that 'partition ... was the only long-term solution to India's foremost problem'. He 'lowered the final curtain on any prospects for a single united independent India'. From that moment Jinnah's determination was fixed; he was set on his seven-year campaign to realize the sovereign state of Pakistan. Evidence to the contrary is either ignored or explained away. It is a vision which should cause little offence to those bred in the traditional historiography of the Islamic republic.

Wolpert's analysis of Jinnah's motivation is less conventional and makes a real contribution. He emphasizes, as others have done before, his vanity, his ambition, his need to play the starring role. His contribution is to show these characteristics continually at work in his career. The centrepiece of the analysis is the study of his interaction with Gandhi. Wolpert makes a good case for Jinnah being obsessed with the Mahatma. It was Gandhi who robbed him of his starring role when he pushed him off centre stage at Nagpur;

this was, Wolpert tells us, the most bitterly humiliating experience of his public life '... the searing memory of his defeat at Nagpur [was] permanently emblazoned on his brain'. It was Gandhi who destroyed the ideals of Hindu–Muslim unity with which the Congress began; 'Mr. Gandhi,' Jinnah told the Muslim League in 1938, turned 'the Congress into an instrument for the revival of Hinduism.' It was Gandhi, Jinnah told a Peshawar audience in 1945, who made no sacrifices in 1920–21 and 'ascends the *gaddi* [throne] of leadership on our skulls'. Here Wolpert adroitly emphasizes the connection between Jinnah's deepest personal grievances and the Muslim cause. The message is that Congress rejected Jinnah in 1920 and continued to do so afterwards. Most of his subsequent actions can be seen as motivated by the need to extract compensation for that rejection. As his old friend, Kanji Dwarkadas, perceptively remarked, after meeting him sick and depressed in December 1946, 'He wanted to keep the fight on because he was badly handled and treated and abused by the Congress leaders ... his self-esteem, his pride, and his feeling of being personally hurt had embittered him.' This is convincing stuff. It goes well with other observations regarding Jinnah's intense psychic drive, Mountbatten's 'psychopathic case'. It dovetails nicely with Robin Moore's recent perception of the identity between Jinnah's feeling of rejection and persecution by Congress and the Muslim sense, although Moore would have done better to talk of the Urdu-speaking Muslim sense, 'of persecution by the Congress denial of their achieved status'.[2]

This contribution acknowledged, Wolpert's *Jinnah* is, nevertheless, a disappointment. On flicking through the pages it seemed to promise much. The subject needs accessible books which can take the fruits of the considerable research devoted to South Asia to a general reading public. Here, perhaps, was a good candidate for the task. But, although the book begins and ends well, it loses the reader for several chapters in a maze of constitutional comings and goings. Then, there is Wolpert's treatment of facts: Mohamed Ali was not an *'alim* (p. 34), Mazharul Haque did not die in 1921 (p. 39), Abd al-Hamid was not Ottoman Caliph in the 1910s (p. 52), Shaukat Ali was not an *'alim* (p. 52), Abul Kalam Azad did not come from Delhi (p. 63), the Moplahs did not riot against Hindus after the abolition of the Khilafat in 1924 (p. 83) and so on. This is too slapdash to breed confidence. Then, there are those patches in the prose. Consider this: 'Jinnah was the "idol of the youth", and "uncrowned king of Bombay". Raven-haired with a moustache almost as full as Kitchener's and lean as a rapier, he sounded like Ronald Coleman, dressed like Anthony Eden, and was adored by most women at first sight, and admired or envied by most men.' Or this: 'Silently, patiently, passionately they waited till Ruttie would attain her majority at eighteen and married just a few months after that, as soon as the last legal obstacle could be slashed aside by Jinnah's invincible courtroom sword.' It is all a matter of taste, of course, but while such mush might draw a few readers from the Georgette Heyer market, one fears that it may well deter others.

The major criticism of Wolpert, however, is that he offers us so little sense of the hard play of power, especially in the years from 1940 to 1947. Given the huge quantity of records newly available in Britain and in Pakistan it is surprising, for instance, that he does not now come to question the purpose of the Lahore resolution or wonder about Jinnah's response to the Cripps offer. It is surprising, too, that he does not show us how consistently weak Jinnah was in relation to the political bosses in the Muslim majority provinces, and how hard he had to work in papering over the cracks in order to present a veneer of unity at the centre. Moreover, because he gives us so little idea of the extent of Jinnah's political weakness, he cannot really tell us the full extent of his political achievement. But, given all the new materials available, it is the more surprising that Wolpert perceives not one single limitation in the orthodox understanding of Jinnah's strategy. He does not see that there may now be hard evidence for the old speculation that the Pakistan demand was less an aim than a bargaining counter, that there might be something in the idea that partition into two sovereign states was for Jinnah less a triumph than a disaster, that it might, in fact, be possible to unravel some of the paradoxes of Jinnah's career. Indeed, Wolpert does not see that when the Quaid seems to doubt the desirability of partition in his first speech to the Constituent assembly of Pakistan, as he himself notes, he might be speaking from his heart, or better put, from the veiled recesses of his mind.[3]

Ayesha Jalal shows us just how much Wolpert failed to see. To be fair, her portrayal of Jinnah's political career up to 1937, although it concentrates more on the structure of opportunities than on the interaction of personalities, does not differ greatly. She identifies Jinnah as a constitutionalist and a nationalist whose prime aims were to assure Muslims a safe position as India moved to independence and to assert himself as their sole spokesman. His natural talent was for the affairs of council chamber and committee room at the centres of all-India politics, so when from 1917 the national movement became increasingly extreme in its forms of action, and from 1920 politics became focused on the provinces, Jinnah found his style out of keeping with the times while there was no longer any stage on which he could play. Politically isolated for the next decade and a half, except for the years 1926–28, he found no opening until 1934 when Muslims from the minority provinces begged him to revive the Muslim League. From then on Jinnah aimed to broaden the basis of League support and to come to terms with the Congress at the all-India level. He and the Congress High Command had a joint interest in destroying both the power of the provincial politicians in their various regional bastions and that which the 1935 Government of India Act gave the British at the centre. The strategy was wrecked by the League's failures and the Congress's success in the general elections of 1937. Now Congress leaders made it clear to Jinnah that they had no need to deal with him or his League. He could, if he wished, join them on their terms.

It is in her understanding of Jinnah's strategy after 1937 that Jalal comes to differ radically from Wolpert. She sees him continuing to pursue a Muslim future within India, and not moving quickly to a decision that the future must be found outside it. Most men after a defeat like that of 1937, she reflects, would have thrown in the towel. But Jinnah, that master of the 'long slow game' sets out once more to build a position of strength from which he could negotiate at the centre with both the British and the Congress. He gained some help as the powerful leaders of the Muslim majority provinces found that they needed someone to represent their interests in Delhi. He gained more when, after the outbreak of the second world war, the British came to appreciate the value of strengthening Jinnah's position as the representative of all India's Muslims at the centre. In this context Jinnah gave new form to his strategy. His presidential speech to the Muslim League session at Lahore, March 1940, asserted that the Muslims were a separate nation on the Indian subcontinent. The session's first resolution announced the Legaue's aim to achieve sovereign and autonomous Muslim states in the northwestern and eastern zones of India. Jinnah was suggesting in the speech and by means of the resolution, later known as the Pakistan resolution, that because there were two nations in India, the transfer of power would necessarily involve the dissolution of British India's unitary structure of central authority, and that any reconstitution of that centre would have to take account of the League's demand that the Muslim majority provinces should be grouped to form a separate state. This was not the end that Jinnah actually sought, merely a means to ensure that his voice was heard when the final constitutional arrangements of independent India came to be negotiated. It should be seen, as Jalal puts it,

> as a bargaining counter, which had the merit of being acceptable (on the face of it) to the majority province Muslims, and of being totally unacceptable to the Congress and in the last resort the British also. This in turn provided the best insurance that the League would not be given what it now apparently was asking for, but which Jinnah in fact did not really want. (p. 57).

From 1940 to 1946 Jinnah developed his strategy with growing success. By 1942 the Cripps Mission was using the terminology of Pakistan and implicitly accepting the two-nation idea. By 1946 most of Muslim India had swung behind the demand for Pakistan demonstrating its support in the sweeping victories of League candidates in the general elections of 1945–46. The Congress, moreover, although it denied the two-nation theory to the end, was unable convincingly to refute it either on the streets or in the ballot box. Throughout Jinnah kept Pakistan's precise form vague, its territories were always undefined. Throughout he managed to play the emotive communal card and undermine independent leaders in the Muslim majority provinces without having to face up to its implications of a partition of Bengal and the Punjab. Then, in May 1946, the Cabinet Mission proposed a three-tier system with compulsory grouping of provinces as the basis for India's constitutional future. Jinnah was offered the prospect of victory in the 'long slow game' he had played from such a weak hand. Here there was the means by which he could discipline the Muslim provinces and bring them into the Indian union on his terms. Jinnah was offered, as Jalal puts it, his 'Pakistan'. This was not, of course, how the Leaguers saw it; the Cabinet Mission did, after all, explicitly reject their Pakistan. Jinnah could only persuade them to accept the Mission's proposal if it was seen as a step towards their Pakistan and if there was the proviso that the League should join no interim gov- ernment without parity with the Congress. At this point, 6 June 1946, Jinnah may well have come closest to winning his game. Within days, however, the prospect of victory began to fade. The Congress refused to enter an interim government based either on parity, or some version of it. The British refused to impose a settlement.

'The last thirteen months of British rule,' declares Jalal, 'saw the tragic collapse of Jinnah's strategy.' He strove desperately to salvage something from the wreckage but as the months passed he had less room for manoeuvre. His followers demanded their Pakistan more and more vociferously; the outbreak of appalling communal rioting underlined their case and the need for settlement. The British wished to leave as soon as they could but were concerned to leave behind them a government strong enough to help to protect their interests in the Indian Ocean region. The Congress wished to take power as soon as possible and they, too, were concerned to take over a strong centre from which they would be able to command independent India. The common interest with the British, which the League had shared during the war, had now shifted to the Congress. At the same time, Jinnah was forced to face up to the fundamental contradictions in his strategy. His Pakistan was enshrined in the groupings of existing provinces proposed by the Cabinet Mission; his two-nation theory was a weapon designed to carve out for the League a share of power, an equal share if possible, at the centre of an independent India. But, as the British searched for ways to transfer power to a strong centre, and the Congress sought ways of achieving one, the attractions of giving Jinnah what he asked for, as opposed to what he really wanted, became overwhelming. And so the two-nation theory came instead to be the 'sword' which cut Jinnah's Pakistan down to size. The principle of national self-determination which he had loudly asserted for the previous seven years came to mean that India's great northwestern and northeastern provinces of the Punjab and Bengal would be partitioned according to the religions of their peoples. In the end 'it was Congress that insisted on partition. It was Jinnah who was against partition.' Power was transferred to two centres. The Quaid was left to savour the irony of becoming the idolized founder of a state whose birth he had long fought to prevent.

What an extraordinary game of poker Jalal lays before our eyes! How deftly Jinnah plays his weak hand over many years! How close he comes to success! How tragic is his failure! By enabling us to peep at Jinnah's cards and by pointing out to us the tricks he was really trying in order to win, Jalal reveals the inner coherence of a career spanning half a century in politics, and more particularly the single-minded purpose which marks its last decade. Those paradoxes are now resolved. Jinnah never deserted his early attachment to Hindu–Muslim unity; his strategy was designed to achieve some form of it in the India of the future. There was no disjunction between a secular ideal. There was no flagging in his zeal for a united India; his Pakistan was never meant to divide it. In some fine analytical set pieces, moreover, Jalal reveals the logic of Jinnah's twists and turns in the complex negotiations surrounding the transfer of power. We understand more fully the wording of the Lahore resolution. We see how his plans were far more fundamentally threatened by the Cripps offer than those of Congress. We feel for him when the Cabinet Mission proposals tease out the contradictions between his rhetoric and his purpose. We perceive the continuing attempts to preserve his strategy in his many shifts and ploys from June 1946, when Congress refused to enter the interim government, down to his May 1947 demand for a corridor through Hindustan to connect the two halves of Pakistan, and his June 1947 proposal that the constituent assemblies of the two new states should both meet in Delhi.

It is hard to believe that this is a first book. A novel thesis is brilliantly sustained from beginning to end. The understanding of politics is mature, the exposition sophisticated, the tone almost unnervingly confident. The style may well jar on some: 'inwardness' is too favourite a word; the prose strains obtrusively for effect; there is that superior and knowing Cambridge air—'full-time worker (almost a contradiction in terms in the enervating climes of Bengal)', big Punjabi families knew 'when expediency demanded them to be turn-coats—an old Punjabi tradition, alive and well to this day'. Such aspects of voice and attitude, however, should not keep readers from a book which transforms the widely held understanding of the role of Jinnah in the making of Pakistan, and does so with a sureness of touch and a depth of scholarship that should quickly establish it both as the orthodox academic interpretation and its author as a scholar of unusual gifts. As a piece of historical revisionism, as an analysis of action in high politics, as a narrative of a dramatic moment when great men played for high stakes, it compares well with the best post-war work of its kind, for instance, Maurice Cowling's *1867 Disraeli, Gladstone and Revolution: The Passing of the Second Reform Bill* (Cambridge, 1967).

It should be understood, however, that this book ventures no more than a treatment of high politics. It concentrates on analysing Jinnah's political strategy and on explaining how Pakistan happened. It has no interest in Jinnah's relationship with his community except to assert that 'his use of the communal factor was a political tactic, not an ideological commitment'. It is not concerned to explain why growing numbers of Muslims should clamour for a Pakistan which many saw as some form of Islamic state. It is innocent of any serious investigation of Indo–Muslim political thought. When it comes to the Congress and the British we are told enough for the main thrust of the argument to make good sense, but no more. The image we are given of the Congress, for instance, is that it wanted the British to go quickly, to inherit a strong centre and to shut the League out; we are given no understanding of how the interactions of people, interests, ideas and events might have fashioned such policies. This limited focus of historical explanation has undoubtedly assisted lucid exposition of Jinnah's strategy, but by the same token it should be clear, as Jalal would be amongst the first to admit, that the full-scale epic of partition, the history of the interplay of men and forces which brought about the division of India, still has to be written. This is not to belittle Jalal's work, merely to give it context. Her achievement, moreover, must be rated favourably against that of Wolpert. She has enriched our understanding of Jinnah's role in one of the great events of the twentieth century; he has added, amid an interpretation of Jinnah's politics in which Jalal reveals we cannot have much faith, to our knowledge of the man. Five distinguished US academics pen puffs of fulsome praise on the jacket of Wolpert's book. Had Professors Keddie, Embree, Rahman, Furber and Palmer had the advantage of reading Jalal's book, they might have couched their comments in more judicious terms.

One further observation is appropriate. Nearly two decades ago the late Jack Gallagher and Anil Seal planned a five-volume series devoted to the interplay of imperialism and nationalism in South Asia from the 1870s to the 1940s. The plan did not work out as intended; such grand plans rarely do. Nevertheless, we can now see a way in which Gallagher and Seal, together with some of their pupils, have brought this plan to a partial fruition. The process begins with Anil Seal's *Emergence of Indian Nationalism* (1968) and Gordon Johnson's *Provincial Politics and Indian Nationalism*

(1973). It continues with Richard Gordon's 'Aspects of the History of the Indian National Congress with reference to the Swarajya Party' (sadly unpublished), Tom Tomlinson's *Indian National Congress and the Raj* (1976) and David Page's *Prelude to Partition* (1982). The imperial backcloth is sketched in Jack Gallagher's *Decline, Revival and Fall of the British Empire* (1982), and the process finds a conclusion of a kind in Ayesha Jalal's *Sole Spokesman*. In these seven works, although it should be said that the so-called Cambridge school has produced others which bear upon the theme, there is the history of that interplay of imperialism and nationalism with an emphasis on high politics from the foundation of the Congress to independence. There is also something more which looks towards the present. There is an analysis of the development and early working of India's multi-level political system. With the publication of Jalal's book historians are nicely poised to study the further development of that system in the politics of India and Pakistan.

NOTES

1. The film was in part financed by the Government of India.
2. R.J. Moore, 'Jinnah and the Pakistan Demand', *Modern Asia Studies*, 17, 4 (1983), p. 535.
3. In a speech, apparently extempore, Jinnah's words were: 'any idea of a United India could never have worked and in my judgement it would have led us to terrific disaster. May be that view is correct; may be it is not; that remains to be seen.' Wolpert, *Jinnah*, p. 338.

Chapter Fifteen

*Congress Muslims and Indian Nationalism**

In the first half of the twentieth century four of the great figures of Indo-Muslim life were Muhammad Ali Jinnah, Muhammad Iqbal, Abul Kalam Azad and Mukhtar Ahmad Ansari. As the second half of the century has worn on, it has become noticeable how differently those who supported the movement for Pakistan have come to be remembered as compared with those who devoted themselves to Indian nationalism. Iqbal's tomb of sandstone, lapis lazuli and white marble, which stands before the main gates of the Badshahi mosque in Lahore, is a place of pilgrimage. Jinnah's Mazar, whose dimensions would not have disgraced a Mughal emperor, is a symbol of Pakistan's identity and one of the first places to which the visitor to Karachi will be taken. Azad's mausoleum before Delhi's Juma Masjid, on the other hand, is not greatly frequented; not once on many visits to the city over twenty years has anyone taken me by the hand and said 'come, let us pay our respects to Abul Kalam.' Ansari, moreover, seems almost entirely forgotten; although I have visited the Jamia Millia Islamia a fair number of times, I had to read the biography under review to learn that he is buried there. It may be said, of course, that regard for great men need not only be displayed at their tombs. But amongst Muslims, the Wahhabi sort apart, it is a natural instinct to respect the resting places of great souls and to frequent them in search of

* Mushirul Hasan, *A Nationalist Conscience: M.A. Ansari, the Congress and the Raj* (New Delhi: Manohar, 1987), pp. xvii, 277. Ian Henderson Douglas, *Abul Kalam Azad: An Intellectual and Religious Biography*, Gail Minault and Christian W. Troll (eds), (New Delhi: Oxford University Press, 1988), pp. xvi, 358.

both solace and inspiration. The relative neglect of the tombs of Azad and Ansari suggests that many Indian Muslims may have lost interest in keeping their memories alive. It also suggests that Indian society as a whole may no longer value as before, and perhaps may not even know, the principles for which they stood.

For the past decade it has been the purpose of Mushirul Hasan, professor of history at the Jamia Millia Islamia, to make up for this neglect. In doing so he has produced a stream of volumes: there is his *Nationalism and Communal Politics in India 1916–1928* and an edited collection of essays, *Communal and Pan-Islamic Trends in Colonial India*; there are four volumes (three of letters and speeches and one of biography) devoted to the nationalist and pan-Islamic leader, Mahomed Ali, who had become estranged from the nationalist cause by the time he died in 1931; there is a volume of correspondence and now a biography devoted to a second nationalist and pan-Islamic leader, Dr M.A. Ansari.[1] Throughout, Hasan's prime concern has been, as Ravinder Kumar tells us in his introduction, to discover why secular nationalism in India failed to create a united nation in 1947 in which all Hindus and Muslims felt that they could equally participate. This biography is by no means the end of Hasan's quest. Three further volumes of Mahomed Ali's letters and speeches have still to appear, while currently he plans a conference on Azad and works on the communal politics of the years 1937 to 1947. Nevertheless, it is an important stage in Hasan's search because no Indian Muslim stood so prominently, or worked so hard, between 1912 and 1936, for a liberal and secular vision of India's national future.

Hasan takes us through Ansari's life and achievements in a straightforward way. He came from an *ashraf* family which traced its ancestry back to an Arab who had migrated to Shiraz in the fourteenth century from where his sons went on to Delhi, one of them being appointed a *qazi* under Muhammad bin Tughlaq. Ansari was as conscious of his family's claim to Arab ancestry as he was of the long tradition of Muslim rule and civilization in Delhi. In the late nineteenth century his family were petty zamindars in Ghazipur district, in eastern UP, and his generation like so many from such background looked to government service and the liberal professions to sustain their fortunes. From 1901 to 1910 he studied medicine in Britain where he met others who were to be leaders of the nationalist movement, and where he, like Jinnah, gained a taste for acting, his Shakespearean role being Othello as compared with the future Quaid's Romeo. On returning to India he quickly established in Delhi what was to be a lucrative practice, and within two years was involved in the rapidly developing pan-Islamic movement, leading the Red Crescent mission to Turkey in 1912–13, focusing attention on the Khilafat issue at the 1918 Delhi Muslim League sessions, conducting the citizens of Delhi through the Rowlatt *satyagraha* of 1919 and the Khilafat non-cooperation and civil disobedience movements of the early 1920s, out of which emerged the most distinctive memorial to his spirit and purpose, the National Muslim University, better known as the Jamia Millia Islamia. There followed his role as the leading Muslim nationalist in the 1920s and 1930s; opposing Council entry in 1922–23, supporting the Nehru Report in 1928, and singlehandedly leading the nationalist Muslims through the second era of civil disobedience, and great difficulties, down to his resignation from politics due to ill-health in March 1935. Throughout, we are in the company of a man with a high sense of public duty, who is respected by almost all—Hindu, Muslim or British—that encounter him, who is competent, practical and pragmatic, and who works tirelessly for the nationalist cause. 'While the spectre of communalism stalked the land and many a nationalist even among the Congressmen fell victim to it,' declared the *Bombay Chronicle* on the date after his death in May 1936, 'Dr Ansari remained unshaken in his faith in democratic nationalism ... His nationalism was pure, unadulterated and undefiled.'

Hasan's approach is the 'life and times' style of biography, or, better put in this case, a 'times and life' style. Often, though not always, his method is to set out the context and then sum up Ansari's contribution to the events concerned. So, on pp. 74–87, he explains the Khilafat movement and then on pp. 88–97 takes us on a tour through Ansari's involvement in the movement and its aftermath. So again, on pp. 175–88, he sets the scene of the aftermath of the Nehru Report and then on pp. 188–209 takes us through Ansari's achievement as the leader of the Nationalist Muslim Party. What comes across most freshly and effectively are those points where Hasan is furthest away from materials with which he has dealt before, for instance Ansari's early life, the founding and early years of the Jamia Millia Islamia, and most particularly his analysis of Ansari's style and weaknesses as the leader of the nationalist

Muslims from 1929 until his death. This last is the point where the book comes most alive. It is from this period too, we should note, that the bulk of Ansari's papers survive. Sadly almost all of Ansari's correspondence which covered the years 1912 to 1925, and which probably would greatly have enriched this volume, did not survive its stay from the mid-1930s to the mid-1960s in a basement of the Jamia library.

There are one or two omissions which may or may not be explained by this lack of private papers. It would be good to know, for instance, if Ansari was actually the originator of the idea of a medical mission to Turkey. True, it is not a matter of great import, but this is Ansari's biography. Then, regarding his relationship with Gandhi we are told (p. 67) that:

> he was genuinely captivated by his personality, his idealism, his concern for the poor and the down-trodden and by his leadership qualities. From now on, the Mahatma was his unquestioned leader; he was to idolize him, follow him and assist him in future political crusades. He enjoyed both his friendship and his confidence ...

That all this is probably true is borne out by Ansari's political career from the Rowlatt *satyagraha* onwards, but such was Gandhi's influence over Ansari's activities, and therefore its significance for the development of Congress Muslim politics, that this bare assertion seems insufficient to establish the relationship. It is one which deserved to be explored in greater depth. In the same vein, it seems a pity that Hasan, who is concerned to establish Ansari's credentials as a major nationalist leader, should restrict himself to a somewhat cursory survey of his activities in the Khilafat–non-cooperation movement from 1919 to 1922. A more thorough demonstration of his leadership of the movement in Delhi, of his involvement in deputations to the authorities, of his influence in committees, conferences and so on, indeed actually to mention the fact that he presided over the Khilafat conference at Gaya in 1922, for instance, would seem to make the point more strongly.

What may irk the reader most it that for much of the book Ansari seems something of a cardboard figure, the gifted doctor, the perfect gentleman, the dedicated nationalist. We rarely hear his voice; we have little sense of his humanity. This may in part be a result of Hasan's eschewing of any form of psycho-history, of respectful reticence regarding Ansari's private life. Although it is surely of some significance, for instance, that he was known to be friendly with the wives of British officials, which is not to suggest that these relationships were not wholly innocent, and that while his first wife was still alive he took a second, a Christian lady, whose son, Ahmad Harold, was rejected by Ansari's family. But the limited sense we are given of the man is probably in part, too, a function of what little remains of his papers. His literary remains are restricted to a medical treatise *The Regeneration of Man*; he left no autobiographical memoir as did Mahomed Ali, Azad, Nehru and Gandhi. His correspondence in any useful sense covers his last eleven years. And how much more he comes to life when we have access to it! 'When I saw the clay feet of my idol,' he wrote to Shaukat Ali in 1929 on the parting of their ways in politics, 'I felt as if the world had turned topsy-turvy.' Life was now to be 'the less fuller, the less richer for want of such friends as you and I have been'.

What new, then, does this biography bring to an explanation of why the cause of secular, liberal nationalism failed? In *Nationalism and Communal Politics* Hasan laid a sizeable chunk of the blame at the door of the Hindu right wing. The parting of the ways took place over the Nehru Report because of the influence of the Hindu Mahasabha over Motilal Nehru and Gandhi. This position is now developed further. On the one hand, Hasan recognizes how out of touch Ansari had become by the late 1920s, as only an Indian politician could be who greeted the Nehru Report with the words: 'Already a new generation is come to the front to which differences between Hindu and Mussulmans are unknown and which will not and cannot think in communal terms.' But, on the other hand, he expands the blame which should be laid at the feet of the Congress leadership. Ansari and the nationalist Muslims were let down by Gandhi and Motilal Nehru who preferred to deal with communalists rather than seriously to back them. He quotes statements from both men to Ansari in 1930 which make it clear that, while the first concern of the Congress had once been to resolve communal differences, now it was to get rid of the British and only then would the communal issue be tackled. Hasan's position is clear. Ansari sustained a nationalist Muslim option but Congress refused to take it. This argument must be noted. But it would be one which would carry greater weight if Hasan nodded a head in the direction of David Page and acknowledged the extent to which the political framework established by the British had by the late 1920s forced the Congress into taking communal forces seriously into account. So, when Gandhi told Ansari that the first priority was to remove the 'evil' British power, he was recognizing political realities.[2]

This said, it should be clear that Hasan has performed a notable service to scholarship. One of the problems of history is that it tends to be written by winners rather than losers, in this case by the historians of the Pakistan movement, of Congress-led Indian nationalism, and even those of British imperialism rather than those of nationalist Muslims. Through his work in general, and through this book in particular, Hasan has made sure that the nationalist Muslim perspective, and the option which it offered the Congress, will not be submerged beneath the rationlizations of the victors. In the process he has added new understanding to the problem of how British India came to be divided in 1947.

The role of Abul Kalam Azad in the 1940s was similar to that of Ansari in the 1920s and 1930s, that of the standard bearer of the Muslim presence in the nationalist movement, a man that the Congress was pleased to have in its leadership although it might not always listen to his views with care. But Azad was much more than just a trump card for Indian nationalists to play against Pakistani separatists: he was for a time India's leading Muslim journalist; the chief rationalizer of Indian Muslim support for the Turkish Khilafat; throughout his political life a fierce opponent of communalism and a distinguished servant of Indian nationalism; both the youngest president of the Congress, aged thirty-five, and the man to hold the office longer than anyone else; for eleven years minister of education until his death in 1958; and finally an outstanding religious thinker whose ideas are of relevance not just to Muslims but to all those, who share a religious vision of man's purpose. No Indian Muslim of his era, Iqbal perhaps excluded, travelled further or more urgently in his encounter with the West. Of all India's Muslims he came closest to Gandhi in his combination of personal religious vision and perspective over political action.

Azad's achievement has never been fully appreciated, in part because there has been no substantial examination of his life and thought in English. This is not to say that biographies do not exist, and some in English. Azad, himself, wrote no less than three autobiographies: the *Tazkira*, which was written while he was interned during the First World War, *Azad ki Kahani Khud Azad ki Zabani*, which he dictated to Abdur Razzaq Malihabadi while they were imprisoned in the 1920s, then *India Wins Freedom*, which was written in collaboration with his private secretary, Humayun Kabir, in the 1950s. Notable amongst the biographical contributions in various forms are: Mahadev Desai's *Maulana Abul Kalam Azad: A Biographical Memoir* (1946), Humayun Kabir's *Maulana Abul Kalam Azad: A Memorial Volume* (1959), and Abid Reza Bedar's, *Maulana Abul Kalam Azad* (1968). This new biography will remedy the situation. The bulk of the book was written by Ian Henderson Douglas, who was Director of the Henry Martyn Institute of Islamic Studies, and presented as an Oxford D.Phil. thesis in 1969. Unfortunately Douglas died before it could be prepared for publication and we have to thank Gail Minault for rediscovering the typescript, and Gail Minault and Christian Troll for editing the text and adding an introduction and conclusion in the light of the past two decades of scholarship. The outcome is a very important and most exciting contribution to the study of Indian Islam.

The richness of Azad's human experience, the distance he travelled as a religious thinker, stand out from this book. Douglas, while always insisting on the consistency and continuity of Azad's thought, divides his life into four phases. The first ends in 1910 when he is twenty-two. There is his childhood and early adolescence in Mecca, Calcutta and Bombay. There are the transitions in his religious understanding: from the attitudes of the old-fashioned *piri* family in which he was raised to detest Wahhabis to the discovery of the world of Urdu music, poetry and prose which helped him reject his father's attitudes and values; from his five-year intoxication with the religious vision of Saiyid Ahmad Khan to his total loss of faith. There is the precocious beginning to his journalistic career aged twelve, which takes him over the next ten years from Calcutta to Bombay, to Lucknow and to Lahore, and which brings him the friendship of Maulana Shibli and a developing political awareness. There is the love affair which consumes him for seventeen months between 1908 and 1910 and which ultimately forms the bridge over which he passes to the recovery of his faith. 'Suddenly the dark curtain was parted. I lifted my eyes and there was the face of lost truth, unveiled before me': as so often happens, earthly passions humbled pride in the all-compassing power of intellect and showed other paths towards truth. Azad's truth now, moreover, was one which found the same essence in all the world's religions. By 1910 the bases of all the main lines of his thought had been laid.

The second phase ran from 1910 to 1922 when Azad had a messianic vision of himself as an instrument of God, and for a time the leader of a Party of God (*Hizbullah*), who was to enable Muslims to exercise their divinely ordained right to govern. He saw himself in spiritual succession to great renewers of the Faith such as Ibn Hanbal, Ibn Taimiya, Shaikh Ahmad Sirhindi and Shah Waliullah. To spread his message he launched *Al-Hilal* and *Al-Balagh*, the greatest Urdu newspapers of the day, in which he expounded his vision in the years from 1912 to 1916 in quasi-prophetic language. His internment from 1916 to the end of 1919 only served to sharpen his sense of mission; the *Tazkira* he wrote during these years showing him to be preparing the way for his acceptance as a *mahdi* of the khalifa of the time. The Khilafat movement brought the climax of this stage of his life when he bid to become *Amir ul-Hind*. The failure both of the movement and his ambition triggered a personal crisis in which during his imprisonment in 1922 he withdrew from all human contact for three months. Now the soaring sense of divine mission was at an end.

From 1922 Azad gave up all ambition to become *Amir* or *Imam ul-Hind* and took his place within the Congress political machinery. No longer did he claim that the Quran gave specific guidance for all political decisions, but instead made his contribution to political life as a man deeply motivated by Quranic religion. If there was any turning point in Azad's religious life after 1909, Douglas tells us, it was this. Hereafter, until the late 1930s, he remained relatively inconspicuous in Congress politics, devoting his prime energies to his Quran commentary, *Tarjuman al-Quran*, in which he developed further his ideas on the essential unity of all religions and which, although unfinished, represents his masterwork as a religious thinker.

In the final phase of his life from 1937 Azad returned to the front rank of politics as the Congress' leading Muslim, as the organization's President from 1939 to 1946, and as the symbol of those Muslims who worked for a united India. During the last years of the freedom struggle he strove to bring Hindu and Muslim together, he opposed partition heart and soul, and was much admired by the Viceroy, Wavell. Few were as saddened as he was by partition. Then as minister of education in the last decade of his life he formulated the educational policy of independent India, setting up many great institutions that exist to this day. His speeches, so Douglas tells us, echoed the themes of his earlier life and writings: communal harmony, religious broad-mindedness, cultural cosmopolitanism and the relevance of religion to public life. Time and time again he came back to the idea of unity in diversity, an understanding which he asserted increasingly was relevant not just to India but to the world at large. But too many ideals had been battered beyond recovery, too many hopes crushed. More and more towards the end of his life he withdrew into himself. With no immediate family and no close friends he came to prefer the company of his books and the solace of the bottle.

This study contains new ideas about Azad and much new information, at least for those who do not read Urdu. Up to now, for instance, it has not been clear just how much Azad was influenced by ideas emanating from the Arab world. Douglas makes the extent of the influence clear. Of course, we would expect there to be some influence on a man whose mother was an Arab, who spent his earliest years in Mecca, who regularly read the Arab press, and who in his teenage years travelled twice, and perhaps three times, to West Asia. But the book really makes clear where that influence was felt. First, there was the great impact of Egyptian nationalism, of Mustafa Kamil and his *Hizb al-Watan* on the early growth of Azad's political consciousness. Indeed, it is arguable that these influences from the Islamic world had a far greater impact on him at this stage than anything going on in India, whether in the world of the Congress or that of the Bengal revolutionaries. Second, there is the impact of the thought of Muhammad Abduh, Rashid Rida and the *Al-Manar* group on the development of his religious thinking. Here we are shown the workings of these influences from his struggles to free himself from the thrall of Saiyid Ahmad Khan to his rationlization of the Khilafat movement, to the style and objectives of his *Tarjuman al-Quran*. Indeed, one happy touch in this book is a photograph of Azad standing behind Rashid Rida, who is the guest of honour at the 1912 session of the Nadwat ul-ulama. This was the occasion when Azad, although assigned to translate Rida's speech into Urdu, just could not sit through it—there were limits to his respect—yet such was his knowledge of Rida's thought that he was able to return at the conclusion and give, so it is said, an acceptable version of the Arab thinker's words.[3]

A second issue, related to the first, concerns the extent of Jamal-uddin al-Afghani's influence on Azad. For it has been assumed that the pan-Islamic vision of this roving revolutionary of the late nineteenth-century Islamic world had great influence on Azad.[4] Douglas argues, and does so with strong support from his editors, that while Azad admired Afghani for his struggles against the West and against the limitations of the *ulema*, he owed little to him in his writing, either on pan-Islam or the Khilafat. In fact, Azad's *Tazkira*, which is the major source for this period of his life, does not mention the man once. If Afghani had any influence at all it was indirectly through the ideas of the *Al-Manar* group.

A further revelation, which may surprise some, is the extent of Azad's knowledge of Western learning. His introduction came through his intoxication with the works of Saiyid Ahmad Khan, which led him to learn English. Admittedly he thoroughly disapproved of Aligarh and of the impact of the movement for Western higher education in divorcing many Muslims from the national movement. He was also scathing about attempts to interpret the Quran in the light of Greek thought. But for Western learning, pure and simple, he maintained interest and respect throughout his life. So he ran a column on science in *Al-Hilal* in which he translated articles from the *Scientific American*.When a young Muslim asked him for advice on how to overcome his loss of faith, he told him to read Bertrand Russell! As minister of education his policies showed great breadth of intellectual sympathy. When he died, his library was found to contain many books in English. Nevertheless, Douglas is also careful to emphasize the limits to Azad's learning in this field and the fact that his great intelligence often enabled him to impress when his knowledge was but slight.

All previous writing on Azad has emphasized his extraordinary memory, his enormous learning and his intellectual power. All that Douglas writes confirms Azad's possession of these gifts. But he is also concerned to go further and to explore the particular quality of his mind and mental process. Azad emerges as a man who saw intellectual scepticism as crucial to human progress, yet also realized that man could not ultimately approach God by intellectual means alone—'only through allowing our emotions free reign can we reach Him'. He talked of his capacity to place his knowledge in separate compartments which he could open and close at will, but it turned out to be a capacity which relieved him of the necessity to make connections between or resolve conflicts amongst what the different compartments contained. He saw no need to create a coherent system of Islamic ideas and was at ease with the inconsistencies in his life and thought. So, as Douglas tells us, he could love music, tobacco and alcohol and yet have great admiration for a theologian such as Ibn Taimiya who stressed the systemic implications of God's transcendence. Ultimately, he was a man whose apprehension of truth was that of a poet rather than an intellectual, of a sufi rather than an *alim*. The editors support this point felicitously by quoting from an article which Azad wrote in 1910:

> Of whatever kind it may be, love (*ishq*) is always the first step towards the station of truth and reality (*haqiqat*) ... Or, better, love is the door to be passed though before man can become man. Whoever's heart is not wounded, and whoever's eyes are not wet with tears—how can he fathom the meaning of humanity?[5]

How different the mind of Azad seems from that of the other great South Asian theologian of the twentieth century, Maulana Maududi! Where Maududi takes refuge in a hermetically sealed Islamic system, Azad for all his erudition knows that the intellect cannot of itself grasp God's full meaning. His understanding seems the more elevated, his attitude the more humble, and the path he wishes to tread the more preferable.

Douglas' emphasis on Azad's capacity to live with inconsistencies, however, should not allow the reader to think that he supports the view, long held by scholars such as I.H. Qureshi, Aziz Ahmad and Peter Hardy, that Azad was inconsistent in the main thrusts of his religious thinking, that in fact there were two stages to his career, the first in which he was primarily an Islamic thinker, and the second in which his thought changed to meet the needs of secular nationalists. An outstanding feature of this book is its analysis of the development of Azad's religious ideas in the context of the changing circumstances of his life from the first to sixth decades of the twentieth century but paying especial attention to *Al-Hilal* and *Tarjuman al-Quran*. What emerges is that Azad's fundamental religious vision, which centred on a belief in *wahdat-e-din* or the essential oneness of all religions, was formulated by 1910 and remained unchanged throughout his life. To illustrate what Azad meant by *wahdat-e-din* the editors quote a telling excerpt from his presidential speech to the Bengal Khilafat conference in 1920:

The tragedy is that the world worships words instead of meanings, and even though all are seeking and worshipping but one truth, they quarrel with one another over differences in mere names ... If one day the veils of 'externals and names' can be lifted so that truth and reality (*haqiqat*) come before all unveiled, then, at once, all quarrels of the world will end, and all who quarrel will see that what we all seek is one and the same.[6]

What accounts for the apparent differences in Azad's thought, says Douglas, is not a fundamental transformation of ideas but a shift of emphasis to meet different contexts. We should note that the editors, while supporting the main thrust of this argument, find the author, like Azad himself, too prepared to gloss over the extent of the changes he made.

From the same quarters, which are of course largely Pakistani ones, Azad is also attacked for changing from advocating pan-Islam and Muslim nationalism in the years up to his internment in 1916 to propounding a vision of composite Indian nationhood and Indian nationalism in order to found the basis for political alliance with the Congress in the Khilafat–non-cooperation movement of 1919 to 1922. Douglas suggests, perhaps too kindly, that the Pakistani approach was developed because the historians concerned, notably Hafeez Malik and Aziz Ahmad, based their assessment on selection from *Al-Hilal* rather than a study of the whole file of the newspaper. Such a study is Douglas' forte and he produces enough evidence to support his conclusion that 'from the first flowering of his political thought to his death, Azad never wavered in his conviction that Muslims in India must work with Hindus and their other fellow citizens.' At the same time, however, he also admits that Hindu–Muslim unity was not the foremost part of Azad's appeal to Muslims in the early years of *Al-Hilal*. Thus, as in his theology so in his politics, we are dealing with shifts of emphasis rather than fundamental transformations.

To come to know a man as a man often brings greater admiration for his works. Douglas asserts that Azad's private life and inner thoughts remain 'enigmatic and contradictory', nevertheless his book does, to an unusual extent in the case of South Asian biography, succeed in interweaving personal and psychological development with changing intellectual and political understandings. We are encouraged to consider the consequences of being a youthful prodigy, who was himself to admit that he 'woke too soon' from the pleasant dream of childhood; if it was not enough that his father's disciples worshipped him as the sufi shaikh's son, they also flocked to marvel at the babblings of a prematurely learned child. We are asked always to remember how old-fashioned and strict his Islamic upbringing was, which was almost bound to bring rebellion in a child who was spirited as well as intelligent; he read, as so many do, forbidden books at night, he took sitar lessons in secret, and struggled hard to give up the habit of prayer. We are constantly reminded of the great egotist, a man who should be visited and not visit, who was always concerned that his superiority to contemporary Muslim rivals should be acknowledged, and who had no difficulty at all in saying how far ahead he was of his fellow Muslims: 'on no path can I go with the caravans of the day ... Whichever way I walk, I get so far ahead [of the caravan] that when I turn to look back, I see nothing but the dust of the way, and even that is the dust raised by the speed of my own passage.' We are reminded constantly of his humanism, the humanism which saw that all men sought the same truth, if in different ways, the humanism that acknowledged that man must accept his humanity to be able to live—'to ensure that life is really life we have to commit errors.' We are introduced to his aesthetic sense: his love of music, his art with words, but most of all his belief that religion should not be against life, should not fashion dour and unsmiling people, but should be a celebration of life—of nature, of beauty, of laughter. Finally, and most tellingly, we are shown a man of deeply felt and highly controlled emotions. Azad is a man who seems incapable of surrendering to a power beyond himself. Indeed, one is left wondering if the greatest sadness of his life was that he was a passionate man who knew that he could only reach God through his heart yet the intellectual surrender involved was the hardest thing of all for him to achieve.

Enough has been said to indicate the importance of this book whose careful scholarship has removed misunderstandings about Azad and offered a more balanced and coherent picture of him than we have had before. With his carapace of austerity and unapproachability prised away a little, we have been able to come close to this man of intellect and passion, faith and complex personality. As with all substantial pieces of research, fresh areas where work needs to be done are illuminated, whether it be on how Azad was influenced by Maulana Shibli, or how, as the editors suggest, he used the Quran differently in *al-Hilal* as compared with *Tarjuman al-Quran*, or the record of his achievement as minister of education. Perhaps most important, a religious understanding, which is drawn from the heart of the Islamic tradition and which speaks most hopefully to Muslim and non-Muslim alike, is set before us:

> In all that a Muslim does, it should be a rule of action that he help whoever may be doing good, even if a non-Muslim or an opponent, and avoid helping whoever may be doing evil, even if a Muslim and a companion ... if even an idolator honour and worship God in his own way, he should not be shown disrespect, for the honour and worship of God is, in any event, the honour and worship of God.[7]

Both these studies of leading Muslims of the first half of the twentieth century bear a pointed message for the South Asian present. To a region increasingly beset by communalism, the life of Ansari shows how during the freedom movement there were Muslims who worked for the highest secular ideals. To a region increasingly beset by religious intolerance, the life of Azad reveals how the finest religious sensibility can fashion the most open and humane outlook in private and public life. These are lives which deserve to be known and studied outside the purely academic community. When they are, we hope that there will be fresh attention to their memorials in Delhi.

NOTES

1. *Nationalism and Communal Politics in India 1916–1928* (Delhi, 1979); *Communal and Pan-Islamic Trends in Colonial India*, 2nd ed, (Delhi, 1985); *Mahomed Ali: Ideology and Politics* (Delhi, 1981); *Mahomed Ali in Indian Politics: Select Writings*, vols I–III (Delhi, 1982, 1983, 1986); *Muslims and the Congress: Select Correspondence of Dr M.A. Ansari 1912–1935* (Delhi, 1979).
2. David Page, *Prelude to Partition: The Indian Muslims and the Imperial System of Control, 1920–1932* (Delhi, 1982).
3. This point is also made quite independently in a recent work: I.H. Azad Faruqi, *The Tarjuman Al-Qur'an: A Critical Analysis of Maulana Abu'l Kalam Azad's Approach to the Understanding of the Qur'an* (Delhi, 1982).
4. See Aziz Ahmad, *Islamic Modernism in India and Pakistan, 1857–1964* (London, 1967), p. 129 and Mushirul Hasan, 'Pan-Islamism versus Indian Nationalism: A Reappraisal' in Paul R. Brass and Francis Robinson (eds), *Indian National Congress and Indian Society 1885–1985: Ideology, Social Structure, and Political Dominance* (Delhi, 1987), p. 148.
5. Douglas, *Azad*, p. 288. The article was devoted to Sarmad, the sufi martyr

of Aurangzeb's reign. This will be translated in full in Christian W. Troll, 'Sarmad, the Martyr, by Abul Kalam Azad' in C. Shackle (ed.), *Festschrift* for Ralph Russell, 1988.

6. Douglas, *Azad*, p. 289.
7. Douglas, *Azad*, p. 215.

Index